"*Please Kill Me* does for the Ramones what the disciples did for Jesus." —*L.A. Weekly*

One of the Top Ten Books of 1996 —*Time Out*

One of the Top Ten Books of 1996—"The riotously funny story of New York punk told by those who were there."
—*New York Daily News*

"*Please Kill Me* might make you shed the kind of tears reserved for lost poets and fuckups, but it almost certainly will also make you laugh. It's an honest, detailed oral history, uncensored—hell, filthy—and fascinating."
—*Rolling Stone*

"Free of historical self-revision or precious musical pontification, [this] book comes as close to capturing the coruscated brilliance and vein-puncturing style of the Blank Generation as the written word is likely to get."
—*Mojo*

"One of the rudest, rowdiest excursions into the dark side, stuffed full of the sickest, most scandalous tales ever assembled on the ongoing epic of sex, drugs, and rock & roll."   —*Paper*

"[*Please Kill Me*] dishes the crud on everyone. . . . As someone who was there at the time, I can vouch for how vividly it recaptures the swampy vitality of the New York scene. . . . Candid, inside and detailed."
—James Wolcott, *The New Yorker*

"*Please Kill Me* is a long-awaited and definitive work."
—*New Musical Express*

"When outrageous movie director John Waters calls a book 'shocking,' it must be something special and *Please Kill Me is* a shocking behind-the-scenes and over-the-top look at the survivors of the '70s New York punk rock scene."   —*New York Post*

"*Please Kill Me* is lurid, insolent, disorderly, funny, sometimes gross, sometimes mean and occasionally touching."
—*The New York Times*

"*Please Kill Me* ranks up there with the great rock & roll books of all time.
—*Time Out*

"There's more gossip, sex, and drugs in *Please Kill Me* than in any book published to date about the Clinton administration. Even if you have no interest in the evolution of punk, I recommend this book."
—*L.A. Weekly*

"McNeil and McCain let the punks do all the talking, [and] as a result, their book is bitchy, graphic, frequently horrifying, and appallingly candid. *Please Kill Me* is a human book, about some humans who all too often were pathetically flawed. Punk rock, [the authors] seem to say, was formulated by the only people suitable for the job: people who didn't give a fuck."
—*Los Angeles Reader*

"Bitchy, contradictory [and] always witty . . . fluent and scabrous as the music itself." —*Esquire* (U.K.)

"*Please Kill Me* is a scenester's paradise, four-hundred pages of person-to-person, 'I was there' testimony fabulously edited for speed and irony. It calls up *Edie*, but it's much richer. A lot about *Edie* was about covering up; in *Please Kill Me*, you rarely, if ever, get the feeling anyone is protecting a reputation or holding back." —Greil Marcus, *Interview*

"The perfect bedtime story for the nineties."
—*Manhattan Mirror*

"McNeil and McCain set the record straight with a vengeance. . . . *Please Kill Me* now stands as the best overview yet of punk rock's first decade or so, and given the wide-ranging and no-nonsense perspective of its contributors, it's likely to be the definitive one."
—*Ann Arbor News*

"An essential accompaniment to the first, still-thrilling punk records, this preposterously entertaining document just reeks with the brilliance and filth of the Blank Generation." —*Kirkus Reviews*

"It's the impossible-to-put-down book . . . hilarious, candid and often tragic." —*Philadelphia Weekly*

"Utterly and shamelessly sensational."
—*Newsday*

"The best rock & roll book ever, and not a word about music."
—Jim "The Hound" Marshall

"It's a tale from the crypt." —Richard Hell

"Legs McNeil and Gillian McCain understand the dangerous excitement of the 1970s punk scene in Manhattan, and tap every source of information for their exhaustive, thrilling, filthy 'uncensored history.' "
—*The Times Literary Supplement* (U.K.)

"[A] saga of nasty lyrics, deafening music, leather jackets, drugs and early death." —*Playboy*

"A no-nonsense insider's view [that] reads like a buddy telling war stories about the good old days over a great many beers in the kitchen . . . a must read." —*New Haven Register*

PENGUIN BOOKS

PLEASE KILL ME

Legs McNeil was born and raised in Connecticut, where the liquor stores still close at 8 P.M. As a teenager he was forced to move to New York City in order to quench his thirst. In 1975, at age 18, he cofounded *Punk* magazine. During the 1980s, Legs worked as a senior editor for *Spin* magazine. He lives alone in New York City and now drinks Pepsi.

Gillian McCain was the program coordinator of the Poetry Project at St. Mark's Church and editor of the *Poetry Project Newsletter.* She is the author of *Tilt,* a collection of prose poems.

The Uncensored Oral History of Punk

Please Kill Me

Legs McNeil and Gillian McCain

PENGUIN BOOKS

PENGUIN BOOKS
Published by the Penguin Group
Penguin Putnam Inc., 375 Hudson Street,
New York, New York 10014, U.S.A.
Penguin Books Ltd, 27 Wrights Lane, London W8 5TZ, England
Penguin Books Australia Ltd, Ringwood, Victoria, Australia
Penguin Books Canada Ltd, 10 Alcorn Avenue,
Toronto, Ontario, Canada M4V 3B2
Penguin Books (N.Z.) Ltd, 182–190 Wairau Road,
Auckland 10, New Zealand

Penguin Books Ltd, Registered Offices:
Harmondsworth, Middlesex, England

First published in the United States of America by Grove Press, 1996
Published in Penguin Books 1997

10

The interviews contained herein have been edited for clarity.

"He'll Have to Go," words and music by Joe Allison and Audrey Allison © 1959
(Renewed 1987). Beechwood Music Corp. All rights reserved.
International Copyright Secured. Used by permission.

THE LIBRARY OF CONGRESS HAS CATALOGUED THE HARDCOVER AS FOLLOWS:
McNeil, Legs.
Please kill me: the uncensored oral history of punk / by Legs McNeil and
Gillian McCain.—1st ed.
p. cm.
Includes index.
ISBN 0-8021-1588-8 (hc.)
ISBN 0 14 02.6690 9 (pbk.)
1. Punk rock music—United States—History and criticism.   2. Punk culture—United States.
3. Rock musicians—United States—Interviews.   I. McCain, Gillian.   II. Title.
ML3534.M46   1996
781.66—dc20   95–49841

Printed in the United States of America
Set in Goudy
Designed by Laura Hammond Hough

Authors' Note

The overwhelming majority of the material in *Please Kill Me* is the result of hundreds of original interviews conducted by the authors. In some cases, interviews and text were excerpted from other sources, including anthologies, magazines, journals, published and unpublished interviews, and other books. A list of these sources and the pages they correspond to in this text appears on page 449. We wish to acknowledge the contributions of these authors and publishers, who have enriched the content of our book.

Acknowledgments

Quite a few people lived through this book and encouraged us through it with their love, support, and humor. The authors would like to express their thanks to the following:

LEGS MCNEIL AND GILLIAN MCCAIN: Susan Lee Cohen, our literary agent, for always performing above and beyond the call of duty; and Dawn Manners, our full-time research/editorial assistant and transcriber, who took care of us through the duration and whose intelligence and insight were always an inspiration. Special thanks as well to all the other transcribers: Liz McKenna, Ann Kottner, David Vogen, Nora Greening, Filiz Swenson, and Allie Morris.

Extra special thanks to Richard Hell for letting us steal the title for our book from his T-shirt.

Also to those friends who invited us into their lives: Abbi Jane, Mariah Acquiar, Billy Altman, Callie Angell, Kathy Asheton, Ron Asheton, Scott Asheton, Laura Allen, Penny Arcade, Al Aronowitz, Bobby Ballderama, Roberta Bayley, Victor Bockris, Angela Bowie, Pam Brown, Bebe Buell, William Burroughs, John Cale, Jan Carmichael, Jim Carroll, James Chance, Bill Cheatham, Leee Black Childers, Cheetah Chrome, Ira Cohen, Tony Conrad, Jayne County, David Croland, Ronnie Cutrone, Jay Dee Daugherty, Maria Del Greco, Liz Derringer, Willie DeVille, Ged Dunn, Mick Farren, Rosebud Feliu-Pettet, Danny Fields, Jules Filer, Cyrinda Foxe, Ed Friedman, Gyda Gash, John Giorno, David Godlis, James Grauerholz, Bob Gruen, Eric Haddix, Steve Hagar, Duncan Hannah, Steve Harris, Mary Harron, Debbie Harry, Richard Hell, John Holmstrom, Mark Jacobson, Urs Jakob, Garland Jefferies, David Johansen, Betsey Johnson, Peter Jordan, Ivan Julian, Lenny Kaye, Scott Kempner, Eliot Kidd, Wayne Kramer, Liz Kurtzman, Mickey Leigh, Richard Lloyd, Matt Lolya, Jeff Magnum, Gerard Malanga, Handsome Dick Manitoba, Ray Manzarek, Philippe Marcade, Jim Marshall, Malcolm McLaren, Jonas Mekas, Alan Midgette, Paul Morrissey, Billy Name, Bobby Neuwirth, Nitebob, Judy Nylon, Pat Olesko, Terry Ork, Andi Ostrowe, Andy Paley, Patti Palladin, Fran Pelzman, Susan Pile, Dustin Pittman, Eileen Polk, Iggy Pop, Howie Pyro, Bob Quine, Dee Dee Ramone, Joey Ramone, Johnny Ramone, Genya Ravan, Lou Reed, Sylvia Reed, Marty Rev, Daniel Rey, Ed Sanders, Jerry Schatzberg, Andy Shernoff, Kate Simon, John Sinclair, Leni Sinclair, James Sliman, Gail Higgins-Smith, Patti Smith, Chris Stamp, Sable Starr, Michael Sticca, Linda Stein, Seymour Stein, Syl Sylvain, Kevin Teare, Marty Thau, Dennis Thompson, Lynne Tillman, Tish & Snookie, Maureen Tucker, Alan Vega, Arturo Vega, Holly Vincent, Ultra Violet, Jack Walls, Russell Wolensky, Mary Woronov, La Monte Young, Marian Zazeela, and Jimmy Zhivago.

Five people passed away during the making of *Please Kill Me* whom we interviewed or were about to interview. We offer our condolences to the families and friends of Sterling Morrison, Patti Giordano, Todd Smith, Fred "Sonic" Smith, and Rockin' Bob Rudnick. We hope we made them come alive in these pages for those who didn't have the pleasure of knowing how special they were.

Special thanks to our publisher and hero, Morgan Entrekin, and all the other wonderful people at Grove Press—Carla Lalli, Colin Dickerman, and John Gall.

Also special thanks to Gina Bone, Doug Simmons, Mary Harron, Victor Bockris, and Jeff Goldberg for letting us use their original material.

For their technical assistance, we'd like to thank Tom Hearn, Stephen Seymour, Drey Hobbs, Christina Berg, and Osako Kitaro.

For their constant support, thanks to Chris Cush and Arlene, owners of Mojo Guitars at 102 St. Marks Place, New York City, where members of the cast of *Please Kill Me* can be found hanging out at any given time.

LEGS MCNEIL: For her love, patience, and insight, I would like to thank Mary C. Greening. For their love, patience, and insight, I'd also like to thank Carol Overby, Patrice Adcroft, Gary Kott, Jonathan Marder, Mrs. Ellen McNeil, Craig McNeil, Rudy Langlais, Adam Roth, Michael Siegal, Tom and Judy Greening (and also for their hospitality in L.A.), Jeff and Susan Goldberg, John Mauceri, Danny Alterman, Jim Tynan, Kevin Kurran, Jack Walls, Yvan Fitch, Lynn Tenpenny, Mim Udovitch, Chris Maguire, Julia Murphy, Kathy Silberger, Susan Dooley, Carl Geary, Shane Doyle, and Jennifer Smith.

And special thanks to Maggie Estep for introducing me to Gillian.

GILLIAN MCCAIN: Most of all, I would like to thank my family for their love, support, and encouragement. My love and gratitude to H.H., my late mother, Billie, Mark, Ann, my late brother, Peter, Laura, Gail, Chris, Joyce, Luke, and John.

I would also like to thank all my friends who were so supportive during the writing of this book: Chris Simunek, David Vogen, Jo Ann Wasserman, Janice and Patrick McGyver, Eric and Filiz Swenson, Diana Rickard, Trinity Dempster and David Hughes, Joan Lakin, Douglas Rothschild, Larry Fagin, Michael Gizzi, Steve Levine, Nancy McCain, Patrick Graham, and my late aunt and uncle, Mr. and Mrs. P. T. Johnson.

Also, for their warm assistance in providing help and support in an assortment of ways, I would like to thank Ian Wright, Brad Sullivan, Yvan Fitch, Goran Andersson, Chris Maguire, Coyote Shivers, Ann Sheroff, Tracy Truran, Carl Geary, Mark Jacobson, Maya Mavjee, Bobby Grossman, and the Poetry Project.

And thanks to Maggie Estep for introducing me to Legs.

Also, to the loving memory of the late Dave Schellenberg and the late Mario Mezzacappa.

This book is dedicated to the memory of Peter McCain (1957–1997), who was always insightful, warm and kind; usually a kidnik, never slow on the uptake, occasionally a going concern, and always a beautiful cat.

And for his gorgeous taste in music, his generous intellect, and his killer sense of humor, this book is dedicated to Danny Fields, forever the coolest guy in the room.

"Them that die'll be the lucky ones."

Long John Silver, *Treasure Island*

CONTENTS

■ Please Kill Me

■ All Tomorrow's Parties
1965–1968

LOU REED: All by myself. No one to talk to. Come over here so I can talk to you . . .

We were playing together a long time ago, in a thirty-dollar-a-month apartment and we really didn't have any money, and we used to eat oatmeal all day and all night and give blood, among other things, or pose for these nickel or fifteen cent tabloids they had every week. And when I posed for them, my picture came out and it said I was a sex maniac killer that had killed fourteen children and tape-recorded it and played it in a barn in Kansas at midnight. And when John Cale's picture came out in the paper, it said he killed his lover because his lover was going to marry his sister, and he didn't want his sister to marry a fag.

STERLING MORRISON: Lou Reed's parents hated the fact that Lou was making music and hanging around with undesirables. I was always afraid of Lou's parents—the only dealings I'd had with them was that there was this constant threat of them seizing Lou and having him thrown in the nuthouse. That was always over our heads. Every time Lou got hepatitis his parents were waiting to seize him and lock him up.

JOHN CALE: That's where all Lou's best work came from. His mother was some sort of ex–beauty queen and I think his father was a wealthy accountant. Anyway, they put him in a hospital where he received shock treatment as a kid. Apparently he was at Syracuse University and was given this compulsory choice to either do gym or the Reserve Officers Training Corps. He claimed he couldn't do gym because he'd break his neck and when he did ROTC he threatened to kill the instructor. Then he put his fist through a window or something, and so he was put in a mental hospital. I don't know the full story. Every time Lou told me about it he'd change it slightly.

LOU REED: They put the thing down your throat so you don't swallow your tongue, and they put electrodes on your head. That's what was recommended in Rockland County then to discourage homosexual feelings. The effect is that you lose your memory and become a vegetable. You can't read a book because you get to page seventeen and have to go right back to page one again.

JOHN CALE: By 1965 Lou Reed had already written "Heroin" and "Waiting for the Man." I first met Lou at a party and he played his songs with an acoustic guitar, so I really didn't pay any attention because I couldn't give a shit about folk music. I hated Joan Baez and Dylan—every song was a fucking question! But Lou kept shoving these lyrics in front of me. I read them, and they weren't what Joan Baez and all those other people were singing.

At the time, I was playing with La Monte Young in the Dream Syndicate and the concept of the group was to sustain notes for two hours at a time.

BILLY NAME: La Monte Young was the best drug connection in New York. He had the best drugs—the best! Great big acid pills, and opium, and grass too.

When you went over to La Monte and Marian's place, you were there for a minimum of seven hours—probably end up to be two or three days. It was a very Turkish type scene. It was a pad with everything on the floor and beads and great hashish and street people coming and scoring—and this droning music going on.

La Monte had this whole thing where he would do a performance that would go on for days and he would have people droning with him. Droning is holding a single note for a whole long time. People would just come in and then be assigned to drone. That's when John Cale was around.

LA MONTE YOUNG: I was—so to speak—the darling of the avant-garde. Yoko Ono was always saying to me, "If only I could be as famous as you."

So I had an affair with Yoko and did a music series at her loft, and I put a warning on the very first flyer: THE PURPOSE OF THIS SERIES IS NOT ENTERTAINMENT. I was one of the first people to destroy an instrument onstage. I burned a violin at the YMHA, and people were shouting things like "Burn the composer!"

John Cale started playing with my group, the Dream Syndicate, which literally rehearsed seven days a week, six hours a day. John played specific drone pitches on the viola—until the end of 1965, when he started rehearsing with the Velvet Underground.

JOHN CALE: The first time Lou played "Heroin" for me it totally knocked me out. The words and music were so raunchy and devastating. What's more, Lou's songs fit perfectly with my concept of music. Lou had these songs where there was an element of character assassination going on. He had strong identification with the characters he was portraying. It was Method acting in song.

AL ARONOWITZ: I gave the Velvet Underground their first gig. I put them on as the opening act at the Summit High School in New Jersey and they stole my wallet-size tape recorder first thing. They were just junkies, crooks, hustlers. Most of the musicians at that time came with all these high-minded ideals, but the Velvets were all full of shit. They were just hustlers.

And their music was inaccessible. That's what Albert Grossman, Bob Dylan's manager, always used to ask—whether music's accessible or inaccessible—and the Velvets' music was totally inaccessible.

But I'd committed myself. So I put them into the Café Bizarre and I said, "You work here and you'll get some exposure, build up your chops, and get it together."

ED SANDERS: Nobody wanted to go to the Café Bizarre because you had to buy these weird drinks—five scoops of ice cream and coconut fizz. It was for tourists. But Barbara Rubin kept saying, "You gotta hear this band!"

PAUL MORRISSEY: Andy Warhol didn't want to get into rock & roll; I wanted to get into rock & roll to make money. Andy didn't want to do it, he never would have thought of it. Even after I thought of it, I had to bludgeon him into doing it. I know that you want to think that ANDY wanted to do this, and ANDY wanted to do that, everything was generated from ANDY. If you knew the actual operation of what happened at the Factory, you'd understand that Andy did nothing, and expected everybody to do everything for him.

So somebody wanted to pay Andy to go to a nightclub in Queens, and he was gonna get paid to do it. I said, "This doesn't make any sense, but it's money."

So I said, "I have a good idea. We'll go to the Queens nightclub, and they'll pay us, but the reason we'll go is because we'll manage a group that appears there."

My idea was that there could be a lot of money managing a rock & roll group that got its name in the papers, and that was the one thing Andy was good for—getting his name in the papers.

What happened then was that Barbara Rubin asked Gerard Malanga if he would come down to the Café Bizarre to take some pictures of this band, the Velvet Underground. There were all these beatnik coffee shops in the West Village that were going out of business, so they were trying to make a transition from beatniks and folk singing to some sort of rock & roll.

So I went over to the Café Bizarre. I think it was the Velvets' first night and they had the electric viola, which was the thing that distinguished them the most. And they had the drummer who was totally androgynous, there was absolutely no way of telling if Maureen Tucker was a boy or a girl. So those were the big attractions.

And John Cale, the viola player, looked wonderful with his Richard III hairstyle, and he was wearing a huge rhinestone necklace. It's hard to believe but that was really weird then.

ROSEBUD: When Andy Warhol swanned into the Café Bizarre with his crew you could tell he was hypnotized right off the bat. Image was all, and the Velvet Underground certainly had it. I could not believe all these tourists were sitting there drinking their bubbly and listening to the Velvets going on about heroin and S&M. I'm sure the audience didn't have a clue because the lyrics were fairly indecipherable. But I thought, This is great!

LOU REED: Music's never loud enough. You should stick your head in a speaker. Louder, louder, louder. Do it, Frankie, do it. Oh, how. Oh do it, do it.

PAUL MORRISSEY: I knew I'd found the right group. I spoke to the Velvets that night and I said, "Are you managed?" And cagey little Lou Reed said, "Well, um, sort of, maybe, um, not really, but, um, yes, no." You know, both answers.

I said, "Well, I'm looking to manage somebody and produce some albums. You'll have a definite job at a nightclub and you'll be managed nominally by Andy Warhol."

They said, "We don't have amplifiers."

I said, "Well, we'll have to get you amplifiers."

They said, "Well, that would be okay, but we don't have a place to live . . ."

I said, "Okay, okay, okay. Well, we'll be back tomorrow to talk about that."

So I told Andy that I had found the group that we were going to manage.

Andy said, "Oh uu-uu-uuuu ohouuuuuuuuuuuuuu!"

Andy was always frightened of doing anything, but once he felt somebody had confidence in what they were doing, especially in my case, he just said, "Oh, oh, oh, oh, oh, oh, oh, oh . . . okay."

STERLING MORRISON: I didn't make any effort to impress Andy Warhol. What did I care? He was just someone from the art crowd who was interested enough in our songs to come down and hear them—but it wasn't like a visit from some big record producer. He was just an artist whom I knew little about—except in terms of notoriety. My taste in art at the time wasn't Pop art, it was probably Flemish, I don't know. Impressionist . . . No, Pre-Raphaelites. I think I was keen on the Pre-Raphaelites, which maybe is a precursor to Pop.

AL ARONOWITZ: I got the Velvet Underground into the Café Bizarre, and the next thing I knew they were leaving with Andy Warhol. They never said a word to me, Warhol never said a word to me, it was highly unethical, there's a law against that really.

It was a handshake deal, but what's a handshake deal to Lou Reed—he was nothing but an opportunist fucking junkie. If I had a signed contract with the Velvets I could have sued the shit out of Warhol.

LOU REED: Andy Warhol told me that what we were doing with the music was the same thing he was doing with painting and movies and writing—i.e., not kidding around. To my mind nobody in music was doing anything that even approximated the real thing, with the exception of us. We were doing a specific thing that was very, very real. It wasn't slick or a lie in any conceivable way, which was the only way we could work with him. Because the very first thing I liked about Andy was that he was very real.

PAUL MORRISSEY: The first thing I realized about the Velvet Underground was that they had no lead singer, because Lou Reed was just such an uncomfortable performer. I think he forced himself to do it because he was so ambitious, but Lou was not a natural performer. So I said to Andy, "They need a singer." I said, "Remember that girl that came up here? Nico? She left her little record, a cute little record she made in London with Andrew Loog Oldham?"

GERARD MALANGA: Nico latched on to Andy and myself when we went to Paris. I just put two and two together that Nico had slept with Dylan. It was kind of obvious. She got a song out of Bob, "I'll Keep It with Mine," so he probably got something in return, quid pro quo.

But Nico was of an independent mind. She was not your typical Hollywood starlet. She had her own personal history going for her—Brian Jones, Bob Dylan, she had been in Fellini's *La Dolce Vita* and she was the mother of Ari, Alain Delon's illegitimate son. Yeah, so Nico already had a life-style when we met up with her.

NICO: In Paris, Edie Sedgwick was too occupied with her lipstick to listen, but Gerard Malanga told me about the studio where they worked in New York. It was called the Factory. He said I would be welcome to visit when I was next in New York, but Edie interrupted with some stupid comment about my hair color. But Andy was interested that I had been in films and was working with the Rolling Stones.

BILLY NAME: All of us at the Factory were very taken with Nico. She was just this fascinating creature who was totally nonflamboyant, nonpretentious, but absolutely magnetically controlling. And she didn't wear all the hippie flowers, she just wore these black pantsuits, or white pantsuits—a real Nordic beauty. She was too much, really, let me tell you, so anything we could think of to have her play a role in our scene, that's what we were gonna do. We wanted her to have a starring role in what we were doing, and since she was a chanteuse, Paul Morrissey thought it would be great to have her sing with the Velvets—which of course was the most wrong thing you could say to them at that point in their development.

PAUL MORRISSEY: Nico was spectacular. She had a definite charisma. She was interesting. She was distinctive. She had a magnificent deep voice. She was extraordinary looking. She was tall. She was somebody.

I said, "She's wonderful and she's looking for work." I said, "We'll put her in the band because the Velvets need somebody who can sing or who can command attention when they stand in front of a microphone, so she can be the lead singer, and the Velvets can still do their thing."

AL ARONOWITZ: Nico was using me, she was cock-teasing me because I knew everybody and had access to everybody. I mean everybody was kissing my ass and Nico was always coming on, promising me pussy, and never delivering.

I was a dumb asshole. Everybody was getting laid and I was being faithful to my wife. Nico said to me, "Come on, take a ride." So we took a ride out to the Delaware Water Gap and she had this little bottle of LSD that she had smuggled in from Switzerland, and she kept dipping her pinkie into it and doing it. She gave some to me and we got pretty stoned and then she wanted to stop at a motel. I said, "Sure."

When a woman says, "Let's stop at a motel," what does that mean to a guy? But it didn't mean anything to her—I don't know why she wanted to stop at a motel. We spent the night under the covers next to each other but nothing happened because she said she liked her lovers half-dead—like Lou Reed. Everybody had had a piece of Nico, except me, ha ha ha. Bob Dylan didn't have an affair with Nico, just a piece. I mean they all had had a piece. They didn't care, they just wanted to get rid of her, not be bothered by her.

I brought Nico to see the Velvet Underground—Nico never had any taste and she had the immediate hots for Lou Reed—because she had visions of being a pop star herself.

And then even Nico started hanging out with Warhol, who had been collecting this freak show. That's all Andy Warhol had—a freak show—and that's what attracted everybody. He had this place called the Factory and it was like a sideshow—"Come look at the freaks!" And all the uptown jet-setters would come down and look.

But I'd always get a bad feeling going over to the Factory because all these arrogant freaks disgusted me, with their arrogance and their put-ons, the way they walked, strutting around. It was all a pose. Nico became one of them—she was doing the same thing—but she got away with it because she was so beautiful, just the way a lot of people used to forgive a lot of things about me because I could write.

PAUL MORRISSEY: Of course Lou Reed almost gagged when I said we need a girl singing with the group so we could get some extra publicity. I didn't want to say they needed somebody who had some sort of talent, but that's what I meant. Lou was very reluctant to go with Nico, but I think John Cale prevailed on him to accept that as part of the deal. And Nico hung out with Lou because she hoped he would write another song for her, but he never did. He gave her two to three little songs and didn't let her do anything else.

JOHN CALE: Lou was very full of himself and faggy in those days. We called him Lulu, and I was Black Jack. Lou wanted to be the queen bitch and spit out the sharpest rebukes of anyone around. Lou always ran with the pack and the Factory was full of queens to run with. But Lou was dazzled by Andy and Nico. He was completely spooked by Andy because he could not believe that someone could have so much goodwill, and yet be so mischievous—in the same transvestite way that Lou was, all that bubbling gay humor.

Lou tried to compete. Unfortunately for him, Nico could do it better—Nico and Andy had a slightly different approach, but they outdid Lou time and time again. Andy was never less than considerate to us. Lou couldn't fully understand this, he couldn't grasp this amity that Andy had.

Even worse, Lou would say something bitchy, but Andy would say something even bitchier—and nicer. This would irritate Lou. Nico had the same effect. She would say things so Lou couldn't answer back. You see, Lou and Nico had some kind of affair, both consummated and constipated, during the time he wrote these psychological love songs for her like "I'll Be Your Mirror" and "Femme Fatale."

When it fell apart, we really learnt how Nico could be the mistress of the destructive one-liner. I remember one morning we had gathered at the Factory for a rehearsal. Nico came in late, as usual. Lou said hello to her in a rather cold way.

Nico simply stood there. You could see she was waiting to reply, in her own time. Ages later, out of the blue, came her first words: "I cannot make love to Jews anymore."

NICO: Lou liked to manipulate women, you know, like program them. He wanted to do that with me. He told me so. Like computerize me.

DANNY FIELDS: Everybody was in love with everybody. We were all kids, and it was like high school. I mean it was like when I was sixteen, this one likes this one this week, and this one doesn't like that one this week, but likes this one, and there are all these triangles, I mean it wasn't terribly serious. It just happened to be people who later on became very famous because they were so sexy and beautiful, but we didn't realize it at the time, we just all were falling in and out of love—who could even fucking keep track?

Everybody was in and out of love with Andy, of course, and Andy was in and out of love with everybody. But people that were most "in-loved-with" were the people, I think, who fucked the least—like Andy. I mean the people who you really know went to bed with Andy, you could count on the fingers of one hand. The people who really went to bed with Edie or Lou or Nico were very, very few. There really wasn't that much sex, there were more crushes than sex. Sex was so messy. It still is.

JONAS MEKAS: I considered Andy Warhol and the Factory in the sixties to be like Sigmund Freud. Andy was Freud. He was the psychoanalyst, there was that big couch in the Factory and Andy was there, he didn't say anything, you could project anything on him, put anything in, unload yourself, give him this, and he wouldn't put you down. Andy was your father and mother and brother, all of them. So that's why those people felt so good around him—they could be in those films, they could just say and do whatever they wanted because they wouldn't be disapproved, that was his genius. Andy admired all the stars, so to please all those sad desperate souls that came into the Factory, Andy called them "Superstars."

STERLING MORRISON: Somebody said, "We're gonna play a psychiatrist convention," and I said, "Is that really the best we can do?"

MAUREEN TUCKER: Why they asked us to play, I have no idea—two hundred psychiatrists and us, these freaks from the Factory. Afterwards people like Gerard and Barbara Rubin just carried on with their tape recorders and cameras, going to tables and asking these ridiculous questions. Those people were flabbergasted. I just sort of sat back and said, "What the hell are we doing here?" Then I realized that maybe the shrinks thought they'd take notes or something.

BILLY NAME: The psych convention started out as a con. We were mingling with them as they arrived, but it was more as if Edie Sedgwick's aunt had thrown a big party. We would naturally talk to everybody, but not like they were guests, more like they were Edie's relatives. I was telling some of them that I read Otto Rank as a teenager, and I said, "Well, you know Rollo May was teaching at the New School so I went to take a couple of courses just to see . . ."

The Velvets were tuning up right out in the open, and then when they did their performance, it was just part of the atmosphere, like a bump in the overall night.

The press played it like it was ironic confrontation, which it wasn't at all. We didn't shock anybody. Psychiatrists may be stiff but they all have a sense of humor, and they're all intelligent. It was more playful than confrontational. Barbara Rubin would do these things like set off light flashes in their eyes, or stick the mike in their faces, you know, that confrontational technique that basically started with the Living Theater. To me it was old. I already knew that number, so I wasn't taken by her.

The psychiatrist convention was important though, because it signaled a new era at the Factory, the *Chelsea Girls* time. Up until Nico and the Velvet Underground came along, it was always Andy Warhol and Edie Sedgwick. Andy and Edie. They were like a double act. You know, she dyed her hair silver for a while, and they would go out as a twosome. They were like the Lucy and Desi of the art world.

But the night of the psychiatrists' convention signaled the end of the Edie Sedgwick era. She danced with the Velvets onstage that night. She danced very cool—Edie was always very cool.

GERARD MALANGA: Right after that the Velvets played a week at the Cinemathèque. Jonas Mekas had proposed to Andy that he do a film retrospective there. Andy came up with the idea of an Edie Sedgwick retrospective, but then when he met the Velvets at the Café Bizarre, the idea turned into something bigger.

PAUL MORRISSEY: The week at the Cinemathèque was supposed to be an Edie Sedgwick film retrospective? Bullshit. That's absurd. We were probably still trying to help Edie, probably had some footage of her wandering around doing nothing.

Jonas Mekas didn't offer the Cinemathèque to Andy. He offered it to me. He said, "Do you have anything you can put in this theater I rent?" And I said, "Why don't you show some movies and we'll launch our group?"

We showed double-screen movies for an hour, and then the Velvet Underground played in front of some more movies for an hour. That's all it was. It was alright. Just a job.

LOU REED: Andy would show his movies on us. We wore black so you could see the movie. But we were all wearing black anyway.

BILLY NAME: It was called "Uptight with Andy Warhol," and it wasn't just a Warhol film festival, it was like a happening with Andy Warhol's films—the films were projected on the people who were in the films, while they were dancing to the music onstage. We actually made a film of the Velvet Underground and Nico so that we could project it on them while they were playing at the Cinemathèque.

The entire thing was first called "Uptight" because when Andy would do something, everybody would get uptight. Andy was sort of the antithesis to what the avant-garde romantic artists were at that time.

Filmmakers like Stan Brakhage and Stan Vanderbeek were still bohemian avant-garde hero artists, whereas Andy was not even an antihero, he was a zero. And it just made them grit their teeth to have Warhol becoming recognized as the core of this thing that they had built. So everybody was always uptight whenever we showed up.

All the other underground filmmakers would cringe like someone was scraping chalk along a blackboard—"Oh no, not Andy Warhol again!"

NICO: My name was somewhere near the bottom of the program and I cried. Andy told me not to care, it was only a rehearsal. They played the record of Bob Dylan's song "I'll Keep It with Mine" because I didn't have enough to sing otherwise. Lou wanted to sing everything. I had to stand there and sing along with it. I had to do this every night for a week. It is the most stupid concert I have ever done.

Edie Sedgwick tried to sing along, but she couldn't do it. We never saw her onstage again. It was Edie's farewell and my premiere at the same time.

BILLY NAME: Edie wasn't happy with the way her career was progressing with Andy, but, of course, she had gotten into amphetamine—crystal stuff, with me and Ondine and Brigid Polk, and that really devastated any possible career, because, you know, you would have to stay in your place and get ready for six hours.

NICO: Some things you are born to, and Edie was born to die from her pleasures. She would have to die from drugs whoever gave them to her.

STERLING MORRISON: When we first showed up, we were downer people—pill people who took Thorazine and all the barbiturates. Seconals and Thorazine were a big favorite. You could get Thorazine from doctors—somebody always had a prescription. It was good, pharmaceutical, drugstore stuff.

They used to give Thorazine to dangerous psychotics—it definitely subdues you. It puts you in kind of a catatonic-like state, ha ha ha. I'd wash it down with alcohol and see if I was alive the next morning.

RONNIE CUTRONE: When you walked out of the elevator at the Factory, Paul Morrissey had a sign up on the door that said ABSOLUTELY NO DRUGS ALLOWED. Meanwhile, everybody was shooting up on the staircase. Nobody actually took drugs in the Factory, except Andy, who took Obetrols, those little orange speed pills. He took one a day to paint, because he was a workaholic. That was really his thing. Everybody else shot up on the staircase.

But only Methedrine. We were purists. The other groups were taking acid. By this time I was basically off of acid, I was into Methedrine, because you had to get uptight. "Uptight" used to have a good connotation—you know, like Stevie Wonder's song "Uptight," but we changed it to mean rigid and paranoid. Hence Methedrine.

ED SANDERS: I knew Andy Warhol before he surrounded himself with those switchblade types. That's why I wouldn't hang out, I just didn't feel comfortable there anymore. It got a little vicious. I was really sick of those people. We called them A-heads, short for "amphetamine heads," because they were all into speed.

In fact, I got into making underground movies specifically to do a documentary on amphetamine heads. So I rented this old loft on Allen

Street and I bought a couple ounces of amphetamine and I put it in the middle of the room and put lights up around the edge. The only rules were that I had to be able to film everything, because I was making this documentary called *Amphetamine Head.* I spread the word, and all these A-heads came, and they were squirting colored ink onto canvas from their syringes, then they'd use the same syringe to shoot up with. That would have been a good flick, but the police confiscated the footage.

SUSAN PILE: People did strange things when they did speed. There was one guy who showed up at Max's Kansas City with his arm in a sling. Everyone was like, "What happened to you?"

He said, "Oh, I took a shot of speed and I couldn't stop brushing my hair for three days."

LOU REED: The old sound was alcoholic. The tradition was finally broken. The music is sex and drugs and happy. And happy is the joke the music understands best. Ultrasonic sounds on records to cause frontal lobotomies. Hey, don't be afraid. You'd better take drugs and learn to love PLASTIC. All different kinds of plastic—pliable, rigid, colored, colorful, nonattached plastic.

RONNIE CUTRONE: The sixties have a reputation for being open and free and cool, but the reality was that everybody was straight. Everybody was totally straight and then there was us—this pocketful of nuts. We had long hair, and we'd get chased down the block. People would chase you for ten blocks, screaming, "Beatle!" They were out of their fucking minds— that was the reality of the sixties. Nobody had long hair—you were a fucking freak, you were a fruit, you were not like the rest of the world.

So for me, there was a strong pull toward the dark side. Lou and Billy Name would go to this Vaseline bar called Ernie's—there would be jars of Vaseline on the bar and there was a back room where the guys would go to fuck each other. While I was never gay, I was into sex, and when you're thirteen or fourteen, sex is not that available from women. So I figured, Gee, wouldn't it be great to be gay?

So I tried it, but I was a miserable failure. I remember I was actually sucking this guy off once, and he said, "Man, you're not into this." I went, "Yeah, I know. I'm sorry."

LOU REED: Honey, I'm a cocksucker. What are you?

BILLY NAME: Lou, Mary Woronov, and I used to go to Max's Kansas City, and also these gay dance clubs in the Village, like the Stonewall. It would close at four o'clock, so Lou and I would still be up, on Methedrine, and still be wanting to do something. So we'd go to after-hours places, where you could still dance. Then when it would get to be daylight, Lou and I would just mosey over to the Factory and do a number. We weren't having an affair or anything, we were just pals hanging around.

I don't think we really did blow jobs. I hate blow jobs. They're just so awkward. I hate having my head so occupied—it's too close and claustrophobic. Lou would just jerk off, get off, and then get up to leave, so I had to say, "Hey, wait a minute. I didn't come yet."

So Lou would sit on my face while I jerked off. It was like smoking corn silk behind the barn, it was just kid stuff. There was no rapture or romance involved. It was just about getting your rocks off at that moment, because going out with girls was still about getting involved, and all that shit. With guys it was just easier.

DANNY FIELDS: I was so in love with Lou Reed. I thought he was the hottest, sexiest thing I had ever seen. I guess he just assumed everybody loved him, you know, he was so cool, and those sunglasses. Oh my god, the emotional energy I expended on that person—what was I thinking?

RONNIE CUTRONE: S&M sex fascinated me even though I knew nothing about it. I had a natural curiosity, so I asked Lou, "What's *Venus in Furs* about?" Lou said, "Ah, you know, it's some trash novel." I said, "Where can I get a copy?" Lou said, "Ah, yeah, just down the block there's a store." So I went and bought the book. I was still in high school, so I'd go to class with my *Venus in Furs* and *Story of O*, and *Justine*, and sit there reading this stuff.

That's why I instantly loved the Velvets' music. It was about urban street stuff, it was about kink, it was about sex—some of it was about sex that I didn't even know about, but I was learning.

Gradually Gerard, Mary, and I formed a great routine for the song "Venus in Furs," because "Venus in Furs" has three basic characters—the Dominatrix, the slave Severin, and the Black Russian Prince, who kills the slave.

I wasn't going to be no slave, and I just didn't have what it takes to be a good dominatrix, so now we had it set—Mary and I dancing with bullwhips, crucifying Gerard.

We basically played only for our own enjoyment—no crowd participation, we didn't say a word to the audience, I mean, an hour and forty-five minute set without a word to the crowd, not "Thank you," not "Glad you could come," not "We're gonna have a real good time tonight."

We'd just come out, shoot up, lift weights, put flashlights in their eyes, whip giant bullwhips across their faces, sort of simulate fucking each other onstage, have Andy's films blaring in the background, and the Velvets would have their backs to the audience.

GERARD MALANGA: After the Cinemathèque, we saw the show as a whole serious entity—the bullwhip dance really went with "Venus in Furs." So I started inventing tableaus for some of the other songs because I wasn't gonna wield my whip for every song onstage, it would have looked ridiculous.

PAUL MORRISSEY: Gerard liked to come along and dance. He would just stand onstage, gyrating next to them. And then he brought a whip and then Mary Woronov stood there and then different people would just get up and . . . let's call them go-go girls or something.

It added a lot. Gerard was great. It added something to see people dancing like that. Because one thing you have to give a lot of credit to the Velvets for, they didn't move onstage. That's an homage. Then of course Nico walked out with this gorgeous face and voice and stood absolutely motionless. Oh, such class and dignity.

So I had to come up with a name for the show—the lights and the dancers that went with the Velvet Underground and Nico, and I was looking at this stupid Dylan album that had always intrigued me a bit, I don't know which one it was, but I seem to recall there's a picture of Barbara Rubin on the back. So I was looking at the gibberish that was typed on the back, and I said, "Look, use the word 'exploding,' something 'plastic,' and whatever that means, 'inevitable'."

ANDY WARHOL: We all knew something revolutionary was happening. We just felt it. Things couldn't look this strange and new without some barrier being broken. "It's like the Red Seeea," Nico said, standing next to me one night on the Dom balcony that looked out over all the action, "paaaaarting."

PAUL MORRISSEY: We performed at the Dom on St. Marks Place for about a month, then I went out to L.A. to set up this gig at a night-club on Sunset Boulevard called the Trip, if you can imagine. Pathetic hippie crap. So we vacated the Dom because there was no air conditioning and summer was coming up, and they all wanted to go to L.A. And it sounded fun.

Then Bill Graham came from San Francisco, begging me to book the Velvet Underground into his toilet, the Fillmore—the Swillmore Vom-itorium. Boy, was he a creep. They always talk about him as a saint. Ucch! I mean, he was really AWFUL! Just a real monster. He came to L.A. crying practically. His argument was that it was a big holiday weekend, and you know, "I've been fighting so hard to keep my place open, and I'm going bankrupt, and the police are closing me, and they're getting me for this and getting me for that and I don't know if I can survive but YOUR act is so famous, that if you came to San Francisco it would save my club . . ."

MARY WORONOV: We didn't even want to go to San Francisco. California was really strange. We weren't like them at all. They hated us.

For one thing, we dressed in black leather, they dressed in wild colors. They were like, "Oh wow man, a happening!" We were like reading Jean Genet. We were S&M and they were free love. We really liked gay people, and the West Coast was totally homophobic. So they thought we were evil and we thought they were stupid.

Plus we were really uptight, because we were all . . . well, I was on speed. And when we walked into the Fillmore, the Mothers of Invention were not just playing like they normally did, but they had people dancing in front of them, just like Gerard and me did with the Velvets. So we were pissed off about that, and Lou was really fucking mad; after the set the band left their instruments near the amplifier, which created feedback, and just walked off the stage.

San Francisco, of course, didn't even know the set was over.

MAUREEN TUCKER: I didn't like that love-peace shit.

GERARD MALANGA: Jim Morrison came to see us at the Trip, because he was a film student in L.A. at the time. That's when, as the theory goes, Jim Morrison adopted my look—the black leather pants—from seeing me dancing onstage at the Trip.

PAUL MORRISSEY: While we were in L.A. we went into the studio and recorded the first album. The first album was done in two nights and it cost about three thousand dollars, which was a lot of money then. Andy never spent that much money on anything. The Warhol movies only cost a couple of hundred dollars a piece. So for me to get that much money out of Andy . . .

ANDY WARHOL: The whole time the album was being made, nobody seemed happy with it, especially Nico. "I want to sound like Bawwwhhhb Deeee-lahhhn," she wailed, so upset because she didn't.

LOU REED: Andy made a point of trying to make sure that on our first album the language remained intact. I think Andy was interested in shocking, in giving people a jolt and not letting them talk us into making compromises. He said, "Oh you've got to make sure you leave the dirty words in." He was adamant about that. He didn't want it to be cleaned up and, because he was there, it wasn't. And, as a consequence of that, we always knew what it was like to have your way.

IGGY POP: The first time I heard the Velvet Underground and Nico record was at a party on the University of Michigan campus. I just hated the sound. You know, "HOW COULD ANYBODY MAKE A RECORD THAT SOUNDS LIKE SUCH A PIECE OF SHIT? THIS IS DISGUSTING! ALL THESE PEOPLE MAKE ME FUCKING SICK! FUCKING DISGUSTING HIPPIE VERMIN! FUCKING BEATNIKS, I WANNA KILL THEM ALL! THIS JUST SOUNDS LIKE TRASH!"

Then about six months later it hit me. "Oh my god! WOW! This is just a fucking great record!" That record became very key for me, not just for what it said, and for how great it was, but also because I heard other people who could make good music—without being any good at music. It gave me hope. It was the same thing the first time I heard Mick Jagger sing. He can only sing one note, there's no tone, and he just goes, "Hey, well baby, baby, I can be oeweowww . . ." Every song is the same monotone, and it's just this kid rapping. It was the same with the Velvets. The sound was so cheap and yet so good.

PAUL MORRISSEY: Verve/MGM didn't know what to do with the *Velvet Underground and Nico* album because it was so peculiar. They didn't release it for almost a year, and I think during that time it was generating in Lou's mind that the album's going to come out and maybe make a lot of money, "So let's get out of this management contract we have with Andy and Paul." Tom Wilson at Verve/MGM only bought the album from me because of Nico. He saw no talent in Lou.

STERLING MORRISON: There were problems with Nico from the very beginning, because there were only so many songs that were appropriate for her, and she wanted to sing them all—"I'm Waiting for the Man," "Heroin," all of them. And she would try and do little sexual-politics things in the band. Whoever seemed to be having undue influence on the course of events, you'd find Nico close to them. So she went from Lou to Cale, but neither of those affairs lasted very long.

RONNIE CUTRONE: Nico was too odd to have any kind of a relationship with. She wasn't one of those women who you stay with or you love or you play with or you hang out with. Nico was really odd. She was very icy and reserved on one level, and then annoyingly insecure on another.

Nico was totally uncool because she couldn't leave the house without looking in the mirror for a hundred hours. "Ronnie, how does this look?" and she'd do a little dance step and I was like, "Fucking Nico, just go out and dance." Yet she was the Ice Princess, she was gorgeous, you know, a killer blonde.

But Nico was a strange one. She was a weirdo. Nico was a fucking weirdo, I mean that's all there is to it. Beautiful, but a weirdo. You didn't have a relationship with Nico.

And Lou didn't really want Nico around because Lou wanted to be the Velvet Underground and play rock & roll. Lou didn't want to be arty anymore. He wanted to be pure rock & roll. You know, enough was enough.

The Velvets weren't getting any radio airplay. There were no big record deals. But that wasn't all Andy's fault, I mean, look what they were writing about: heroin, and naked sailors dead on the floor. I mean, they were not going to get radio airplay with "Venus in Furs"!

NICO: Everybody in the Velvet Underground was so egomaniac. Everybody wanted to be the star. I mean like Lou wanted to be the star—of course he always was—but all the newspapers came to me all the time. I always wanted to sing "I'm Waiting for the Man," but Lou wouldn't let me. Lou was the boss and was very bossy. Have you met Lou? What do you think of him—sarcastic? It's because he takes so many pills—the combination of all the pills he takes . . . He's real quick, incredibly quick. I'm very slow.

RONNIE CUTRONE: You also have to realize we were on Methedrine nine days a week. So even now, I don't know what the truth was, because when you stay up for nine days straight, anything can happen, the paranoia is so thick you can cut it with an ax. And all the resentments would stay swallowed up for months, even years.

I'll never forget one night we got bad speed, but we went out onstage, and we found out later that everybody thought that the other person was out to get them. During "Venus in Furs" I would throw down my bullwhip and wiggle it on the floor and Mary would dance toward it, but on this night when I threw down my bullwhip, Mary *stepped* on it, and I couldn't pull it back. Gerard was doing the same thing, and everybody was thinking that the other one was out to get them.

That was not untypical. There would be "I know so and so's talking behind my back" or "He's trying to do this" or "He's trying to get there."

Everybody was vying for Andy's attention. There was always this subliminal, and sometimes not so subliminal, level of rivalry and deep, deep, deep paranoia. I mean, you're up for nine days, your peripheral vision is raining, everything is moving in the room, you don't know nothing from nothing, so a casual remark takes on deep, deep, deep meaning that is so important to the cosmos. It really fucks you up.

DANNY FIELDS: I told Lou and John, repeatedly, "You know you guys are too good for this. Why don't you try and make it as a band?" I thought the visual effects of the Exploding Plastic Inevitable were stupid and corny, I thought the whip dancing was stupid and corny, and I thought that Barbara Rubin's slide projections were stupid and corny. The Exploding Plastic Inevitable was just like kindergarten, it had nowhere near the power of the music. The music was the real stuff. Had the lights been as good as the music, maybe, but they weren't—I mean polka dots and films?

So I thought that the Velvet Underground were better as a band, but I suppose they felt secure under the aegis of Andy Warhol and it gave them an opportunity that they might not have had. So when I'd tell Lou and John that they were better than the Exploding Plastic Inevitable, they'd tell me, "But Andy's so good to us. How could we ever leave Andy?"

JOHN CALE: Warhol was a good catalyst. Whoever he worked with, he took and he set them off really well. It wasn't very good when he started losing interest in the whole project. We were touring around the country and Warhol just wasn't interested anymore, and there was a lot of backbiting going on in the band. For one thing, traveling with seventeen people and a light show and everything is a kind of mania if you don't get enough money. And the only reason we got a lot of money was because Andy was with us.

PAUL MORRISSEY: Lou more or less disbanded the group before the *Velvet Underground and Nico* album even came out and announced that he wanted out of the contract. He wanted to go with better managers. Better managers? They would have gone back to Queens and remained unknown if I hadn't come along.

LOU REED: Warhol was furious. I'd never seen Andy angry, but I did that day. He was really mad. He turned bright red and called me a rat. That was the worst thing he could think of. This was like leaving the nest.

PAUL MORRISSEY: Andy was so ill at ease around Lou Reed. Andy was ill at ease around anybody—but a billion times more ill at ease around Lou, who he realized was a double-faced, insincere, grasping type. So any confrontation Lou passes off as something between him and Andy is pretty much invented.

Andy would say, "Oh that Lou is coming around, you got to get rid of him. Say I'm not here." Andy just didn't want to deal with people like that. And I can't blame him. I dealt with Lou all the time, on Andy's behalf, and Lou always had a little agenda of his own.

JOHN CALE: Lou was starting to act funny. He brought in this real snake, Steve Sesnick, to be our manager, and all this intrigue started to take place. Lou was calling us *his* band, and Sesnick was trying to get him to go solo. Maybe it was the drugs Lou was doing at that time. They certainly didn't help.

RONNIE CUTRONE: I remember when we broke up as the Exploding Plastic Inevitable. We were playing the Scene. In those days, nobody could dance, so if you were dancing onstage, people watched you, like, "Wooow, cool." But after fifty to a hundred performances of the EPI, people caught on.

The stage at the Scene was really low, and all of a sudden, out of nowhere, five or ten people came up and joined us. Mary and I just looked at each other: "Like, it's over, isn't it?"

I was actually relieved. I had a girlfriend and I just couldn't lead the groupie life-style anymore. I used to wear eight rings, and I always had a bullwhip around my waist, so I went backstage, took off all the rings and threw them out the window, untied my bullwhip and threw it out the window, too. I turned to my girlfriend and said, "I love you. I'm not doing this anymore." She probably said to herself, Oh goody, he's all mine. Now we can go home and shoot up alone.

ED SANDERS: There's a problem with opening your act to the gutter. I mean, it's like dabbling in Satanism, or experimenting in certain life-styles, or certain types of drugs, that open you up—I mean, I'm not a religious person, but you open up that crack, it can get you. So you have to be careful.

The problem with the hippies was that there developed a hostility within the counterculture itself, between those who had, like, the equivalent of a trust fund versus those who had to live by their wits. It's true, for instance, that blacks were somewhat resentful of the hippies by the Summer of Love, 1967, because their perception was that these kids were drawing paisley swirls on their Sam Flax writing pads, burning incense, and taking acid, but those kids could get out of there any time they wanted to.

They could go back home. They could call their mom and say, "Get me outta here." Whereas someone who was raised in a project on Columbia Street and was hanging out on the edge of Tompkins Square Park can't escape. Those kids don't have anyplace to go. They can't go back to Great Neck, they can't go back to Connecticut. They can't go back to boarding school in Baltimore. They're trapped.

So there developed another kind, more of a lumpen hippie, who really came from an abused childhood—from parents that hated them, from parents that threw them out. Maybe they came from a religious family that would call them sluts or say "You had an abortion, get out of here" or "I found birth control pills in your purse, get out of here, go away." And those kids fermented into a kind of hostile street person. Punk types.

LOU REED: There is a lot to be said for not being in the limelight. In other words, Andy didn't have to wear the sunglasses and the black leather jacket, the two things that drew attention to him. Anybody knows if you go out and do that, you're going to attract a certain bunch of people, both on the negative and positive side.

PAUL MORRISSEY: Andy Warhol gave Valerie Solanis handouts because he was a nice guy. Then Andy said to her, "Why don't you earn the money once, Valerie. You can appear in a movie." So instead of giving her twenty-five dollars—just to get rid of her—he was trying to rehabilitate her, as he was always trying to do with everybody, trying to make them useful. He said, "Well, say something in front of the camera, and then when we give you twenty-five dollars it'll look like you earned it." *I, A Man* was done in one night. The whole movie was made in two to three hours, and Valerie showed up and did a five- or ten-minute scene and that was it.

ULTRA VIOLET: Valerie Solanis was a bit scary, but I liked her, because I think she was brilliant. If you read her manifesto, *SCUM*—for "The Society for Cutting Up Men"—it's mad but brilliant and witty. I was not born a feminist, but when I read her manifesto I thought it had a lot of good points—that men have been controlling the world ever since Adam and it's about time it stopped.

PAUL MORRISSEY: I tried to get rid of Valerie Solanis three times. And then one day she came in with Andy and when nobody was looking, she just took out a gun and started shooting. Stupid idiot. She wanted to shoot somebody else that day and he wasn't home, so she just decided to shoot Andy. What do you make of someone like that? You can't analyze that. There were no deeper meanings in there. It had nothing to do with Andy.

BILLY NAME: I heard the shots from inside the darkroom. I heard an unrecognized sound, but I was working on something, and I knew

Fred Hughes and Paul were up front, so whatever it was, I was sure they'd be able to take care of it. So I wanted to finish up and then go see if something fell down.

When I opened that door and I walked into the front part of the Factory, there was Andy on the floor in a pool of blood. I was immediately down on my knees at his side, to see what I could do. I had my hand under him, and I was just crying. This was really strange—Andy said to me, "Don't . . . don't . . . don't make me laugh. It hurts too much." By that time the ambulance driver came and I didn't really pay much attention to anybody else . . .

GERARD MALANGA: It was bad. He almost did die. His pulse was so low that he was pretty much pronounced clinically dead. There was at least two, maybe three bullets. He lost his spleen. He lost part of a lung or a liver. For a year he had to wear a corset to keep his intestines in place.

LOU REED: I was scared to call Warhol, and in the end I did, and he asked me, "Why didn't you come?"

RONNIE CUTRONE: After Andy got shot, he was very, very, very paranoid about the whole scene. I think he thought that maybe he had taken some wrong turns in his life and shouldn't be around people who were that crazy. That's when the new Factory came in, with the suits and ties.

Andy was different after he got shot. I mean Andy would say hello to me and talk to me but he was really scared. He was scared about what that kind of insanity could bring—which was six bullets in the chest.

So Andy was trying to change his life, I was trying to change my life, Lou was trying to become commercial, and Nico, I don't even know what happened to Nico. She just drifted off, maybe she thought that she'd get back into the movies . . . I'm not even really sure, because it wasn't a time when people expressed their feelings.

STERLING MORRISON: Lou called Maureen Tucker and I to a meeting at the Riviera Café in the West Village to announce that John Cale was out of the band.

I said, "You mean out for today or for this week?" And Lou said, "No, he's out." I said that we were the band, that was it, graven on the tablets. So then there was a long and bitter argument, with much banging on tables, and finally Lou said, "You don't go for it? Okay, the band is dissolved."

Now I could say that it was more important to keep the band together than to worry about John Cale, but that wasn't really what decided me. I just wanted to keep on doing it. So finally I weighed my self-interest against

John Cale's interests and sold him out. I told Lou I'd swallow it, but I didn't like it.

I'd have to say that Lou bumped John because of jealousy. One friend said that Lou had always told him he wanted to be a solo star. Lou never confided that to us, but John and I always knew that he really wanted some kind of recognition apart from the band.

JOHN CALE: In the beginning, Lou and I had an almost religious fervor about what we were doing—like trying to figure ways to integrate some of La Monte Young's or Andy Warhol's concepts into rock & roll. But after the first record we lost our patience and diligence. We couldn't even remember what our precepts were.

LOU REED: Rock & roll is so great, people should start dying for it. You don't understand. The music gave you back your beat so you could dream. A whole generation running with a Fender bass . . .

The people just have to die for the music. People are dying for everything else, so why not the music? Die for it. Isn't it pretty? Wouldn't you die for something pretty?

Perhaps I should die. After all, all the great blues singers did die. But life is getting better now.

I don't want to die. Do I?

Part One

■ I Wanna Be Your Dog
1967–1971

Chapter 1

■ Poetry? You Call This Poetry?

DANNY FIELDS: When I wasn't getting laid elsewhere I went to Max's Kansas City every night. It was a bar and restaurant two blocks away from where I lived and you could sit there all night and bring yourself coffee. It was free. And you always signed the check and never paid the bill. I felt so guilty, I had an unpaid bill of about two or three thousand dollars. I guess that was a lot in the sixties. I had friends that would sign the check "Donald Duck" and "Fatty Arbuckle." It was just so wonderful and all the waitresses were beautiful . . . and all the busboys . . .

You could have sex with all the busboys. I mean, not right there, but later. And anybody who walked into the room, you could fuck, because they all wanted to be in the back room. And you would say, "You'll have to fuck me and I'll let you sit at a good table."

So it was wide open, but it wasn't gay, thank god. We hated gay bars. Gay bars? Oh please, who wanted to go to gay bars? At Max's you could fuck anyone in the room, and that was what was sweet about it.

LEEE CHILDERS: Danny was the company freak at Elektra Records. His job was to keep the stupid record company executives somehow in touch with the street. That was an actual job title then: "company freak." He told them what was good and what wasn't, but mostly what was cool.

The record companies were wise to actually admit that they weren't cool. In the sixties, they had to admit they didn't have a clue. So they hired people whose job it was to be cool. It was a wonderful idea.

DANNY FIELDS: They hired someone at a low level who wore bell-bottoms and smoked dope and took LSD in the office—me. And I really would take LSD in the office. I would sit around and just lick it. My hands would be all orange.

STEVE HARRIS: I was working for Elektra Records and was in California with Jac Holzman, the president of Elektra, when he went to see the Doors at the Whiskey for the first time. He came back and said, "I saw a really interesting group and I think I'm gonna sign them." And he did. Then they came to New York to do a show at Ondine's, on Fifty-eighth Street, under the bridge.

DANNY FIELDS: I remember Morrison did "Light My Fire" that night, because it was the only good song that he did.

TOM BAKER: I sat with Andy Warhol and his entourage at a long table near the stage. Pam Courson, Morrison's girlfriend, sat alongside me and was very excited. She said to me, "Jim's really up for tonight's show. Forget that shit at Gazzari's, now you're going to see the *real* Jim Morrison."

When I saw them at Gazzari's, the club on Sunset Strip, Jim was high on LSD and staggering drunk. His performance was unspectacular, except for one moment—while stumbling through a song early in the set, he suddenly let out with a deep-throated, bloodcurdling scream. Pam was furious with him and kept telling me I wasn't seeing him at his best. I told her he was a good guy, but he should keep his day job.

But when he finished the show at Ondine's, I sat there stunned. I looked over at Pamela. She leaned toward me and said, "I told you so."

Afterwards, the Doors gave a party in a club to celebrate their success. When it was over, Jim and I stood talking at the bottom of the stairs that led up to Forty-sixth Street. It was late, and the area was full of various cops and creeps. Suddenly, Morrison started throwing empty glasses up the stairs.

I grabbed him by the arm and yelled, "What the fuck are you doing, for Christ's sake?"

He ignored me and threw another glass up the stairs, simultaneously letting out one of his bloodcurdling screams. I expected a small army of cops to come charging down. After one final glass and one final scream, Jim turned and was gone. I was frustrated because I wanted to tell him that finally I had met someone who was truly possessed.

DANNY FIELDS: The next day I had to go to the record company, so I told them there was this song about fire, and, "If you're putting out a Doors single, put that one out."

They said, "Uh uh, it's too long."

Then other people started to tell them to do that. At first they thought it was impossible, but after deejays reported back to them that they had a potential hit here, without that pretentious nonsense in the middle, they started to listen. It was a catchy tune.

So they sent Paul Rothchild into the studio and said, "Paul, cut it." And Paul did. You can hear the separation in the middle. And it worked. It went to number one.

STEVE HARRIS: I think Danny had problems with Jim Morrison because Danny thought he could lead Jim around. They had a falling out at the Castle in California, when Jim was fooling around with Nico. They were hanging around in the Castle and Jim was very drunk, and very high, and Danny was afraid that he would die if he drove. So Danny took the keys to Jim's car. And Jim got really pissed at Danny for that.

DANNY FIELDS: I was in L.A. staying at the Castle with Edie Sedgwick and Nico, who were in Hollywood for some reason that I can't remember. The Castle was this two-story house, owned by some old Hollywood queen who rented it out to rock bands. Everyone had stayed there—Dylan, the Jefferson Airplane, the Velvets. The owner would rent it out to rock & roll bands because it was in such a state of ruin that it didn't really matter what happened to it.

Just before I arrived in L.A., I was in San Francisco to see the Doors play at the Winterland. After the show I'd gone backstage and Morrison was surrounded by very slovenly and ugly groupies. I thought that was bad for his image. So I decided to fix Morrison up with Nico. It was a *shiddach*, which is Yiddish for a fix-up. I wanted him to meet Nico so that he would fall in love with her and see what kind of girl he should hang out with. I mean, it was a lot of nerve on my part. It was really none of my business to meddle in, but . . .

I've never had any respect for Oliver Stone, but after seeing his version of the Morrison/Nico meeting in the Doors movie—"Hello, I am Nico, would you like to go to bed with me?"—the reality of it couldn't have been more different.

What really happened was that I met Morrison at the Elektra office in Los Angeles and he followed me back to the Castle in his rented car. Morrison walked into the kitchen and Nico was there and they stood and circled each other.

Then they stared at the floor and didn't say a word to each other. They were both too poetic to say anything. It was a very boring, poetic, silent thing that was going on between them. They formed a mystical bond immediately—I think Morrison pulled Nico's hair and then he proceeded to get extremely drunk and I fed him whatever was left of my drugs that Edie Sedgwick hadn't stolen.

In those days, I never traveled without my little supply of everything. My father was a doctor, so I had access to reds, yellows, blacks, Tuinals—

everything. But since I had lived with Edie in New York, I knew she was a kleptomaniac of extraordinary skill, especially when it came to drugs. Edie just had a bloodhound's nose for prescription drugs. So the minute I got to the Castle, when I knew Edie's back was turned—she was kissing Dino Valenti good-bye in the driveway—I'd snuck upstairs and hid my drugs carefully in what I thought was a safe place, under a double mattress in a back bedroom.

When I went back to them later, sure enough, they were decimated. Edie had found them. So I took what was left, some acid, and gave it to Morrison, and he got so stoned and so horrendously drunk that he wanted to drive away.

So I took the keys out of his ignition and hid them under the mat of his car. I was afraid he would drive drunk and you know, go off a cliff and kill himself, and I'd be fired from Elektra. I was there on Elektra's money and it wouldn't be seemly to lose the lead singer on account of the publicist getting him so stoned, so I kidnapped him.

There was no phone in the Castle. He couldn't get outta there. Morrison knew that I had taken the keys, but he was so stoned . . . finally I went to bed.

While I was sleeping, Nico came into my room, crying, "Oh, he's going to kill me! Oh, he's going to kill me!"

I said, "Oh, leave me alone, Nico! I'm trying to sleep!"

She was sobbing, "Whoo hoo hoo." She went back outside, and then I heard her screaming. I looked through the window into the courtyard, and Morrison was just pulling her hair, so I went back to bed. Then David Numan, who was also staying at the Castle, came running into my room and said, "You'd better check this out."

So I got up again and Nico was out in the driveway, still sobbing, while Morrison was naked in the moonlight, climbing around the rooftop. He was jumping from one turret to the other, while Nico sobbed.

I went back to sleep, and that was the affair—he pulled her hair, he walked naked, she screamed, and I kept his car keys hidden for a day or two until he straightened up.

And of course he hated me from that moment on for kidnapping him.

NICO: I argued with Jim. He asked if I would walk along the edge of the Castle. I said to him, "Why?" and he couldn't answer.

It was not a positive act, and not a destructive act; it didn't change anything. So why should I do something that is so vain, just to follow him? It was not spiritual or philosophical. It was a drunk man displaying himself.

RONNIE CUTRONE: I loved Jim Morrison dearly, but Jim was not fun to go out with. I hung out with him every night for just about a year, and Jim would go out, lean up against the bar, order eight screwdrivers, put down six Tuinals on the bar, drink two or three screwdrivers, take two Tuinals, then he'd have to pee, but he couldn't leave the other five screwdrivers, so he'd take his dick out and pee, and some girl would come up and blow his dick, and then he'd finish the other five screwdrivers and then he'd finish up the other four Tuinals, and then he'd pee in his pants, and then Eric Emerson and I would take him home.

That was a typical night out with Jim. But when he was on acid, then Jim was really fun and great. But most of the time he was just a lush pill head.

RAY MANZAREK: Jim was a shaman.

DANNY FIELDS: Jim Morrison was a callous asshole, an abusive, mean person. I took Morrison to Max's and he was a monster, a prick. And his poetry sucked. He demeaned rock & roll as literature. Sophomoric bullshit babble. Maybe one or two good images.

Patti Smith was a poet. I think she elevated rock & roll to literature. Bob Dylan elevated it. Morrison's wasn't poetry. It was garbage disguised as teenybopper. It was good rock & roll for thirteen-year-olds. Or eleven-year-olds.

As a person, I think Morrison's magic and power went beyond the quality of his versifying. He was bigger than that. He was sexier than his poetry—more mysterious, more problematic, more difficult, more charismatic as a performer. There has got to be a reason why women like Nico and Gloria Stavers, the editor of 16 magazine, fell so deeply in love with him, because he was essentially an abusive man to women.

But it sure wasn't his poetry. I've got to tell you, it wasn't his poetry. He had a big dick. That was probably it.

GERARD MALANGA: I was walking down Eighth Street and I heard these two girls behind me say, "Isn't that Jim Morrison?" Ha ha ha. I felt like saying, "No, my jaw is a bit more angular." I felt a little eclipsed but I didn't give a shit, really.

DANNY FIELDS: The ultimate rock star is a child. How can you not be spoiled by everything that's going to come along? For most rock stars, what's in store for them, realistically, is a lot of spoilage, denting and banging around, exploitation, being used up, and ruination.

And what happens if you get fat like Jim Morrison? You don't look cute in those clothes anymore.

Jim Morrison really had it on his first trip here, which was the winter of 1966. Even when the first album was released in 1967, he looked wonderful. That's when he was at his best. He became a teen idol about a year later and then started putting on weight. His genes had an unfortunate tendency to send all the weight to his cheeks, so his eyes, which were never his best feature, disappeared.

Then he grew a beard and became fat and drunk and sloppy.

So my thinking was, Bring me another one. Bring me that one's head on a plate. Bring me a new one.

Chapter 2

■ The World's Forgotten Boys

RON ASHETON: My younger brother, Scotty, and our neighbor Dave Alexander were stone punks. I was just the weird guy. In school, I was either the complete oddball, the nerd, or the freak, and then they always called me "the Fat Beatle" when I used to wear Beatle suits on dress-up day.

I didn't have a lot of friends. I was mostly into Nazi stuff. I took German class and did Hitler speeches. I'd wear SS pins to school, draw swastikas all over my books, draw Hitler mustaches on everyone's pictures, and draw little SS bolts on my arm. So I wasn't so much a stone-punk-kinda-hoodlum-guy as Scotty and Dave.

We just didn't fit in. I remember one year we all tried to go back to high school on the first day. I made bets with Scotty and Dave about how long they were gonna last. I said, "Dave, you'll probably make it three hours, and Scotty, you'll probably make it half the day, and I'll probably make a whole day."

Dave turned to me, he had a sixty-ounce—a big can of Colt 45 in his hand. He already had drank two of them, it was like nine in the morning, and he said, "You lost. I'm leaving now."

Scotty wanted to get thrown out, so he went up to some kid at his locker, grabbed him by the back of the arms, and squeezed and twisted him with a pair of needle-nose pliers. So the kid runs down to the office, and we heard over the PA, "Scott Asheton come to the office!" He went down and got thrown out.

IGGY POP: These guys were the laziest, delinquent sort of pig slobs ever born. Really spoiled rotten and babied by their mothers. Scotty Asheton— he was the juvenile delinquent. His dad had died, his and Ron's, so they didn't have much discipline at home . . . I mean, Dave Alexander and Ron Asheton had skipped school and gone to Liverpool, to be near the Beatles.

RON ASHETON: Me and Dave Alexander were supergeeked on bands. We were always sitting around listening to records and talking about the Beatles or the Stones.

We even had a band—well, sort of a band. We were called the Dirty Shames. We would play along to records and say, "We're great!" Then we'd take the record off and say, "Whaaa? Hey, maybe this isn't sounding too good."

We built up the reputation that we were a great band, because we never played. We were actually called down to Discount Records one time, to meet this guy who was promoting the first Rolling Stones show at the Olympia Stadium in Detroit. He wanted the Dirty Shames to open for the Stones. We were all excited, until we realized, Wow, we can't even play! So we told the guy, "I think we're going to be auditioning out in L.A."

A little while after that Dave tells me, "Hey, I'm going to England, you wanna go?" So I sold my motorcycle. I had a Honda 305 that I got instead of getting a car, when I got my driver's license. So we sold the bike and flew to England.

We went to see the Who at the Cavern. It was wall to fucking wall of people. We muscled through to about ten feet from the stage, and Townshend started smashing his twelve-string Rickenbacker.

It was my first experience of total pandemonium. It was like a dog pile of people, just trying to grab pieces of Townshend's guitar, and people were scrambling to dive up onstage and he'd swing the guitar at their heads. The audience weren't cheering; it was more like animal noises, howling. The whole room turned really primitive—like a pack of starving animals that hadn't eaten in a week and somebody throws out a piece of meat. I was afraid. For me it wasn't fun, but it was mesmerizing. It was like, "The plane's burning, the ship's sinking, so let's crush each other." Never had I seen people driven so nuts—that music could drive people to such dangerous extremes. That's when I realized, This is definitely what I wanna do.

When Dave and I got home we got kicked out of school because we had superlong hair. I'd also grown the giant sideburns. I had knee-high Beatle boots—the big leather kind with the big Cuban heels—a leather vest, and a turtleneck. The counselor completely freaked and said, "This won't do!" So I said, "Fuck it," and started hanging out in front of Discount Records, where Iggy worked inside.

In 1966, Iggy was still Jim Osterberg, who was a straight kid when I met him in high school. He hung out with the popular kids that wore chinos, cashmere sweaters, and penny loafers. Iggy didn't smoke cigarettes, didn't get high, didn't drink. He worked in the Discount Records store after school, and that's when I got to know him better.

That's where my brother Scott and Dave Alexander always hung out—out front of Discount Records, spitting on cars.

WAYNE KRAMER: The important thing about Scotty Asheton, which needs to be told, is that he was a great fighter. He saved me and Fred Smith's ass.

We went to Ann Arbor one night to see Iggy play drums in the Prime Movers—this blues band that did a lot of really eclectic stuff. Iggy was certainly the best drummer in Ann Arbor. He was just unbeatable, man.

At that time, I was still combing my hair back, I still hadn't switched over to the new thing. Fred was combing his hair down and it was almost over his ears, which was radically long for the time. We were just being cool, watching the band, and a bunch of fraternity guys came up and started fucking with Fred, slapping him on the back of the head and saying, "Are you a boy or a girl?"

There was a bunch of them, so I thought, Aw, it's just me and Fred, and in about two minutes, man, we're gonna get killed. This is really not gonna be good.

Just as the tension was building, Scotty Asheton came over. He picked this guy up and kicked his ass across the dance floor, telling him to leave us the fuck alone, we were friends of his.

I mean, I was just so impressed, "Yeeaaahh, right on, man," because I didn't really know the guy. I only knew Scotty as the brother of a girl that Fred was dating.

KATHY ASHETON: The first time I saw Iggy's band, the Prime Movers, was at a club in Ann Arbor called Mother's. I was fourteen, still in my innocent, virginal days, and the very next night the MC5 played. They were from Detroit and no one knew who they were.

The MC5 were Detroit hoods. Greasers. Wayne Kramer was completely greased out, but Fred had long hair, which was rare at that time. So I instantly got a crush on Fred. He actually came offstage and asked me if I wanted to slow dance, while the rest of the band played on. I told him, "NO!"

Fred was sort of taken aback by that, like he thought I was just going to leap at him. Anyway, he convinced me to dance—a slow dance.

WAYNE KRAMER: We had existed in a couple of forms before we were known as the MC5. Me and Fred Smith had been in rival neighborhood bands in Lincoln Park, a suburb of Detroit. Fred's band had been called the Vibratones and mine was the Bounty Hunters, named after Conrad Colletta's dragster of the same name.

We all shared a love of hot rods and big-assed engines. I even took a job at the drag strip selling ice cream—"ICE COLD, ICE COLD ICE CREAM!"—just so I could be there every week. Drag racing was in our blood. I mean, it was loud and fast, just like the music.

It's funny about the cross-pollination between drag racing and rock & roll—my first experience seeing live rock & roll was at the drag strip. It was Del Shannon, backed by this Detroit instrumental band called the Ramrods. They had matching red blazers, all new Fender gear, and they did choreographed moves on the return road at the drag strip. I thought it was the coolest thing I'd ever seen.

So Fred Smith and me formed a neighborhood supergroup by combining the best players of our two bands. Later we got Rob Tyner, who was a beatnik kind of a guy, and he came up with the name the MC5. Rob said it sounded like a serial number—it fit the whole auto factory life.

You know, we were from Detroit, and the MC5 sounded like it had been stamped out of the auto factories. And we had the juvenile delinquent look, the grease look. We combed our hair back in a kind of pompadour, and wore our trousers tight.

KATHY ASHETON: After the MC5 show at Mother's, Fred Smith gave me a ride home. I was with a girlfriend, who was spending the night at my house, so I told her to go inside first, since I wanted some time alone with Fred.

I said, "Just go break the news that I'm right behind you."

Fred turned out to be a great kisser. In fact, he's probably one of the best kissers that I ever had.

Of course my brothers were flipping that I was out front with this total stranger. My mom found out and she was furious. I was only fourteen. But when Fred walked me to the door, my brother Ronnie came popping out, and Ronnie had long hair at that time, and so did Fred, so it was instantly like, "Well, it's an okay kind of thing."

But I was flipped. I had the girl crush kind of thing on Fred. I definitely had a TV Eye on him.

RON ASHETON: After Dave and I got back from England, I played with this band, the Chosen Few, and when that band broke up, after high school, I played with the band Iggy was the drummer for, the Prime Movers.

But I got fired. Then I went back and roadied for them. They let me sit in and play a couple songs every time, but then Iggy quit. He decided Sam Lay, the famous black blues drummer, was going to be his mentor, so he went to Chicago.

IGGY POP: Once I heard the Paul Butterfield Blues Band and John Lee Hooker and Muddy Waters, and even Chuck Berry playing his own tune, I couldn't go back and listen to the British Invasion, you know, a band like the Kinks. I'm sorry, the Kinks are great, but when you're a young guy and you're trying to find out where your balls are, you go, "Those guys sound like pussies!"

I had tried to go to college, but I couldn't do it. I had met Paul Butterfield's guitarist, Mike Bloomfield, who said, "If you really want to play, you've got to go to Chicago." So I went to Chicago with nineteen cents.

I got a ride with some girls that worked at Discount Records. They dumped me off at a guy named Bob Koester's house. Bob was white and ran the Jazz Record Mart there. I crashed with him and then I went out to Sam's neighborhood. I really was the only white guy there. It was scary, but it was also a travel adventure—all these little record stores, and Mojos hanging, and people wearing colorful clothes. I went to Sam's place and his wife was very surprised that I was looking for him. She said, "Well, he's not here, but would you like some fried chicken?"

So I hooked up with Sam Lay. He was playing with Jimmy Cotton and I'd go see them play and learned what I could. And very occasionally, I would get to sit in, I'd get a cheap gig for five or ten bucks. I played for Johnny Young once—he was hired to play for a white church group, and I could play cheap, so he let me play.

It was a thrill, you know? It was a thrill to be really close to some of those guys—they all had an attitude, like jive motherfuckers, you know? What I noticed about these black guys was that their music was like honey off their fingers. Real childlike and charming in its simplicity. It was just a very natural mode of expression and life-style. They were drunk all the time and it was all sexy-sexy and dudey-dudey, and it was just a bunch of guys that didn't want to work and who played good.

I realized that these guys were way over my head, and that what they were doing was so natural to them that it was ridiculous for me to make a studious copy of it, which is what most white blues bands did.

Then one night, I smoked a joint. I'd always wanted to take drugs, but I'd never been able to because the only drug I knew about was marijuana and I was a really bad asthmatic. Before that, I wasn't interested in drugs, or getting drunk, either. I just wanted to play and get something going, that was all I cared about. But this girl, Vivian, who had given me the ride to Chicago, left me with a little grass.

So one night I went down by the sewage treatment plant by the Loop, where the river is entirely industrialized. It's all concrete banks and effluvia by the Marina Towers. So I smoked this joint and then it hit me.

I thought, What you gotta do is play your own simple blues. I could describe my experience based on the way those guys are describing theirs . . .

So that's what I did. I appropriated a lot of their vocal forms, and also their turns of phrase—either heard or misheard or twisted from blues songs. So "I Wanna Be Your Dog" is probably my mishearing of "Baby Please Don't Go."

RON ASHETON: Iggy called me up from Chicago and said, "Hey, how about you guys coming to pick me up?" That was the beginning of Iggy deciding, "Hey, why don't we start a band?"

IGGY POP: When we first started rehearsing, it was in the winter and I was living with my mother and father because I had no money. I'd have to walk about a half a mile through the snow to the bus stop. Then, after about a forty-minute bus ride, I'd have to walk another ten minutes to get to the Ashetons' house.

RON ASHETON: Iggy lived in a trailer on Carpenter Road, which is on the fringe of Ann Arbor. He'd take the bus into Ann Arbor to our house. I remember once, in order to get some money to buy an organ, his mother made him cut off all of his hair. She said, "I'll buy the organ for you if you cut your hair."

So he got this Raymond Burr haircut. Have you ever seen when Raymond Burr plays the mentally retarded insane guy with Natalie Wood? He had these little teeny bangs, almost a crew cut kind of thing?

Well, for some reason Iggy got a haircut like that, and he wound up wearing some baggy white pants, like coveralls, and the cops stopped him because they thought he was an escaped mental patient.

IGGY POP: The trick would be to get Ronnie or Scotty to open the door, because they'd always sleep until noon. I'd ring, ring, ring, ring the bell, and sometimes they'd answer, sometimes they wouldn't.

So I had to turn on the garden hose and spray their windows, throw rocks, yell weird things, throw snowballs. Finally I'd get in, and then I'd have to wake them up a couple more times. They were really moody guys— I'd spin a few records to get them in the mood. Later on Dave Alexander, who lived down the street, would pop over.

Ronnie, Scotty, and Dave were very good dreamers, which is mostly what my dusty Midwest is all about. The land that time forgot. Pete Townshend said something nice about that. He said it must be really difficult for a bright person in the Midwest because you don't have a London or a New York City that can provide you with fresh input, that can rub against you and rub off any illusions . . .

RON ASHETON: The first time Iggy saw the Doors was when they played at the Yost Field House for the University of Michigan graduating class. We all went down, but Iggy was the only one who got in, probably because he used to go to the University of Michigan and had an old ID card.

I hung around outside because I could hear the band playing. Morrison was really drunk and the kids kept yelling for "Light My Fire."

Morrison was making fun of them. He'd say, "The men of Michigan!" then do gorilla imitations. I think they threw beer at him and kept on screaming, " 'Light My Fire'!" all during the set.

IGGY POP: I was not yet a firm fan of the Doors before the gig at the Yost Field House, because their musical approach was so different from the Detroit rock approach. And the MC5 did not like the Doors. Fred Smith used to say, "God, I hate those pussies."

But I went to see them at this gymnasium, and the concert was the homecoming dance for all these big, butch American clods and their girls. They were going there to see the band that did "Light My Fire."

The band got out onstage first, without Morrison, and they just sounded like pure shit. It sounded awful, worse than pussy—it was old pussy, ha ha ha. It sounded decrepit and disgusting and unbalanced—they were playing the riff to "Soul Kitchen" over and over, until the singer was gonna make his entrance.

Finally, Morrison lurched on the stage, but very sensuously. He looked incredible. I remember thinking, Hedy Lamarr in *Samson and Delilah*, because his hair was Hollywood-coiffed ringlets, and it was blue-black, greased and shiny. It was some good hair, I'll tell you.

Morrison had big, almost black eyes, because the pupils were totally enlarged, so obviously he was taking something, or maybe he was just excited. Yeah, right. And he was dressed really well in the black leather jacket, black leather pants, felt boots, and ruffled shirt, and he just sorta lurched forward, like "I'm gonna sing, but not yet . . ."

And the regular American guys were thinking, Who is this pussy?

When Morrison opened his mouth to sing, he sang in a pussy voice—a falsetto. He sang like Betty Boop and refused to sing in a normal voice. I think they got near to the end of the song and then just stopped. Morrison looked around, went over to the guitar player, and said, "Hey, my man, play that one . . ."

I think it might have been "Love Me Two Times," and it was happening. Until Morrison started singing in the Betty Boop voice again.

Basically the concert proceeded like that. I was very excited. I loved the antagonism; I loved that he was pissing them off. Yes, yes, yes. They were all frat people, football killers, the future leaders of America—the people who today are the rock stars of America—and not only was Morrison pissing them off, but he was mesmerizing them at the same time. I was humping this little girl that I brought with me, thinking, This is great!

The gig lasted only fifteen or twenty minutes because they had to pull Morrison offstage and get him out of there fast, because the people were gonna attack him. It made a big impression on me.

That's when I thought, Look how awful they are, and they've got the number-one single in the country! If this guy can do it, I can do it. And I gotta do it now. I can't wait any longer.

RON ASHETON: The first gig we had was at the Grande Ballroom. I said, "Hey, let's just get Dave Alexander to play the bass, I'll pick up the guitar, and my brother will play whatever weird drums we get for him."

The night before the show, we didn't know what Iggy was going to wear, so he said, "Don't worry, I'll come up with something."

So we go to pick him up and he's wearing like an old white nightshirt from the 1800s that went all the way down to his ankles. He had painted his face white like a mime, and he had made an Afro wig out of twisted aluminum foil.

As we were driving to the Grande Ballroom we were smoking joints. It was our first show and we were kind of nervous. Then this bunch of hoodlums pulls up next to us and tries to run us off the road. So we were a nervous wreck by the time we got to the Ballroom. When we got out of the car, the black security guard in the parking lot said, "Motherfucker, is that a mechanical man, or what?" He was just laughing his ass off.

SCOTT ASHETON: Iggy had shaved off his eyebrows. We had a friend named Jim Pop who had a nervous condition and had lost all his hair, including his eyebrows. So when Iggy shaved his eyebrows we started calling him Pop.

It was real hot in the Ballroom that night, and Iggy started sweating, and then he realized what you need eyebrows for. By the end of the set, his eyes were totally swollen because of all that oil and glitter.

JOHN SINCLAIR: It was just so fucking real it was just unbelievable. Iggy was like nothing that you ever saw. It wasn't like a band, it wasn't like the MC5, it wasn't like Jeff Beck, it wasn't like anything. It wasn't rock & roll.

Iggy kind of created this psychedelic drone act as a backdrop for his front-man antics. The other guys were literally his stooges. They'd just get this tremendous drone going, but they weren't songs, they were like demented grooves—"trances" I called them. They were closer to North African music than they were to rock.

And there's Iggy dancing around like *Waiting for Godot* meets the ballet. He wasn't like Roger Daltrey, you know what I mean?

RON ASHETON: We invented some instruments that we used at that first show. We had a blender with a little bit of water in it and put a mike right down in it, and just turned it on. We played that for like fifteen minutes before we went onstage. It was a great sound, especially going through the PA, all cranked up. Then we had a washboard with contact mikes. So Iggy would put on golf shoes and get on the washboard and he would just kind of shuffle around. We had contact mikes on the fifty-gallon oil drums that Scotty played, and he used two hammers as drumsticks.

I even borrowed my ma's vacuum cleaner because it sounded like a jet engine. I always loved jet airplanes. VVVVVRRRRR!

SCOTT ASHETON: People didn't know what to think. John Sinclair, the MC5's manager, was just standing there with his mouth wide open. That was the master plan—knock down the walls and blow people's shit away. All we wanted to do was make it different.

There were a lot of people that didn't like it, and those were the people who started showing up at every gig. They'd yell to get a response, and Iggy would tell them to fuck off.

IGGY POP: On my twenty-first birthday we opened for Cream. I had spent the day transporting a two-hundred-gallon oil drum from Ann Arbor to Detroit so that we could put a contact mike on it and Jimmy Silver would hit it on the one beat of our best song. I got it up the three flights of stairs into the Grande Ballroom, by myself, and then we discovered that our amps didn't work. And when we went out onstage everybody yelled, "We want Cream! We want Cream! Get off, we want Cream!"

I'm standing there, having taken two hits of orange acid, going, "Fuck you!" It was one of our worst gigs ever.

I went back to Dave Alexander's house with him. I was heartbroken. I thought, My god, this is twenty-one. This is it. Things are just not going well.

Dave's mom served me a cheeseburger with a candle in the middle of it. The idea was to keep going and things would get better. Don't give up.

Chapter 3

■ The Music We've Been Waiting to Hear

STEVE HARRIS: With the success of the Doors' single, "Light My Fire," Elektra Records really became competitive, because we then had the leverage to sign other acts. We weren't just your nice little folk label anymore . . .

DANNY FIELDS: Bob Rudnick and Dennis Frawley had a column in the *East Village Other* called "Kocaine Karma," and the two of them were relentless in loading me with propaganda about this band from Detroit, the MC5, which stood for "The Motor City Five."

Rudnick and Frawley would say, "You gotta see this band! You gotta sign this band! This is the greatest band! They're so popular! They sell out the Grande Ballroom! They sell out all over the Midwest! It's not just a band, it's a way of life!"

And the MC5 became legendary for being the only band that played at the riots at the Chicago Democratic National Convention. Norman Mailer had written about them.

WAYNE KRAMER: Being the young hustlers we were, the MC5 started to see that this hippie thing was gonna go, man. That it was gonna be big, because all these kids would come into Detroit from the suburbs, dressed like hippies on the weekend. So we figured the way to get the hippies to like us was to get the chief hippie to like us, who was John Sinclair.

Sinclair was doing six months for reefer in the Detroit House of Corrections and his getting-out-of-jail party was going to be the cultural event of the summer. We showed up and had to wait all day to play—there were all these poets reading and dancers dancing—so we didn't get to play until four in the morning. So we cranked up our fucking hundred-watt amps and were blasting away all the hippies and the beatniks. They didn't care what you played—hippies would dance to anything. So we were in the middle of our set, dedicating a song to this guy John Sinclair, and his wife pulls the plug on us.

Our relationship with John had started on a sour note. He had a column in the local underground paper, so he wrote about us saying, "What's with these jive rock & rollers? If only they'd pay attention to real music like Sun Ra and John Coltrane." I took exception with it, you know? I went over to his house and said, "Hey man, what's up with all this? We're in the Community, too. And we know about John Coltrane and we need a place to rehearse and can't we use the Artist Workshop too?" So we smoked a joint and everything was cool.

DANNY FIELDS: In 1968 the mood of the country was changing. The night President Lyndon Johnson announced, "I will not seek, I will not run," I couldn't believe it. I mean, who were you gonna hate now?

Of course, then came the Chicago Democratic National Convention . . .

JOHN SINCLAIR: We insisted we play at the Festival of Life outside the 1968 Democratic Convention in Chicago. We were this hungry band from Detroit—you know, we're trying to get over, we're trying to get recognized, we're trying to get a record contract. I mean, let's say it in so many words.

At the same time, we just wanted to be a part of it because it completely coincided with our world view. So on both of those fronts, we said, "Man, we can go there and be part of the Festival of Life and there'll probably be some people from the papers and shit." You know, "Maybe Norman Mailer will see us!"

WAYNE KRAMER: About an hour before we played, a couple of people came up to us and offered us some hash cookies. They said, "Just eat one, because they're very strong," so naturally we all ate one and then we all split four or five of 'em: "Oh yeah, take another bite, yeah, I'm not getting off, you getting off? No, man, I need some more."

So it came time to play and I started getting off, man. Getting off seriously. I think we were doing our song "Starship," and we're in this space-music thing and we're talking about the war and the human being–lawn mower and everything, and the Chicago police helicopters started buzzing above us.

They were coming down on top of us, and the helicopter sound fit in with what I was playing on the guitar—"Yeah, it's perfect man, waaaaahhhhh!"

There were all these police agent provocateurs in the audience starting fights and pushing people around—guys in army fatigue jackets with short hair and sunglasses. There were real bad vibes. And the whole thing just made absolutely perfect sense to me.

As high as I was, it all made perfect sense. It all fit.

DENNIS THOMPSON: When I saw all those cops, the only thing I could think was, Jesus Christ, if this is the revolution, we lost. I was thinking, It's over, right now. I looked over my shoulder and didn't see any other band trucks.

"Hey, John Sinclair, where's everybody else?"

It was like Custer and the Indians, you know—"Where's the cavalry? There's no one here! I thought there was supposed to be all these other bands! Where's Janis Joplin? She was gonna be here, she was bringing the beer . . . Oh shit!"

There must have been four or five thousand kids all sitting in Lincoln Park. We played about five or six songs, and then the police troopers came marching into the park with their three-foot batons.

The entire park was surrounded by cops. Literally surrounded—helicopters, everything, the whole nine yards.

JOHN SINCLAIR: Abbie Hoffman came up onstage, grabbed the microphone, and started rapping about "the pigs" and "the siege of Chicago."

I said, "Oh dear, this does not bode well for us." So I kind of signaled to the guys, "Let's get the fuck outta here . . ."

All the equipment guys started packing everything away, everything except the one mike that Abbie was using. Finally they said, "Uh, Abbie, excuse me, we're gonna have to . . . get out of here."

WAYNE KRAMER: We just pulled the van right up and the minute we stopped playing we threw the shit in the truck, man. I was so high, and I knew the minute we stopped playing there was gonna be a riot. We had seen it happen a lot of times before—we knew as soon as we stopped playing the crowd wouldn't have anything to focus on anymore and the riot would start. And it did.

JOHN SINCLAIR: I looked back and saw these waves of cops descending on people. We were driving in the van across the field, we didn't bother with no road, we were just going the fastest way toward the exit. And there was the Up, they were in a van coming in from Ann Arbor, and we said, "You gotta go back!"

Fortunately we escaped, ha ha ha. We headed right back home. But after that we were kind of *in* it, you know?

But I was always happy that we got out of Chicago with our gear intact, because we had to keep playing—you know, we weren't going to catch a plane to the next college to do a speech for five thousand bucks, we were going back to Michigan to play some teen club for two hundred dollars.

DENNIS THOMPSON: Chicago was supposed to be the show of solidarity, goddamn it. This is the alternative culture? Come on. Where were all the other bands?

No one showed up but us. That's what pissed me off. I knew the revolution was over at that moment—I looked over my shoulder, and no one else was there. We were the ones who were gonna get hanged. I said, "This is it. There ain't no revolution. It doesn't exist. It's bullshit. The movement is dead."

DANNY FIELDS: I went out to see the MC5 the first weekend of autumn 1968. They met me at the airport and took me back to their house. Of course I was just stunned. I'd never seen anything like it. John Sinclair, the MC5's manager, was bursting with charm, vigor, and intellect. Just the look and size of him—he was one of the most impressive people I had ever met— and that house!

WAYNE KRAMER: Before the Chicago riots, we moved from Detroit to Ann Arbor because of the 1967 Detroit race riots. It was real scary. I was living in an apartment at Second and Alexandrine, and the first couple of killings were right in that neighborhood. It was all police murders. The police just went insane and shot the place up for a week—killed forty or fifty people.

Shit started getting real tense after that. Some of our girlfriends got raped and our gear got ripped off a few times. I mean, we'd get to the place where we practiced and the door would be busted open and three more guitars would be gone. So we moved into two fraternity houses in Ann Arbor.

DANNY FIELDS: It was sort of like a Viking commune on Fraternity Row. Each place had hundreds of bedrooms, and each bedroom was decorated by its inhabitants, sort of psychedelically. A lot of beds on the floor, draperies hanging from the ceiling, your typical sixties stuff. The basement was filled with printing presses, design studios, workshops, and darkrooms. A lot of their propaganda posters were produced in that factory downstairs. And there were Red Books everywhere. Mao's Red Books were everywhere. You had to have a Red Book. They came in all sizes, and they were all over the place.

WAYNE KRAMER: Self-righteousness flowed like water in that house. In fact, "righteousness" was an expression that we used all the time. "That's not righteous, man . . . No, this'll be really righteous, man . . ."

We knew the world generally sucked and we didn't want to be a part of it. We wanted to do something else, which amounts to not wanting to get up in the morning and have a real job.

You know, it was "This sucks, that sucks, this is square" or "This isn't any fun." Working at Big Boy is not fun, playing in a band is *fun*, going to the drag strip is *fun*, riding around in the car drinking beer is *fun*. It was just on a gut level—that was the level of our politics—we wanted to make up different ways to be.

So our political program became dope, rock & roll, and fucking in the streets. That was our original three-point political program, which later got expanded to our ten-point program when we started to pretend we were serious. Then we started the White Panther party, which was originally the MC5's fan club. Originally it was called "The MC5's Social and Athletic Club." Then we started hearing about the Black Panthers and how the revolution was bubbling under, so it was, "Oh, let's change it to the White Panthers. Yeah, we'll be the White Panthers."

DANNY FIELDS: On the one hand you had the politics of revolution and equality and liberation and on the other hand you had silent women in long dresses, gathered in the kitchen, preparing great meals of meat, which were brought out and served to the men—who ate alone.

The men and women didn't eat together. The men ate before a gig or after a gig. They'd come home and pound on the table like cavemen. And the women were very quiet. You weren't supposed to hear from them. Each one was supposed to service her man quietly.

KATHY ASHETON: John Sinclair was a pig. He really took over the MC5 as far as instilling them with his political garbage. They got really into all that "brother and sister" kind of stuff, which was good for a live show, but . . .

I never took it seriously. Neither did my brothers or Iggy, so there was a parting of the ways between the Stooges and the MC5. The MC5 were still a good band, but they weren't as much fun anymore.

They were really chauvinistic. I definitely wasn't into this live-in maid thing and that's what they all gravitated toward. I wasn't friendly with any of the girls at Trans-Love. The girls were all big-time submissives, and I'd come over in the party mode, all primped to go out for the night, and they'd all be on their knees scrubbing the floor. I thought they were insane letting themselves be treated like that.

WAYNE KRAMER: We were sexist bastards. We were not politically correct at all. We had all the rhetoric of being revolutionary and new and different, but really what it was, was the boys get to go fuck and the girls can't complain about it.

And if the girls did complain, they were being bourgeois bitches—counterrevolutionary. Yep, we were really shitty about it. We tried free love and that didn't work so we went back to the traditional way—"No, honey, I didn't fuck nobody on the road, and by the way, I gotta go to the VD clinic."

I was the second runner-up in our band, I think I had the clap nine times. But Dennis beat me—he had it twelve times.

DANNY FIELDS: Of course, I thought all that male bonding was sexy. It was a world I never knew. I mean, there was the myth of the Beatles living in adjoining rooms in *Help!* But everyone knew that was a myth, that bands didn't really live in the same house with the living rooms connected. But this band did!

So I thought that was wild. I just thought they were the sexiest thing I'd ever seen. I just thought it was quaint! I mean, there was a minister of defense carrying a rifle! Wearing one of those bullet things—a cartridge belt! With real bullets in it! I never saw a man wearing a cartridge belt. Even the girls were wearing these things. And they were serious!

WAYNE KRAMER: I was walking up to our house one day and I heard KABOOM! And then all these sirens, coming from just a couple blocks away. Just then, John Sinclair's buddy, Pun, came riding up on his bicycle and gave his girlfriend, Genie, a revolutionary hug.

Pun was a tough guy. He was just out of the penitentiary for reefer and was real surly. Pun really got into left-wing rhetoric and the ersatz politics of the day. He became the minister of defense of the White Panther party.

I said to Pun, "What did you just bomb?"

He whispered, "The CIA."

I said, "Right on! Power to the people!"

He had tossed a bomb at the CIA recruiting office at the University of Michigan. It didn't kill anybody. It just blew a hole in the sidewalk and freaked everybody out.

IGGY POP: John Sinclair was always saying, "You've got to get with the People!"

I was like, "AWWWHHHH, THE PEOPLE? Oh man, what is this? Gimme a break! The People don't give a fuck."

Sinclair would say, "We are going to politicize the Youth!" But the kids were like, "WHAT? Just gimme some dope." They didn't care. That's how it really was.

JOHN SINCLAIR: Lumpen hippies. Those were our people. That was the White Panther party. We were the voice of the lumpen hippie, just like the Black Panther party was the voice of the lumpen proletariat—which means working class without jobs.

My writing from the period was tailored precisely for the lumpen hippie, to the point where my work was ridiculed by the more erudite motherfuckers that came out of the SDS. Oh yeah, they thought we were a joke.

IGGY POP: The MC5 went beyond having a sense of humor about themselves, they were a parody. They just acted like black thugs with guitars. In Detroit, if you were a white kid, your dream would be to be a black thug with a guitar and play like one.

I mean, the Stooges were the same way—a nasty bunch of people, but nice to each other. I can't say how political the MC5 really were, but I certainly didn't feel it. But on a basic level, would they share their peanut butter with me?

Yeah.

And sometimes I would have to walk two or three miles to the Trans-Love house to get a sandwich, because I didn't have any money, and they would never say, "Hey, don't eat that sandwich." And their girlfriends would sew my pants.

So they were a decent bunch of guys—a nice bunch of guys to have around to blow up your local CIA recruiting office.

DANNY FIELDS: I don't know what they expected, or who they were going to fight off, but they had ministers of everything. Ministers of propaganda, ministers of defense. Of course they named themselves the White Panther party because their role models, musically and politically, were black radical musicians and politicians. Bobby Seale and Huey Newton and Eldridge Cleaver were their political heroes. Albert Ayler, Sun Ra, and Pharaoh Sanders were their musical heroes.

It was a midwesternized version of anarchy. Tear down the walls, get the government out of our lives, smoke lots of dope, have lots of sex, and make lots of noise.

WAYNE KRAMER: The official party line from the Black Panther party in Oakland was that we were "psychedelic clowns." They said we were idiots and to keep the fuck away from us. But we got along well with the Ann Arbor chapter of the Black Panthers. They were neighborhood guys and they used to come to the house to hang out, and then we'd go have shooting practice.

We had all these M1s and pistols and sawed-off shotguns, so everyone would set up in the woods behind our house and blow the shit out of everything imaginable. Bla-bla-bla-bla-bla-pow-pow-pow-pow-pow-pow-bam-bam-bam-bam.

Then we'd drink this concoction the Black Panthers called the "Bitter Motherfucker." It was half a bottle of Rose's lime juice poured into a bottle of Gallo port. So we'd sit down, smoke reefer, drink that, and shoot guns. I guess we thought, We're all gonna end up in a shoot-out with the Man, you know, we'll shoot it out with the pigs.

Like we were gonna be trapped one day yelling, "WE'LL NEVER COME OUT, COPPER. YEAH? KKR! KKR! KKR! TAKE THAT, PIG! POW-POW-POW! POWER TO THE PEOPLE! KKR-KKR-KKR! TAKE THAT, OPPRESSOR!"

DANNY FIELDS: Of course the MC5 sold out the Grande Ballroom the night I came to see them. They dressed up—they all wore satin—and they spun around really fast. It was a great show, but they weren't breaking the barriers of rock & roll. I had no criticism of it. It was fine blues-based rock & roll. The energy was great, and Wayne Kramer, who was very smart, must have sensed something, because the next day he said to me, "If you liked us, you will really love our little brother band, Iggy and the Stooges."

I think he knew something, intuitively, about my own taste in music. So that Sunday afternoon I went to see Iggy and the Stooges play at the student union on the campus of the University of Michigan. It was September 22, 1968. I can't minimize what I saw onstage. I never saw anyone dance or move like Iggy. I'd never seen such high atomic energy coming from one person. He was driven by the music like only true dancers are driven by the music.

It was the music I had been waiting to hear all my life.

IGGY POP: It got to the end of our show, so I was just wandering around. I had this maternity dress on and a white face and I was doing unattractive things, spitting on people, things like that.

DANNY FIELDS: I went up to Iggy when he came offstage and I said, "I'm from Elektra Records."

He just said, "Yeah."

He didn't believe me. He thought I was like some janitor or some weirdo, because no one had ever said "I'm from a record company" to Iggy. So Iggy turned to me and said, "Yeah, see my manager." And that was the beginning of our relationship.

IGGY POP: So this guy, Danny Fields, says to me, "You're a star!" just like in the movies. He said he worked for Elektra, so I figured he cleaned up as a janitor or something. I didn't believe it, you know, like, "Get away from me, man."

DANNY FIELDS: I called New York on that Monday morning from the kitchen of the MC5 house. I had John Sinclair and Jim Silver, the manager of the Stooges, in the room with me while I called Jac Holzman in New York and said, "I'm in Ann Arbor looking at that group the MC5 I told you about. Well, they're really going to be big. They sold out four thousand tickets on Saturday night; the crowd went wild, and there were crowds around the street. They're also the most professional and ready-to-go act I've ever seen."

And I added, "And what's more, they have a baby brother group called Iggy and the Stooges, which is the most incredibly advanced music I've ever heard. And the lead singer is a star—he's really mesmerizing."

And Jac Holzman said, "So what are you telling me?"

I said, "I think we should take both groups."

He said, "See if you can get the big group for twenty grand and the little group for five."

I put my hand over the mouthpiece and said to John Sinclair, "Would you take twenty grand?"

Sinclair went white and fell backwards.

And I said to Jim Silver, "Would you take five?"

They both needed chairs or to have spirits brought to them. And that was the deal. They were signed.

Chapter 4

■ Your Pretty Face Is Going to Hell

KATHY ASHETON: About a month after the Stooges and the MC5 got signed to Elektra, Iggy got married. I remember the day of his wedding because that was the day Iggy and I started our romantic relationship.

You see, I never wore skirts or dresses, I hated all that, but the day of the wedding I decided to wear this really skimpy halter dress. That was the first time anybody saw my legs. And I guess you could say that Iggy was much more attentive to me than a man should be on his wedding day. He had a TV Eye on me . . .

"TV Eye" was my term. It was girl stuff. My girlfriends and I developed a code. It was a way for us to communicate with each other if we thought some guy was staring at us. It meant "Twat Vibe Eye." Like, "He's got a TV Eye on you." And if we had it, then of course we'd use, "I have . . ."

Iggy overheard us and thought it was really funny. That's when he wrote the song "TV Eye."

SCOTT ASHETON: It used to blow my mind how Iggy could get the girls to just flock around him. You know, they'd sit around and watch him eat boogers. Don't say that Iggy sat around and ate boogers, but he did. But he could be worse than that. Once I saw him pick up his usual five girls, and he's walking back to the house and he's got all these young girls just grouped around him—"Oh Iggy, oh Iggy . . ."

I came home about fifteen minutes later and he was sitting on the floor, playing an album, and they were all around him in a semicircle, just staring and gawking at him. All of a sudden, he blew his nose into his hand, and then just guided it right down into his mouth.

And I swear, they were still gazing at him like they didn't even notice.

RON ASHETON: We called Iggy's wife the "Potato Girl." She was pretty, but her face looked like a nice potato. I told Iggy, "Don't marry her, man," but the wedding was fun.

I wore my *Luftwaffe* fighter pilot's jacket, with a white shirt, with a Nazi Knight's Cross with oak leaves and swords. On the jacket I had my Iron Cross first class, the ribbon bars, the Russian front Iron Cross second class, and my riding boots and jodhpurs.

I was the best man. Our manager, Jimmy Silver, who is Jewish, was the minister. Iggy's wife was Jewish also. Her father owned a large chain of discount stores, they were like the Kmart of Ohio and Michigan. Her parents refused to acknowledge the marriage so no one in her family showed up.

It was just the MC5, our manager, Jimmy Silver, John Sinclair, Danny Fields, and all our friends. Because we were into macrobiotics, we had buckwheat casserole, and the MC5 were flipping: "Where's the food? Where's the hot dogs? Where's the hamburgers?"

So the MC5 wound up eating nothing and just getting blasted. It was fun. The cops even came. They said, "Hey, wait a minute, you're flying the Sears Roebuck flag on the flagpole—that's against the law."

They said it was unlawful to fly any flag on the flagpole except the American flag. So I put up a Swiss flag. They told me I couldn't fly that one, so I said, "Okay, if you're gonna bust me, it's gonna be big time," and I ran up the old swastika.

BILL CHEATHAM: Dave Alexander and I went and bought new tennis shoes for the wedding. I remember going through the line and Dave saying, "Bet you these tennis shoes last longer than Iggy's marriage."

IGGY POP: The boys in the band were sitting on the front porch drinking beer and flipping coins, taking bets on how long it was going to last. Really loud: "Hey! I'll give you five to four on two months."

"No, one day, I say. I know Pop."

Danny Fields is saying, "Iggy, what are you doing? Think about your image."

And Jimmy Silver, my macrobiotic Zen manager, is going, "Hey, reality, truth—that's where Iggy is at."

Danny Fields just looked at him and said, "Fuck reality! Who cares about reality?"

RON ASHETON: The Potato Girl moved in with us and brought all this neat wicker furniture for Iggy's room. They had their own little refrigerator up there, with a lock on it, so every time they were gone, Scotty, Dave, and I would sneak up there and jimmy open the refrigerator and eat all their food.

Iggy's wife had money, so she was getting all these nice cheeses and stuff. And we only had rice and beans. Then Iggy wanted to be with us more than her, and she just couldn't take the way we were.

IGGY POP: She liked to sleep at night, of all things, and I liked to sleep whenever I wanted to. I like to play my guitar any old time. So one night I got an idea for a song—just right in the middle of the night—but here's this woman in my bed.

It suddenly hit me, then and there: It was impossible. It had to be one or the other: her or a career.

Mind you, I loved her very much. I then proceeded to write one of my best tunes ever, "Down on the Street." I went into a closet with my amplifier and played my guitar muffled and quiet—a real stomp, very tribal. It sounded nice—muffled and intense. But then I wanted to go to the next musical idea for the song, and I thought, Oh, I gotta be quiet.

And then I thought, No man, you don't gotta be quiet!

So I stepped out of the closet and the next part was this huge noise—a thundering fucking chord. That just shattered her immensely. But it was okay: I had the song stuck together. That was a funny moment—birth! So finally I had to tell her to go.

RON ASHETON: She ended up leaving after a month. I said it would only last one month, and it lasted one month! I won.

When the divorce papers came we hung them up on the wall. They were so funny. A whole thick document saying that there was no consummation, that Iggy was a homosexual. We had it up on the wall for ages, man.

Iggy went back to the usual. He would bring home girls after a gig, they'd go upstairs, and after a while they'd come downstairs crying, because Iggy had just banged them and then said, "Get out."

So they would wind up staying with me. A couple of them even became long-term girlfriends. Ann Arbor girls—they always wanted to drink Bali Hai wine, and they'd get shit-faced, and then I'd have to baby-sit them. The puking girls—I baby-sat all the basket cases.

Iggy would also give girls acid for the first time. I'd be like, "Don't give it to them, man."

So when Iggy's peaking and having fun I'd wind up spending my whole trip with the girl that's on a bummer. The psychedelic doctor, that's me.

For fifteen hours I'd be sitting in a stairwell with a girl who's freaking out, and Iggy would just go, "Oh, fuck it." Then he'd go out and have *more* fun.

One of the girls that flipped out disappeared. She had been totally straight, and she came back a month later, wearing suede hip-hugger pants with a halter top, and carrying tons of hash, man. I got fucked-up with her and she said, "I wanted to thank you guys for turning me on."

IGGY POP: I was free again. I could roam the streets looking like I used to. I walked into a hamburger joint where the kids went after school. It's actually where I wrote the first Stooges record. I'd just observe their social patterns, which became material for my songs. So I went there and saw Betsy. I never saw anything like that. She was very cute. She was the exact opposite of my wife—blond, white as snow. She was thirteen and she looked at me penetratingly. So I guess you can figure out what happened next.

RON ASHETON: Betsy was fourteen years old, just a cute little funny-faced kid. Iggy would still fuck other girls on the side, but he'd always go back to Betsy. I'd be going, "Goddamn it, Iggy, she's been here for two fucking days and she's only fourteen years old!"

But then Iggy introduced me to Danielle, who was Betsy's best friend. And I'm going, "What am I doing, man? I'm fucking a fourteen-year-old girl!"

So I got rid of that one, because I didn't want to get in trouble, even though Iggy never got in trouble over Betsy. He actually met her parents. I guess they were really liberal.

JOHN CALE: Danny Fields and I went to see the MC5 in Detroit, and the opening act was the Stooges, and I fell in love with them.

RON ASHETON: I'd been to New York with Iggy a few times before we went to record the first album. The first time we went, before we got signed to Elektra, was when Iggy took STP for the first time. He didn't know it was a three-day trip, so guess who got to watch him? Me.

I tied a rope around his waist and led him around town. Iggy kept saying, "Wow, I can see right through the buildings, man."

Iggy kept having to get up and do stuff and I said, "Oh man, I'm tired." So when I wanted to go to sleep, I tied the rope that was around his waist to my wrist, so every time he moved it would wake me up.

That was our first trip to New York. When we showed up to do the record, Jac Holzman had asked me, "You guys got enough material to do an album, right?"

We said, "Oh sure."

We only had three songs. So I went back to the hotel and in an hour came up with the riffs for "Little Doll," "Not Right," and "Real Cool Time."

IGGY POP: Even though I was a very big Velvet Underground fan, I wasn't excited about John Cale producing the first album because I wasn't excited about anybody producing me. I wasn't excited about anybody touching my music any more than you want somebody that you don't know to touch you anywhere else, ha ha ha.

It's very personal, but hearing that John Cale was going to produce the album, I thought, This is good. I can work with this. Obviously this is gonna be an intelligent, sensitive, cool guy. Somebody I can have a dialogue with—not a dick. What I was excited about was the thought of getting him to play on something.

RON ASHETON: We'd never been into a recording studio before and we set up Marshall stacks, and set them on ten. So we started to play and John Cale just says, "Oh no, this is not the way . . ."

We were like, "There is no way. We play loud, and this is how we play."

So Cale kept trying to tell us what to do and being the stubborn youth that we were, we had a sit-down strike. We put our instruments down, went in one of the sound booths, and started smoking hash.

But Cale kept trying to talk to us. He tried to tell us about recording. "You can't get the right sound with these big amps, it just doesn't work."

But that's all we knew. We couldn't play unless it was high volume. We didn't have enough expertise on our instruments, it was all power chords. We had opened up for Blue Cheer at the Grande, and they had like triple Marshall stacks, and they were so loud it was painful, but we loved it— "wow, triple stacks, man." That was the only way we knew how to play.

So our compromise was, "Okay, we'll put it on nine." Finally he just said, "Fuck it," and he just went with it.

IGGY POP: When we started recording, Nico and John Cale used to sit in the booth looking like they were in the Addams family—Cale was wearing a Dracula cape with a great big collar on it. He looked like Z-Man in *Beyond the Valley of the Dolls* and he had this funny haircut. And Nico was knitting. Throughout that whole album, she sat there knitting something, maybe a sweater.

RON ASHETON: Danny took us to meet Andy Warhol at the Factory after the record came out. The Factory was decorated in tinfoil and kind of grungy. We were midwestern kids and it was too weird for us—all these New York speed freaks and homosexuals. I didn't even talk to Warhol. Scotty, Dave, and I were so freaked that we just sat together on the couch. We wound up thinking it was too creepy and left after a half hour.

The next night or so, we went to Steve Paul's club, the Scene, to see Terry Reid play. Jimi Hendrix showed up and jammed with him. After the show, Iggy and I had a beer with Hendrix. Iggy was walking around with Nico, and I was just sitting there snickering, because she was leading him around like he was her kid. She was so tall and he's so short—they were holding hands, real lovey-dovey. She wouldn't let him out of her sight.

DANNY FIELDS: You kind of expected that Iggy would be someone Nico would fall in love with. He was everything she would like in a guy: wounded, brilliant, fragile but made of steel, insane, demented.

So it was no surprise. Nico fell in love with everyone who was extremely brilliant, insane, or a junkie. I don't want to seem cynical, and if I knew it was going to make such history I would have had a tape recorder, but at the time it was, "Ho hum, Nico's in love with another poet."

IGGY POP: I was making love to Nico a lot. All day pretty much. Nico was really something special. I really dug her a lot. I couldn't fall in love with anybody, but I was really thrilled and excited to be around her. She was older and she was from somewhere else. I really liked that—her accent was from somewhere else, everything about her was from somewhere else.

Also, she was extremely strong. I was like hanging out with a guy except she had girl's parts; that was the only difference, otherwise it was like hanging out with a tough-minded, egotistical, artiste kinda guy.

She'd be very opinionated about my work, and this, that, and the other thing—then all of a sudden that veneer would fall off and she would show tremendous vulnerability. And then I would see her: Here's someone over thirty, not a model anymore, not a commercial entity of any kind in the big business called America, and what the fuck is she gonna do?

Nico had a great sadness about her. You know, she had all the accoutrements of a really groovy international gal—the right boots, the right sheepskin coat, the right hair, and she knew people on the right level, and yet she was fucked-up—she had a twist to her. She was a great, great artist. It was just a real kick to be around her.

I'm absolutely convinced that some day, when people have ears to hear her, in the same way that people have eyes to see a van Gogh now, that people are gonna just go, "WHOOOAAA!"

Then she came with me to Ann Arbor and lived in the band house with me.

RON ASHETON: When Iggy said, "Nico's coming," it was like, "Hey, well cool, we don't care." When Nico moved into the Fun House, we hardly saw her, because Iggy kept her up in the attic. The only time we saw her was when we practiced, and we resented her being there because we had a big rule—nobody allowed in the practice room, *especially* a woman.

But then she'd make these great curry dishes and just leave them on the table with really expensive wines. That's what got us all back into drinking, the great wines Nico turned us on to.

IGGY POP: The Stooges didn't want any girl in the house, especially one who had a very deep voice. They would imitate how she talked. Nico would try to cook for us, but she would cook a pot of brown rice and pour half a container of Tabasco sauce in it. She had an ear infection and she felt the Tabasco would clear her ear out.

And Nico liked to drink. And she got me into that, too, and while she was living with us my shows started getting really, really bad. Because Nico was a bad seed. You know, she was not like the girl next door.

RON ASHETON: Nico got some filmmaker to come to Michigan and make some sixteen-millimeter movie with Iggy. We all went out to this farm, and Nico got John Adams to be in it, too, because he looked like a sphinx: big, long, tight, curly red hair. It was the dead of winter and we were sitting looking out this picture window, laughing, while they put these mannequin arms all over the field—John with no shirt on, and Iggy with no shirt on, doing nothing. Boy, it was real artsy.

IGGY POP: We ran around and around this potato field and mimed with plastic limbs. I never made much sense of it. It was jive. But I needed dinner that day. What had happened was that François de Menil of Texas money wanted to do a film with Nico and she said, "If you wanna do a film, you gotta come out to Michigan and put Jimmy in it." So he said, "Well, okay."

DANNY FIELDS: Nico would call me all the time from Ann Arbor, saying, "I don't know eeeff he looves meee enymore, he's ignoring meee, oooh, he's meeeean to meee!"

I'd say, "Well, I guess you picked kind of a hard guy to have an affair with." You know, sorry, but what else is new?

IGGY POP: Nico used to say to me, "Zhimmy, oh Zhimmy, you must be totally poisoned to do what you do. You are only mostly poisoned, you must be *totally* poisoned."

She meant I had too much humanity. Then she'd feed me red wines with French names I never heard of. That's how I learned all that bullshit;

that's how I learned to modulate my voice . . . wear light blue suits and speak to record company executives.

RON ASHETON: Nico stayed a long time, about three months. Iggy never said if he was in love with her or not. But I remember after she left, Iggy came downstairs looking for some advice. He came up to me and said, "Well, I, I think something's wrong, maybe you can tell me what this is?" So he whips out his cock, squeezes it, and green goo comes out. I said, "Buddy, you got the clap."

Nico gave Iggy his first dose of the clap.

Chapter 5

■ There's a Riot Going On

DANNY FIELDS: The night the MC5 played at the Fillmore East was a historic night in the history of rock & roll and alternative culture. It was just after *Kick out the Jams* was released.

The background is that the Motherfuckers were a radical East Village group who had been demanding that Bill Graham turn the Fillmore East over to them one night a week because it was in the "Community." My favorite word, the "Community." They wanted to cook meals in there and have their babies make doody on the seats. These were really disgusting people. They were bearded and fat and Earth motherish and angry and belligerent and old and ugly and losers. And they were hard.

So Bill Graham and the Fillmore were under pressure from the Community and the radical elements of the Lower East Side to turn the theater over to them. Meanwhile, the MC5 album came out and Jac Holzman thought, Wouldn't it be a great idea if we present the band at the Fillmore and give all the tickets away free! The "people's band"! This way the Fillmore gets a lot of publicity and we can promote the show on the radio and everyone will be happy!

So they booked a Thursday night, and to placate the Community five hundred tickets were given to the Motherfuckers to distribute to their fat, smelly, ugly people. Then we found out later the tickets were locked in Kit Cohen's desk. The tickets never left his desk! The time for the show approached and the Community was getting more and more angry about what happened to their entrée into the show. And since the MC5 were legendary as the band of the Movement, the only band to have played Chicago in 1968, the audience was composed of the leaders of the antiwar movement in America, people like Abbie Hoffman and Jerry Rubin. This was very high level underground stuff.

And then I did perhaps the stupidest thing in my life. There I was, sitting up at the Elektra offices, smoking cigarettes, sucking acid, smoking pot, saying, "Aaww, I have to get this band downtown? What do I do?"

So I called ABC Limo Company. We arrived downtown in the midst of the Motherfuckers banging on the doors of the Fillmore to be let in free. And right at that moment comes this big symbol of capitalist pigism, a huge stretch limo, and the MC5 get out. The Motherfuckers start screaming, "TRAITORS! BETRAYAL! YOU'RE ONE OF THEM, NOT ONE OF US!"

And the MC5 are going, "What did we do wrong?" Maybe I should have sent them in a jeep or a psychedelic van. It didn't occur to me. I didn't anticipate how the image of a limo was going to affect these loathsome people. You can imagine, a bunch of people that would call themselves the "Motherfuckers," what they would be like.

WAYNE KRAMER: Rob Tyner sometimes had the uncanny ability to put his foot in his mouth. He'd get nervous and make a stand on something—but he'd say the wrong thing.

So he gets up onstage at the Fillmore and tells the audience, "We didn't come to New York for politics, we came to New York for rock & roll!"

Of course all the Motherfuckers go, "GRRRRRR!"

The place erupted in a riot. They started trashing our gear. I was standing behind a curtain, and I saw knives cutting the curtain down.

DENNIS THOMPSON: We were warned that there were true revolutionaries out there—and here they were, smashing our equipment, setting the seats on fire, and coming through the curtain after us. So they grabbed us and escorted us out into the middle of the theater. We were surrounded by about five hundred Motherfuckers, ha ha ha. Then all this revolutionary banter starts going back and forth. One guy would get up and say, "You guys preach revolution, so why don't you put up or shut up? Time to get started right now, don't you think?"

Then we'd go, "But uh, but uh, we don't mean to blah, blah, blah, we just want to blah, blah, blah."

Another one would pop up, "You guys are a bunch of fucking pussies. You're pussy motherfuckers. This is the time for revolution. You guys are either gonna be the real thing or if not, we're gonna kill you."

It was getting more and more intense—they weren't giving us much time to say anything—and then this knife comes out and goes right for Wayne Kramer's back.

Jesse Crawford grabs this guy's hand with the knife in it, wrestles it away, and we're all being spun around, and it's getting very violent. I grab Wayne, we just sorta plow our way through these people, and I said, "RUN!"

WAYNE KRAMER: We ran outside, and there's this limousine waiting and there's all the Motherfuckers and their women, crying and screaming. We gave away a bunch of free records and they started smashing the records on the limousine screaming, "YOU SOLD US OUT! YOU SOLD US OUT!"

DENNIS THOMPSON: They're all over the car, jumping on it, hitting it, throwing rocks and bottles. It's just like we're down in one of those domino countries, where the politico shows up and everyone jumps the car, and we're driving away with these monkeys falling off.

So we finally escape and we're all going like, "OOHHH! What are we doing? Fuck this revolution shit. We should have just stayed in Detroit."

DANNY FIELDS: People were swinging chains. Bill Graham got hit on the nose with a chain and he claimed it was Rob Tyner who did it. The idea of poor Robin Tyner hitting anyone with anything is just so preposterous. It must have been some other guy with a big Afro.

Bill Graham never forgave them. He blackballed the MC5, and he had the power because he controlled every market. He put out the word to other promoters across the country, "Watch out for this band. Don't have anything to do with them or any of their ilk."

DENNIS THOMPSON: We kidnapped Janis Joplin on our first tour. We were playing with her at one of the shows in San Francisco, and afterwards we pulled her into our station wagon. She had a couple cases of beer, and Fred Smith was like, "Hey, bitch, you're coming with me."

For Janis, that was unheard of, she controlled everybody. But Fred wanted the beer. Fred gave one case of beer to us, and he took the other when he and Janis disappeared. They became a little bit of a number, which was nice, because Fred and Janis were perfect together, you know?

They were a Jack Daniel's dream all the way down the line. They could go one for one, and Fred could still get it up. I think Janis liked that in a man.

STEVE HARRIS: I was having lunch one day with Jac Holzman, the phone rings and it's a call from our distributor in Detroit. They said they were throwing all of the Elektra Records and Nonesuch Records out of the stores. They said they would never distribute another Elektra record again.

What had happened was that Hudson's, this chain store in Detroit, had refused to sell the MC5 album because they had used the word "motherfucker" in the liner notes on the back of the album. So what the MC5 did was they took out a full-page ad in an underground newspaper that said "Fuck Hudson's."

And they put the Elektra logo in the ad. So Hudson's thought Elektra had something to do with it and got crazed. It was like having Tower Records say they wouldn't sell your records anymore.

DANNY FIELDS: There had been an earlier dispute about the line "Kick out the jams, motherfuckers," but the band had agreed to change that to "Kick out the jams, brothers and sisters." They already agreed that "motherfucker" couldn't be sung on the song.

The band understood that that would be radio suicide. What were they going to say—"You gotta keep the word 'fuck' on the record?" I mean, this was 1968. If it were a perfect world, and you could say "fuck" all over the radio, then what would the revolution be about? We would have already won and there'd be no fight to be fought.

But they put out the record with the word "fuck" in the liner notes and Hudson's refused to carry the album. So the MC5, in their own newspaper, put in a full-page ad advertising the album. I think it was just a picture of Rob Tyner, and the only copy was "Fuck Hudson's." And it had the Elektra logo. That "E."

So Hudson's wasn't pleased and refused to carry any Elektra product, which included Judy Collins, the Paul Butterfield Blues Band, and Theodore Bikel singing songs of Yiddish theater. This was a substantial outlet and Elektra was not happy. It had to be explained to the band that you could say "Fuck Hudson's," signed the MC5, but you could not say "Fuck Hudson's" and sign somebody else's name to it.

STEVE HARRIS: I thought it was the funniest thing I had ever heard. But Jac was very serious about it, because it represented a lot of money. And some of our other acts resented it. They were saying, "Hey, why aren't we getting sold? This isn't fair."

The Hudson's incident was the beginning of the end for the MC5. I think we solved the problem by giving the head buyer or owner of the store some original artwork from Nonesuch Records. He was a classical freak and the artwork pacified him.

The problem with the MC5, on the other hand, was that they never really broke out. They certainly got enough press, and everybody thought it was a hip group, but that didn't equal sales.

DANNY FIELDS: The album went to maybe number thirty on the *Billboard* charts, on account of the publicity. They did have the cover of *Rolling Stone* magazine, but they weren't selling that many records. They weren't getting on the radio and they were too hot to handle. So Elektra dropped them.

Chapter 6

■ Real Cool Time

STEVE HARRIS: Right after the Hudson's incident with the MC5, I went to see Iggy and the Stooges at the Pavilion on the World's Fairground in Queens. It was his first New York gig. Iggy looked at the audience, picked his nose, somebody threw a beer can, Iggy threw it back, sang a couple of lines, somebody threw another bottle, the bottle broke on the stage, and Iggy rolled around in it and cut himself all over the place.

ALAN VEGA: This guy with blond bangs—who looked like Brian Jones—came out onstage and at first I thought he was a chick. He had on torn dungarees and these ridiculous-looking loafers. He was just wild looking—staring at the crowd and going, "Fuck you! Fuck you!"

Then the Stooges launched into one of their songs, and the next thing you knew, Iggy was diving off the stage onto the concrete, and cutting himself up with a broken guitar.

It wasn't theatrical, it was theater. Alice Cooper was theatrical, he had all the accoutrements, but with Iggy, this was not acting. It was the real thing.

Iggy's set ended in twenty minutes, and somebody had the fucking genius to play Bach's Brandenburg Concerto through the speaker system. The audience was throwing bottles and roses at him. I swear it was beautiful.

Do you know what I'm saying, man? It changed my life because it made me realize everything I was doing was bullshit.

STEVE HARRIS: Someone at the office was reading a review of the show aloud to a bunch of us sitting around eating lunch, and the writer described the show pretty much as I just did. Somebody at the table said, "Who would want to see that?" And everybody in the office who was listening to the review said, "Me."

So that kind of word of mouth got around.

DANNY FIELDS: The bill at the New York State Pavilion at the World's Fair was David Peel, the Stooges, and the MC5. It was a famous show. Howard Stein, the promoter, claimed that the Stooges gave his wife a miscarriage. He called all the promoters and said, "Go see the Stooges and they'll give you a miscarriage!"

ALAN VEGA: Nineteen sixty-nine was the turning point for everything. Before that, it looked like the sixties was going to change the world, that everything was gonna go THIS way, but instead everything went THAT way. The MC5 were one of my favorite bands, but I couldn't watch them after the Stooges. They knew it, too. They were just boogying their ass off all night TRYING, but baby, they knew they were outdone by Iggy.

STEVE HARRIS: When *The Stooges*, the first Stooges album, came out on Elektra in August of 1969, I sat around the table with the promotion people. These were the people that I thought of as being in the promotion trenches—the people from Denver, from Philadelphia, wherever. They listened to Iggy and said, "Oh, this isn't the Doors, this isn't Love, this isn't Judy Collins, this isn't Tom Paxton, what the hell is this? This is a bunch of noise!"

I said, "But it's going somewhere. It's salable. You don't understand—what he's doing is rock & roll!"

It was hard trying to sell Iggy. People just didn't understand the act. People at the record company would say behind my back, "There's Steve, he likes Iggy. Can you believe that?"

I was Iggy's biggest booster at the record company. Of course there was Danny Fields kicking it to me, but I was a tremendous booster of Iggy's everywhere. And I tried to use all my influence at that time, which was considerable, since I had at my disposal Judy Collins and the Doors, but the resistance to Iggy was tremendous.

SCOTT ASHETON: Iggy started doing stuff to himself at the Cincinnati Pop Festival, where that famous photo was taken where he's walking on people's hands. He brought two jars of peanut butter and a couple pounds of hamburger onstage with him, so he broke out the peanut butter and started smearing it all over himself, and then he took the hamburger and was flopping on it and tossing it into the audience.

RON ASHETON: Dave Alexander got fired from the band at the Goose Lake Pop Festival because he got too fucked-up. He was nervous to be in front of all those people—he drank a pint of Kessler, smoked a bunch of pot, and took some downers. And when he got onstage, he forgot all the songs.

So we just charged ahead and played the tunes. It actually turned out good, but when we got offstage, Iggy was furious. As soon as Iggy saw Dave, he said, "You're fired."

Dave left right away. I was thinking, No way, but Iggy was adamant.

SCOTT ASHETON: I think Dave wanted to move back to his parents' house—he spent most of his time there anyhow. Dave had everything he needed at his parents' house: his stereo, his books, and his TV. He was taken care of there, and I think he liked it that way.

IGGY POP: When we came to New York to play Ungano's, I went up to see Bill Harvey, the general manager of Elektra, and said, "I can't possibly do four gigs in a row without drugs—hard drugs. Now it's gonna cost this much money, and then we'll pay you back . . ."

It was like a business proposition, right? And he's looking at me like, "I do not believe this!"

But to me it was very official, and very logical, you know, "What's wrong with that?"

LEEE CHILDERS: The show at Ungano's was one of the greatest rock & roll shows I'd ever seen. It was very powerful, very dangerous—I mean, before that was the Beatles and the Dave Clark Five singing love songs, and suddenly here's Iggy wearing a dog collar and singing "I Wanna Be Your Dog."

The incredibly beautiful photographer, Dustin Pittman, was sitting by the side taking pictures of Iggy, and Iggy straddled him while Dustin took pictures of him at the same time. It was so sexual, so outrageous, it was so un-allowed! To me, that's what rock & roll should always come down to—the un-allowed.

RON ASHETON: Every time we played New York, this guy would come by our show and give the Stooges a little bottle of coke, completely on his own volition. So we're sitting backstage with Miles Davis, and this guy finally arrives and just throws down a big old pile. We already had the straws ready. Imagine that great scene—Miles Davis's head right next to all the heads of the Stooges going "SNNNORRRT!"

We all just devoured that fucking pile, man. Later, Miles Davis said, "The Stooges are original—they've got spirit," or something like that. It was great. My head next to Miles Davis, man.

SCOTT KEMPNER: I was terrified watching the Stooges at Ungano's. I was going down there to see this amazing band and be ready for anything, but it was ten times more than I bargained for.

I mean, I was scared, actually nervous, but so exhilarated, and so involved in the sound of this band and this unbelievable guy Iggy—this wiry little thing—who could cause more damage than all the tough guys I knew in my neighborhood.

Other guys would punch you in the mouth, that would heal, but Iggy was wounding me psychically, forever. I was never gonna be able to be the same after the first twenty seconds of that night—and I haven't been.

We went back the next night, and it was the exact same songs, but it was totally brand-new. This had nothing to do with last night, this had nothing to do with rehearsal, this had nothing to do with sound check—this was living and being born and coming for your fucking children in the middle of the night right in front of you . . .

And every time I saw that band it was the same thing—there was never a yesterday, there was never a set they'd played before, there was never a set they were ever gonna play again. Iggy put life and limb into every show. I saw him bloody every single show. Every single show involved actual fucking blood.

From then on, rock & roll could never be anything less to me. Whatever I did—whether I was writing, or playing—there was blood on the pages, there was blood on the strings, because anything less than that was just bullshit, and a waste of fucking time.

ALAN VEGA: Iggy came out and he's wearing dungarees with holes, with this red bikini underwear with his balls hanging out. He went to sing and he just pukes all over, man. He's running through the audience and shit, and he jumped Johnny Winter, who was sitting beside Miles Davis. Johnny Winter hated them, but Miles Davis loved it. It was one of the greatest shows I've ever seen in my life.

JIM CARROLL: Patti Smith took me to see the Stooges for the first time. Iggy took his shirt off and came out in the crowd, and he was looking right at us, and Patti goes, "I think he's gonna come to us."

I said, "If he pushes me, I'm gonna fucking clock him." I thought, What is this bullshit? Performance art? Ha ha ha. But Patti was into anything like that, man. Raw energy in any form just lit her up.

STEVE HARRIS: Iggy took out his dick and put it on the speaker. It was just vibrating around. He was very well endowed.

LEEE CHILDERS: Iggy's performance went beyond being just sexual. Geri Miller, the Warhol Superstar, was sitting in a chair in what could be loosely described as the front row, and Iggy walked over to her, put his hand on her face, grabbed hold real tight, then dragged her by the face across the floor, with her hanging on to the metal folding chair. What Iggy was doing to her wasn't sexual, it was just brutal. No one knew what to think.

Iggy was the first time I ever saw what was to become my rock & roll.

IGGY POP: I was out of my mind doing those gigs for four days. After that, I understood what it was that the audience needed out of me. And my attitude toward them was that I welcomed any support.

I mean, it could've been Charles Manson in the front row, and I would have gone, "Yeah, Charlie, good to see you baby, right on, hey, we got a fellow here in the front row tonight who's really standing America on its ear, let's have a hand for him."

You know, it wouldn't have mattered. It was like what Hitler said, "Go for the lowest common denominator."

With the Stooges that was really necessary, because those were the only people that really dug us. When we first started out, our fans were JUST A MESS—it was like early Christianity. It was the ugliest chicks and the most illiterate guys—people with skin problems, people with sexual problems, weight problems, employment problems, mental problems, you name it, they were a mess.

DANNY FIELDS: When it comes to Iggy, everyone hangs on me that I was doing a generational overturn—promoting Iggy as the next generation's Jim Morrison. That was not on my mind at all. I saw nothing similar between Jim Morrison and Iggy Pop. Iggy was dangerous.

Jim Morrison never went out, like Iggy did, and raised a four-hundred-pound bench over the heads of the first rows of kids in the audience like he was going to slam it down, and you thought the momentum of the swing was such that he couldn't stop it. You thought that the kids were going to get squashed to death. And then Iggy would seem to stop it in midair, like he was Nadia Comaneci.

As I later got to know him, and knew that no one was going to get killed at the show, I was never quite sure that that night wasn't going to be the exception.

Chapter 7

■ Jailhouse Rock

WAYNE KRAMER: Things started unraveling for the MC5 for bigger reasons than just the record company stuff. Anytime you take a political stance, especially when you start throwing around violent political rhetoric, you're guaranteed a violent reaction from the powers that be.

There was an attitude that prevailed in the Detroit area, amongst parents, teachers, policemen, and prosecutors: "When is somebody gonna do something about the MC5? We cannot allow them to say what they're saying!"

We were telling people at our shows to smoke reefer, to burn their bras, to fuck in the streets—it wasn't just a matter of "Well, they were a little too wild for the record industry," which we were, but it went beyond that. Peace and love worked in the realm of the music business, but once you went beyond that, to revolution . . . that's bad.

DENNIS THOMPSON: Nixon and the smart boys in the green room back in the brain trust sat down and said, "Here's the easiest way to handle this damn thing. Just take away their party favors."

The government figured it out. It was obvious. "These people do pot and hash and psychedelics and then they get revolutionary, and they come up with all these new ideas like 'Hey let's change this world. And let's eliminate these fascist politicians!'

"Well, the smartest thing to do is give them what's been in the ghettos for a long time because that's been working pretty good there." All of a sudden all you can find anywhere you go is heroin. It's cheap, and there it is.

So heroin became the next drug of choice, mainly because you couldn't buy a kilo of pot to save your soul. And there's no doubt about it, music is affected by the substances that you abuse.

DANNY FIELDS: I was fired from Elektra Records on the day Richard Nixon was inaugurated president, January 20, 1969. The guy who fired me beat me up and punched me in the head because I repeated some bit of gossip about one of his family members getting pregnant.

I think that was the last straw. I think they wanted me out of there because I was bringing elements into their carefully nurtured folkie-yuppie environment that were troublemaking. I don't know that I brought in so much money as caused them grief.

When I think of what I did at Elektra—I fought with the Doors (Jim Morrison and I hated each other); I signed the MC5, who they fired; I signed the Stooges, who they dropped; I signed Nico, who never sold any records; and I signed David Peel and the Lower East Side, who embarrassed them with his record, *Have a Marijuana*, which sold close to a million copies and cost three thousand dollars to make.

Right after I was fired, John Sinclair was arrested for two joints of marijuana and sentenced to nine years in prison.

WAYNE KRAMER: Warner Stringfellow was a Detroit narcotics detective who busted John the first time for reefer. So John decided to write "The Poem for Warner Stringfellow."

The poem went something like: "Warner, what are you gonna do when your kids smoke pot? What are you gonna do when all the lawyers in the world smoke pot? Warner, what are you gonna do, you small-minded asshole?"

Needless to say, Warner really got it in for John and was always trying to slide these undercover cops in on us all the time. They'd be hanging out, helping us lug equipment or run the mimeograph machine and say, "Come on, man, lay a joint on me."

LENI SINCLAIR: The person who busted John was the same guy who busted him before, in a completely different disguise. He was a master actor. This time he looked like a hippie and he came with a girlfriend attached. And his girlfriend was really young, had a short bob hairstyle, wore miniskirts. They would come to the potluck dinners and help us mimeograph.

One time the girl came by herself and said to John, "Can I have a couple joints? I'm on my way to a party."

So John, sexist that he is, didn't think anything of it, because it was a girl. So he gave her two joints. Nothing happened for about a month, and then all of a sudden there was a lightning raid. They busted fifty-six people—you know, "BIG DOPE RING SMASHED!"

It was obvious that they weren't really interested in anybody but John, because everybody got their charges dismissed except for him.

See, Warner Stringfellow had a daughter who was one of us. She used to tell us that he would talk about John Sinclair like he was the evil incarnate. He'd talk about this heathen with dirty toenails. And his daughter eventually got into junk and he blamed it all on John Sinclair. So John was the symbol to him of everything that had gone wrong in society, so he thought if he socked it to him he could stop the revolution, ha ha ha.

So the two undercover cops got an award from the governor for doing such excellent police work.

DANNY FIELDS: John Sinclair was an easy target. I think the marijuana advocacy is what did John Sinclair in, more so than the revolution or "fucking in the streets."

All the forces of law and order were galvanized in those early years of the Nixon administration—this was a time when Attorney General John Mitchell had just come to power with a very strong antidrug, antiyouth, law and order message. And John Sinclair was big and strong and they figured they could cut the head off this movement by getting him. So they arrested him for two joints and gave him the maximum penalty. There were draconian laws on the books then, which were rarely enforced, except if they wanted you.

And they wanted John Sinclair.

JOHN SINCLAIR: Warner Stringfellow was my nemesis. I was a trouble-maker. Oh man, we were in their face. I mean, we were on acid, you know what I'm saying?

I wasn't pissed. It was inevitable to me that I was going to do time or get killed. I didn't care. I had no idea that I would do two and a half years in prison on this fucking case where I was challenged on marijuana laws and they ruled that I was a danger to society.

But I would have been offended if they *hadn't* said I was a danger to their society. I was determined to be one.

WAYNE KRAMER: I talked it over with Jon Landau and we tried to figure out a percentage of our earnings that we could give John Sinclair while he was locked up. Fred Smith and I had a meeting with his wife right after John got locked up to see if they needed any money. She told us that they didn't, that everything was okay.

JOHN SINCLAIR: When the jury came back and said guilty, I went straight to jail and I didn't come out for two and a half years. There was no chance to straighten my affairs or anything. My wife was pregnant, I had a two-year-old girl, and I was just taken away. And the MC5 just left me there, you know what I mean? They kinda just left me in prison.

WAYNE KRAMER: John was hurt and angry. I think he felt like we were crossing him out of the picture. He said he was never in it for the money, he was in it because he loved the music. He said, "You guys wanted to be bigger than the Beatles, but I wanted you to be bigger than Chairman Mao."

DENNIS THOMPSON: We didn't wanna be Chairman Mao. We didn't want to be supporting everybody—like two hundred people.

We were supporting a band called the Up, who probably had twenty people living in the house next door—roadies, cooks, bottle washers, girlfriends, girls that made clothes. So I'm seeing where all our money is going—our money is buying brown rice and raisins for everybody, ha ha ha.

We were treated like good little communists, but I'd rather be a great drummer in a great rock & roll band.

John Sinclair used to get mad at me, you know, "Oh, you Polack college boy."

So I'd say, "Well, John, you're just a beatnik hippie that gets busted by the same cop with a different mustache." Ha ha ha.

WAYNE KRAMER: What happens generally when people get locked up is that they freak out. It's a real traumatic thing to get locked up and it was almost like John was being punished for his work with the MC5.

So I think he may have felt that I was trying to cross him out of it. And of course he had a legion of people behind him that were way more over the top about it than he was—his wife, the minister of defense, and his brother. They all hated us.

You see, after we got dropped from Elektra, Danny Fields came to the rescue again and engineered this deal with Jerry Wexler at Atlantic Records—they gave the MC5 $50,000, because Wexler believed in the band.

But even with the $50,000, we had no money. None of us ever got anything out of being in the band. The money always went into one central account that paid the bills. We had a place to live, we had food, we had clothes, but for guys that smoked, we had to beg spare change to go buy a pack of cigarettes.

I mean, we had reefer, but we never had any money and we never had any personal possessions.

JOHN SINCLAIR: Jon Landau produced their next record, and he was a bad influence on them in terms of telling them they would never get anywhere if they were associted with us—you know, "Those people are nuts, they're ripping you off, they're taking all your money, they just wanna use you . . ."

You know, I was the guy who carried these guys for two years when they were making twenty-five dollars a night. I was the one who drove them around and set up their equipment and wrote their press releases, and all of a sudden I'm using them?

All because they had gotten a record contract.

DENNIS THOMPSON: After we signed, it came down to a thousand bucks apiece, woopie doo. So we all got our parents to cosign for cars.

Wayne Kramer got an XKE Jaguar, Mike Davis got a Buick Riviera, Fred Smith got a '66 Fastback Corvette with a 327, and Rob Tyner got a station wagon, ha ha ha.

I got the best one out of the group—I got a '67 Corvette, six taillights, 427, 390 horse, purple hard top. That car was a beast. You're talking 400 horsepower. I got thirty-six points off my license in a matter of about eight months. I lost my license three or four times, and was thrown in jail for driving on a suspended license.

Michael and I drove that car down to Florida and it was the fastest trip to Florida I ever made in a car—we were averaging 120 mph. It was fun. What did cars have to do with people getting mad at us?

WAYNE KRAMER: We were purged from the White Panther party for counterrevolutionary ideals, because we bought sports cars that our parents signed for. I got a Jaguar XKE. Yeah, man, it was about the coolest thing I've ever had from playing rock & roll. I still have dreams about that car. Oh, it was sweet. Fred Smith bought a used Corvette. Dennis bought a Corvette Stingray—a big 427 muscle car. Michael Davis bought a Riviera.

And Rob Tyner got the band station wagon.

We were awful. Not long after Rob got the station wagon, he came out of the supermarket with his arms loaded down with groceries, and the car was gone. Nobody had made any of the payments on it, so they had repossessed it.

DENNIS THOMPSON: I mean, we all grew up at the drag races. But fast cars and drinking beers doesn't quite go with brown rice and Zen. There's the clash right there. It's not even a political clash, it's a cultural clash.

We didn't abandon Sinclair at all, it's just that there was nothing we could do. Along with the rest of the dippy hippies across the country, John

Sinclair actually believed that the revolution would win. Sorry, Nixon had a lot of Nazi troopers out there and it was just NOT gonna happen, folks.

RON ASHETON: Eventually the Five got tired of all that sharing. They always knew when the Stooges had good hash, and they'd come over to the Fun House and say, "Can we smoke some hash and just hang out? It's weird over at our house man, all that sharing."

DANNY FIELDS: After John was put in jail, I spent a lot of time commuting between New York and Ann Arbor because Jon Landau and I managed the MC5 between us. We would take turns baby-sitting them.

Jon Landau had brought both me and the band to Atlantic Records. Jerry Wexler was the president of Atlantic and he liked young, smart, hip people. So Lisa Robinson, Lenny Kaye, and I would hang out at his house and drop a lot of acid.

I can remember the acid trips better than I can remember what happened from that time. I was flying through the universe, you know, talking to God—I was on my knees seeing things going into the future. On one trip I decided I had an IQ of 3,000. Not only that, I could easily visualize beings with IQs of 300,000 . . .

I wouldn't want to be higher than LSD.

Chapter 8

■ Fun House

SCOTT ASHETON: After the first album, we didn't get much immediate recognition and sales weren't going great, but we were contracted for three albums, and Elektra decided that we were going to do the second album in their L.A. studios, so we recorded out there.

On *Fun House,* our second album, we were trying to sound more like the original band before the first album—more a free-form, jamming thing, and we added Steve MacKay on saxophone. It was basically a live album in the studio.

Peace and love wasn't a big part of it. We really didn't care that much about trying to make someone feel good. We were more into what was really going on, and how boring crap was, and how you're really treated.

"Dirt" is a perfect example of what our attitude was. You know, "Fuck all this shit, we're dirt, we don't care."

IGGY POP: In April or May of 1970, we returned to Detroit from doing the album in California, and things were changing. Suddenly unemployment was driving people out of Detroit. The whole atmosphere had changed, and we started sliding into hard drugs.

KATHY ASHETON: One night I walked into the house and a total stranger was sitting there. This guy had literally broken into the Fun House and was hanging around waiting for the Stooges. I thought the guy was a groupie. He knew about the band, he obviously knew where they lived, and he had clearly made up his mind that he was going to be involved with them.

In retrospect, James Williamson was like a black cloud descending.

RON ASHETON: I met James Williamson because we were in the same band for one gig in high school. His father was an ex–army colonel who wanted to get James away from his rock & roll environment, so he sent him to a school in New York for troubled kids that needed discipline. The colonel hated long hair, so we weren't allowed in their house—but we could stand on the front porch.

I didn't see James again until he showed up at the Chelsea Hotel when we were recording the first album. We hung out for a couple days and then he disappeared.

After Dave Alexander got fired from the Stooges, our bass player was Bill Cheatham, our road manager, who couldn't play at all. I taught him some rudimentary chords. He played six shows, and then he said, "Please let me be road manager again."

So we started auditioning people, and somehow James Williamson showed up at the audition. I was playing mainly power chords and stuff, and he was playing more melodic type chording, so he was a little further ahead of my Stooge style. So that was great—someone I already knew, and he was a good guitar player.

After I told him he could be in the band, one of the first things he did was sell his amplifier for seven hundred and fifty bucks. He said he'd split it with all of us so we could have some eating money. So he divvies it up and I'm thinking, Alright, I got a little bit of money.

Then Iggy comes up to me and says, "Everybody else is giving me their money to buy some heroin, and I'm getting some extra to sell, so you'll get back twice the money that you give me right now."

I said, "No way."

But he kept badgering the hell out of me so finally I said, "Just take the fucking money and leave me alone!"

SCOTT ASHETON: I was friends with one of the equipment guys from the MC5, and we went to a free concert where Parliament/Funkadelic were playing. We were hanging out in the backstage area, and we asked one of the band members if he wanted to go smoke some hash.

So we climbed into the front of one of Parliament's equipment trucks, and this guy broke out these little packets of white powder.

I said, "Is that coke?"

He said, "No man, this is horse!"

I had done a couple lines of coke before, but I didn't know what horse was.

He said, "Wanna try some?"

"I guess."

After that I remember standing out in the woods in the pouring rain. I was trying to take a leak and I couldn't do it, but it felt really good.

John Adams was clean and pure all the way—he followed a strict macrobiotic diet, didn't drink, didn't smoke, and didn't do drugs. But to us, he was still the older guy with the bad past. He had been a junkie. He had a real gangster attitude, and he was twenty-seven, so he seemed really old.

So I went back to the house, and having heard stories about John Adams' past, I went to him and told him what I had done. I guess I woke up some worm or something, because he got all excited and wanted to go out and get some. Then Brother Ig wanted to get some, too.

So that's how that whole thing started.

RON ASHETON: John Adams, our road manager, was a former junkie, but he fell back into it and took Scotty and Iggy with him at the same time.

One day I happened to be alone in Fun House with John, and he calls to me, "Come on down here!"

So I went down to his room in the basement, and there was a baby-fist-sized pile of white powder on the table.

I asked, "Wow, is that coke?"

He had his face right down in it, looking at it, and I had my face right down in it, looking at it. We were both staring at it, and he said. "No, man."

I said, "It's not heroin?"

He said, "Yeah."

I started going, "Oh, no, you can't do this, man!"

I was really upset, but John didn't pay attention because the other guys were filtering in, and that evening was the first time that they snorted heroin. I didn't do it. I never got into it.

They started chipping then, just tooting some, and finally "The Fellow," as we called John Adams, introduced them to shooting up. It was done in secrecy, behind my back, because I didn't approve of it. So I became the outcast.

KATHY ASHETON: The first time the heroin got up close and personal to me was when Iggy called me from a sleazy hotel in Romulus, which is a funky part of Detroit, and asked me to bring him some pot. Iggy wanted to trade the pot for heroin. He gave me this address, but it wasn't until I got to the area that I realized that I was going to this sleazed-out hotel.

I knocked on the door and Iggy opened it and there was my brother Scotty and these black dudes with guns. I was one of the very few people that was not into heroin that Iggy would let come around him, which was very unusual because from what I understand about junkies, they only want to be around other junkies.

RON ASHETON: The shooting gallery in Fun House was my brother's apartment. It had a bedroom, a bathroom, and it was perfect for shooting

Amphetamine times: The scene at the Factory. Top row (from left to right): Nico, Brigid Polk, Louis Waldon, Taylor Mead, Ultra Violet, Paul Morrissey, Viva, International Velvet, and unidentified man. Bottom row (from left to right): Ingrid Superstar, Ondine, Tom Baker, Tiger Morse, Billy Name, and Andy Warhol. © *Archives Malanga*.

Juvenile delinquency merges with art: Andy Warhol in his trademark black leather jacket. © *Archives Malanga*.

Nico. © *Archives Malanga*.

Gerard Malanga, Andy Warhol, and John Cale at the champagne breakfast at the Horn and Hardart Automat in Times Square following the film premiere of *Our Man Flint*, 1966. © *Archives Malanga*.

Our hero: Danny Fields on the phone in his loft on West Twentieth Street, New York City, 1971. © *Gerard Malanga*.

Iggy Pop and fan at a 1968 free concert in Ann Arbor. *Photo by Leni Sinclair*.

The Elektra "signing" party at the Trans-Love house in Ann Arbor, October 1968. Top row (left to right): Jac Holzman, Danny Fields (in sunglasses), John Sinclair (with all the hair), Fred "Sonic" Smith (arms crossed), Ron Asheton (fifth from left), Steve Harnadek (sixth), Iggy Pop (seventh), Dave Alexander (peeping out from behind Iggy), Scott Asheton, John Adams, Wayne Kramer, Ron Levine, Emil Bacilla, Jimmy Silver, Susan Silver, Barbara Holiday, and Bill Harvey (far right). Middle row: Michael Davis, Dennis Thompson, Rob Tyner, Jessie Crawford. Bottom row: Sigrid Dobat, Chris Havnanian, Becky Tyner. *Photo by Leni Sinclair.*

John Sinclair and Wayne Kramer at the White Panther party headquarters, 1510 Hill Street, Ann Arbor, Michigan, 1969. *Photo by Leni Sinclair.*

The king of Manhattan nightlife: Mickey Ruskin, owner and proprietor of Max's Kansas City. © *Archives Malanga*.

The seventies couple: Todd Rundgren and Bebe Buell. *Photo by Bob Gruen*.

The Stooges: Second lineup.
From left to right: Ron
Asheton, James Williamson
(seated), Jimmy Recca, Iggy
Pop, and Scott Asheton.
*Danny Fields Archives. Photo by
Peter Hujar.*

Glitter on Saint Marks Place:
Iggy performing at the Electric
Circus, 1971. © *Gerard
Malanga.*

The original New York Dolls. Clockwise from top: Billy Murcia, Arthur Kane, Johnny Thunders, David Johansen, Syl Sylvain. *Photo by Leee Black Childers.*

The Doll's house: The New York Dolls onstage at the Mercer Arts Center, New Year's Eve, 1973. *Photo by Bob Gruen.*

The poetry all-stars: Patti Smith, Victor Bockris, Andrew Wylie, and Gerard Malanga the morning after the Better Books poetry reading, February 3, 1972, London. Photo taken by Sam Shepard with Gerard Malanga's camera. © *Archives Malanga.*

Jim Carroll at Andy Warhol's Union Square Factory, 1970. © *Gerard Malanga.*

Iggy meets the Dolls in L.A. Left to right: Arthur Kane, unidentified, unidentified, Shaun Cassidy, David Johansen, unidentified (top), and unidentified. Front row: Coral Shields, Iggy Pop, Kim Fowley (peeking out from behind Iggy), and unidentified. *Photo by Bob Gruen.*

"Two writers, in love, onstage." Sam Shepard and Patti Smith, coauthors of the play *Cowboy Mouth*, at their one and only performance at the American Place Theater, 1971. *© Gerard Malanga.*

dope—a dark green tile floor, a big round table, and those kind of cheap white acoustical ceiling things they used to have in doctors' offices. Very fifties. The walls were already kind of brown, but the worst thing was that the acoustical tiles were all bloodstained. And there were big blood drips on the floor and on the walls, because when you pull a needle out of your arm after shooting up, some blood gets in the syringe, and to clean it out, you squirt it.

So they squirted the walls and the ceiling a lot. *Shhhhtick* . . . blood on the ceiling, blood on the walls, just good drops, like if you took a squirt gun and just shot water up there. This went on for a long time. It wasn't all red, just big ugly brown stains, but a lot of times there would be fresh red stuff. Then it would drip on the table or on the floor, where they'd throw their cotton balls. Such degradation.

I wish I was smart enough to take pictures of it because it would have been a masterpiece, but I was so disgusted.

DANNY FIELDS: By 1971, the Stooges were getting ready to do a third album. Jim Silver left as the Stooges' manager because he was dabbling in health foods and it started being a lot more profitable than managing the Stooges, who were like an oven that burned money. So he just started backing away from the Stooges, and I became the Stooges' de facto manager.

I worked with them long-distance since I was working for Atlantic Records in New York. The Stooges had their songs ready for their next album—what was to become *Raw Power*—and I loved it. I was just thrilled.

So I called Bill Harvey, the executive from Elektra who had fired me—we still hated each other, but I still had to have a relationship with him since the Stooges were still signed to his label—and I said, "It's time to pick up the option."

I think he had determined beforehand that he wasn't going to pick up the option. He just went through the motions.

RON ASHETON: Iggy had moved out of Fun House to the University Towers in downtown Ann Arbor to be closer to his dope connection. Fun House was too far on the outskirts of the city for Iggy and Scotty because nobody had cars. They had to be in the city to be closer to their dope connection.

Iggy couldn't drive a car—you'd think with all his coordination on-stage, but he can't drive. We had this rented car that we were supposed to keep for a few days, but Iggy kept it for a month. The cops picked him up going down Sharon Street with two wheels up on the curb, stoned on 'ludes, just plowing into everything.

So Iggy moved to the University Towers, and right across the street from it was Biff's, a twenty-four-hour, all-night diner. They used to score right at fucking Biff's diner. They'd be sitting there at three in the morning getting their dope.

WAYNE KRAMER: Iggy and I had a little dope business going. I used to hook him up with a few of my connections in Detroit and we'd use some of his connections in Ann Arbor, and then we went into the dope business ourselves. All these kids would come over to the University Towers and buy from him, and I had some connections, so we both put up a couple hundred dollars and bought a piece of dope, which was nine spoons or something like that. But then I had to go out on tour with the MC5.

RON ASHETON: Iggy was taking his parents' checks to Discount Records and cashing them. Shit, it was several thousand dollars. The cops finally busted him, but his parents paid back all the money.

WAYNE KRAMER: I was expecting that when I got back to town, my money would be doubled and I'd have eighteen spoons of dope. It was your typical pyramid scheme, "Let's-double-it-up" dope deal. It worked one time. The second time, I had to go on tour, and when I got back, I asked my girlfriend, "Well, where's the drugs?" My girlfriend said, "Oh, uh, Iggy's veins collapsed and he was in the hospital and the money's all gone and the drugs are all gone."

So I went over to his place because all I heard was there were major problems. His apartment was always a real disaster. So I get to his place and it's all clean and neat. His mother had come and cleaned up the whole apartment and folded the clothes. Iggy was real apologetic about the money, he said I was gonna be the very first one he was gonna pay back . . .

DANNY FIELDS: Bill Harvey and I flew together to Ann Arbor so he could hear the audition of the Stooges' new material and I thought that they had carried off the audition so well that Bill Harvey would have to say, "Yeah, well, this band is living up to its promises."

I was just so proud and pleased.

RON ASHETON: I got Bill Harvey earplugs to wear while we played. He tried to be nice and gracious, but he was very uncomfortable.

DANNY FIELDS: We went back to the motel in Ann Arbor and I was sort of beaming and said, "So?"

Bill Harvey said, "Frankly, I heard nothing at all."

That's when the Stooges were dropped from Elektra.

I was appalled. I thought *Raw Power* was genius. "Search and Destroy" was one of the greatest rock & roll songs of all time. It just doesn't get any better than that.

I think Bill Harvey just didn't want this band and didn't think they were commercial enough. Which he was right about; they weren't commercially viable. They never sold any records. I thought they would make this investment in art for art's sake. I thought eventually the public would catch up with this great music if you just kept putting it out and believing in it. The irony is that I guess he was right, because more than twenty years later, *Raw Power* still sounds advanced.

So I had to tell Iggy, "They're dropping you."

He said, "I don't believe it. We played so great, and the songs were so great."

I said, "I did too, but what are you gonna do? They don't want you."

BILL CHEATHAM: Ronnie got this call from a guy at the IRS who said that the band owed a lot of money in back taxes. Ronnie said, "I don't know anything about it."

The IRS guy said, "Well, you'd better find out."

So Ronnie said, "Hey look, man, we're all drug addicts, we don't know where the fuck the money is."

The guy went, "Oh," and hung up. The Stooges never heard another word from the IRS.

DANNY FIELDS: It was hell managing Iggy. We were all in New York, and they were out in Detroit and no one understood anything about money. Actually, there was no money. The record company didn't support them and they didn't sell any records.

And Iggy had a drug problem. The Alice Cooper band and the Stooges would play the same show and they'd get paid $1,500 a night. It would come showtime and there would be the guys in Alice's band looking for the mirror to put on eye makeup—you know, being real professional—and then we'd have to go look for Iggy.

And I'd find him lying there, down around the toilet bowl with a spike in his arm, and I'd have to pull it out, with blood spurting all over the place, and I'd be slapping his face, saying, "It's showtime!"

Was that fun? Yeah, right.

DEE DEE RAMONE: The first time I saw Iggy was at the Stooges' show at the Electric Circus on St. Marks Place in June of 1971. They went on real late because Iggy couldn't find any veins to shoot dope into anymore because his arms were so fucked-up. He was pissed off and wouldn't come out of the bathroom, so we had to wait.

IGGY POP: I was backstage looking for a vein and screaming, "Get out! Get out!" to everybody, even my friends—and they were all thinking, God, he's going to die, blah, blah, blah.

Finally, I'm up there on the stage, and as soon as I walked on that stage, I could feel it. I knew I just had to puke. I wasn't going to leave the stage, though, because I felt that would have been considered deserting one's audience.

DEE DEE RAMONE: The band finally came out and Iggy seemed very upset. He was all painted in silver paint and all he had on was a pair of underwear. The silver paint was smeared all over him, even in his hair. But his hair and fingernails were gold. And someone had also sparkled him up with glitter. They went on and played the same song over and over. It only had three chords. And the only words to it were "I want your name, I want your number."

Then Iggy just looked at everybody and said, "You people make me sick!" Then he threw up.

LEEE CHILDERS: Geri Miller was down front again. She had this horrible little voice and she was right down front screaming, "Throw up! Throw up! When are you gonna throw up?" And he did! He threw up. Iggy always satisfied his audience.

IGGY POP: It was very professional. I don't think I hit anyone.

RUSSELL WOLENSKY: I was up front. I did get thrown up on. Iggy got me on the shoulder.

RON ASHETON: By then, I was used to Iggy throwing up. He used to go behind the amps to hide it, but it became common knowledge what was happening. Such degradation . . .

I gave up saying anything because nobody listened to me anyway. I mean, just before the gig they took my vintage pre-CBS Stratocaster up to Harlem and traded it for forty dollars' worth of smack. They said it got ripped off. I was heartbroken, man. Years later, my brother, Scotty, told me what really happened. Yeah, by the time of the Electric Circus gig, I'd given up . . .

DANNY FIELDS: Everything was falling apart as far as my relationship with the Stooges was concerned. I was bailing them out of hotels and putting my own credit on the line for them. I couldn't afford it. I had no money coming in. There were rumors that they were holding up gas stations on the weekend to pay rent on the house, and the house was getting torn down and a highway was coming through where the Fun House was.

And then came the phone call at four o'clock in the morning from the Stooges saying they'd just driven a fourteen-foot truck under a thirteen-foot bridge in Ann Arbor.

RON ASHETON: The Washington Street Bridge—it ate so many trucks. Scotty was driving. He was doing like thirty-five miles per hour and BAM! It took the top right off—peeled back the top of the truck.

I was at Fun House and the phone rang: "Whaaat?"

I went to the hospital and you know how those desk nurses are, they won't say nothing, all she would say was, "They're all in very serious condition, that's all I can say right now."

I'm going, "Oh, man!"

So I went to the bridge and the truck was all fucked-up, then went back to the hospital. When I walked into the waiting room, they were all sitting there, the two roadies, Larry and Jimmy, and my brother, Scotty.

They looked just like the Three Stooges—Larry with teeth missing, my brother with stitches in his tongue, and Jimmy all bandaged up. So I was driving home with Larry and Scotty, and Larry says, "Take me back to the bridge!"

I said, "Huh? Okay . . ."

We get there, and they jump out and start rummaging through the weeds. That's when I found out they were on reds. When the cops had come, they threw the bag of reds out the window. So we had to go back and get them.

I said, "You motherfucking idiots!"

SCOTT ASHETON: Nobody told me it was a twelve-foot-six truck and a ten-foot-six bridge. I got thrown out of the truck about fifteen yards. One guy hit the dashboard and knocked all his teeth out, he was unconscious, and the other guy hit the windshield, which put a big gash in his head and he was wandering around with blood all over his face. I thought the other guy was dead.

I was going, "Oh no," still not knowing what the hell happened, and then I turned around and saw that the truck didn't fit under the bridge.

So they made the gig that night without me. They had to put six stitches in my chin, but what I'll never forget is that stitch they put in my tongue. It was the worst pain I ever had in my whole life. I thought I was gonna snap. I thought I was just gonna lose it.

You can look at the bridge even now, and you can tell. That bridge is still fucked-up.

DANNY FIELDS: They destroyed the truck, destroyed the musical instruments, which were rented, and destroyed the bridge. So they were being sued by the owners of the truck, the owners of the instruments, and the city of Ann Arbor. And they wanted to know, at four o'clock in the morning, what was I gonna do about that.

What was I gonna do about it? I was gonna go back to sleep.

BILL CHEATHAM: Somehow Scotty Asheton ended up owing this motorcycle gang money and they were coming after him. Scotty owed them money, so they were gonna come out and kick our ass, steal the equipment, and bust up the place.

So there was a siege at the Fun House. We turned the Fun House into a fortress, literally. We put up plywood on all the lower-floor windows and we had a lot of guns—shotguns, pistols, rifles—virtually everything.

For the first couple days, we took turns standing watch. Scotty decided he didn't want to live at the house right then, so he would stop by for practice and then split. But the thing was, that to get into the house we had to tear out the police lock and then rebuild it once somebody got back in. So the door was getting more and more full of holes.

After about four days, Scottie came back to stay, and the bikers never showed up, so we just sorta got trigger-happy, you know, "Goddamn it, I'm in the mood to use this thing."

We were sitting on the couch, and there was a picture of Elvis across the room, and Scottie just kept staring at it. Finally he just cocked his shotgun, and KABOOM, he blew a hole in Elvis. So then I just opened fire, too, and we just started blowing holes all through this wall.

All of a sudden we heard this screaming: "Hold your fire! Hold your fire!"

We didn't know that John Adams was down in the basement, sleeping. He came upstairs—he was completely covered in plaster—sees us, and just goes, "What the fuck is going on?"

After we found out that the city was going to destroy the building, we just said, "Oh screw it," and totally shot the place to hell.

But Ronnie stayed till the bitter end.

RON ASHETON: After we got dropped, Danny came back to Ann Arbor because he had heard all these terrible junkie stories. In my apartment, Danny fired John Adams. We were all quiet, because we loved him. But I didn't know that John Adams was carrying dope all over the United States. I would have been too freaked out to fly with him. And a little while after he fired John, Danny said he couldn't do it anymore.

DANNY FIELDS: It became impossible. I couldn't handle it. They were stoned, I was probably stoned too, and I just said, "I can't do this anymore."

It was all too much for me. I needed a real job. So I went to work for *16* magazine.

Part Two

■ The Lipstick Killers
1971–1974

Chapter 9

■ Personality Crisis

PENNY ARCADE: My family thought I was the Devil's child. So, by the time I was seventeen, I ran away from home. What happened was my mother had signed a complaint against me and I spent a night in jail in my hometown of New Britain, Connecticut. The next day my mother came to get me, and while I was walking home with my mother, I just kept walking. After going to Provincetown and Boston, I ended up in the East Village.

This was the era of crash pads and floating shooting galleries, a whole junkie culture that went from the Chelsea Hotel to the Hotel Earle, to the Henry Hudson to the Seville. Somebody would go into the hotel and get a suite and fifteen people would move in. But there was always an issue of somebody trying to fuck you, and I was just a kid looking for a place to sleep.

So I started hanging out at this pizza place on the corner of Seventh Street and Second Avenue, and that's where I met the speed freaks. That's where I was introduced to the "A Set," which was short for the "Amphetamine Set"—Brooklyn Frankie and Short-Haired Sammy and Black Frank. It was a really wild scene because they weren't hippies, they were a criminal, homosexual, drug-taking, spiritual-seeking, artistic crowd of men. Real con artists. Flim-flam men. Second-story men. Legendary characters who'd been doing it for years. And it felt like I was the newest addition into this long history.

Those were the real street-level members of the A Set. Then there was also a higher echelon, people like Ruby Lynn Rainer, the legendary amphetamine dealer, Ondine, the Velvet Underground, and all those other people from Andy Warhol's Factory. At that time, the drug world and the art world ran through each other.

At first I hung around with the A Set without shooting speed, because I could stay up for three days at a time, but after a couple of months they wanted me to get high with them, so I started shooting speed. And I liked it. It was my drug. I understood speed and I liked the people who took it.

Then one day, while I was speeding my brains out at a coffee shop on Greenwich Avenue, somebody passed me a note that said, "To the girl in the green dress, what time do you get off work?" I looked at it and said, "What's this?" The note was from Jackie Curtis, who was sitting at another table with a shopping bag filled with his plays and press clippings and God knows what.

Jackie came over because he wanted to meet me. We became instant friends and spent the rest of the day hanging out together. He was still a boy then; he still dressed as a boy and he loved speed too, though he wasn't shooting it. Just pills. I started hanging out with Jackie and soon after I discovered John Vaccaro's Playhouse of the Ridiculous Theater.

LEEE CHILDERS: The outrageous underground theater that John Vaccaro, Charles Ludlam, and Tony Ingrassia were doing in the late sixties and early seventies became known as "ridiculous theater," a label like "theater of the absurd." And of course, John Vaccaro thought that the Playhouse of the Theater of the Ridiculous was his banner, and Charles Ludlam thought Ridiculous Theater Company was his banner, but it had become a genre, a type of theater—"ridiculous theater."

In my opinion, John Vaccaro was more important than Charles Ludlam, because Ludlam followed theatrical traditions and used a lot of drag. People felt very comfortable with Charles Ludlam. Everyone's attitude going to see Charles's plays was that they were going to see a really funny, irreverent, slapstick drag show. They never felt embarrassed.

But John Vaccaro was way past that. Way, way past that. John Vaccaro was dangerous. John Vaccaro could be very embarrassing on many levels. He used thalidomide babies and Siamese triplets joined together at the asshole. One actor had this huge papier-mâché prop of a big cock coming out of his shorts, down to his knees. He also couldn't control his bowel movements, so shit was dripping down his legs the whole time and everyone loved it. People loved that kind of visually confrontational theater. And John Vaccaro used tons of glitter, that was his trademark. Everyone wore glitter. The whole cast was always covered with glitter.

People had been wearing glitter for a long time and the drag queens were wearing it on the street, but I think "glitter" really took off when John Vaccaro went shopping for costume material and he came across this little place in Chinatown that was having a big clearance sale on their glitter. He bought it all—giant shopping-bag-size bags of glitter in all colors.

John brought it back to the theater and encouraged everyone to use as much of it as they possibly could, anywhere they could possibly put it. Of course their faces were covered with glitter, their hair was full of glitter, the actors who played the Moon Reindeer had their entire bodies covered in green glitter. Baby Betty, who was playing a thalidomide baby, had glitter coming out of her pussy—so it was because of John Vaccaro that glitter became synonymous with outrageousness.

His whole stage was covered in it. And not only were the people covered with glitter, but because they were constantly moving, dancing, bumping into each other, and jumping off things, there was all this glitter in the air—just floating around. So the whole atmosphere of the stage with the lights on it was one that was constantly in motion with glitter.

JOHN VACCARO: I never thought of anything as the "glitter movement." I'd been using glitter in theater since the mid-fifties. But I really wasn't interested in campy things. I wasn't interested in promoting homosexuality. My sensibility is different than camp. There were two schools: the homosexuals and the theater people. Some of the homosexuals did what they thought was theater: "Why not go into a nightclub and do a drag act like *La Cage Aux Folles?*" That's exactly what it was. But it wasn't theater. It was not theater at all.

The height of the theater has always been man versus himself: Hamlet, King Lear, Willie Loman, Blanche DuBois. And I always thought the height of theater was the world versus itself. Fuck "man." I've given up on "man." I'm more interested in the world. Nevertheless, there were two different schools. Mine had social content, the others didn't.

And I used glitter as a way of presentation. Nothing more. Glitter was the gaudiness of America, that's what I interpreted it as. And it was pretty. Glitter was makeup. I used it because it was shoving America back into the American faces. It was the gaudiness of Times Square. You know, take away the lights and what do you have in Times Square? Nothing.

LEEE CHILDERS: While Jackie Curtis was in rehearsals for *Heaven Grand in Amber Orbit*, a play she had written and was starring in, and which was being directed by John Vaccaro, things got a little out of hand. John Vaccaro was a very difficult man to work with because he used anger to draw a performance out of a person. And Jackie was a speed freak who was extremely paranoid and accusatory—the slightest thing would throw her into a frenzy. So she and John fought constantly, and he eventually took all her clothes and ripped them to shreds, threw her shoes at her, fired her, and kicked her down the stairs, which he was famous for doing, and Ruby Lynn Rainer took over the title role.

A few days after the fight, Jackie Curtis showed up at my door and said she had the ultimate showdown with John Vaccaro, that she left the play, and that she wanted everyone in New York to think that she had committed suicide. So she had to stay at my apartment, and no one could know she was staying there, because everyone was supposed to assume she was dead.

Which I thought was fabulous. I loved that idea. I said, "Come right in!" The next day, Holly Woodlawn showed up, dressed entirely in black cut velvet, with black ostrich feathers in her hair, saying, "I'm in mourning." So then Holly moved in, too.

JOHN VACCARO: Jackie Curtis was the least talented of the people who worked for me. Jackie Curtis was a drag queen who carried his clippings around in a shopping bag everywhere he went. That's what these people did. They carried their clippings. This was their crutch. They couldn't live without having these things with them.

I did one of Jackie's plays, but I didn't do it as Jackie had written it. Jackie had written a homosexual play about a Forty-second Street cafeteria and a cashier at it called *Heaven Grand in Amber Orbit*, which was the name of the lead character. Jackie wrote the play using the names from horse-racing forms.

I changed *Heaven Grand in Amber Orbit* to a circus with Siamese triplets. I turned it into a musical and a sideshow—what it was about was the problem of the world, and if the people in power took a really good shit, there wouldn't be any war. So all throughout the play, I had this woman sitting on a toilet, delivering her lines out of constipation. Someone else had a toilet plunger to her asshole—none of this was in the Jackie Curtis play.

LEEE CHILDERS: I don't know if anyone actually thought Jackie had killed herself or if everyone in New York knew exactly what was going on, but it was the most fabulous lie. It went on for about six weeks. A charade. An event. With Holly Woodlawn showing up in the back room of Max's in increasingly outrageous black drag, with veils and things, mourning Jackie. All of us still went to Max's every night and people would say, "Have you heard anything? Has anyone heard anything of Jackie?" and we were all saying, "No."

Meanwhile, we're taking plastic bags and filling them full of food to take back to Jackie. So that's how we all ended up living together, and once you got Jackie and Holly in the apartment, it was an easy step to Candy Darling dropping by. At the most crowded it was Jackie, Holly, Rio Grande,

Rita Red, Johnny Patten, Wayne County, and me all in a Lower East Side one-bedroom apartment.

To me, Jackie Curtis and Holly Woodlawn and the rest of them were the most glamorous people. They weren't drag queens. They weren't crazy. These were just people who lived twenty-four hours in dresses and old ladies' shoes. Jackie didn't wash, so she stunk to high heaven half the time. Holly was a complete speed freak. She didn't really care whether other people knew she was a man or a woman or a Martian.

The stove immediately became coated with zip wax from them zipping their faces, because in those days you zip-waxed your beard, and what it achieved wasn't a feminine look.

You took hot, molten wax, put it on your face, let it dry, and then grabbed it and pulled it off. So what it did was rip out your beard by the roots, which made your face swell up all red, bloated, and ugly. Then they'd put this Woolworth's makeup on, because that was all they could afford— this Woolworth's orange makeup all over their red faces and then go out in public! No one thought they were women, no one thought they were men! No one knew what they were! And they dressed in old-lady dresses. This old lady died next door to us, and Jackie walked the ledge from our window to her window and broke into her apartment to steal all her clothes. Those were the clothes that Jackie wore, the dead old lady's dresses!

Holly just wore anything. She'd just wrap a sheet around her. In fact, Holly got in trouble with the welfare people. She was on welfare, everyone was. She would show up at the welfare office to get her welfare check in ostrich feathers and false eyelashes. One day they took her into an office and said, "Sir, this is the welfare office. You're showing up in evening gowns and ostrich feathers. The other welfare recipients are getting very upset about this."

Holly said, "Buy me some jeans, I'll wear them, otherwise I'll spend my money as I please, and I please to spend it on ostrich feathers."

PENNY ARCADE: Anybody could be in the Playhouse of the Ridiculous Theater. It was all street stars. Homosexuals, heterosexuals, lesbians—it didn't matter, nobody cared about those things. It was all outsiders. So John Vaccaro wanted me to join and I said no.

But they got me the way people always get me, which was, "John Vaccaro just called, and they need somebody to help." And of course, if somebody needs help, I'm there. My job was to hold Elsie Sorrentino's costumes, one of the actresses who was the actual role model for the character Tralala in Hubert Selby Jr.'s *Last Exit to Brooklyn*. Then one night John Vaccaro came up to me, took the costumes out of my arms, and literally pushed me onstage, saying, "GET OUT THERE AND DO SOMETHING!"

LEEE CHILDERS: John Vaccaro was notorious for his megalomaniac fits—throwing things, screaming obscenities, and humiliating these teenage kids in his theater company who were already on speed, sleeping on someone's floor, and didn't have money for a McDonald's hamburger. He frightened them, and it frightened him, I think that's why he'd let it go so far sometimes.

One New Year's Eve, John Vaccaro literally did kick Candy Darling down two flights of stairs. She fell seven or eight steps and started to get up, but he was right behind her and kicked her again. There was a blizzard outside, three feet of snow, and he kicked her right out into the snow in her evening gown. But make no mistake about it, Candy loved being kicked out into the snow. She lived for drama. I'm sure she was probably back up there the next day, sitting around, having tea and talking it all over with him.

You see, everyone was on speed, which lent itself to great dramas and outbursts of emotion. The scenes were always extremely dramatic *and* publicly dramatic—lots of slappings, drinks in the face, and bottles over the head in the back room of Max's.

PENNY ARCADE: Jackie Curtis wrote a play called *Femme Fatale* based on the experiences that Jackie Curtis, me, and a guy named John Christian had hanging around together. But John Christian had turned into a major junkie and agoraphobic. He refused to come out of his apartment or be in the show. So Jackie announced to me that John's part was gonna be played by this girl, Patti Smith.

Some people thought Patti was this ugly girl, you know, when ugly was a sin. But she wasn't ugly, it was just that nobody looked like that then. She was really skinny and dressed weird. She had this look that was completely her own, which in retrospect was a precursor of the whole punk thing. She wore these espadrille-type wrestler's shoes, skinny black pants, and usually a white man's shirt, tucked in, with a Guido type of undershirt underneath. She didn't wear a bra, and she had a very gaunt face and very dark hair. And Patti had all these scars on her stomach from when she was pregnant. She'd wear her pants real low and you could see all these scars.

When Jackie and I first met Patti, Jackie said to me, "I don't trust that girl, she's a social climber."

But I didn't think one way or another. While we were rehearsing *Femme Fatale* I had gotten pregnant and abortion was illegal. I had heard if you had an IUD implanted it would force a miscarriage. It was really stupid and dangerous, but I went to a doctor in Allenville and had an IUD put in. I felt fine, so I went to rehearsal. Then I started to black out, so I left. I was going down in the elevator with Patti. I was losing it and Patti kept saying to me, "Do I look like Keith Richards?" You know, "How does my hair look? Does it look like Keith Richards?"

I said, "Yeah, kind of," because I didn't understand why anybody would wanna look like Keith Richards.

I didn't show up the next day for rehearsal nor did I call, so when I did go back to rehearsal everybody was really mad at me; Tony Ingrassia, Jackie Curtis, everybody was like, "You didn't show up, blah, blah, blah."

Just as I was standing there listening to them yell at me, Patti Smith came up to me with this page torn out of her diary. It said, "Today I met a girl named Penny Arcade, she's really cool, I really like her, I want her to be my friend."

So Patti and I started to be friends. I think originally she was living in the Chelsea with Robert Mapplethorpe, but then they'd gotten their own place, a loft a few doors down from the Chelsea.

JAYNE COUNTY*: Jackie Curtis was brilliant in *Femme Fatale*. At the end of the play she was crucified to an IBM card. We had this giant IBM card and we stapled her to it.

After we did *Femme Fatale* we were in another play called *Island*, where I played the transvestite revolutionary and Patti Smith played this speed freak who's into Brian Jones and shoots up onstage. Actually, it was simulation of shooting up speed while shrieking, "Brian Jones is dead!" That was Patti Smith's big moment on the New York underground stage. She had a little thing of putty in her arm and the needle would actually go into the putty. And while she was shooting up she'd go, "Brian Jones is dead! Brian Jones is dead! Brian Jones is dead! Look, it says right here, Brian Jones is dead!"

LEEE CHILDERS: *Island* had a huge cast—Cherry Vanilla, Patti Smith, Wayne County—and it was set on Fire Island. It was episodic and it didn't really have a plot; everybody got killed in the end because the government decided to blow up Fire Island from battleships. Andy Warhol loved it. He thought it was genius, so he said to Tony Ingrassia, the director, "I've been making tapes . . ."

Of course Andy Warhol made audiotapes of everything. He was always standing there with his little tape recorder, taping every phone call,

---

*Jayne County was formerly Wayne County, before the sex change.

every single word that was said to him. So Andy had boxes and boxes of cassette tapes and he said to Tony Ingrassia, "These would probably make a good play." Tony said, "But what am I supposed to do with them?" Andy gave him the boxes and said, "Oh, I'm sure you'll find some good stuff in here."

Tony actually did it. He went through the tapes, found interesting snippets of conversation, mostly from telephone conversations, and constructed this play called *Pork*. The play consisted of an actor playing Andy Warhol sitting in a wheelchair on this empty, white, sterile hospital stage, with all the other characters spread around, talking on white telephones. The Pork character was supposed to be Brigid Polk. The Vulva character was Viva, and she would talk on the phone to Andy and say things like, "Andy, have you ever thought about monkey shit, what do you think monkey shit looks like? Has anyone ever seen monkey shit? I guess zoo-keepers must see monkey shit, I've never seen monkey shit, how about cow shit, isn't cow shit . . ."

JAYNE COUNTY: *Pork* was basically about someone playing Brigid Polk—shooting up speed all the time and just rapping. Everyone else in the play revolved around her, talking about their fetishes and their perversions. Jane Callalots, who was also in *Heaven Grand in Amber Orbit*, played Paul Morrissey. She wheeled the Andy Warhol character, played by Tony Zanetta, around in a chair with rollers on it. He would just sit there and go, "Um hum, aaah."

LEEE CHILDERS: That was basically the play. I was the assistant director of both the productions—it ran for six weeks in New York, then it ran six weeks in London. But it was in London that the production created a huge, giant scandal of a sensation. We were such kids, we didn't know anything about the London tabloid press. Geri Miller went for a photo session in front of the Queen Mother's house, popped her tits out, and got arrested. It made the front page of every tabloid: "PORK PORNO ACTRESS POPS TITS IN FRONT OF THE QUEEN MOTHER'S HOUSE!" They would quote her: "WHAT'S WRONG WITH TITS, THE QUEEN'S GOT 'EM."

We were really a major media event and we didn't even know it, but Cherry Vanilla decided that we could pass ourselves off as New York rock & roll journalists. Cherry was the only one who realized that we could pull a few scams there. She called an editor at *Circus* magazine and he told her, "Okay, anything you want to try to get away with, use my name, but I know nothing should the phone ring."

So we passed ourselves off as rock & roll journalists from *Circus* magazine—Cherry was the writer, I was the photographer, and it worked like a charm. We went backstage everywhere. We would get *New Musical Express* every week and look to see who was playing so we could go. We went to see everyone—Marc Bolan, Rod Stewart . . .

Then I saw a tiny ad, like one column inch, that said "David Bowie at the Country Club." I'd read an article by John Mendelssohn on him, so I said, "I've heard of David Bowie. He dresses up in dresses." Everyone said, "Oh, that's good—let's go see him." So we called and got on the guest list—me, Cherry, and Wayne County. It was a tiny club and the audience couldn't have been more than thirty people. And my first impression of David Bowie was, "Oh dear, what a disappointment. How boring." He was wearing yellow bell-bottom pants and a big hat.

JAYNE COUNTY: We'd heard that this David Bowie was supposed to be androgynous and everything, but then he came out with long hair, folky clothes, and sat on a stool and played folk songs. We were so disappointed with him. We looked over at him and said, "Just look at that folky old hippie!"

We were sitting in the audience with our black fingernails and dyed hair. You couldn't get any of those bright punk colors then, but Leee Childers had gotten a Magic Marker and colored his hair all different bright colors. At one point David Bowie said, "And the people from Andy Warhol's *Pork* are here tonight, stand up."

We all had to stand up—Cherry stood up, took her top off, and shook her tits. It was great. We were being scandalous everywhere.

LEEE CHILDERS: David was disappointing, but we loved his wife, Angela Bowie. Angie was loud, she was pregnant, she was crazy, she was grabbing our crotches, laughing it up, and having a good time.

So we came away talking about Angie, not about David. The very next night they invited us out to this gay bar called Yours and Mine on Highgrove, and we got to know David a little more and saw his sense of humor and began to appreciate him more. By the time we left England, we were very much in love with him.

JAYNE COUNTY: Of course we influenced David to change his image. After us, David started getting dressed up. I'd gotten the shaved eyebrows thing from Jackie Curtis, and David started shaving his eyebrows, painting his nails, even wearing painted nails out at nightclubs, like we were doing. He changed his whole image and started getting more and more freaky.

Chapter 10

■ Land of a Thousand Dances

DANNY FIELDS: To me, Max's Kansas City was always the downstairs back room. Later, when they started having bands play upstairs in 1973, on a regular basis, Max's became a whole other place. There was a disco upstairs, and Wayne County would play records, and it was okay. But it wasn't downstairs. It wasn't the back room. The really fun period ended as soon as they started bringing the bands in, because it brought in a lot of riffraff. Max's had been an exclusive downstairs enclave and only people who knew about it knew about it. As soon as there were lines in the street waiting to see the bands upstairs, it was the end of Max's.

EILEEN POLK: I went to Max's every night. Every single night. At first it was full of Warhol people. During that period you'd see Andy Warhol there with his entourage: Viva, Jane Forth, Joe Dallesandro. Taylor Mead would be hanging out in the corner, drinking. Or some crazy girl with dreadlocks, holding a baby doll, talking to herself. Warhol's Factory had been up on Forty-seventh Street, but then they moved it to Seventeenth Street, right off of Union Square Park, a few blocks away from Max's. So you could just walk across the park and hang out at the Factory when Max's closed. And that was usually the place where everybody had video cameras following them. It was pretty much like that scene in the Doors movie where they meet Nico and go off and do heroin.

Then the Warhol people started getting replaced by all these glitter bands: Jo Jo Gun, the New York Dolls, Slade, Sir Lord Baltimore. I would usually pick up some guy in an up-and-coming band. I wouldn't meet rock stars and have sex with them. I would meet them and be afraid to have sex with them. So I wouldn't have sex with guys who would come in to get the groupies drunk and pick them up. I'd usually end up having sex with a friend. I liked people who were willing to make assholes of themselves, instead of people who were like, "I only want to be seen with the coolest-looking guy."

DUNCAN HANNAH: I was hanging out at Max's with Danny Fields at his usual booth. We were having a couple of brandies and in walks Lou Reed with the Maltese crosses sculpted into his head. It was 1973, and Lou comes over and says, "Hey, Danny!" Danny says, "Oh, Lou, sit down, sit down." So it's the three of us. And I'm introduced and Lou goes, "Hey, he looks like David Cassidy, you know that?"

And I said, "Oh, I don't really like David Cassidy." And he goes, "Yeah, you look just . . . doesn't he, Danny? Doesn't he look just like David Cassidy?" And then they started talking about me in the third person, "Doesn't *she* look like David Cassidy?"

That goes on for a while and then they started talking about Raymond Chandler. And I'd just read all of Raymond Chandler. So I'm thinking, Hey, I know about this, and I'm sitting with my hero, Lou Reed, and we're going to have an intellectual conversation about Raymond Chandler. Alright!

So Lou is making some point, talking about a scene that was in *The High Window*. And I said, "Oh no, that's in *The Little Sister*." He goes, "Wha?" I said, "That's in *The Little Sister*. I just read that, too, it's great, I know that piece . . ."

So Lou turns to Danny and says, "Hey, Danny. She speaks. Does she think? I guess she reads, huh?"

I thought, I get it. I'm just a dumb blond.

So Lou says, "Hey, Danny, what does she do anyhow?" And Danny says, "Oh, she's an art student." So Lou goes, "Oh, an art student." And it was horrible. It's horrible being with your heroes when you're an art student. It sounds like nothing. So I got the message: Be seen and not heard. I'm a bauble. I'm an accessory. Oh, great. Here's my hero, I finally meet my hero! And I can't talk.

So then Danny goes to the bathroom and Lou turns to me and says, "Say, are you Danny's?" And I said, "No, no, Danny's my friend." He said, "So you don't belong to Danny?" And I said, "No, you know, he's my *friend*." Lou goes, "Well, will you be my David Cassidy then?" I said, "Uh, no, I don't think so." And he said, "Well, look, why don't you come back to my hotel with me?" I said, "And?" He said, "And you can shit in my mouth. How'd you like that?" I said, "I don't think I would like that."

I was really ashen. And Lou started whispering, like it was supposed to make me hot, and said, "Does that, does that repulse you?" I said, "Yeah." And he said, "Well, I'll put a—I'll put a plate over my face, then you can shit on the plate. How'd you like that?"

I said, "No, I don't think I'd like that either."

He said, "Well, you're really missing out. Come on and we'll just go have fun."

I said, "Ah, no, I don't think so. I think I'll just stay here." So he said, "Okay. And nuts to you," or something like that. So then Danny came back and Lou says, "Gotta split, Danny!" And he left, and I was really depressed because I'd imagined something really different. It wasn't like it was in the books: "God, I met my hero and we were talking about Raymond Chandler!" Instead it was, "Can I shit in your mouth?"

After Lou splits, Danny says, "Hey, I think Lou liked you." I said, "I don't think so." I think I told him, "Lou asked if I belong to you," and Danny liked it because he was with something that his friend wanted. Danny said, "Well, if you wanna go with him, go if you like." And I said, "No, I don't think so."

JAYNE COUNTY: The back room was vicious. Vicious. Everyone was on a different drug, and if you got up to use the bathroom you didn't dare turn your back. The bathroom was on your left, and you had to back out of the back room to get there, because if you turned your back, people would talk about you. People would say horrible things about you the minute you got up.

LEEE CHILDERS: When they first started coming around Max's, Patti Smith and Robert Mapplethorpe couldn't get in. Visually they were a little tacky—Robert would wear big hats, these big, suede floppy hats and big college shirts, and he did look pretty bad. Patti looked a little cooler, she'd be in ugly, dirty ripped clothes.

I guess Mickey Ruskin thought they didn't have the right look. And to their great credit, because it's something I probably wouldn't of had the nerve to do, Patti and Robert would sit on the curb out in front of Max's and would talk to everyone as they came and went. That seemed fabulous to me. I wouldn't have dared do that if I couldn't have gotten in. I would have just disappeared. I admired Patti's guts to sit there and say, "This is where I want to go, and if they don't let me, I'm just going to sit out front." It was a very punk attitude way before there was a punk attitude.

TERRY ORK: Patti Smith and Robert Mapplethorpe were very much a couple. They had a real tactile sensual perversity to them, definitely unique. I used to go over to the Chelsea Hotel to see them and we'd dress up together to go to Max's. They were an enchanting little couple and the darling of everyone at the Chelsea Hotel—that included Viva, some other

Warhol Superstars, and Bobby Neuwirth. Mapplethorpe was still straight, very much a young Catholic boy gone astray.

JACK WALLS: I believe Patti and Robert were entertaining some notion of becoming Warhol Superstars and made a production out of going to Max's to try and get in. They used anything to get attention—eyeliner, lipstick, black nail polish, anything that was going to get them into the back room. But no one gave them the fucking time of day.

DANNY FIELDS: Patti tells this story wonderfully. She and Robert used to come to Max's every night, stand in the doorway, and stare at all the chic people and wish that they would be invited to sit down or hang out with them. Those of us who were sitting down used to look at this adorable, sexy young couple in the doorway, wondering who they were, wishing that they would come over and sit down with us. And this tension, this stasis, went on for a while. Finally I said, "Well, come and sit down you two, who are you?" And Patti remembers that I'm the first person at Max's to ask her to sit down. It was funny: "Come on already, stop hovering in the doorway, you're cute, who are you?"

PENNY ARCADE: Patti was a girl who would wake me up at nine o'clock in the morning going, "Penny?" I'd say, "What is it, Patti?" "It's Bobby's birthday." "Bobby who?" "Bobby Dylan." Patti lived her whole life pretending to be John Lennon or Paul McCartney or Brian Jones or some other rock star.

I was with her the night that Brian Jones died. She was just hysterical. Just crying hysterically. I mean I was upset too, but she just kept talking about "Baby Brian Jones" and "Baby Brian Jones's bones." It was like she was involved with these people, but it was all in her head. Other people have imaginary playmates, but Patti had imaginary playmates who were Keith Richards and people like that. Patti told me the story about when she met Eric Clapton. She was with Bobby Neuwirth and she kept hanging around Clapton, until finally he said to her, "Do I know you?"

Patti said, "Naa, I'm just one of the little people."

JACK WALLS: Tinkerbell called Patti up at her mother's house in New Jersey and told her that Robert was a fag. It broke Patti's heart. I mean, how you gonna compete? If it's another girl, that's understandable, but if the person you love tells you that they are homosexual, then you've got a *big* problem.

Before that, the only thing Patti and Robert argued about was who was gonna do the laundry.

DUNCAN HANNAH: Robert and Patti were still going out when I first got to New York. They were so cool. I ran into Patti one night and mentioned Mapplethorpe and Patti said, "Oh, I split up with my old man." She said, with this great confidence, "You know, he's turned to men, and there's nothing a woman can do when her guy turns to men."

It was like she was exempt. It wasn't her fault and she really wanted me to know this, which to me was incredibly generous. I was so flattered that she really didn't want me to think ill of her, right? I was just like, "WOW!" but I just nodded like, "Uh huh," like these are truisms: That's how it goes when a woman loses her man to another man. Yup.

JACK WALLS: Robert Mapplethorpe was a child of the fifties and when the Stonewall riots happened in 1969 that signaled the beginning of gay liberation, Robert was nineteen or twenty years old. It was a movement, and people were coming out even if they weren't gay. By the early seventies people started going to the extremes of being gay. And Robert went to the extremes right away. The "trucks" were happening then—a bunch of empty flatbed trucks on Fourteenth Street in the meat-packing district, where gay men started going for anonymous sex.

Then someone got enough sense to open some clubs, because everyone was over there anyway, so might as well get them a drink. So the Mineshaft and the Anvil sprang up and it was a whole scene of decadent sex—piss, shit, fist fucking, gloryholes, doing as many people as you could—just fucking like there was no tomorrow.

TERRY ORK: I dunno what came first, if Robert's gayness began to show itself, or if Patti began to fool around with rock stars. I think Patti was living a very public persona. Patti would always kiss somebody and then look at you to make sure you'd noticed, almost as if she were acting out a sort of nineteen-twenties Paris kind of bohemian role. She was very self-conscious about living as if she were onstage and about being a starfucker. She had that New York bravado about it. And then Patti ended up having a pretty long love affair with Todd Rundgren.

PATTI SMITH: If I didn't think so much of myself, I'd think I was a name dropper. You can read my book, *Seventh Heaven*, and who do you get out of it?

Edie Sedgwick, Marianne Faithful, Joan of Arc, Frank Sinatra; all people I really like. But I'm not doing it to drop names. I'm doing it to say this is another piece of who I am. I'm shrouded in the lives of my heroes.

BEBE BUELL: Todd Rundgren introduced me to Patti. She was his girlfriend before me. I liked her immediately. She told me I looked like Anita Pallenberg, Nico, and Marianne Faithfull all rolled into one cream puff. Those were her exact words to me. Then she said, "You gotta cut your hair into bangs." At the time I had long hair and Patti told me to cut it with the bangs and stuff, so I did. Then she tried to talk me into dyeing it white, but I wouldn't

I used to drive Patti crazy. I'd go visit her every day. I would just show up on Twenty-third Street where she was living with Allen Lanier, you know, right after they'd just fucked or she was fixing one of her shrines or she was writing, but she'd always let me come in.

We'd sit and talk and she told me, "I really want to sing." I'd told her, "So do I." This is way before she started singing. So we'd put on records and sing to them at the top of our lungs. We'd put on "Gimme Danger" and try to imitate the attitude on the vocals, trying to get it right in our throats. Patti would say, "Yeah, this is how you learn how to sing." We'd use hairbrushes for microphones and stand in front of the mirror and sing. I had great times with her like that—she was really fun. Sometimes I would bring pot and Patti could not smoke a lot because she's just so smart and crazy that after two hits, she'd be like off, man—in the stratosphere, with philosophy and telling me stories about Sam Shepard.

I was so young and crazy—I would always go running to Patti every time I had a problem with Todd. Patti still loved Todd a little, so it was hard for her to have this little brat coming over, asking her for advice about Todd when she still had a lot of feeling for him, even though she was living with Allen. Sometimes I would catch Todd and Patti hugging or something, and I would get very teenage about it. I'd go over to Patti and say, "Why you hugging my boyfriend?" She'd say, "Relax. It's okay, just cool out, little girl."

PENNY ARCADE: Patti was a very demanding person to know because she was extremely driven. Patti wanted to look like Keith Richards, smoke like Jeanne Moreau, walk like Bob Dylan, and write like Arthur Rimbaud. She had this incredible pantheon of icons that she was patterning herself on. She really had a romantic vision of herself. Patti had gone to teacher's college and was gonna be a teacher, but then she made the leap out of the New Jersey working-class life.

At the time I didn't realize you could do that. I didn't realize that being an artist was better than being a home-economics teacher.

BEBE BUELL: The person who talked me into posing for *Playboy* magazine was Patti Smith. At the time I was doing well as a cover-girl model for Revlon, Intimate, and Wella. I had four or five big accounts. But my role models weren't models. I admired girls like Anita Pallenberg and Marianne Faithfull, those were the girls I looked up to and aspired to be like.

So when *Playboy* asked me to pose, Patti said, "I wish *Playboy* would ask me. I'd do it." Patti had really big boobs, a lot of people don't realize that. She was extremely well endowed and she always thought that kind of stuff was really cool. She showed me pictures of Brigitte Bardot, Ursula Andress, Raquel Welch, and all these *Playboy* pictures. She'd say, "Being in *Playboy* is like Coca-Cola. It's Andy Warhol. It's American, you know it's part of America, this magazine." She said, "Do it. It'll be great. It'll fuck up that fashion thing."

At that point I was having fantasies about starting a band, and Patti was trying to explain to me that if I modeled too long it would be harder for me to make the transition. She thought the fastest way to kill the fashion thing and to get rid of the teen stigma and the rock & roll girlfriend thing was to do something daring. But to do it really classy like in *Playboy*.

Patti's idea of feminism seemed to me to be about not being a victim—that women should make choices in full control of their faculties and make a rebel stand.

Posing for *Playboy* was a rebel move. It almost ruined my career in this country as far as legitimate fashion work went. The only magazines that would book me after that were like *Cosmopolitan* and stuff. I lost all my bread-and-butter clients. I lost Avon and Butterick. All the straight fashion magazines stopped booking me.

But how could I regret it?

PENNY ARCADE: I always perceived Patti and Robert as brother and sister. I always perceived Robert as gay, but Patti always talked about him as her boyfriend. I'd been a fag hag since I was fourteen years old, so I was familiar with the idea of deeply passionate but nonsexual relationships with gay men. So I don't think that I ever really believed that Patti had a sexual relationship with Robert, although they probably did. I always saw Patti as being like me—a fag hag. So I knew that there were problems. I knew Patti was frustrated and angry. And I loved Patti. You know, I was in love with Patti, and I think Patti was in love with me, too.

I always had this very romantic friendship with her. It was kind of a Victorian thing—it wasn't very physical, though it did get physical.

PATTI SMITH: I tried to make it with a chick once and I thought it was a drag. She was too soft. I like hardness. I like to feel a male chest. I like bone. I like muscle. I don't like all that soft breast.

PENNY ARCADE: I mean, I wasn't physically attracted to Patti, and Patti probably wasn't physically attracted to me. So when we got physical it was only a one-time thing. It definitely came out of an emotional attachment rather than a physical one. My emotional relationship to Patti was so much more . . .

But then things changed. We were hanging out at Max's one night and Patti and I were goofing around. We were sitting with Miss Christine from the GTO's, and we decided we were gonna do a band. It was gonna be me, Patti, and Miss Christine.

For me and Miss Christine doing this band was just one big goof. I mean, I did want to do a band, but I had no idea of what that meant. Word got around that we wanted to do this band, and apparently Danny Fields talked to Steve Paul and told him that we were putting something together, because a few nights later, when I got to Max's at my usual time, there was a telegram waiting for me. It was from Steve Paul saying, "Don't sign with anyone else!"

I was like, "What the fuck is this?"

I had no idea, but the thing that was weird was that I noticed Patti got very antsy about this whole band thing. For me it was a goof, but for Patti something else was going on, which I didn't get.

I didn't understand that Patti saw that something really could be done.

Chapter 11

■ The Poetry All-Stars

JIM CARROLL: One night I was walking home to the Chelsea Hotel and Patti Smith and Robert Mapplethorpe were out in front of the hotel having this big fight. But when Patti saw me, she stopped fighting, came over to me, and said, "Hey, you're Jim Carroll, right? I'm Patti. Hi."

I'd seen Patti around—I could see her checking me out at Max's and at readings at the Poetry Project at St. Mark's Church. By that time I was pretty established as a poet.

So she said, "How about if I come see you tomorrow? I have a book I wanna give you."

So I said, "Sure. I'm in room—"

Patti said, "I know what room you're in."

She came over the next day and that was when we really met. We made it that day, as I recall. And she did have a book. I think it was about some Native American Indian tribe.

What was scary was that she was really pursuing me to move into the loft that she shared with Robert. She knew that I was going out with this fashion model, Devra, who was like the archetypal sixties-type model—in the Jean Shrimpton sense, not the Twiggy sense—and I really had the hots for Devra. And Patti would say, "Man, you're blowing it, you should get rid of her. You're only going out with her because she looks good on your arm. I'm really the girl for you."

In the Mapplethorpe biography, the writer Patricia Morrisroe makes it out like Patti wore me down to move into the place. I mean yeah, I guess she did, but I didn't stop seeing the fashion model.

Our relationship didn't last all that long. I was the first guy she took up with that she actually moved into the loft, but Robert Mapplethorpe didn't feel threatened by me at all. Robert and I got on really well. He'd ask me a lot of questions about different things—he wanted to know how to make class transitions, and he knew that I was this street kid who had gone to this very prestigious private school on a scholarship.

So he knew that I knew a lot of rich people, and it wasn't like he was soliciting me to meet them, but he wanted to learn how to be more sophisticated. But it wasn't something I could teach him, though I did tell him that he should read a lot more books, because Robert didn't read at all, you know. And those works that he had then were so baroque, I mean they were like motorcycles on a bed of velvet and stuff—it was like something out of *Great Expectations*, Miss Havisham's wedding cake or something. But a lot of it was just finding himself—both his own self and his artistic self.

And Robert also used to talk to me about how I knew I wasn't gay, since I was hustling guys. You know, didn't I like it? I'd say, "Yeah, but I always ask them for the money first, Robert. You know, that's how I know. And that I tell them I can't see them again afterwards."

It had to be a one-time thing. So Robert was still trying to convince himself he was at least bisexual, but he pretty much knew that he was gay, and there was no turning back.

I just took it for granted, Patti didn't speak about Robert as a boyfriend to me. She made it sound like they were like brother and sister. In her own way, Patti is extremely old-fashioned. Before I moved in to the loft, she'd bring me over breakfast at the Chelsea every morning—coffee, chocolate donuts, and a pint of chocolate Italian ice. Brigid Polk had been trying to get me off heroin by shooting speed, which was ridiculous. I was ten times worse that summer. I had to get back on junk to get my health together. Patti was working at Scribner's bookstore, so she'd rip off money from there and give me money to get junk, so it was one of my worst drug periods, but it was great. I always thought she was a total speed freak, but Patti never took any drugs, which was amazing to me, because it was like she was vicariously nodding with me.

Patti used to watch me sleep, man, I'd wake up and she'd be looking right at me. Somebody else told me that she liked to watch guys sleep . . .

I only saw the sweet side of Patti—very, very faithful and very loving. I mean it's just that I didn't get rid of that fashion model and when Sam Shepard came along, it was like, "Okay, *hasta la vista!*"

LENNY KAYE: I'd written this piece for *Jazz and Pop* called "The Best of A Cappella," and Patti called me up because it had touched her. I was working at Village Oldies, so she started coming down on Saturday nights and we'd put on the Deauvilles or the Moonglows and dance, so that's how we got friendly. She asked me if I would play guitar with her at this reading she was going to be doing at St. Mark's Church.

GERARD MALANGA: Terry Ork introduced me to Patti Smith and Robert Mapplethorpe. She sent me some of her poems and I wrote back a very glowing letter about them. I must say that she was a punk true to heart, right from the start, because in her letter back to me she says, "I still think I'm a better poet than you." She was half-joking, but probably half-serious too.

I got into Patti immediately and saw real talent there, so I arranged for her to read with me at the Poetry Project at St. Mark's Church.

LENNY KAYE: The first thing we did was "Mack the Knife," because it was Bertolt Brecht's birthday, and then Patti read a bunch of poems including "Oath," which was "Jesus died for somebody's sins . . ."

Then we did this song that she had written about Jesse James, then a song called "Ballad of the Bad Boy," which was all suspense and buildup, and getting faster and faster, and then at the end I got to do the car crash. That seemed to me the set that we always would do—your cool oldie, your pop song, and your piece of maniac car-crash music.

The reading was a hit. I think Gerard had one eye up. In a way you could feel the generations change at Max's, and he was definitely part of the Warhol crowd who helped invent Max's, but as the seventies progressed, the rockers took it over, and the order changed.

JIM CARROLL: Somebody had asked Nico if she wanted to do a reading at the Poetry Project, so Nico said to me, "You are the young poet, eh, I have my poems they want me to read at St. Mark's, have you read there?"

I said, "Yeah, I did." I was totally overwhelmed, man—she was this Teutonic beauty asking me about my poetry, she was reading me her poems that she had memorized.

They were terrible, ha ha ha.

GERARD MALANGA: After Patti and I read together I arranged for her to have a book published by Telegraph Books. Victor Bockris and Andrew Wylie had approached me about publishing a book of my poetry, and I in turn told them that they should do a book of Patti Smith's poetry. I also arranged for them to do Brigid Polk's scar book. I arranged two or three books for them.

VICTOR BOCKRIS: Andrew Wylie had a storefront on Jones Street, and that became our headquarters for Telegraph Books. Andrew lived in the back, and I would come up from Philadelphia once a week to meet with him.

Andrew and I talked on the phone every day. He would call me in Philadelphia and say, "I'm hanging out with Patti Smith now, she's really great, blah blah blah, her boyfriend is the guy in Blue Oyster Cult."

Andrew finally took me to meet Patti Smith where she was living on Twenty-third Street with Robert Mapplethorpe, and he was sort of lurking about. Mapplethorpe had a lot of Polaroid photographs up on the wall that were largely sexual. They weren't all gay sex, but there were enough of them that were gay sex that it made me uncomfortable. I was very uptight about gay people in those days, very uncool.

The next time I saw Patti was when I came up to New York to bring her copies of her first book that we published, called *Seventh Heaven*. Normally when someone publishes a book, we'd give them like six copies, but we decided to give Patti forty copies because we realized that she was a great publicity machine, and that she could get them to well-known people.

So I went up to her loft, carrying these big stacks of books, and Patti was really uptight because someone had said to her, "You're an idiot to let these people publish your book without a contract because when you become famous, they'll be able to sell millions of copies and make a lot of money."

So she confronted me about this. Even though I wasn't cool and confident at that point, I said to Patti, "What the fuck are you talking about?"

I was sort of offended because I'd worked my ass off getting the book done. Patti said, "You guys are gonna make a lot of money outta this!"

I said, "Patti, nobody buys poetry books, even for a buck, so we're not gonna make any MONEY, unfortunately it's not the way these things work. We did this for fun and because we think you're great."

She sort of mellowed, and I did our trip—which we'd done a million times—which is to make people feel good about themselves. So I said, "I think you're really great. I wanna do an interview with you! I can do an interview with you and get it published in this really hip magazine in Philadelphia!"

Patti said, "Great," and I think we did the interview that night. It was probably the first interview she ever gave. It was long and really good—it was like Patti telling her story the way she does.

PATTI SMITH: I was working in a factory and I was inspecting baby-buggy-bumper-beepers and it was my lunch break. This guy would come around with this little cart that had these genius sausage sandwiches in it, and I really wanted one. They were like, a dollar-forty-five. I really wanted one, but the thing was, the guy only brought two a day. And the two ladies who ruled the factory, Stella Dragon and Dotty Hook, took those sausage sandwiches.

So there was nothing else I wanted. You get obsessed with certain tastes. My mouth was really dying for this hot sausage sandwich, so I was real depressed. So I went across the railroad tracks to this little bookstore. I was roaming around there, looking for something to read, and I saw *Illuminations*. You know, the cheap paperback of *Illuminations* by Rimbaud. I mean, every kid has had it. There's that grainy picture of Rimbaud in it and I thought he was so neat looking. Rimbaud looks so genius. I instantly snatched it up. I didn't even know what it was about, I just thought Rimbaud was a neat name. I probably called him "Rimbawd," and I thought he was so cool.

So I went back to the factory. And I was reading it. It was in French on one side and English on the other, and this almost cost me my job, cause Dotty Hook saw that I was reading something that had foreign language in it, and she said, "What are you reading that foreign stuff for?"

I said, "It's not foreign."

She said, "It's foreign and it's communist. Anything foreign is communist."

She said it so loud that everybody thought I was reading the *Communist Manifesto* or something. They all ran up, of course it was complete chaos, and I just left the factory in a big huff. I went home and so, of course, I attached a lot of importance to that book before I had even read it.

I just really fell in love with it. It was gracious Son of Pan that I fell in love with, cause it was so sexy.

JIM CARROLL: An ex-girlfriend of mine sent me this mimeo magazine from Philadelphia, which had an interview with Patti in it. One of the questions was, "What three poets would you like to tour with?" And Patti answered, "Muhammad Ali, Jim Carroll, and Bernadette Mayer." She said that I was "the only true poet in America."

Patti gave me a copy of *Seventh Heaven*, and of course she told me which poems were about me, but I think Patti was probably telling the same thing to other people. The only poems I trusted that Patti really wrote for me were ones that she showed me at the time.

GERARD MALANGA: I was a little pissed off at Patti because when the book came out she thanked Anita Pallenberg, who she didn't even know, Bobby Neuwirth, and somebody else.

Not that I looked for gratitude or acknowledgment, but I'm the one who arranged for her to get her book published. I put a lot of energy into

promoting her talent. Here she was—somebody who was totally unknown—
and I was pushing her, because I believed in her as an artist. I went out of my
way to twist a few arms and get her work known and then she just turns
around and she's thanking Bobby Neuwirth?

I mean, what the fuck's that all about? I never broached the subject
with her, but I was very deeply disturbed about this. She must have had an
affair with Bobby Neuwirth for her to make that acknowledgment like she
did. Yeah, but what did she get out of Bobby Neuwirth? Maybe she got to
meet Dylan. I thought it was a bit of brownnosing.

ED FRIEDMAN: One night at a reading, Patti was introducing Ruth
Kligman, who had been a mistress of Jackson Pollock, and Patti starts off
her introduction by saying, "When I was growing up in Jersey, you know,
like the coolest thing in the world was like to be the mistress of a great
artist, you know, and the first thing I did when I left home was become
Robert Mapplethorpe's lover. You know, Ruth Kligman—how much bigger
can you get? How much bigger can you get?"

I think Ruth was pissed off—I would have been if I was trying to present
myself as a serious poet and I was introduced as an artist fucker.

So afterward I said, "Ah, Patti, that introduction . . ."

Patti just sort of looked at me and said, "Oh, was I bad?"

JIM CARROLL: Patti was complaining to me that she couldn't get
another reading at the Poetry Project—you know, "They're just jealous,
everybody liked me that night," which I think was true. So the next reading
I had I told them that I wanted to do a reading with Patti.

The day of the reading I was in Rye, New York, staying at my friend
Willie's house, who was a character in *The Basketball Diaries*. Willie was like
one of the few heads in that area, and that morning the fucking sheriff of Rye
decides he's gonna pull a bust on him. I just happened to be there when they
raided his house at dawn. The only thing they found were hash pipes with
residue, but they brought us in for that. We had to go to the jail there—but I
ordered one of the best meals I ever had from this Italian restaurant, and then
they took us down to White Plains to book us, but then the judge threw it out.

By then it was around midnight. Fortunately we didn't have to spend
the night in jail. But it wasn't that bad, for jail, it was kinda nice, actually.
But I had missed the reading. Nobody knew where I was, and Patti got up to
read and kind of prefaced her reading with, "Well, we all know that Jim has
his problems . . ."

But I think that Anne Waldman and everybody at the Poetry Project
were really pissed—you know, "Jim's just so unreliable!"

So Patti said something like, "You love the fact that he's a rebel, but when it gets in your face and bothers you, then you don't like it so much do you? Well, I say, *Here's to Jim Carroll* . . ."

But it also gave her the whole show, so she could dig that. I was good enough to get busted and give her twice as much air time.

PATTI SMITH: The St. Mark's poets are so namby-pamby, they're frauds, they write about, "Today at 9:15, I shot speed with Brigid . . ." They're real cute about putting it in a poem, but if Jim Carroll comes into the church stoned and throws up, that's not a poem to them—that's not cool.

If you could play with it in your poetry, that's okay, but if you're really with it, that's something else—they don't want to face it. Jim Carroll was the St. Mark's Poetry Project's chance to have something real among them. Jim Carroll is one of America's true poets. I mean, he is a true poet. He's a junkie. He's bisexual. He's been fucked by every male and female genius in America. He's been fucked over by all those people. He lives all over. He lives a disgusting life. Sometimes you have to pull him out of a gutter. He's been in prison. He's a total fuck-up. But what great poet wasn't? It kills me that at twenty-three Jim Carroll wrote all his best poems—the same year of his life as Rimbaud did. He had the same intellectual quality and bravado as Rimbaud.

But they blackballed him because he fucked up. He didn't come to his poetry reading. He was in jail. Good for him. They said, "Oh well, we can't ask him to do poetry readings anymore." It was ridiculous.

DUNCAN HANNAH: I knew of Patti Smith before I moved to New York. She was this great mix of rock chick, poet chick, and kind of a historian, a beatnik. French existentialism and rock & roll, everything that I liked. I thought, Wow! Cool.

What was great about Patti was she was such a fan. Her poems were like fan letters. Like mash notes to Rimbaud. And I could identify with her because I was doing the same thing, keeping journals, writing mash notes to dead people, and here she was doing it in a much more confident way, a little older, right? And making art out of it.

We were always looking for the obscure, kinda left of center, right? These fringe things. When I came to New York, I remember seeing Patti one night and saying, "Hey, are you onto Egon Schiele?"

Egon Schiele was a Viennese expressionist that had great hair, got busted for pornography, and died at twenty-eight. You know, like perfect.

So Patti goes, "Oh, yeah, I been onto him."

"Yeah, you must be crazy about him."

"Oh, totally."

It's a big hero-worship thing, right? And in being obscure about it, that was cool.

JIM CARROLL: I was up at Sandy Daley's room at the Chelsea about a year after Patti and I had split up, and I put my hand around her waist and said, "We should get together again, Patti."

I guess she must of been really hot for Sam Shepard, because she looked at Sandy and they started laughing—obviously all this girl talk had gone on—it was like, "Man, are you kidding? A year ago if you had said that to me I woulda jumped out the window, baby. But not now. Sorry, Jim."

You know, she was like, "I told you you were gonna blow it if you didn't stay with me."

So I did feel that, man, maybe it was a big mistake, but through all those vacillations that Patti went through I don't know if I could of handled that.

In the Mapplethorpe book it says she left me, after she picked my mind about poetry and got some recognition of her own, but it didn't happen that way. We just kinda drifted apart . . . you know, she was like, "I was faithful to you and you kept fucking the fashion model!"

But we did talk a lot about poetry. Patti's poems were very different than mine—she had this whole Dionysian thing, whereas I was pretty Apollonian. That's why she was so successful with rock—she could just go nuts and counterpoint it with this sweet self and let go with this weird-angry-magic self, too.

She could just let it all loose, but formwise she wasn't that disciplined, and to me that was really important. Patti was taking in everything I was saying about form, and a longer line, but I mean that was all technical stuff, and neither of us were going to change. I didn't like all her poems, but she had some really good lines in there.

VICTOR BOCKRIS: John Calder, who ran Calder and Boyars, which was like the Grove Press of England, agreed to publish an anthology of the Telegraph writers. So Andrew Wylie, Gerard Malanga, Patti Smith, and I went to London together in 1972.

Gerard's visit was written up in the New Musical Express—and the article said that Gerard Malanga was reading with Patti Smith and Andrew Wylie.

GERARD MALANGA: We all gave great readings—we really put out. I went on last. The place was very plush. It was cushioned in red velvet, like something out of a cowboy movie. I was wearing all white at the time—I was going through my spiritual period, I was on a Don Juan trip, reading J. D. Salinger and Castaneda and getting all worked up, ha ha ha.

VICTOR BOCKRIS: In those days, Gerard wore totally white. He'd just come back from India or something. Everyone was milling around, and he just sat on the ground cross-legged, and started reading without being announced, and suddenly everyone was going, "SSSSHHHHH, Gerard's reading."

He was reading this Robert Creeley–type poetry, like, "I looked but YOU were not THERE in the ROOM and you were the LIGHT coming through the window . . ."

Then Patti came out and she was really brilliant. She knew what she was doing. Back then she was very clever about the way she dressed. She was wearing a sort of baggy white T-shirt that really accented her breasts. Patti has big breasts. She'd been on the cover of *Time Out*, naked from the waist up, holding a hammer—naked except for a necklace—and she had the black Keith Richards hairdo.

That night she read stuff from *Seventh Heaven*, but then she told this poemlike story, and she said, "I haven't finished writing this yet, but it goes like this, 'The boy looked at Jesus as he came down the steps,' " and she got confused in the middle, but she said, "Oh fuck it, I forgot it."

Everyone was completely with her—"Oh, that's really cool, she forgot her poem"—but then she said, "But I'll make it up anyway, what the fuck," and she made it up as she went along.

So she was really a punk, a punkette, and it was very, very effective. The audience was completely blown away. Nobody had ever seen anything like it.

Then Andrew Wylie came on, and because he'd insisted on reading last, he had less time than the rest of us, because the porn-theater owner had to close the place or he would get busted. So Andrew was under a lot of time pressure, and I think he realized that Patti was the star act, and once you see the star act you don't really wanna see anything else.

So we went out for a drink afterwards, and everyone said, "You guys changed London overnight, blah blah blah." Patti and Gerard disappeared. Gerard was living in his own little world, and Patti was too aloof to be hanging out with us—I think she spent the night with Sam Shepard.

GERARD MALANGA: It was a coincidence that Sam Shepard was in London, and so when I got wind that Patti needed a place, I gave her the key to my hotel room and said, "Hey, take my room for the afternoon."

The morning after the poetry reading we all went out to breakfast together in Knightsbridge in front of the church that Ezra Pound used to go to. Then we went to the photo session for Telegraph Books.

VICTOR BOCKRIS: Gerard said to me, "Don't tell anyone. Sam Shepard's not supposed to be here." I said, "Okay," even though I didn't know who Sam Shepard was. He was very gaudy and had long hair—he just stood off to the side, you know, like, "Don't tell anyone I'm here." He was married, and he wasn't supposed to be seeing Patti.

There's a whole series of those publicity photographs taken—Andrew in his beret and black leather jacket, me with my long white scarf, Patti with her black hair. You know, we all had our little number.

GERARD MALANGA: Back in New York, Patti Smith and Sam Shepard did a play together called *Cowboy Mouth*. Here were these two writers, having an affair, and they wrote this play together, and it was kind of like having a love affair onstage.

TERRY ORK: When Sam Shepard and Patti Smith were rehearsing *Cowboy Mouth*, I was bringing Nick Ray, who directed *Rebel Without a Cause*, to see the production. I had the full intention of trying to get money to film an actual performance of it, but after opening night Sam got cold feet and left town. He couldn't face performing this adulterous relationship in front of his wife and kid. I mean, he just OD'd. He just fried out.

ED FRIEDMAN: I saw Patti at a group reading at the Poetry Project at St. Mark's Church, and Patti was head and shoulders above everybody else—in terms of having real crowd magnetism. She was able to really BE this star presence as a poet—this mix of Rimbaud and Keith Richards and the Velvet Underground and Janis Joplin. And she would talk about these people—but the work had this romantic quality and it also had this real goofy pop quality to it. And in her performance, she was able to play at being this male presence, sort of alternatively female and male, or androgynous.

She had that poem "Rape," and at a certain point she took the role of the man—she was calling the rapee "Lambie Pie."

During that time feminism was really rising as a public discourse, and I don't think they ever cited Patti as one of their favorite authors, ha ha ha. But I think that was part of her appeal—she could be one of the guys.

One time she told me, "Allen Ginsberg thought I was a cute boy and he tried to pick me up, so I said, 'LOOK AT THE TITS, ALLEN! NOTICE THE TITS!'"

PATTI SMITH: I didn't have no confidence in myself. So I used to write stuff mostly about girls getting rid of their virginity, and I used to write like Lorca. I wrote this one thing about this brother raping his cold sister under the white moon, it was called "The Almond Tree." He looked at her cadaver and said, "You are cold in death and even colder to me than you were in life."

Most of my poems are written to women because women are most inspiring. Who are most artists? Men. Who do they get inspired by? Women. The masculinity in me gets inspired by the female. I fall in love with men and they take me over. I ain't no women's lib chick. So I can't write about a man, because I'm under his thumb, but a woman I can be male with. I can use her as my muse. I use women.

JOEY RAMONE: I saw Patti at Kenny's Castaways, real early on. She was reading poetry. And every time she'd read a poem, she scrunched up the paper in a ball and threw it on the floor—or she'd be reading something and she'd pick up a chair—and throw it across the room, smash it into a wall or something. I thought that was great. I never knew anything about her, but I was real impressed.

RICHARD HELL: I went to see Patti read when she used to play these gay clubs, like Le Jardin, and they just would go nuts for her. That amazed me. "This crowd turned out for this girl doing poetry?"

Patti would just reel this stuff off and it was so hot and she was so sharp, but she was so sweet and vulnerable at the same time. She was the real thing, there was no mistaking it.

Chapter 12

■ A Doll's House

LEEE CHILDERS: When *Pork* ended its London engagement, I returned to New York and started working for *16* magazine. Then Lisa Robinson got Roy Hollingworth, the correspondent for *Melody Maker* in London, to hire me as his photographer. So Roy said, "I've heard about this band, the New York Dolls, they're supposed to be really incredible, really fabulous. Let's go take their pictures and do an interview."

I went with Roy to a loft on the Bowery, and of course the New York Dolls were well prepared for us; obviously, with *Melody Maker* coming, they were all in women's clothes and makeup. Women's clothes were especially cool then. So here's David Johansen in a little see-through polka-dot blouse. But I went for it. It was 1970 and I was all for these gorgeous boys in women's clothes. I didn't think any of them were heterosexual.

JERRY NOLAN: In the beginning, a lot of the New York Dolls' audience was gay, but of course, we were all straight. We were all girl crazy. And let me tell you something: it turns out women knew immediately. It was the men who were confused. The women knew, I don't care what we wore. And they loved us for it, that we had the balls to look and act the way we did. It was fun for them.

LEEE CHILDERS: I thought they were all gay. I was wrong, of course. But they were very, very funny. Very funny, which is more important to me than a woman's blouse, or hetero, or homosexual, which I thought they were, because they talked very gay. They were playing gay. I don't remember specifically what we talked about, but it was very sexual, it was a lot about "cocks and big cocks" and stuff like that.

I was still young enough, and naïve enough, and wanting it to be true enough, that when Johnny Thunders talked to me about big cocks, I believed that he was into that. Of course, he was only saying it because he wanted to get a record contract. Isn't it funny that those times were so fortuitous? I took really great pictures of them, totally great pictures, because I was entranced, not with anything sexual, but with their vision. And so they invited me down to the next show, which was that weekend at the Mercer Arts Center, and to their credit and to my credit, all thoughts of sexuality, makeup, women's blouses—everything else went right out the window the minute I heard them. I am a true lover of rock & roll, and they were a true rock & roll band.

DAVID JOHANSEN: There wasn't a lot of intellectualizing going on when we started the New York Dolls. It was just a bunch of guys practicing in a storefront who started playing together. The Dolls consisted of myself on lead vocals, Johnny Thunders on lead guitar, Syl Sylvain on rhythm guitar, Arthur Kane on bass, and Billy Murcia on drums. None of us said to each other, "You wear this or you do that."

I don't know where the glitter thing came from. We were just very ecological about clothes. It was just about taking old clothes and wearing them again. I think they called it glitter rock because some of the kids who used to come to see us put glitter in their hair or on their faces. The press figured it was glitter rock—the term itself came from some writer, but it was just classical rock & roll. We used to do Otis Redding songs, Sonny Boy Williamson songs, Archie Bell and the Drells songs, so we didn't consider ourselves glitter rock, we were just rock & roll.

And we thought that's the way you were supposed to be if you were in a rock & roll band. Flamboyant.

CYRINDA FOXE: David Johansen borrowed the outrageousness of the ridiculous theater and put it into rock & roll by starting the New York Dolls. He was certainly the one that did it, because he wanted to be hip, and I think he very much wanted to be part of the theater scene. The ridiculous theater was much more exciting than rock & roll. It was more alive—it wasn't all cut up, patched up, cleaned up, and sold to the mass media the way rock & roll had been.

David had an intellectual side to him and he very much wanted to be in with the whole Charles Ludlam gang. David and Charles were good friends, I think he even played a small part in a Charles Ludlam play—I think he carried a spear or something. He didn't have a speaking part.

But I think that was as close as he could get to that world, because David was a little more heterosexual than they wanted him to be. They were a little set back by this babe on David's arm. I think that hurt him. David wanted out of Staten Island and Warhol wasn't interested in him, Ludlam wasn't. Then he started doing the New York Dolls and he didn't need the theater scene anymore. And there was definitely nothing exciting and glittery and fun and sparkly and wild going on in rock & roll until the Dolls came along.

JERRY NOLAN: The Dolls started playing around, mostly at a place called the Mercer Arts Center, every Tuesday, and the Diplomat Hotel. I fell in love with them right away. I said, "Holy shit! These kids are doing what nobody else is doing. They're bringing back the three-minute song!" These were the days of the ten-minute drum solo, the twenty-minute guitar solo. A song might take up a whole side of an album. I was fed up with that shit. Who could outplay who? It was really boring. It had nothing to do with rock & roll. Then there was Top Forty, which was steady work and you made a few bucks, but I just hated playing Top Forty.

The Dolls not only appealed to the kids, they were drawing the young art crowd: Andy Warhol, actors and actresses, other musicians. One time I saw Jimi Hendrix just sitting around. He sent his girlfriend over to get me, and she introduced us. He said, "I was admiring your suit"—this red velveteen suit with velvet cuffs and collar, red on red. He asked me if he could touch it. "Where'd you buy it?" I said, "I had it made."

That's the kind of scene it was. I used to go out with Bette Midler and hadn't seen her in a while, but I ran into her again at the Mercer. People don't realize it, but New York really wasn't a meeting ground for anybody then. You did your shit, then went back home again. But the Diplomat Hotel and the Mercer Arts Center brought everyone together.

DAVID JOHANSEN: The Mercer Arts Center was this multiroomed entrepreneurial scheme to get people to spend money on the Lower East Side. They used to have plays in one room—*One Flew over the Cuckoo's Nest* was one of their mainstays, that was what paid the rent. And they had a small theater and a cabaret room, a bar, and they had these plastic seats that were very modern at the time. Now it seems tacky. *Ciao! Manhattan* chic. In the cabaret room they had some guy named Louis St. Louis and his St. Louis Express playing the piano with these black girls singing. They had another room called the Kitchen, which was the conceptual art room, or the zoo room, where anything could happen. Then they had this other room called the Oscar Wilde Room that they didn't know what to do with. That's the room we wound up in first.

JERRY NOLAN: I used to watch the Dolls and think to myself, Boy, could I play the shit out of that song! Or *that* song, or *that* song.

I'd get into these incredible arguments with musicians my own age, friends of mine. They couldn't understand why these guys were getting so much attention—the Dolls were not what you'd call great technical musicians.

I'd say, "You're missing the fucking point. They're bringing back the magic of the fifties!"

They were wild *and* they were natural. Every move they made seemed to hit the papers. Their popularity just kept growing. Everybody talked about those guys. Their songs were like nobody had ever heard for ten years: beginning, middle, end, boom-boom-boom.

DAVID JOHANSEN: The audiences there were pretty depraved, so we had to be in there with them. We couldn't come out in three-piece suits and entertain that bunch. They wanted something more for their money. And we were very confrontational. We were very raw. We were really into confronting the audience: "HEY YOU STUPID BASTARDS, GET UP AND DANCE!" We were not polite.

We were also the first ones with those really big high-heeled shoes. Billy Murcia's mother used to go to England all the time and we used to see these pictures in the English papers of all these girls wearing these shoes and we'd put in our orders with Billy's mother. We used to put our feet on the ground and draw an outline and give them to her and she'd go to London and come back with twenty pairs of boots. And we would all wear them and paint them and trade them.

LEEE CHILDERS: The Dolls created a huge scene and it became extremely fashionable to go see them. You didn't just go see the Dolls—you had to be seen seeing the Dolls.

It was an actual participatory thing. And the people not onstage were just as much a part of the show as the people onstage. Everybody in the audience was just as outlandish as the Dolls were. There was Wayne County, the Harlots of 42nd Street, Sylvia Miles, Don Johnson, Patti D'Arbanville, all that kind of gang, were all in the audience, dancing.

Then of course there was David Bowie and Lou Reed, watching and learning. David Bowie came to see the New York Dolls a lot. Lou came to see them a few times.

So when the Dolls played the Mercer Arts Center, it was one of those rare times when the fashionable place to be was actually the right place to be, because it was the best rock & roll in a long time. Real rock & roll.

DAVID JOHANSEN: People who saw the Dolls said, "Hell, anybody can do this." I think what the Dolls did as far as being an influence on punk was that we showed that anybody could do it.

It used to be when we were kids, man, rock & roll stars were like, "Wow, I got my satin jacket and I'm really cool and I live in this gilded cage and I drive a pink Cadillac." Or some crap like that. The Dolls debunked that whole myth and that whole sexuality.

Because basically we were these kids from New York City who spit and fart in public, were raunchy and just debunked everything. It was just so obvious what we were doing to rock & roll—we were bringing it back to the street.

RICHARD HELL: Music had just become so bloated. It was all these leftover sixties guys playing stadiums, you know, being treated like they were very important people, and acting like they were very important people. It wasn't rock & roll, it was like some kind of stage act. It was all about the lights and the poses. With the Dolls, it was just like the street put onstage, you know? That was another cool thing about them, they were exactly the same offstage as they were on.

DAVID JOHANSEN: It was real easy to take over because there was nothing happening. There weren't any bands around so we just came in and everybody said the Dolls are the greatest thing since Bosco. But we were the only band around, really, so we didn't have to be that good.

Chapter 13

■ Raw Power

JAYNE COUNTY: After we all came back from London was when David Bowie started getting his Ziggy Stardust trip together. They convinced him to cut his hair and to dye it orange—the whole spaceman trip.

Angela was pushing him to do it. And Tony DeFries hired Cherry Vanilla, Leee Childers, Tony Zanetta, Jamie DeCarlo—they had all these freaky people around, trying to make David look good. But if it hadn't been for Andy Warhol's *Pork*, there would never have been a MainMan, or for that matter a Ziggy Stardust.

LEEE CHILDERS: David Bowie was beginning to build his legend in London. Suddenly he became a really huge sensation—the old guitar-string-chewing act with Mick Ronson. When it came time to bring David Bowie to America, Tony DeFries, who was David's manager, was in touch with Tony Zanetta, who had played Andy Warhol in *Pork*, and the two of them had formed some sort of bond. God knows why.

Anyway, Tony DeFries and Tony Zanetta took me out to dinner at Pete's Tavern and I just jabbered away, the way I have jabbered all my life: "Oh, I think we should do this! Oh that'd be great!" At the end of the dinner Tony DeFries said, "Well, Z"—which is what he called Tony Zanetta—"I think we have our vice president."

I didn't even realize it was a job interview. I thought I was just out having dinner, but that's when I became vice president of MainMan, David Bowie's management company. Then, of course, we dragged Cherry Vanilla straight in as secretary and suddenly we were the American company.

PAUL MORRISSEY: Tony DeFries brought funny little David Bowie to Warhol's Factory. I had to deal with all the business there—people didn't discuss anything with Andy because Andy didn't know what to say, so I had to do all the discussing.

So I'm talking with Tony DeFries, and he says, "RCA has given me a lot of money to promote this guy in America," and he points to Bowie—this funny little white-skinned guy sitting over in the corner.

Tony says, "We think he's gonna go through the roof. He's big. And RCA has given me a lot of money, so my idea to promote Bowie is that Andy Warhol come with us on the U.S. tour."

There's Andy in one corner, and this shy little Bowie thing in another corner—they're sort of eyeing each other across the room, and here's DeFries proposing that Andy be paid as a groupie! For David Bowie!

I just couldn't believe it. I said, "RCA will pay YOU money and then you'll pay ANDY? Why don't they just pay us to promote our own album like we did with the Velvet Underground?"

It was all stupid—to take a fee for promoting somebody if you're not part of it, just because DeFries wanted David Bowie to be the new Velvet Underground.

So I said, "Gee, I don't think so. We're just a little too busy right now."

BEBE BUELL: I met David Bowie at Max's. I was there with Todd Rundgren and a group of people. He was with his wife, and they came over to our table and David told me he thought I was very beautiful and so did his wife, and that his name was David, and this was his wife, Angela, and what was my name?

I told him, "I'm Bebe Buell and this is my boyfriend, Todd Rundgren."

He looked at Todd and said, "I've heard of you, you're supposed to be pretty fucking smart."

Todd said, "Yes I am, and I hear you're supposed to be ripping me off."

David looked at him like he was out of his mind. There was an immediate tête-à-tête between David and Todd, like "Hmmmmmmpphh!"

The next day my phone rang and it was David Bowie. Somehow he found out where I lived and tracked me down. He invited me to go to Radio City Music Hall to see the Rockettes, then he wanted me to be his guest sightseeing around New York City.

He was sweet. I went shopping with him. He bought me a couple of pairs of shoes and a couple of dresses and some glitter paste-on stars. We pasted the stars on our faces when I took him to see the Dolls about a week later.

David picked me up in this fucking huge limousine and I said to him, "How do you pay for all of this?"

He said, "Oh, my manager pays for it." David was very extravagant for somebody that had not yet made it on our shores.

So we went and made out through the whole show. The Dolls were fucking incredible, and Bowie had a big smile on his face in between kissing me. Yeah, I was the big slut again because it got in the papers and got all over town—"The Slut Strikes Again!"

DAVID JOHANSEN: Bowie used to come see us play at the Mercer Arts Center. I had never heard of him before. I remember he used to come around in these quilted drag outfits, and he asked me, "Who does your hair?"

I said, "Johnny Thunders," which was the truth.

STEVE HARRIS: When David Bowie was being sought after because he was about to sign with RCA Records, someone at Elektra saw him and said, "Why don't you go and see Elektra, it's a really good company." So he did, and the question people usually asked when they visited Elektra was always "Tell me about Jim Morrison." But when David Bowie came up it was, "Tell me about Iggy."

DANNY FIELDS: Lisa Robinson called from Max's one night. She was there with David Bowie and David wanted to meet Iggy. Iggy happened to be watching television at my house, so I said, "You have to be nice to him, he mentioned you in *Melody Maker,* in a poll of favorite new singers."

I was amazed that anyone in England had even heard of Iggy. So I said, "Be nice to this David Bowie person. Besides, he's pretty and I want to meet him. So let's go."

So we went over and I don't know what they talked about—you know, "Hey, man, I like your music."

LEEE CHILDERS: I think David Bowie's infatuation with Iggy had to do with Bowie wanting to tap into the rock & roll reality that Iggy lived—and that David Bowie could never live because he was a wimpy little South London art student and Iggy was a Detroit trash bag. David Bowie knew he could never achieve the reality that Iggy was born into. So he thought he'd buy it.

DANNY FIELDS: I gladly started seeing less of Iggy when he started hanging out with David Bowie. My history with him and his band was too fraught with disaster for me to really feel good about continuing to work with them. It was going nowhere. So I was glad to see Iggy with anybody who could help him, especially when that person was David Bowie.

RON ASHETON: I ended up being the last guy in Fun House. Iggy had gone to New York. David Bowie was there, found out Iggy was in town, invited him to lunch, and introduced him to Tony DeFries. The next day Tony DeFries goes to Clive Davis at CBS and gets Iggy a hundred-thousand-dollar deal.

ANGELA BOWIE: Tony DeFries was just enchanted by Iggy. He looked at him and saw money. Tony enjoyed playing God and he played God very successfully with Iggy. Before he took Iggy in to see Clive Davis at CBS, he told Iggy that this was a make-or-break deal for getting a real "recording contract."

So Iggy jumped up on the desk and sang "My Funny Valentine" to Clive Davis. I'm sure that Tony probably made Iggy aware that Clive would be, how shall I say, *receptive* to a good-looking young entertainer jumping up on his desk and singing "My Funny Valentine."

STEVE HARRIS: When I left Elektra in 1970, I became a vice president at CBS and Clive Davis said to me, "You know, I should really sign Iggy."

I said, "Well, you'll have to be prepared to market this guy because it's not the usual thing. You're not signing Barry Manilow."

About two months before Clive left CBS, we were both leaving the office at the same time, and he offered me a ride home. So we're sitting in this limo, talking about Iggy.

I said, "The important thing is that the company understand that this is attitude over music, and it could sell if it was marketed properly."

IGGY POP: I sang "The Shadow of Your Smile" for Clive Davis and just did a little soft-shoe. He'd ask me if I'd do this or that or the other thing, I'd say no:

"Will you do Simon and Garfunkel?"

"No I won't."

"Will you be more melodic?"

"No I won't . . . but I can sing, ya wanna hear it?" And I just sang "Shadow of Your Smile."

He said, "Okay, enough! Enough!" Then he just picked up the phone and said, "Call the legal department." And that was it.

RON ASHETON: They split up the property we lived on in Ann Arbor after they tore down the Fun House. On part of it they built a highway, then they put in a bank on the other part. I was left with nothing.

So one night I went into town and somebody said, "There's a party at the SRC studio."

So I went. Iggy and James Williamson were there. So I'm talking to Iggy and he says, "Oh yeah, by the way, I signed a deal. James and I are going to England."

It was just like somebody punched me in the stomach or hit me over the head with a sledgehammer. I was flabbergasted, because I thought that eventually we would get back together again. I just walked out, grabbed a tree, and started crying for about a half hour.

I was so dazed. I ended up walking home, fifteen miles, in complete shock. Iggy was just so casual, "Oh yeah, by the way, I just signed a deal, James and I are going to England . . ."

ANGELA BOWIE: David Bowie always lined himself up with people that he felt he could sell, or were influential and movers. I think he felt that way about Andy Warhol. After he met Warhol, David came back to England to promote Iggy Pop, he came back to England talking about Lou Reed and the Velvet Underground, and then *Pork* came to London.

So David Bowie ended up making an album with Iggy, and he made an album with Lou Reed. If you look back and look at his m.o., it's a fairly coherent, fluid way of operating. And I don't say that in a bad way. I'm impressed, I think it's incredible. *Raw Power* was something David could see; he could visualize. And that he could sell Iggy the idea of doing an album with him, which was David's way of buying into America.

RON ASHETON: Iggy and James went to England and three months later—this was perfect Iggy—he calls me from London and says, "Well, we tried out a hundred drummers and bass players, and we can't find anybody good enough, so how would you and your brother like to come over and play drums and bass?"

Well, of course I wanted to do it, because it was something to do, but just the way he said it—they tried everybody they could think of, and then couldn't find anybody good enough, so the last choice is us. The original members.

At first I was like, "Huh?" Like, "Well, god, that's a weird way to ask me." But I was just so excited to be doing something, especially going back to England. So Scotty and I went over to London and it looked like a good situation—we had a driver and the basement of a beautiful mews house on Seymour Walk.

The first day I was there, I met David Bowie. He showed up at the house, drunk, with these two Jamaican girls with identical David Bowie carrot-top haircuts, and they went down to the dining room to drink wine and stuff. I really didn't participate. David kind of got disoriented in the house, so I showed him to the front door, and then he grabbed me by the ass and kissed me. My arm went back to coldcock him, then I thought, Whoa, can't do that.

I didn't hit him.

ANGELA BOWIE: It was very easy to impress David because England is so backward. I mean, it was against the law to commit sodomy. You've got to understand where David was coming from, so when Lou Reed would talk about the New York drag queens, for David that meant that America was the most wide open, wonderful place.

When David said in *Melody Maker* that he was gay—then he changed it, and said he was bisexual, which was what he really meant—he never would have had the balls to do that unless he'd been hanging around with Iggy and Lou. Because they represented this place across the ocean where things were changing, so fuck all the English hypocrites.

IGGY POP: I used to walk around London, through the park and stuff, with this leopard jacket I had, a cheetah-skin jacket actually—it had a big cheetah on the back—and all the old men in London would drive by in their cars and they'd stop and try to cruise me.

All I liked to do was walk around the streets with a heart full of napalm. I always thought "Heart Full of Soul" was a good song so I thought, What's my heart full of?

I decided it was basically full of napalm.

RON ASHETON: Bowie was rehearsing for his show at the Rainbow, and we went to the rehearsal. It was cool—we're watching these guys get ready for their first big David Bowie/Spiders from Mars show. That night we go to the show, we got prime seats, David's singing, the place is packed, me and my brother said, "Ah, we already seen this shit, let's go get a beer."

We were so obvious—Bowie's doing his show, here's me and Scotty getting up and going down the aisle. We went to the bar and there was Lou Reed. He was drunk and taking Mandrax, an English downer. Lou gave us each a Mandrax and I pretended I took mine, but Scotty took his, and we just hung out with Lou and were just getting fucked-up. I'm going, "Oh great, now I gotta take care of *two* guys."

The next day I get a phone call that I'm supposed to go down to the MainMan office. Tony DeFries chewed me out for getting up after the first three songs of David's show. They were furious that I walked out of the show. I was like, "Fuck you, man, every seat was full. I just didn't wanna be there."

ANGELA BOWIE: I suppose Lou was a little more sophisticated than Iggy, but whereas Lou didn't do the reading, Iggy did the reading. Iggy had school teachers for parents, and he actually read, you know, Dostoevsky and all that kinda crap. Lou had that New York thing—he could make out like he'd read it even though he hadn't. But he covered enough ground and it was superficial enough that you didn't get a headache by the end of the conversation.

With Iggy, if you ever did have a serious conversation with him, the whole idea he would point out was that you were ignorant and stupid, and that he was as smart as a whip. And that having been said and established, now he was gonna use you any possible way he could—either to eat, get drugs, or cop a piece of ass.

RON ASHETON: James was playing lead guitar, I was playing bass, and Scotty was on drums. We practiced from midnight to six, just like that great Pretty Things song, "Midnight to Six," and then we made the record *Raw Power*.

ANGELA BOWIE: Iggy really felt that Tony DeFries was going to save him. So Iggy was making a big effort to keep his shit together. I understood that Iggy liked heroin and that made me nervous, because I had never been able to understand the motivation for doing heroin.

But I was trying to be the perfect hostess and that's why I got the macrobiotic cook. I was such a jerk, I thought it would help, ha ha ha. I was really just trying to be all things for all men. You know, I thought, "Well, maybe they think they're being poisoned, maybe they think life isn't worth living, maybe they need hippie-fying . . ."

MALCOLM MCLAREN: During the *Raw Power* days, when Iggy was in London with Bowie, I found Iggy incredibly vain, because he was an incredibly handsome character. But I wasn't taken with Iggy in the same way as I was with the Dolls.

I think one of the reasons was because Iggy was less about fashion. I think it's a stupid thing to say, but it's the truth; I didn't see the fashion about Iggy.

What I saw was a very tough, incredibly sexual, wonderfully enjoyable singer. I adored the album *Raw Power*—but I didn't wanna walk into a guy with a lion's head full of drugs and pills, shouting and screaming "RAW POWER" at me.

I didn't want to throw myself into a junkie's lap like that, I just wasn't set up for it. I was too naïve, I didn't fancy the notion. It didn't sound trendy-nice, there was no lipstick there. It didn't have the fashion element that the New York Dolls had, that fashion twist—just like that crappy old lipstick on the collar. It's kind of pathetic when I think about it now, all that tartiness, but that's what I liked. I always thought the parties were gonna be better, I always thought the scene was gonna be better. The Dolls just looked more attractive.

RON ASHETON: Just before we left England, after the album was recorded, the boys found out that they could walk right around the corner and get liquid codeine over the counter. So fucking James, the last month we were there, his room was nothing but codeine bottles. Him and my brother were just drinking codeine all the time.

Then there was heroin, and a lotta downers, and cocaine, and everything. They did get a little bit of a habit again and then they were gonna fire my brother for being a junkie. I said, "Waaaait a minute, I'll go if her goes, and you guys are junkies too, man, now this is not right that you're picking on my brother as a scapegoat for your problems!"

LEEE CHILDERS: They wrecked the house and disrupted the neighborhood totally until they were thrown out. That's why they ended up being brought back from England. MainMan could find no place for them and they were afraid Iggy was going to be deported any minute.

RON ASHETON: While David Bowie was palling around with Iggy, I was fucking David's wife. He didn't mind, I didn't mind, we never felt weird about any of that.

When it came time to leave London we flew back to Ann Arbor. Angie came a few days later and moved into the Campus Inn. She called me up and said, "I'm in town."

I wound up living with her in the hotel for a couple of weeks. Then I introduced her to my friend Scott Richardson. I went by the hotel one day to tell Angie that it was time for me to move on, and there was a note on the pillow that said, "I left with Scott Richardson, blah, blah, blah, see you later." So Angie took Scott back to England and he ended up hanging out with David and Angie for a year.

Angie was just a kind of perfect person. She loved sex, but it wasn't just sex, she liked nice people. And she did women too.

Chapter 14

◼ Billy Doll

MARTY THAU: The very first thing we did once Steve Leber, David Krebs, and I signed the New York Dolls to a management contract was to send them to England. We concluded that America was going to be a strange place to break the Dolls, so we thought, Let's go to England and sign a major deal and in doing that, we'll come back to our home country and get an even bigger deal. We went to England and opened for Rod Stewart in front of 13,000 people, never having played before more than 350 people at the Mercer Arts Center.

SYL SYLVAIN: The reason why we went to England was because *Melody Maker* had given us a big spread—"From NYC: The New York Dolls—The Next Sensation!"

JERRY NOLAN: The Dolls went to England to open for Rod Stewart. No group in the history of rock & roll had ever gone on a tour with a major star and not had a record out, not even a single. They didn't even have a record company behind them. And they tore the fucking place up. Everyone was telling me how they were the toast of the town. But then I got worried. They were hardcore, wild kids. They drank, but they really weren't into hard drugs. Well, okay, once in a while. All of a sudden I said to my girlfriend, "You know something, Corrine, something's wrong. Something happened in England. I have these bad vibes."

MARTY THAU: The writers of the English weeklies were so blown out of their seats after the Dolls opened for Rod Stewart that they were printing things like "I have seen the future of rock and roll!" Of course, others said, "This is the worst fucking piece of shit I've ever seen."

There was big, big hysteria, and everyone wanted to sign them. We were talking with Phonogram, the Who, the Stones, and Virgin. And we were receiving telegrams from New York. We received a telegram from

Ahmet Ertegun saying, "I haven't even seen the group, but I'll give you fifty grand for the United States."

Richard Branson, the guy who owns Virgin Airlines and Virgin Records, sends a messenger to the hotel saying, "Please come to my houseboat, I want to talk to you about the New York Dolls."

We go over there and he arrogantly opens with, "I'll give you five thousand dollars for the Dolls." We weren't on that boat for more than three minutes.

I said, "You're gonna give us five thousand dollars? We're here talking to people about three hundred fifty thousand dollars. Thank you. It was nice meeting you, good-bye."

It was in a meeting, two nights later, at Tony Secunda's flat in London, with me, my wife Betty, Steve Leber, Tony Secunda, his girlfriend Zelda, Chris Stamp, and Kit Rambler, when I got the phone call.

"Marty, come quickly to"—whatever the address was—"Billy Murcia just died."

I said, "What?"

I dropped the phone, I looked at everybody, I didn't say a thing, I was just in shock. I ran out the door.

I don't know what they must have thought. They must have thought, What kind of a lunatic is this? I immediately hailed a cab and I was over there in about four minutes.

What had happened was Billy had stopped down at my room earlier in the evening, before we went out, and asked if he could have five pounds. Then he got a phone call, which went up to his room, and it was someone inviting him to a party. But that wasn't his original plan. When he came down for the five pounds, he didn't know what he was going to do. Just knockin' around.

So Billy ended up going to that party, and through a combination of alcohol and what was listed on the autopsy report as Quaaludes he started choking. He was turning colors and passed out and this whole flat was loaded with people who ran away. They didn't give a fuck about this poor kid who was choking to death. Everybody ran out looking to save their own hides. The few that remained didn't want a scandal, so they put him in an ice-cold bathtub and ran the water.

He drowned. What they should have done immediately was called for an ambulance, rushed him to the hospital, pumped out his stomach, and he would have been fine.

By the time I got there, Scotland Yard was there with four people from the party and Billy was dead.

I identified his body.

Syl Sylvain: Billy Murcia was the first member of the New York Dolls that I met. I was going to Van Wyck Junior High School out in Queens, and his brother came up to me and said, "Hey, my brother wants to fight you, three o'clock today."

I was a Syrian Jew, born in Cairo, and my family was exiled from Egypt in 1956 during the Suez Canal incident. We were brought to America by some Jewish committee, the same one that was bringing over the Russian Jews. We came over by boat and I was probably one of the last immigrants to sail into New York Harbor to be greeted by the Statue of Liberty.

The first words I learned when I got off the boat were "Fuck you!" I would be standing there in my fucking brown shoes and people would say, "You speak English?" I'd say, "No." They'd say, "Fuck you."

After relocating all over, we finally ended up in Jamaica, Queens. Billy Murcia lived three blocks away. His family had just come from Colombia, South America. We were both immigrants. He had five brothers and sisters: Alfonso, Billy, Hoffman, Edgar, Heidi, and then two others from another marriage. But he lived in a pretty big house, and we lived in an apartment building.

I wasn't a tough guy, but I had girlfriends, so maybe that gave me the appearance that I was a tough guy. I had a good haircut, so maybe that was why Alfonso said, "You're going to fight my brother."

It's funny, but I had seen Billy fight the day before, because his big brother had set it up. Alfonso was like Billy's manager—he was in the eighth grade and we were only in the seventh grade. Billy fought some guy across the street from the school where they were building new houses. It was raining, and they were getting all muddy. I couldn't believe it, because Billy wasn't a tough guy or anything, but his brother was working Billy—his brother was working him up to the biggest guys with knives.

So when Alfonso said I had to fight, I was thinking, Hey, wait a minute, what is this shit? Then I ran into Billy in the lunchroom and he said, "You? You're the one?"

We had seen each other in class and we kinda got along, we'd said a word or two. So Billy turned to his brother and said, "No, man." He said it in Spanish: "That's my friend, *mi amigo*." You know, "He's my friend."

So Alfonso said, "Okay, Billy, you know, no problem, let's go find somebody else whose ass we can kick."

Then I got Billy a job working with me at my uncle's store—Michelle Novelties on Jamaica Avenue. We sold earrings—you know, fifty-nine-cent earrings that black girls used to wear. Then we worked selling clothes at Truth and Soul just before the Dolls happened. That's where we got the name for the band. The New York Doll Hospital, a place where they fix rare dolls, was right across the street.

It was hard when Billy died—I had to call his mother and tell her since I knew the whole family. She just couldn't believe it—I never heard anybody screaming that much in my life.

MARTY THAU: The very first thing I did was make all the Dolls pack their bags and I put them on the first flight out. I figured they would probably be forced to answer a lot of inquiries, probably forced to stay there for weeks or months, and it might get very scandalous. I wanted to spare them the agony of it all. I didn't appreciate the thought of a scandal so I sent them back to New York in the middle of the night. Then I stayed on with Steve Leber to answer the Scotland Yard deposition.

JERRY NOLAN: That night a friend calls. He says, "Jerry, you ain't going to fuckin' believe this. Guess who just died?"

At first I thought it was Johnny Thunders. You know, everybody used to think that Johnny was the type of guy who'd OD. Billy's death may not have been foul play, but it was real abuse. He went to a party with a lot of highbrow, stuck-up, rich teenage English kids. They had these pills called Mandies. They were a heavy barbiturate down. And all day long kids kept giving him these pills. When Billy fell asleep everybody fucking panicked.

So you know what they do? They throw him in the goddamn fucking bathtub to try to shake him out of it. They fucking drowned him! They drowned the kid! These fucking rich kids freaked out and ran away. They all split on the guy. What a fucking waste.

MARTY THAU: When I got back home, I came down with a case of the mumps that I got from my daughter, and I was in bed for a month, receiving phone calls from all over the world—*Rolling Stone*, *Bravo*, the *New Musical Express*—giving them quotes and explanations.

But there were no Dolls once Billy died. Everything came to a halt when that happened. It took about a month for Billy's body to be returned. Billy's funeral was up in Westchester or Yonkers, somewhere up in that area. It was the first day I was out of bed. Shortly after that, the band had a meeting and we decided that we were going on. So we started looking for a new drummer.

JERRY NOLAN: After Billy died, the Dolls were going to break up. Then I got to talking to David Johansen. I said, "Look, David, I come from the old school."

I probably talked in the-show-must-go-on terms, because I'm like that. "The music is so important that it would be wrong to break up. You've got to keep going, in memory of Billy."

There was one thing I knew about the Dolls—simplicity. And I knew my rock & roll. These kids had the right idea and knew what they were, but they weren't as professional as I was. I said to David, "Look, David, there's only one guy who can fill that job and do it well. I'm the guy."

Well, I played the whole set in the audition like I had been playing with them for ten years. I added a little bit more. Each song I would change a little bit. I didn't want to overdo it, because they would get lost. Like I say, they weren't very professional yet. I gave them just enough so they'd notice that there could be more done with a song than they had been doing. I was so on it was pathetic. I remember Arthur walked over to me after we played "Personality Crisis." He said, "Wow, I've never played that song so fast in my life."

I loved that group so much you wouldn't believe it. Even though I was the last guy in the group, no one was more dedicated or loved that group more than me. They were my dream come true.

MARTY THAU: December 19, 1972, was the first performance of the new New York Dolls and, of course, they became bigger than ever because of the sinisterism of Billy's death. There was a story that the *Village Voice* printed about how that death never should have happened. And the record companies, who already thought the Dolls were transvestites, now thought they were also drug addicts. Dangerous drug addicts. Dangerous to society and transvestites to boot.

So we went through a series of shows all around town—Kenny's Castaways, Max's—and just built up the heat. The band got bigger and bigger and bigger, and Paul Nelson, who was an A&R guy at Mercury, came to every show. Finally after months and months of negotiations with record companies who just couldn't muster up the balls to sign the New York Dolls, Paul Nelson finally got it together. The Dolls signed to Mercury Records. I must say, Mercury wasn't our first choice, but they had the guts.

BOB GRUEN: The first time I saw the Dolls was after Billy died, right at the time they got signed. I was hanging out, flipping knives with the Hell's Angels on Third Street. The Mercer Arts Center was nearby, and a friend had told me to drop by there, so one night on my way home, I did. I went upstairs and saw a strange assortment of people, not the kind of people I tended to hang out with. Some guy I knew walked past me with eyeliner on and I freaked out. I left.

I always had quite a strange mix of friends—Alice Cooper, John Lennon, and I went to a lot of different kinds of shows, but I didn't have friends who wore makeup. Yet.

The Hell's Angels were shocking, but I didn't feel threatened by knives and guns, I felt threatened by guys in makeup and dresses. During the week, my friend said, "No, no, come back, it's really cool, it's not so bad, come back. You gotta see this band, the New York Dolls, they're good."

So I went back. I got a beer, and instead of noticing all the guys in makeup, I started noticing all of the girls in makeup. They were very attractive girls, and I thought, This is getting a lot more interesting.

I'm waiting to see the band come out on the bandstand, but I needed to use the bathroom. So I went through a door, and on the other side was the Oscar Wilde Room and it was completely packed. Everyone was dressed really wild, and the stage was completely packed, and in the middle of all the people onstage was the band.

But you couldn't really tell who was in the band from who was onstage. There was a whole row of bleacher seats that went up really steep around the stage and it looked like a wall of people. Everybody was sort of milling around and dancing and singing and yelling all at once and that was the first time I saw the New York Dolls. It was just the most exciting thing I had ever seen in my life.

Chapter 15

■ Open Up and Bleed

LEEE CHILDERS: My first assignment for MainMan was to go get Iggy at the airport. David Bowie was on tour with the Rise and Fall of Ziggy Stardust and the Spiders from Mars, his first big tour, and I had to collect Iggy and bring him to the show. I knew Iggy from the Danny Fields days, so I didn't have to say, "Hi, I'm your MainMan representative." He hugged me when he got off the plane, we started talking, and what he wanted to know was if MainMan was for real. You know, "What am I involved in here?" I couldn't give him any straight answers because I didn't know. But what did I care? I was traveling all over the country, ordering room service. So I said to Iggy, "Well, what do any of us have to lose at this point?"

CYRINDA FOXE: David Bowie and his wife Angela had a very open marriage. They were sleeping with anybody they felt like sleeping with. David and Angela and I had a ménage à trois for about five minutes, but then I made her leave because David and I were gonna play. Angela was fucking David's black bodyguard, and David and I used to get down on all fours and peek in their keyhole and watch them fuck. I was sort of like a new toy for David on the Ziggy Stardust tour. But while we were in San Francisco, David asked me, "Are you in love with me?"

I said, "No." I wasn't about to say, "Yes!" I was still tripping around. I had no flies on me then. No salt on my tail. I didn't want to get tied down. Besides, Tony DeFries wanted everybody to be this Bowie thing. I didn't want to cut my hair like that. So I wasn't impressed with them. I mean, okay, I get to go on a plane and go somewhere, but that's all I thought it was. So when David Bowie asked if I was in love with him, and I told him no, he left me there.

LEEE CHILDERS: I was in Kansas City, on my way to Los Angeles, working as the advance man on Bowie's Ziggy Stardust tour, when I happened to be talking on the phone to Lisa Robinson. I said, "They're going to put us up at the Chateau Marmont, do you know anything about it?"

Lisa said, "Oh sure, it's fine, but don't stay there, stay at the Beverly Hills Hotel." I asked why. Lisa said, "Oh, it's so gorgeous, it's pink, and I'm going to be there." So I said, "Okay." I called RCA and said, "We won't stay at the Chateau Marmont, we wanna stay at the Beverly Hills Hotel." The RCA guy said, "The Beverly Hills Hotel?" I said, "The Beverly Hills Hotel, we're all staying at the Beverly Hills Hotel." And he said, "Okay."

None of us at MainMan had any experience in the rock & roll business at all, but that was one of the things that Tony DeFries was very smart about—he knew we'd go to RCA Records and make the demands that he wanted us to make, because we thought that was what you did.

DeFries's philosophy seemed to be to make outrageous demands on a giant record company for an artist who hadn't sold more than three records. We were demanding unlimited air travel, limousines for everyone, all our hotel bills, giant advances in cash—and because we were loud and crazy looking, we got all the demands.

It was easier for a huge company like RCA to give us whatever we wanted than to listen to us. They didn't want us there at all. So when I'd come in with this blond hair flying and say, "I need fourteen tickets to Kansas City," they'd just go, "Okay, fine. You got 'em, just go away."

It was a totally unheard-of tactic, but it worked. We lived off the credit. I had no idea how much we went into debt with RCA, but of course the philosophy was, once you went so far into debt, they didn't dare cut you off then, because then they'd never make it back again.

So I arrived at the Beverly Hills Hotel three or four days before the whole entourage—forty-eight people at the Beverly Hills Hotel. I had Olivia De Havilland's suite, and David had one of the bungalows out back. He never came out of his room. Angela was fucking his bodyguard in the pool.

The funniest thing was that the roadies would go up to Sunset Strip and pick up tourists and bring them back to their rooms and order dinner on room service and the tourists would pay them for the dinner. All our expenses were paid for, so the roadies would go to the Strip three or four times a day, bring back these tours, sit them down in their room, and serve them these fabulous lobster dinners with chocolate soufflés, and then charge them for it. The tourists would get cut-rate dinners at the Beverly Hills Hotel, and the roadies were making fortunes.

CYRINDA FOXE: I didn't want to go back to New York yet. I was kind of embarrassed and didn't want to face Andy Warhol and everybody. I had run out of money and had bleached my hair, which broke my hair off. I didn't like myself. So when I found out Leee had gotten everyone into the Beverly Hills Hotel, I thought, Well, I could hang out here for a while.

So I went to the Beverly Hills Hotel and Iggy and the guys showed up and it was cool. Iggy and I always had a real brother and sister relationship, and I was convinced that *Raw Power* was his last stab at making it. We had a really long talk about it being his last chance to do something, and that he'd better get his shit together and not fuck it up.

Then I went and crashed with that guy, what's his name? James Williamson. He had the hots for me big-time. What was I doing with that guy? He was so uncool.

Yeah, I slept with him, so people keep reminding me. But James wasn't from the same litter as Iggy, Ronnie, and Scotty. He was just some stray dog that found his way into the pack. James Williamson ruined the Stooges. They didn't need him. Somebody should have chewed his ass out. Left him to die.

LEEE CHILDERS: I guess Iggy decided he wanted to live in California. I mean once you're getting free hamburgers from David Bowie, the next thing you see is a house in the Hollywood Hills. I mean, you get what you can. So Iggy said, "I want to live in Hollywood." Then it was our job to find him a house. I had to go back to New York, so I left, of all people, Cyrinda Foxe in Hollywood to house hunt for Iggy, while he lived at the Beverly Hills Hotel.

Cyrinda found this amazing house. It was right up off Mulholland Drive, at the very peak of the mountain, and it had a huge swimming pool and four bedrooms. Once Iggy had the house, I was dispatched back to live in the apartment over the garage, like the chauffeur. And be Iggy's caretaker.

It was difficult living with Iggy because he was at the height of his junkiedom. And I was inexperienced in the ways of a true rock & roll junkie—how he would deceive, cajole, flirt, and manipulate in order for me not to realize the massive amounts of treachery he was up to. My job was to keep him straight, but he was too quick for me. With all the roadies, groupies, and band members hanging around, I could never cut off his supply.

CYRINDA FOXE: James Williamson got sick one night, threw up some wine or something, and he didn't make it to the toilet. It was all over the bathroom. So gross. And then he just left it. I said, "You gotta be kidding! I'm not cleaning this shit!" I think that's when I said, "I'm outta here." I was

GONE. That's when I went back to New York and started hanging out with David Johansen again.

RON ASHETON: In the beginning, living in the house on Torrenson Drive was great—we'd come back from practice and there'd be naked girls in the pool. It was classic rock & roll: naked girls in the pool, Cadillac in the driveway, getting paid, maids, plenty of pot . . .

We had a gig at the Whiskey-A-Go-Go when we first moved out there and that's when we met Sable Starr, who was a really nice girl. First she was Iggy's groupie, then with me, then go back to Iggy, then back to me, and then go to my brother and back to me. We would do two sets at the Whiskey, and in between sets, Sable would say, "Can I suck your dick?" She was real open about stuff, that's what I always liked about her. So in between our sets Sable would suck my dick in the upstairs men's bathroom.

SABLE STARR: I didn't really live in Hollywood, I was about forty-five minutes away. But my friend called me up one day and said, "Do you wanna go to the Whiskey-A-Go-Go?" This was when I was fourteen. And I was nuts to begin with, I always liked getting in trouble, so I said sure. *Hollywood*—I thought I'd see movie stars or something. So I went to the Whiskey, and I'll never forget the girls there, I was so intrigued. I was still ugly then, I had to work on it for about a year when I was hanging out in Hollywood. I didn't get my nose fixed until I was fifteen.

BEBE BUELL: I always liked Sable Starr and Laurie Maddox—the two big groupies in L.A. They got completely trashed by Pamela Des Barres in her book *I'm with the Band*. God, who does Miss Pamela think she is, Queen of the Pussies? Miss Pamela took down everyone she thought was competition. Laurie and Sable didn't give a fuck. They weren't competitive. They didn't have to be. Every rock star that came to L.A. wanted to meet them, it wasn't the other way around. It was like, "We've got to meet this Sable Starr and Laurie Maddox, and we got to meet Rodney Bingenheimer and Kim Fowley." There was a certain crowd you had to meet when you were in L.A.

SABLE STARR: David Bowie came into town and wanted to meet me, so it wasn't a thing where I had to go running after him. Those days were crazy, every day I was on the go, from one hotel to another, cause Silverhead were staying at the Hyatt House and Bowie was staying at the Hilton, and it was just back and forth all the time. So I went up to meet David Bowie. It's funny, cause he's bisexual, and he had this guy traveling with him, Freddy. Freddy was really pretty.

I sat on David's lap and said, "It is true, you've got different-colored eyes." Just the whole trip, and I was very good at that. Most girls are really shy, they just sit down and wait. But I'd jump right on their laps.

David said, "Oh, you're very cute. Freddy, isn't she cute?" I said, "Are we gonna fuck tonight?" I just came out and said it. And David started laughing and I said, "Really." He goes, "I'd like to, but I don't like Queenie. But I like Laurie." I said, "Well, we'll get rid of Queenie and we'll meet you at the Rainbow later." So he said okay. So me and Laurie went back to the Hyatt House and were just screaming, "We're gonna fuck David Bowie!" We were so excited. And so we went to the Rainbow, and that was another neat thing about being a groupie. Upstairs at the Rainbow they have like just one table. Me and David were sitting there, with a couple of other people. And to have all your friends look up and see you—that was cool. That was really cool.

Then this guy came up and said, "David Bowie, I'm going to kill you." Some hippie was freaking out and started like trying to punch him. So David's bodyguard was throwing the guy down the stairs and David was really freaking because he's very paranoid about that—he had voodoo dolls and stuff—"Oh, I'd better go home and chant, he's trying to kill me!" So he's dragging me down the stairs and all these girls came up to him saying, "David, do you want to take me home?" And he said, "No, I'm with her tonight." So we get out to the car and this guy's going, "I'm coming to your show tomorrow night and I'm going to fucking kill you! I've got a gun." It was very heavy.

Back at the hotel we were sitting around. I had to go to the bathroom, and David came in and had a cigarette in his hand and a glass of wine. And he started kissing me—and I couldn't believe it was happening to me, because there'd been Roxy Music and J. Geils, but David Bowie was the first heavy.

So we went to the bedroom and fucked for hours, and he was great. I don't know where Laurie was. She was always there, but she never was, you know? So I woke up that morning and he said I had to go because his wife Angie was coming. I kept saying I wanted to meet her and stuff. He said he had a surprise for me and gave me tickets for that night's show in Long Beach. He really liked me a lot, David Bowie. I became very famous and popular after that, because it was established that I was cool. I had been accepted by a real rock star.

RON ASHETON: Iggy would say about Sable, "I love her," then, "I hate her," then, "I love her," but he wound up falling for Coral, Sable's sister, who was a pretty straight girl—not a real groupie. Coral, she was beautiful. Really beautiful. She had superlong, Crystal Gayle long hair. Coral was real quiet, real straight, didn't really get fucked-up, and always looked out after Sable.

SABLE STARR: The one thing my parents were always strict on was school. They let me stay out until six o'clock in the morning, just as long as I went to school. Oh, I *hated* school when I was fifteen. I had to have a probation officer, that's when I started living with Iggy Pop in the Hollywood Hills and I didn't go to school for about a month.

LEEE CHILDERS: Iggy brought Sable up to the house and wanted her to move in, but I wouldn't let him move her in. Meanwhile, of course, I had this gorgeous little boy that Cyrinda picked up for me at the Whiskey, living in my apartment over the garage. I didn't have much ground to stand on about not letting Sable move in, but I managed to prevail. She never really moved in, she was just there a lot.

Sable had a good heart and I liked her, but she was on a general rampage of buying *Billboard* magazine and working her way down the list to someone she hadn't fucked yet. Wayne County came to stay with us at the house and Sable came on to Wayne very heavy. Wayne said, "BUT I'M A FAG!" Sable's thinking was probably, But you're next on the list! So Sable took all her clothes off, cut her wrists, and dove into the pool. She was floating facedown in the deep end with blood going everywhere, and I was saying, "Wayne, we have to get her out of here!"

Wayne said, "Why not let her drown? We'll take her over there to the cliff and pitch her off. Nobody'll know where she came from." I finally managed to reach her by hanging on to the side of the pool, got a hold of her, dragged her out, wrapped her in a blanket, bandaged her up, and gave her to Coral, who put her in the car and took her away.

RON ASHETON: One day I was at practice and Leee Childers called up and said, "You gotta come back to the house, Sable's locked herself in your room and she's threatening to kill herself."

I thought, What the fuck? It wasn't like we were in love or anything. It was just nice to get my dick sucked when I woke up. I liked her and we were friends, but I didn't know why she was so distraught. It definitely wasn't over me.

So I go back to the house and our road manager, Eric Haddix, had to kick in the bedroom door. Sable was locked in the bathroom and I had to coax her out: "Come on, open the door!"

She finally opened it and she was just downed-out. She was naked except for some bikini underwear and she had taken my razor and tried to cut her wrists. There were these two little lines on her wrist because it was a Trac II, and I just started laughing and Leee said, "Get her the fuck out of here!"

And there was poor Sable, being hauled out of the house half-naked. Her sister, Coral, got some friends to pick her up in their car. Leee was saying, "That's it! No more of this bullshit, man! This is a business—I can get into trouble for this!"

Thank god I was using Trac IIs then, because usually I used a straight razor.

LEEE CHILDERS: I learned how to swim because of Iggy. As a child my mother used to take me to pools and hold me like mothers are supposed to, under the stomach, and let me thrash about, but none of it worked. But when I moved into the house with Iggy, he would get stoned and almost certainly fall into the pool, and be floating there, facedown. I'd be saying, "I can't swim, somebody grab him! Somebody grab him!" The rest of the band would say, "Fuck 'im, he gets what he deserves."

I'd get in the pool, holding on to the sides in the deep end, thinking, I'm gonna die, I'm gonna die! I'd be reaching for him, trying to grab his ankle and pull him in—and eventually I learned how to swim.

IGGY POP: MainMan were skillful at putting us off. Once the album *Raw Power* was done, they wouldn't tour us, they would not let us play. We were supposed to do an American tour, but it ended up being one gig in Detroit, but the people loved it. The gig was very successful artistically, but of course I had a problem at the radio station. Everything was a problem with me. Ha. I was a problem. I *am* a problem.

What happened was by the time I finished *Raw Power*, my standards were different than other people's. That's the only way I can put it. I wanted the music to come out of the speakers and just grab you by the throat and just knock your head against the wall and just basically kill you.

That's what I wanted. And it never did that enough for me. No matter what I did, I couldn't get it. I couldn't get the treble to hurt enough, I couldn't get the bass to hit you enough, I couldn't get the beat hard enough, and so on, and so on, and so on. So I kept doing mix after mix after mix until I was crazier and crazier.

But it still was not *hard* enough, you know?

Basically, I'd lost perspective—artists do this. And probably the drug use blew that outta proportion. So I just went to the radio station, I don't remember why, but I'm just not the kind of person that can go like a door-to-door salesman, "Hi, I'm really jolly. It's great to be like in the rock & roll business and here's my new tape, heh, heh, heh." Everything's gotta be like something's happening, right? So I went there and took off all my clothes inside the radio station, and started talking on the air, "Yeah, I'm naked here . . ."

LEEE CHILDERS: Iggy took off all his clothes and was jerking off on the radio! He was saying, "I've got all my clothes off now, I'm playing with my balls . . ."

Later he locked himself in the radio station's elevator with Cherry Vanilla and tried to rape her!

Tony DeFries was beside himself with anger.

IGGY POP: The radio station nearly lost their FCC license. The deejay, Mark Farrento, got into a lot of trouble. But my attitude was like . . . I mean, a month before, Tony DeFries had come to L.A. to see his new acquisition, Iggy and the Stooges, and he took me out for a ride in a giant stretch limousine and said, "Now we want to think about film projects for you, and what we see you as is Peter Pan."

I went, "I ain't no fucking Peter Pan! We're gonna do MANSON! CHARLIE MANSON, I'M GONNA BE MANSON, I AM MANSON!"

RON ASHETON: Tony DeFries's plan was to break David Bowie first and then concentrate on Iggy and the Stooges. So he just kept us fat, dumb, and happy. I remember we were sitting by the pool one day, I was drinking rye and ginger, and Leee came over and he was very upset. He gave us our paychecks and said, "I have some very bad news for you. MainMan just fired you."

LEEE CHILDERS: I can't believe I'm telling this very bad story about myself, but Tony DeFries called me and said, "Tell Iggy and the rest of the band that MainMan isn't handling them anymore and to get out and get out now."

I went to Iggy and said, "Sorry, MainMan doesn't like you anymore, you have to leave." Not, "Here are tickets home to Detroit." Not, "You have two weeks." Not, "Would you like a hamburger?" Not anything, just, "The company doesn't want you anymore, you're dumped. Go. Now."

IGGY POP: Leee said, "Yeah, they dropped you and I have evidence." They had a blackened spoon from my room. Ha ha ha. They sent Leee Childers on orders, MainMan sent him into my bedroom to gather evidence.

Now in their defense I've got to say, from their point of view, the Stooges were an impossible band to tour. I mean they must have thought, These guys are maniacs, you know, the singer attacks the audience, they're all loaded, they don't communicate nicely with us, their songs won't go on the radio, the drummer won't even talk to us, he won't talk to the manager. He'd grunt, say, "Uhh-uh" like a juvenile delinquent kid: "Don't talk to me, grrr . . . rrr . . ."

So I could see their point. But, hey, I didn't know we were that way, I saw it differently. I thought we were great. I thought we were the best band in the world. We knew what we were doing was better than anybody and certainly more rocking.

RON ASHETON: We got kicked out of the house, and luckily for Iggy and Scotty, I'm a saver of money and I had squirreled away about five grand. I literally had it hid in my mattress, there was a hole in the box springs and I'd stick my arm way in there and stash it. James Williamson had moved down to the Riviera Hotel, so he said, "Hey you guys, you gotta come down to the Riviera, it's only seventy bucks a week."

So I got Iggy, Scotty, and myself a room. I paid the whole week up front, that way you got the discount, and I put those guys on a per diem, ten bucks a day. Then it was five bucks a day . . .

LEEE CHILDERS: Iggy literally hit the streets. He had a place to stay, Iggy's nobody's fool, but he'd land in the gutter. He'd fall over, stoned, laying in the gutter on Sunset Boulevard, and people wouldn't even pick him up. People didn't care, he was a joke. That's how unimportant Iggy Pop was in the minds of the rock & roll world at the time. And to my great discredit, I didn't hop in a cab and go down and get him. I didn't say, "Come up here, I don't care what Tony DeFries has to say, you come up here and stay here and be safe."

Instead, I heard the stories: "Oh, Iggy fell over in front of the Whiskey last night, everyone laughed, he was lying in the gutter, a taxi almost hit him . . ."

IGGY POP: Coral had had enough of me. I was no longer happening. I was fucking up, and fucking up, and losing, and losing—and she could see it. I was also losing my charms. If you don't have the goods and the charms, you don't get the girls. This is America, you know.

STEVE HARRIS: A year after it was recorded, *Raw Power* finally came out in May of '73. CBS was even much more out of my grasp than Elektra because CBS is just so vast. But when *Raw Power* came out, I came up with an idea that I thought was really good. I called up a guy named Sam Hood who booked Max's and I said, "Let's put on Iggy for a week at midnight." He said, "That's great, we'll do it." So Iggy starts doing his week at Max's and the company sees him, he was still a joke to them, but he starts getting this incredible amount of press because he's rolling around in broken glass. By the third night, he rolled around in so much glass I think he was really injured. Really hurt.

BEBE BUELL: We had a great table. I was sitting with Alice Cooper, Todd Rundgren, Jane Forth, Cindy Lang, and Eric Emerson, who was dressed exactly like Iggy that night—in some little bikini–porn thing with glitter all over it. The whole crowd was there and Iggy did the most brilliant show I have ever seen. It was totally amazing. He started off the set with "Search and Destroy". . .

NITEBOB: Iggy was trying to walk on tables. Max's had tables all the way up to the front, the stage was too small, and sometimes Iggy would go walking out on tables. Max's was a lot smaller than the places the Stooges were used to playing. I was working the stage that night, and Iggy fell off a table. I remember seeing him walking out and going, "Oh, that's not a good idea," and then he went down and came back up with a cut.

He was twenty minutes into the set and I asked him if he wanted to stop the show because he was cut pretty bad. He was pumping some blood out. It wasn't the kinda thing you could solve with a Band-Aid. It wasn't just a scratch.

BEBE BUELL: All of a sudden, blood just started to pour out of this very neat little slice on Iggy's chest.

NITEBOB: Iggy was a mess. He had a pretty good gusher going. But he wanted to finish the show, so he went on playing. I was blown away. I told him, "Just stop!" The band kept saying, "Let's stop!" But Iggy kept on pushing on.

When he came off the stage, I said, "You're cut, man, what are we gonna do about this?" He didn't think it seemed to be that much of a problem, but then Alice Cooper wanted him to go to the hospital.

STEVE HARRIS: After the show, I said to Iggy, "I'm going home," and he said, "I'll drop you off cause I have an appointment uptown."

So we took a cab and when we got to Seventy-second Street and Park Avenue, Iggy said, "Why don't you come up and have a drink?"

So I said, "Okay," and we got out. Iggy was wearing a pair of shorts and a T-shirt that were now all bloody, and when we walked into the building there was a doorman who looked at Iggy and said, "Who should I say is calling?"

Iggy wanted to play it to the hilt, because he would usually say, "Jim Osterberg," but he said, "Iggy."

It was like something you would see in a movie. So we went up to the apartment and this voluptuous woman in a negligee opened the door. She was incredible looking.

Anyway, the next day Iggy came over to my place and he was really cut up. He didn't know how badly he was hurt. He needed stitches. So I called Sam Hood at Max's and said we were just gonna have to skip a night or two.

BEBE BUELL: Everybody thought the stitches were really sexy. It was while Iggy was recuperating for those two days he took off from Max's that I met him for the first time at a New York Dolls concert at the Felt Forum. Iggy was really fucked-up. Somebody had smashed him in the head with something and his head was bleeding. Nobody was paying any attention to him, people were just walking by him.

IGGY POP: The night of the Dolls' gig, I was at Lou Reed's apartment and I asked him for a bunch of Valiums, which he gave me, and then I said, "Well, I gotta go, I wanna go see the New York Dolls."

By the time I got inside the Felt Forum, I had already walked straight into a door, and I had this big unicorn sticking out of my forehead.

BEBE BUELL: Iggy was really a mess. He was stumbling and falling and embarrassing everybody. I really felt sorry for him. I thought it was sort of sad, because he was Iggy and he was really helpless. He was fucked-up and couldn't get up. He kept banging himself and gashed himself pretty bad on the head. Blood was all over and nobody was helping him, not even David Johansen, who always had a big heart. David was going, "Oh fuck, this is all we need, to have Iggy fucked-up on our floor . . ." Todd Rundgren was going, "Leave him alone." And I was going, "No, I'm gonna go get him a rag or something."

So I went and got him a rag. I mean, it's really corny, but I ragged his head, and Iggy said, "You really care." You know, just like in a fucking soap opera. He just went, "Wow, you really care." And I said, "Well, I don't know you well enough to care, but if you died and didn't make any more records, I'd be very unhappy."

Iggy said, "Where do you live, man?" You know, like, "I like you, got an apartment, got any money?" I told him, "I'm Todd's girlfriend and we have a house on Horatio Street."

I swear to God—this is where the brilliance of Iggy comes in—he was totally fucked-up, and the one time I said my address, guess who was on my doorstep the next day?

Iggy. I never thought he would remember 51 Horatio Street in the condition he was in. And not only did he show up at the house the next day, pretending like he was there to see Todd, who he'd never met in his life, but he looked fucking amazing. He was totally sober and had just exercised, had gone swimming, and looked like a sun-kissed blond beauty.

Todd was not being nice to me that day because he thought I was acting too wild—going out too much, hanging out at Max's too much, going to see the Dolls too much. So Todd is packing because he has to leave for San Diego, and in the three seconds Todd went out to buy some socks, Iggy showed up. Todd came home to finish packing and there was Iggy. I told Todd, "I didn't invite him." But Todd didn't believe me. Iggy was saying, "I just came over to hang out because you two are the nicest people I met last night. I like the fact that you don't do drugs and you're just nice and you have a clean house. You wouldn't believe some of the places I've been staying. I haven't taken a bath in about three weeks, can I borrow your tub?"

Iggy's a charming fucker and he knows it.

Todd pulled me aside and said, "You know he will steal from you because he's a junkie. He'll walk off with half the house, you really shouldn't let him stay here. But I'm leaving now, I'm going to play some gigs, and I'm expecting you to use your best judgment in this situation."

I lived with Todd Rundgren for five years and we always fooled around with other people, but we didn't always talk about it or flaunt it. You see, when I first met him, fidelity was very important to me. I was really young, seventeen going on eighteen, and he formed a lot of my opinions about men and about relationships. And I realized I didn't stand a chance with the fidelity philosophy. My heart would have been in fifty thousand pieces because he cheated on me from the very beginning.

So when Iggy came over, I could tell that Todd was trying to be mature and cool and very seventies, but I still couldn't wait for him to get the hell outta there. I was nuts about Iggy. I was completely wild about him. But it didn't start off passionate and sexy. We went to the movies, we went to see *Paper Moon*, we ate some hamburgers—and I couldn't understand why he kept passing out all the time.

He was always falling asleep everywhere. I didn't know what the fuck was going on because whatever drugs he was doing, he was doing them very discreetly. I just remember my friend David Croland dropped by, saw Iggy, and said, "Bebe, he's nodding." I said, "Oh no, he's just really tired. He's been on the road for a long time . . ."

David rolled his eyes and said, "Right, he's tired, Bebe. Oh god, I'm outta here."

So Iggy became my boyfriend for two weeks, but I had a boyfriend, so he couldn't really be my official boyfriend. So we had an affair, as they say in the trades, but Iggy was bummed out about Todd the whole time we dated. He didn't like the fact that I had a boyfriend I lived with. So he made me refill the water in the waterbed—don't ask me the significance of that.

LENNY KAYE (REVIEW IN *ROCK SCENE*): "You can't slander the Stooges," Iggy said after a round of band introductions, followed by a cooling bath of beer borrowed from an adjacent table. It was then that the newly written encore, "Open Up and Bleed," abruptly assumed its final shape. The words had been changing all week, but suddenly mumbled passages became clear, the lyrics in flick of the wrist focus, the music delivered with nary a falter or misstep. "I've been burned . . . ," he sang at one point, "I've been pushed aside, sometimes I even been fixed and died." Then, "It ain't gonna be that way no more . . ."

STEVE HARRIS: *Raw Power* was released on Columbia, and at CBS we had the same problems with Iggy that we'd had at Elektra. Nobody took his music seriously. Nobody thought of it as rock & roll, but I kept saying, "You might not like it, but there are kids out there who understand this . . ."

And I thought to myself, And the men don't know what the little girls understand.

Chapter 16

■ Separation Anxiety

SYL SYLVAIN: The Dolls had just finished playing a week at Max's, and Connie got wind that we were supposed to go to L.A. for six days to play the Whiskey-A-Go-Go. Connie Gripp supposedly was in the GTO's, which I don't believe, I think she was this maniac who thought she was in all things, but who was in nothing. She was a big-mouthed talker, that's basically who she was. She got mad at him. They were living out on East Third Street and Avenue A. She said to him, "Hey, aren't you going to take me to California?" Arthur said, "No, we aren't going to take none of our girlfriends, we have no money." So that night, when he's sleeping, she fucking stabs him in his thumb and gets him in his tendon.

PETER JORDAN: Connie was one of these babes that would just smack you in the face, you know, even just joking around, like, "Oh, that's funny," SCHMACK!

She was a big fucking girl, and could really booze up for fucking days—you'd be having a ball, and then she'd fucking smack you on the head with a bottle because you called her a crybaby. You know, "Don't be a bimmy . . ." "You can't call *me* a bimmy, you big asshole!" SCHMACK!

Arthur had a thing for tall girls. He always found these fucking enormous fucking tall girls, and the nuttier the better. He was very tall himself, maybe six foot two, and he liked to walk around at night. He'd roam through Times Square at four in the morning—he just loved roaming around the street—where he'd meet these enormous women. He had a knack for it.

Arthur came up with a tremendous succession of Amazons. It was incredible. I couldn't believe that there was so many spaced-out fucking chicks with dyed hair and torn black stockings in every city in the United States.

Where did they come from? A million of them—all enormous and with similar characteristics—all about six foot one, would drink fucking whiskey out of the bottle, and be the kind of girls who would have a broken heel on their shoe. And Arthur would find them everywhere.

Connie was one of them. She was pretty big—big butt, big tits, big laugh. She was hooking at that point, so Connie was the kind of girl who'd carry a knife, because she was peddling her ass and probably needed one for protection. Also, she and Arthur were not the type of people to have a kitchen. So she didn't go to the fucking kitchen and get a knife out of the goddamn drawer—she had to have a fucking knife in her bag.

EILEEN POLK: Arthur told me that he woke up to find Connie kneeling on his chest with the knife, in a kind of ritualistic position. It was like she had taken a knife and slit the part of his thumb that he needed to play the bass with.

She didn't really cut his thumb off. So he woke up, saw what she was doing, and tried to grab the knife away. She didn't try to cut his thumb off, she was going to do something weird to him with the knife, and he tried to stop her. She might have been play-acting, because Arthur told me all sorts of weird stories about those groupie girls.

He told me about these two other girls, Ginny and Debbie. They were huge, both like six feet tall, and they would play dolls together. They would have tea parties—this was their little play-acting routine. The groupies were like that. They thought it was fascinating to play out these roles, like an S&M role, or "I'm going to be a witch for a week" or "I'm going to get into tarot" or "I'm going to play with Barbie dolls and pretend I'm three years old" or "I'm going to have tea parties with my friends and drink opium instead of tea."

DEE DEE RAMONE: All those girls that hung around those glitter bands at Max's were evil. All those girls worked in massage parlors—which were a thriving industry in New York at that time. You'd go in, supposedly to get a massage, but it was really for a hand job or a blow job. And all your girlfriends worked in massage parlors, "massaging" all day.

EILEEN POLK: All these girls lived in fantasy worlds. And they could afford to not work because they were whores or strippers and made a lot of money. And the way they got these guys interested in them was by being so weird, paying for all their drugs, and paying their rent.

And once one of these guys had one of these girls on his tail, he couldn't get away from her. Because that was their profession, to follow you. If they were interested in a guy in a band, they had to make sure that they gave blow jobs to the security guards at every concert they played, and spent three hundred dollars on cab rides to follow the tour bus, and got plane tickets to California.

Whatever it took. And that's the kind of girl Connie was. She would do whatever she needed to do to get what she wanted, including threatening people and beating them up and just being crazy.

MALCOLM MCLAREN: The day after Connie attacked Arthur was absolutely horrific. But I wasn't shocked because I'd sensed the violence of New York already—people were too fucked-up—and Arthur was an alcoholic, and Connie was crazy.

When I first got to New York, I was very naïve, you've got to realize. I'd only had one girlfriend in my life. I never quite thought of that kind of jealousy, I was just learning to grow up. I had come to New York to seduce a girl—but when I got to New York I didn't recognize her, because she'd changed her face. She had gotten plastic surgery.

I mean, things like this were quite shocking to me. Here was a girl I was partly in love with, that I thought I knew, and when I came here—she didn't look the same.

So, no, I wasn't shocked by Connie stabbing Arthur—I wasn't even sad. I was just disappointed, that's the word.

I was disappointed with the fact that much of their behavior was wasted energy—I didn't think it even had any philosophical purpose. It was a trashy energy, easily disposable energy, an energy that didn't really bear any genuine point of view, except jealousy, which is so time wasting.

SYL SYLVAIN: Arthur called me up from Beth Israel Hospital and said, "Sylvain, aughh!" I was the first one he talked to. After that, I called David Johansen, then went straight to the hospital, and David met me. We said, "What happened? What happened?" But what was Arthur gonna say? The doctor told me that it wasn't too bad, he just threw in a couple stitches and put a cast on him.

PETER JORDAN: The Dolls still had one more night to do at Max's, so we all immediately ran up to Leber and Krebs and Johnny Thunders says to me, "Well, you know all the fucking songs, why don't you play them?" Leber and Krebs asked me, "You can do it?" I said, "Of course I can do it." We rehearsed for two hours and then I played the show.

CYRINDA FOXE: Even after she tried to cut off his thumb, Connie still wanted to be with Arthur, and I think Arthur still intended to be with Connie. I don't think he knew it was wrong. Syl was the one who told Arthur, "NO! NO! NO! NO! She's gotta go, she's horrible, look what she's done!"

BOB GRUEN: We walked into the lobby of the Continental Hyatt House and there was at least a dozen groupies waiting for the Dolls. I had traveled with a lot of groups, with more well-known groups, like Alice Cooper, and they'd walk into the hotel and there'd just be the desk clerk saying, "Fill out this form." But wherever the Dolls went, there was a scene surrounding them—there would be people waiting for them. We'd go to Detroit, there'd be thirty people in the lobby, dressed like Dolls fans. The Dolls had never been to L.A., but there were all these people waiting for them in the lobby: Rodney Bingenheimer was there, and Sable Starr was there . . .

NANCY SPUNGEN: The New York Dolls started a scene. They were the center of attention. Everything came after them. They were different. Nobody ever dressed the way they did or talked the way they did, or played music the way they did.

And they were the first band that I was hanging out with all the time. I slept with David Johansen, I slept with Johnny Thunders, I slept with Syl Sylvain, I slept with Jerry Nolan—everybody but Arthur Kane.

JERRY NOLAN: Musicians always get chicks, but not like the Dolls. The Dolls took all the chicks from any other musician, from any other band. Anybody! If the Dolls were in town, we owned it. I mean, *we owned it.*

There were times that I was with the most beautiful girls that I just couldn't believe it. I couldn't believe the things I was doing with girls. I couldn't believe that some of these girls were going home with and going to bed with me. They were so beautiful.

We had the beautifulest women. I would say to Johansen, "Jesus Christ, David, we could never touch a girl like that. They're just too beautiful."

Then that same night we'd be in bed with those same women with their toes pointed at the ceiling, and we'd be looking at each other and laughing. One time we were both having sex with these girls and "Looking for a Kiss" came on the radio. Wow, we were tickled. We laughed so hard we lost our hard-ons.

SABLE STARR: The Dolls pull up in this limousine and Johnny Thunders was the first to get out of the car. He had this red leather suit on—the one on the back of the first album cover. And I just knew something would happen with Johnny. And it did. He asked me to stay the night and the next day he started laying all this heavy stuff on me: "I really like you, I mean I really care about you, I mean *really* like—I love you. Will you marry me? Will you come back to New York and live with me?"

PETER JORDAN: Johnny and Sable's eyes met, their loins locked, and they spent quite a bit of time together. I think Sable was quite surprised that Johnny was so intensely and passionately interested in her, as opposed to just screwing her and kicking her out of the room. At the time, Johnny had been going out with Cindy Lang, who was Alice Cooper's girlfriend. Cindy was living with Alice, but he was never in town, he was always on tour, making money. So Cindy used to come see Johnny all the time. It was not that uncommon, you know, these things happen, as they say . . .

I think Sable's big romance previous to Johnny had been some schmuck from Led Zeppelin or something, who probably pissed on her, you know, literally. So I think Sable was surprised that Johnny wanted to become so intensely involved.

SABLE STARR: I had just turned sixteen, it was summer, and my mother was starting to make me register for school. So I ran away. The Dolls manager wouldn't let me go to San Francisco. He said, "If she comes I'm going to call the tour off," so I came straight to New York. My mother called the police and they followed the Dolls with detectives, and they grabbed another groupie instead of me. She was going, "I'm not Sable Starr, I'm Cyrinda Foxe, and don't you forget it." She had white hair just like me.

CYRINDA FOXE: I had a modeling job in Texas and the Dolls were playing so I went to meet them at the airport. I'm waiting for them at the airport and all of a sudden I see all these huge state troopers, like Texas Rangers, fucking scary guys, come walking up and surround the gate.

I thought, Oooh, I've been in this state before, and they don't come around unless . . . Then I see that they have a woman with them, a female Texas Ranger, and I knew that something scary was gonna happen to me. I knew the men weren't gonna touch me, but here was a woman and she kept looking at me. I'd get up and move to another seat to see if they were still looking at me. They were. I was so afraid. I wanted to go over and say, "Are you looking at me?" Then the Dolls came in, WOOF, and the cops jumped on me.

They thought I was Sable Starr, a sixteen-year-old runaway. I was like, "OH really? OH, this is SO good!" because I was twenty-one, but still in lust with that sixteen-year-old thing.

Of course Sable wasn't with them, Johnny was smart enough to send her straight to New York. But they thought I was Sable. I had to show them my pictures in *Life* magazine. I had a full-color page that month, me and Elvis Presley. I had all the proofs of me and Elvis together, and me and the guys from *Grease*. They finally said, "Well, I guess you're not Sable."

God, I really hated Johnny Thunders for that, but he got his. The Dolls were being driven in a Rolls-Royce while they were in Texas and the police stopped us. I guess they knew the Dolls. Johnny had on these red leather pants and no underwear and we all had to get out of the car. It was really funny, all the Dolls with their hair bouffanted like roosters and Johnny in these red leather pants with no underwear, so tight they left nothing to the imagination. And kind of a lot not to leave to the imagination. So the cops thought maybe he had drugs in his pants, maybe he had a stash. Johnny was so bad. He undid his pants and whipped out everything he owned . . . and it wasn't a big bag of pot!

Guess where Johnny went? Right to jail. We had to come up with some bucks to get him out.

EILEEN POLK: Right after the Dolls came back from that tour was when I met Arthur at the Cobra, which was an after-hours club that had a cobra snake in a little glass tank. We got drunk together and everybody said, "Oh, what a great couple. Arthur, break up with Connie and go out with her, she's so nice."

I didn't know who this Connie was. I'd seen her, but I didn't know what her relationship was to Arthur, because we'd only just met at the Cobra. So that night, Arthur told me he'd been going out with this woman who was driving him crazy. He told me, "She tried to cut my thumb off and I hate her and I never want to see her again, and I love you, blah, blah, blah."

So I said to Arthur, after he finished showing me the scar on his thumb, "Well, good. Break up with her and go out with me."

A little while later I met Connie for the first time in the back room at Max's and she tried to beat me up, but Arthur stopped her. Connie screamed, "You cunt, what are you doing with my boyfriend?"

And a growl came from Arthur. He could be really nasty too. When he got mad, it was scary. So Arthur body-blocked Connie so she couldn't hit me. I was this nineteen-year-old girl from Garden City, Long Island, and to me, fighting with a girl was just inconceivable. I wasn't raised to have street brawls with women. That's what men did.

But the fights that Connie and I had when I was with Arthur were nothing compared to the fights we had a year later when we both started going out with Dee Dee Ramone. The fights Connie and I had over Arthur were just teeny spats compared to the ones over Dee Dee Ramone. That's when it got *really* nasty.

PETER JORDAN: What happened to Johnny and Sable was that Johnny became a fucking totally fucking paranoid fucking speed freak. The Dolls had this guy Frenchie who worked with us for years. He was the band's valet, a kind of general odd-job man on the road crew. Frenchie was a total amphetamine freak and Johnny started taking speed with Frenchie. Johnny got completely fucking into it. He got so fucking into it that he fucking went like literally nuts. He wasn't taking like, you know, diet pills—he was fucking taking amphetamine to the max.

And Johnny became a fucking, raving fucking classic paranoid speed freak—like, "Let's pull down the blinds because there's somebody over there watching us," that type of paranoid routine. And Johnny was convinced that Sable was fucking around. And Sable was enough of a wiseass to tell him, "Yeah, sure I'm fucking around, you prick, you big baby, you stupid WOP!"

Yeah, Johnny became a complete fascist fucking speed freak, and I think that's what led him into smack. He needed something to come down.

SABLE STARR: I lived with Johnny in New York but it didn't work out. Johnny and I were going to get married. We were going to have a baby, too. I did get pregnant, but had an abortion.

Johnny tried to destroy my personality. He wanted me to sit there and be quiet and tell him I loved him twenty-four hours a day. I liked to run around and have a good time, but I did change for him. I mean I was becoming the type of person he wanted me to be—just stay home every day.

After I was with him, I just wasn't Sable Starr anymore. He really destroyed the Sable Starr thing. He made me throw all my diaries and all my phone numbers down the incinerator and he ripped up my scrapbook. It was a good one, too. It had everything in it.

After that I was just kind of destroyed. That's why I felt so bad, to have been such a hot shit and to be let down to such a low level.

RON ASHETON: I ran into Johnny Thunders one night at Max's Kansas City. I was real happy to see him, but Johnny snubbed me and then started yelling at Sable. She came up to me and said, "Johnny's mad because I was with you, that's why he hates Iggy too, cause I was fucking you guys."

I thought, God, Johnny, for a guy that's such a sleazebag, you're mad at that? That's when I said, "You know, fuck you, Johnny. You're an asshole."

CYRINDA FOXE: I could tell Sable wasn't going to fit in. She wasn't hip enough. She was a real L.A. girl, where she lived at home and could go home and change her clothes and then go out and play. She thought it was just a lot of glitter and glam—and then she hit New York. These streets are tough, aren't they?

Johnny Thunders was genuinely into Sable, but he hit girls he was involved with. The first time I actually met Sable was after one of her fights with Johnny. The whole area under her lip was cut. She was beaten up. She was dirty. And her clothes weren't cute like I'm sure they were when she met him. I said to her, "What are you doing? Just go home!"

SABLE STARR: Johnny was *crazy!* Crazy and vicious. Sick. Disturbed. Being Italian had a lot to do with it as far as the crazy jealousies go. If I was ever caught talking to a guy . . . So after Johnny tried to kill me four or five times, I thought I'd take a trip back home.

SYL SYLVAIN: Johnny Thunders was the most prudest guy you could ever imagine. Oh god, and even when we played the Club 82, when we finally played in drag, right? He never would dress in drag. Do you think Johnny wore a dress that night? No way. Johnny had a few hangups, you know, let's face it.

PETER JORDAN: I don't know if anyone ever really thought we were gay. I mean there was only that one show where they wore dresses. Everybody wore a dress, except for Johnny, who said, "Fuck you, I'm not wearing a dress!"

ROBERTA BAYLEY: I had just moved to New York from London and had a phone number of a guy who lived here. I called him up. "What do you want to do, what can I show you in New York?"

I said, "Well, I'd really like to see the New York Dolls."

So we went to see them at Club 82. That's the show they did in drag, so the first time I ever saw them they were all wearing dresses. I didn't really get it, I didn't know they were dressed in drag as a joke. you heard all this stuff about the New York Dolls, they're a bunch of fags, they wear makeup, and then I went, and it was true.

RONNIE CUTRONE: The 82 Club was a famous old drag place where Errol Flynn used to ship out his dick and play the piano with it. It was a wild place, and then it completely died. One night my girlfriend Gigi said, "You gotta come visit my family." So we went into the 82 Club and there was an old man named Pete and two very old Dyke bartenders, Tommy and Butch. That was the whole place—one john at the bar and three transvestites. So Pete, Tommy, and Butch said to Gigi, "Hey, maybe you could drum up some business for us." Gigi and I ruled New York then. Gigi was wild. I was really wild again because I had just split up with my girlfriend and was drinking heavily with Gigi—we fucked six times a day, we went out dancing every night, that was our life.

We were New York's fun couple. Whatever we said, people listened. If we said something was good, it was good. So we'd go to Max's and say, "Hey, there's this great place that's just right for having fun, the 82 Club on Fourth Street." Pretty soon it became THE place to be.

EILEEN POLK: Everybody hung out at Max's, and then the New York Dolls played their famous show in drag at the 82 Club. I started hanging out there. The 82 Club was a famous drag-queen bar on Fourth Street, around the corner from CBGB's, which wasn't happening yet. I started going to the 82 Club real early on and made friends with all the drag queens. That's where I met Rachel, Lou Reed's girlfriend. Rachel was a drag queen who was very feminine and really nice. The drag queens liked me, but Rachel was especially nice. One night when she was really drunk she told me that she could never be a guy because she had such a small dick. Then she showed it to me, and it was really small. I said, "That's okay, Rachel. That's okay." And she said, "Well, it better be, because I make a better woman than I do a man."

Then she met Lou Reed, and he was the man of her dreams. Apparently it was love at first sight. Rachel told me, "I've met Lou Reed! I've made it! This is it! I knew this was gonna happen! Something good was gonna happen to me, and this is it and I'm in love!" She was just ecstatic.

Lou would just sit in the corner and Rachel would keep everyone away from him. She announced to everyone, "I don't want anyone near him. I don't want anyone to talk to him. He's mine." And everyone respected that at the 82 Club. All the other drag queens stayed away from him, and all the women did too. Rachel said, "He's mine," but she didn't threaten anybody. I felt like everybody wanted something good to happen for her. And when it did, everyone was happy.

DUNCAN HANNAH: It was around that time that I saw the Dolls at the Waldorf-Astoria. I think it was my first Halloween in New York City, I'd been here two months. I was wearing this black velvet overalls I got in King's Road in London that both David Bowie and Mark Bolan wore.

The thing to do was to wear it without a shirt, if you were skinny enough and pale enough, so it really looked like—I mean, I looked like bait, right? I was trying to bait a rock chick, but I wound up with Danny Fields.

I was watching the Dolls gig and this guy starts talking to me, he says something like, "You oughta be in pictures," or something like that. I laughed.

Then he said his name was Danny Fields and I thought, Wait a second, Danny Fields?

I thought, No way. The back of the Doors album, that Danny Fields? The Danny Fields who did the Stooges and the MC5?

I was thinking, Whoa! Like, do I know about you, pal! So I said, "You're *that* Danny Fields?"

He said, "Yeah, you wanna come over?"

I said, "Well I'm with my friends," because I was a little nervous, right?

Danny said, "Oh, bring your friends."

So we went to Danny's loft on Twentieth Street and smoked some hash. We were all looking around his house, at all the pictures on the walls— because he had photos of everyone—so I was pumping him for what they were like. I kept saying, "Well, what's Iggy like?"

He'd say, "Well, he's an asshole."

Then I'd say, "Well what's—God you must know everyone—well, what's Wayne Kramer like?"

And he'd say, "Well, he's an asshole. All musicians are assholes."

You know, he was like, "Why do you ask?" Danny was looking at us, saying, "These people are jerks."

I said, "I know, but they're so great."

And Danny said, "Of course they're great, they're the best. But they're just complete assholes."

So Danny and I became friends and I took him to CBGB's because I kept raving about this new band called Television.

Part Three

■ The Piss Factory
1974–1975

Chapter 17

■ Go Rimbaud!

PATTI SMITH: The thing that gave me hope for the future of poetry was this Rolling Stones concert at Madison Square Garden that I saw. Jagger was real tired and fucked-up. It was a Tuesday, he had done two concerts and was really on the brink of collapse—but the kind of collapse that transcends into magic.

Jagger was so tired that he needed the energy of the audience. He was not a rock & roller that Tuesday night. He was closer to a poet than he ever has been, because he was so tired, he could hardly sing. I love the music of the Rolling Stones, but what was foremost was not the music but the performance, the naked performance. It was his naked performance, his rhythm, his movement, his talk—he was so tired, he was saying things like, "Very warm here/warm warm warm/it's very hot here/hot, hot/New York, New York, New York/band, bang, bang."

I mean, none of that stuff was genius—it was his presence and his power to hold the audience in his palm. I mean there was electricity. If the Rolling Stones had walked off that night and left Mick Jagger alone, he could've been as great as any poet that night. He could've spoken some of his best lyrics and had the audience just as magnetized.

And that excited me so much I almost blew apart, because I saw the complete future of poetry. I really saw it, I really felt it, I got so excited I could hardly stand being in my skin and that gave me faith to keep on going.

DUNCAN HANNAH: On New Year's Eve of 1973 I went with Danny Fields to see the New York Dolls, Kiss, and Iggy and the Stooges at the Academy of Music. I was wearing this gold satin suit I had gotten on King's Road and I went to Danny's house. We had some cocaine and champagne, and we both put on makeup, cause it was like, "Glam rock! Glitter! Yippee!"

So we go to the show, the Dolls were great, "Jet Boy" was just incredible, and everyone was there: Todd Rundgren, Mackenzie Phillips falling over on Quaaludes, really fucked-up—a really decadent scene.

So in between sets, Danny takes me up to the dressing room to see Iggy. I'd never met him, and we're climbing all these stairs to the dressing room, and I hear him howling up there, and I'm getting scared. It was like, "God! Meeting Iggy!"

Danny said, "Oh, he's great—he's just Jim, you know, don't worry about it, he's my old buddy." So we meet Iggy and he says, "Hiya, Danny, who's your friend?" I was like, "Hi, Iggy. Boy, knock 'em dead tonight!" It was great, the Stooges were all psyched, you know, it was *Raw Power* time, right? So I thought, This is really gonna be incredible. Like, history!

Iggy was stoked. He was bouncing off the ceiling. He was in perfect form. He looked great, and the Stooges were looking deadly, you know, just severe. I was thinking, Oh, this is gonna be so good! So we had a drink, then go back down to our seats, and wait for the show to start. The Stooges don't come on, and they don't come on, and they don't come on.

Finally the band comes out, but no Iggy. We're thinking, God, where is he? He was ready to go! Then he comes onstage, and he was just a complete fucking mess. Somehow, in like fifteen minutes, he'd gone from perfection to . . . I don't know what he did, it was like he shot two quarts of vodka or something. He comes out and he barfs all over everything, he falls off the stage, he can't remember any of the lyrics, the band starts a song, they stop, they start, they stop. They're mad as hell, but Iggy just can't stand up. He just doesn't know what's going on.

PATTI SMITH: Physical presentation in performing is more important than what you're saying. Quality comes through of course, but if your quality of intellect is high, and your love of the audience is evident, and you have a strong physical presence, you can get away with anything.

VICTOR BOCKRIS: The next day, I was sitting on the stage at the Poetry Project at St. Mark's Church during the 1974 New Year's Day reading, and Patti Smith came up and SPAT on me as she walked to the podium. I mean, she didn't spit on me, she spat on the ground right in front of me and said, "You owe me money, motherfucker!" And I was like, "Fuck you!"

I mean, I thought, She's an asshole, but she's really good.

JAMES GRAUERHOLZ: Patti performed with Lenny Kaye and she was a showstopper. She just had so much show-biz sense, it was just overwhelming. Patti knew how to capture the attention of her audience and to take them along through every twist of her little soul journey. She'd take them up way high—then drop them, and catch them, and set them down.

When she finished her piece at St. Mark's, she stormed out of the building—marched through the crowds, right through the packed church and out the front door—leaving Lenny onstage to unplug his amplifier as the crowd went crazy. She blew the place away.

I was sitting with William Burroughs—who has always had a very strong sense of show biz—and he turned to me and said, "She's really got it."

WILLIAM BURROUGHS: You see, Patti started out as a poet, then turned to painting, and then she suddenly emerges as a real rock star. Which was strange, because I don't think she could have gone very far either in her poetry or her writing, just from scratch. But suddenly, she's a rock star. There was no question of that.

PATTI SMITH: I started getting successful writing these long, almost rock & roll poems. And I liked to perform them, but I realized that, though they were great performed, they weren't such hot shit written down. I'm not saying I didn't stand behind them, but there's a certain kind of poetry that's performance poetry. It's like the American Indians weren't writing conscious poetry. They were making chants, they were making ritual language—and the language of ritual is the language of the moment.

But as far as being frozen on a piece of paper—they weren't inspiring. You can do anything you want as long as you're a great performer, you know, you can repeat a word over and over and over, just as long as you're a fantastic performer. I mean, Billy Graham is a great performer, even though he is a hunk of shit. Adolf Hitler was a fantastic performer. He was a black magician. And I learned from that. You can seduce people into mass consciousness.

So I write to have somebody. Everything I write has a motive behind it. I write the same way I perform. I mean you only perform because you want people to fall in love with you. You want them to react to you.

The other thing is that through performance, I reach such states, in which my brain feels so open—so full of light, it feels huge, it feels as big as the Empire State Building—and if I can develop a communication with an audience, a bunch of people, when my brain is that big and receptive, imagine the energy and the intelligence and all the things I can steal from them.

DUNCAN HANNAH: Patti Smith asked me, "Do you know any piano players?" I said, "Yeah, I live with one." She said, "Well, is he a rocker?" I said, "Yeah, I mean he's a classical piano player, but he's been playing around."

Eric Lee auditioned for Patti and played with her for about a week. So they were working out her tunes, and she was doing "Land of a Thousand Dances," and she finally turned to him and said, "Eric, when I say, 'Do you know how to pony?' I'm not talking about dancing."

He said, "Yeah, I know," but he was really embarrassed that she was talking about sex.

DANNY FIELDS: I was having an affair with Richard Sohl, and Patti Smith and Lenny Kaye said something about wanting a keyboard player, so I introduced them to Rickie Sohl, and that worked out very well. But I don't know what was said between them: "Hey, I have an idea, you recite poems and I'll strike a few chords. . . ."

PATTI SMITH: Right now I've been in this room in this city for so long I don't see it anymore and you know I'm not being stimulated. Lately I've just been doing a lot of cleaning inside my brain. My eyes are not seeing anything around me. So I've been dreaming a lot, recording dreams and trying to look within, but I'm not worried about it. I'm just waiting for the moment when I'll get to take a train or plane someplace and I know I'll spurt out because I've just got to see new things. I think Rimbaud said he needs new scenery and a new noise, and I need that.

Chapter 18

■ Down at the Rock & Roll Club

RICHARD HELL: Me and Tom Verlaine went together to see the New York Dolls at the Mercer Arts Center—and the Dolls had a lot to do with me wanting to do a band. There was just so much more excitement in rock & roll than sitting at home writing poetry. The possibilities were endless. I mean I could deal with the same matters that I'd be sweating over alone in my room, to put out little mimeograph magazines that five people would ever see. And we definitely thought we were as cool as the next people, so why not get out there and sell it?

Up until we went to see the Dolls, Tom would take his acoustic guitar to a hootenanny night, to some club in the West Village, once every couple of months. It was the most he would do. He didn't pursue anything very hard here. But he did write some songs, I don't know how many—five or six. Really funny ones. And we used to goof off. With me improvising shit while he was playing guitar. Just goofing off.

After seeing the Dolls, I kept pressing Tom to get together a band instead of just this acoustic hootenanny stuff. An electric band. And he would just stall and prevaricate and nothing ever happened. And I don't remember exactly how it came about, but finally he sat down and showed me how simple bass playing was for rock & roll. I thought it took some skill to play a musical instrument, and I didn't have any. But he showed me and that sealed it. There was the beginning of a band, because Tom already knew this drummer from Delaware, and so we started rehearsing together. But it was the Dolls that really inspired us.

DUNCAN HANNAH: There was a real pecking order at Max's. If a pretty boy would come in the back, I'd go, "Who's that? Good, very good. Nice threads. He didn't get that here, he got that in London. Hmmm. Very cool."

And I remember the first time I saw Richard Lloyd. I thought his hair looked like an Easter chick. He was really pretty.

I said, "Wow. Who's that?"

"He's new—he's a male hustler and he's a great guitarist too."

"You're kidding. Cool."

"He was living in Los Angeles."

"Cool. Cool."

RICHARD HELL: Tom Verlaine and I were both working at this film bookstore called Cinemabilia, and Terry Ork was the manager of the store. He was always interested in cute young boys and so he was really friendly to us. We had a lot in common in our tastes and Terry said he knew this kid who played guitar and who he thought might be what we were looking for, because he knew we were trying to make a band.

And that was Richard Lloyd.

RICHARD LLOYD: I was looking for a place to live and I met this guy at Max's Kansas City who worked for Andy Warhol named Terry Ork.

I was a bum. I had stayed at Danny Fields' house for two weeks and he had made it clear that I had a definite time limit. So I was like, "Does anybody have a floor that I can sleep on and hopefully not get too many advances made upon me?"

At that time, that's what I provided in a relationship: ME. No money, no effort, no work, but you did get ME. I would go up to girls in a bar and I would say, "God, I'm in love with you, do you wanna take me home and I'll just live with you?"

You know, "I won't pay the rent, I will keep my own hours, I will do what I wanna do, but you'll have me—AROUND." And I had a lotta takers.

Terry Ork said, "I have a huge loft in Chinatown with an extra room— the guy that lived there just moved out and you can have it if you want it."

The deal we cut was that I was supposed to provide the drugs, and Terry would provide everything else. Of course, as it turned out, I didn't provide the drugs, because providing the drugs would have meant coming up with some money. But I moved in anyway.

TERRY ORK: I felt pretty cocky about my taste. I felt like I could walk into a room and say, "Oh, that kid's got it, that kid hasn't got it." Yeah, Svengali, thank you. Heroin makes you real smart, huh?

RICHARD LLOYD: Terry began to pursue this band idea, but Tom Verlaine wasn't interested, from what I gather. Richard, Tom, and Billy Ficca had been in this band the Neon Boys and they'd actually put an ad in *Creem*. It said something like "Wanted: Rhythm guitarist. Talent not necessary." Dee Dee Ramone had shown up, and Chris Stein too, but I guess they didn't possess the sufficient "no talent," or whatever.

RICHARD HELL: Dee Dee showed up at an audition we held when Verlaine and I were trying to find a second guitar player for Television. We put ads out and not very many people showed up. It was funny, we couldn't have auditioned more than four or five people, and two of them were Chris Stein and Dee Dee Ramone. This was before we'd ever met either one of them.

DEE DEE RAMONE: Tom Verlaine and Richard Hell were very calculating, grownup, determined people. Everyone else was just kind of blundering into everything, but they were different. I thought they were beatniks.

RICHARD HELL: We tried to show Dee Dee a song and he was just dying. He would just play bar chords, because that's all he knew. You only need one finger to play a bar chord. And we'd tell him, "Okay, this is in C." And he'd start playing, and we'd say, "C." And he'd say, "Oh! Oh!" And just start playing something else. It was total trial and error. And we'd say, "No. No. No, man; C!"

Dee Dee would look up with this quizzical look and move his finger a little bit . . . We'd shake our heads no and he'd move it a little bit further . . . He was really funny. He was just like a little puppy dog coming to this audition. But eventually we had to say, "Sorry."

DEE DEE RAMONE: I was kicked outta there because I couldn't play good.

RICHARD LLOYD: Terry Ork finally told Tom Verlaine that he was willing to have them rehearse in his loft, buy them amplifiers, support the band, and put in money so they would be able to do shows. And I guess that I was part of that bargain.

At that time, Terry had been doing heroin once a week, you know, as a vacation. It was part of being hip; it wasn't grotesque sticking needles in your arm. And personally, by this time, I was in such an alcoholic state that I needed something to calm down my shakes. I needed to get away from alcohol. So I began to ask Terry to let me try some heroin.

TERRY ORK: I think Jim Carroll was the first one to shoot me up with heroin. Yeah, in his room, overlooking the basketball court. Gerard Malanga and I were living on Fifty-third Street and Third Avenue—which was the place where male prostitution thrived in New York City—and we had a great apartment there. So we were giving a party that night, and we went back to Jim's house to get some heroin or some shit.

I think it was his parents' house, above the Catholic school, where Jim injected me for the first time. I had no idea he was a male hustler or I would've grabbed him right there.

By the time I met Richard Lloyd, I had moved to a loft in Chinatown and was a weekend junkie. Using heroin was like taking a vacation a few days a week.

RICHARD HELL: My first experience with junk was with Terry Ork. I loved it. Yeah, I used to look forward to the dates we'd make to get high.

I didn't have any reservations about junk. It was just the ideal state as far as I was concerned. Not only did it physically make you feel as good as you possibly could—after all, it's a painkiller—but it felt like the fulfillment of all my fantasies, the way you got to dream but direct your dreams like a movie director.

RICHARD LLOYD: You could do dope, and then you could drink all night, and you wouldn't shake at all, you wouldn't get drunk, nothing would hurt, you could play guitar like you've never played before, you could fuck for six or seven hours, straight—you know, like a machine, "Mr. Machine."

You could do no wrong. I was one of these people with whom heroin had the opposite reaction. Instead of falling asleep, I would be awake for like months—thinking profundities and having phantasmagorical opium dreams.

So I began pressing Terry to do it twice a week, then three times a week . . .

RICHARD HELL: Just nod out and dream. And some sort of scenario would fade in and you'd really be living it—I mean, when you're dreaming you're actually having an experience, you're actually going through whatever you're dreaming, you only realize when you wake up that it was a dream.

And when you're nodding, you're not just watching it, you can change it—you could nudge it this way and that—as if you could make whatever you wanted to happen, happen.

So yeah, I liked it, ha ha ha, and heroin seemed so safe at the time, you know? Because it's true that you'd have to do it every day for two or three weeks to develop the mildest habit. And that seemed like such an easy thing to avoid. How could people be afraid of that? What kind of risk is that? No risk—but it's amazing how it catches up with you.

TERRY ORK: Tom Verlaine was very priggish; he didn't smoke marijuana, inject heroin, and he didn't even drink that much. I think Verlaine was scared of any derangement of the senses, and Hell was just the opposite. He would just luxuriate in it.

Tom Verlaine was a very bright boy, very learned, but there was some tightness within him. He was just so tightly wound. He was always concerned about men coming on to him. I mean, he was pretty, but I think he didn't really know what life was about. He had just accrued experience from books—it was all read, and not lived. He was very naïve in a lot of ways. As opposed to Richard Hell, who had both feet in the ooze.

Hell was definitely the one thinking in subversive terms. Hell was the one who always had the most awareness of what the text was trying to denote. Hell was a boulevard surrealist, groping for the breakthrough, the one grasping for liberation.

RICHARD HELL: Tom Verlaine and I had gone to boarding school together off in the hills of Delaware. We got to be good friends when we started rubbing each other up with this plan to run away from school.

It happened pretty quick—I got suspended in twelfth grade for taking morning glory seeds. Tom was in the schoolyard the day I got back from suspension. It was the week of my seventeenth birthday. Tom and I just wanted to be out living on our own. We figured we'd go to Florida where it would be warm, and be artists, writers, poets—something like that. But mostly we'd just beachcomb and live off the fat of the land. And try to seduce girls.

We put together fifty dollars or something. And we spent most of that getting the train as far as Washington. Then we started hitching back to Lexington because I wanted to pass through my hometown and be like the conquering, returning hero.

A rich guy I knew had a farm with an extra house on his property. It was like a servant's house way out in the fields. They put us up there and they'd come out and we'd party at night. They'd bring liquor and girls. There was a girl there who I'd known before. What happened in the year and a half since I'd met her, she'd become a slut and it was great. I remember looking between her legs with a flashlight—she was available for whatever I wanted to do. So we stayed there for maybe a week then we started off for Florida again.

We spent the next couple of days hitchhiking south. We got to Alabama, about two hundred miles from the Florida border. We were stranded on this country road late at night and it was cold. We were also getting taunted by rednecks who would drive by, pretend to stop, and when we came up to the car, they'd step on the gas and spray us with gravel. And we were getting really disgusted and furious, so we figured we'd have to give up for the night.

We built a campfire in the field by the road and started pushing each other, getting ourselves giddy with our freedom and our anger. We somehow broke into throwing the burning sticks from the fire around the field. We were so disgusted with Alabama. Pretty soon the whole place was going up in flames and we were still laughing and dancing and getting off on it and then the sirens come on and outta nowhere this police car and fire engines . . .

They caught us. We made up some story that we were kids returning to school in Florida but they didn't go for it. Anyway, they found out it wasn't true when they checked us against missing persons. So we were found out.

My mother had relatives in Alabama who came and got me. Tom's dad came and took him outta jail. Tom went back to school. I was very disappointed in him because I got a bus ticket to New York and left home. He finished high school, then went to college for a year before he came to New York.

But when he moved to New York, we would go to Max's and be like spies. People thought Tom and I were brothers. We were inseparable.

TERRY ORK: There was a definite love/hate relationship going on between Richard Hell and Tom Verlaine, and Richard Lloyd fit in beautifully to that mix.

I was in love with Richard Lloyd and I was in love with the way that Lloyd interacted with Hell and Verlaine. I was in love with the guitar duels and how they all just played against each other in that marvelous way.

And Lloyd was certainly even more "lived" than Hell or Verlaine. I mean, for god's sake, he had really been fucked-up by being in the hospital, all that chemical shock therapy. He said that he sensed that he couldn't connect in the same ways anymore, and that he was a little crazy.

RICHARD LLOYD: I wasn't sane, I had been insane. After I was hospitalized a number of times, in increments of nine months to a year, I would go insane. I would be placed into a hospital or an institution, do the *One Flew over the Cuckoo's Nest* thing, and then come out. And after whatever they had done to me—shock therapy—would wear off, I would look around and see that I had my life back, and then there would be this certain fear, like, "Is it gonna happen again?"

My parents would not sign for electroshock, so the doctors got them to accede to giving me chemical shock therapy, which consisted of them giving you a drug that puts you to sleep, administered every four hours, by injection. The thinking was that after you got a tolerance to the sleep drug, when it no longer kept you asleep for the four hours, they took you off that medication and put you on the opposite medication—like a high-powered speed—and let it wring you out like a sponge.

I slept for about eight days. It was a very pleasant drug, you know, just sleeping for a week—then it started wearing off. And I knew something was about to happen when I kept coming up to consciousness. It was like air bubbles coming up from the sea—you're down there and it's so quiet, there's no tension and the air bubbles are coming up.

Then one day, they said, "Okay, I think he's ready." And then they gave me this other injection and I started feeling not so good. And they took me and put me in this room, and I was like, "Wait a minute, it's rubber . . . I'm in the RUBBER ROOM!"

By then I was starting to kick and bounce around like a rubber ball—and they'd come every half an hour and open the little window, and watch me, until I stopped moving.

Right after the chemical shock treatment, I had a friend come visit me at Greystone State Mental Hospital in New Jersey. He just started weeping in front of me—because, later on, he told me that he didn't see me, that I had been erased.

RICHARD HELL: I had been really impressed with how the New York Dolls had managed to make things happen for themselves. When they were first going, they would play the same night every week at the Mercer Arts Center. They were associated with the Mercer Arts Center and I thought that was perfect, because people could depend on that. They didn't have to read the paper in order to follow you.

I liked it that if there was a cool band and if you wanted to see them, they'd always be playing on Friday nights at the Pit, or wherever. It seemed like the ideal way, if you were good, to draw the people who would be interested in you as quickly as possible.

So that's what I proposed: that we find a place where we could do that. And I figured, "Where is a bar where nothing is happening? With nothing to lose if we tell them to let us play there one night a week? We'll charge a door price, but you can let in any of your regular customers. You can't lose, because the people who come in will be buying drinks who wouldn't have been there otherwise, and we'll have an audience."

So we all decided we were going to keep our eyes open.

We used to take a bus down Second Avenue or Third Avenue or something to get to Chinatown to go to our rehearsal loft. Verlaine and

Lloyd were apparently walking to a bus stop to go to rehearsal and they spotted CBGB's. They went in and talked to Hilly Kristal, the owner, and asked him if our idea appealed to him.

RICHARD LLOYD: Hilly was like, "What kinda music do you play?" We said, "Well, what does 'CBGB-OMFUG' stand for?" He said, "Country, Bluegrass, Blues, and Other Music for Uplifting Gourmandizers." So we said, "Oh yeah, we play a little of that, a little rock, a little country, a little blues, a little bluegrass . . ."

And Hilly said, "Oh, okay, maybe . . ."

He was gonna have the place be like a drive-in. He was gonna put the stage in the front of the place, so people could hear the music from the street, too. We said, "Hilly, that's not gonna work—first of all, the person taking money at the door won't be able to hear what anybody's saying; second of all, when people leave they're gonna walk right in front of the band; and third of all, you're gonna get complaints from the street."

That just shows you the kind of bizarre ideas that Hilly had from the get go. So Terry Ork ended up going on our behalf, to guarantee Hilly an audience. He said, "Look, the band's playing around, we do our own postering, we take an ad out in the *Voice*, we'll guarantee you a bar."

So Hilly gave us three Sundays, in three weeks' time.

DUNCAN HANNAH: Onstage, Richard Hell and Tom Verlaine looked like they could blow up at any minute—like they were just trying to keep the peace. Sometimes they'd have a fight onstage. It would be like a Sunday night, there'd only be like fifteen people there, and someone would play something wrong, and Tom Verlaine would start yelling at Richard, "Ah, fuck you." And Richard would yell back, "Don't take it so seriously, asshole."

DANNY FIELDS: I thought Television was fabulous! The arms of Richard Hell and the neck of Tom Verlaine were so entrancing that I needed no more art, music, life, love, or poetry to make me happy after that. They were the most gorgeous thing I'd ever seen. The skin between the two of them . . . they had the most perfect skin in the world. Tom Verlaine's skin and Richard Hell's skin were in a class of like "God made that and then threw away the skin formula." And then there was Richard Lloyd, who I fucked.

Everybody fucked Richard Lloyd. He was another one with gorgeous skin. He was another gorgeous beauty. It was the band of beauties.

DUNCAN HANNAH: Patti Smith wasn't at the Television shows at the absolute beginning, but as word spread, then she got there. Patti always acted like she was old, but, I mean, how old could she have been? Twenty-nine? So she'd come down to CBGB's and be checking out these boys.

RICHARD LLOYD: Patti Smith started coming to see Television play at CBGB's. Everybody knew that Patti was nuts for Tom. It was like, nudge-nudge-wink-wink, you know, "Go for it." I think Tom was ambivalent. I don't think he wanted to get swallowed up by anybody, but frankly, I wasn't paying attention.

TERRY ORK: Patti Smith just came up to me and said, "I want him. I want Tom Verlaine. He has such a Egon Schiele look." She just told me, "You gotta get that boy for me."

It was pretty cut and dry. So I told Tom. He was very enamored with Patti as a poet and a scenemaker. I guess he knew that she was gonna get signed to a record deal. Plus, I guess he liked her physically, I mean they had the same kind of body structure.

RICHARD HELL: I wasn't upset when Patti started going out with Tom, except that it made me nervous to have Tom do anything that was gonna boost his ego further, ha ha ha, because it was getting pretty dicey. Tom thought he was a big deal when he started going out with Patti. But I never hung out with them—that was when I couldn't be around Tom, I was just hating him.

DUNCAN HANNAH: I knew that Allen Lanier was Patti Smith's old man. I lived on Thompson Street and Patti lived nearby, and I would run into her at the laundromat, which was a very Shangri-Las kind of thing—washing Allen's clothes.

I said, "What are you doing?"

Patti said, "Oh, washing my old man's clothes."

I mean, feminism existed, right? And this seemed kind of like a servile thing, but Patti was traditional that way. I didn't know anybody that would talk like that: "Yeah, I got to wash my old man's clothes, cause I'm his old lady."

Wash clothes? Shit, nobody cool would wash their clothes.

But Patti told me about the triangle between Allen Lanier, Tom Verlaine, and herself, which that song "We Three" is about. It was like a problem. Patti knew that I knew Allen—I knew them as a couple—and now I knew Tom and Patti as a couple, so Patti was in two couples. It was kind of a little neighborhood scandal, but she was trying to work it out.

DEBBIE HARRY: I remember the look on Patti's and Tom's faces when they were caught kissing behind CBGB's, whoaa. Tom blushed and Patti went, "Fuck off."

Patti didn't really ever talk to me much. We weren't very friendly at all—especially when she showed up at one of Blondie's auditions for drummers. All of a sudden Patti walked into the room—I had Clem Burke there—and she said, "Heeey, you're pretty good, what's your name?"

I said, "Patti, I'm working with this guy."

She just went, "Oh." You know, instead of, "Oh pardon me," like she hadn't done anything.

RICHARD LLOYD: Patti really liked us. She had the crush on Tom Verlaine, and she really wanted to help us. Her own band was just getting fleshed out and they were starting to draw, so she asked Tom, "Do you think it would be a good move for me to play at CBGB's?"

Tom was like, "I think it'd be a great move for you. Why don't we do some shows together, because then you'll bring in new people for us, and we'll give you a new audience, too."

TERRY ORK: Patti was being managed by Jane Friedman, and I guess Clive Davis, the president of Arista Records, was already showing interest in signing Patti, but Patti and Jane were still nervous about getting a record deal.

So I went to Patti and said, "Hey listen, I think that we got something happening here. Let's try you and Television for a few weekends. Let's rip."

So they played Thursday, Friday, Saturday, and Sunday nights at CBGB's, and it just became huge. Each weekend got bigger and bigger. It lasted for six weekends. After that, I went to Hilly and said, "You can't beat these figures with your country and bluegrass, dude!"

And I considered that the official beginning of the scene.

RICHARD HELL: The scene definitely started snowballing. CBGB's was clearly where things were happening, from the very first time we played there. We were really unique. There was not another rock & roll band in the world with short hair. There was not another rock & roll band with torn clothes. Everybody was still wearing glitter and women's clothes. We were these notch-thin, homeless hoodlums, playing really powerful, passionate, aggressive music that was also lyrical.

I think we were the best band in the world that year. Well, for the first four or five months.

Bob Gruen: The first time I saw Richard Hell, he walked into CBGB's wearing a white T-shirt with a bull's-eye painted on it, and the words Please Kill Me written on it.

That was one of the most shocking things I had ever seen. People had a lot of wild ideas back then, but for somebody to walk the streets of New York with a target on his chest, with an invitation to be killed—that's quite a statement.

Richard Hell: I don't ever remember wearing the Please Kill Me T-shirt, though I do remember forcing Richard Lloyd to wear it. I was too much of a coward.

Richard Lloyd: Richard Hell had designed a T-shirt for himself that said Please Kill Me, but he wouldn't wear it. I was like, "I'll wear it." So I wore it when we played upstairs at Max's Kansas City, and afterwards these kids came up to me. These fans gave me this really psychotic look— they looked as deep into my eyes as they possibly could—and said, "Are you serious?"

Then they said, "If that's what you want, we'll be glad to oblige because we're such big fans!" They were just looking at me, with that wild-eyed look, and I thought, I'm not wearing this shirt again.

Terry Ork: I approached Hilly and I said, "Listen, I wanna come back here with Television and I wanna book the club." I said, "Hilly, look what you got, look at the crowds we had here!" I gave him a big pitch because I wanted control. I said, "You gotta go new music every night." The music didn't have a name yet.

Hilly said, "Okay, okay."

So we did.

And that's when it really began to break, and we started getting other great bands, like the Ramones.

Chapter 19

■ 53rd & 3rd

JIM CARROLL: I was a terrible hustler. When I was fourteen or fifteen years old, I'd be down on fucking Greenwich Avenue and Christopher Street—until somebody hipped me to the fact that if everybody's giving it away for free, you ain't going to make no money.

A lot of runaway kids would go to Forty-second Street, like in Larry Clark's *Teenage Lust* book, but that was just *Midnight Cowboy* shit to me. Then some older guy tipped me off to go to Fifty-third and Third, which was the boy-hustling place in New York City.

So I went up there and I'd get offered a lot of money, but then I'd have to renegotiate, because unless I had poppers, I'd only let guys suck my dick. Or I'd jerk them off or something. I would never let guys fuck me. And I wouldn't fuck guys, unless they had poppers. If they had poppers I would fuck them. Fuck 'em good, ha ha ha. I'd like it if they were fat, with a lotta money, ha ha ha.

MICKEY LEIGH: I remember driving by Fifty-third Street and Third Avenue and seeing Dee Dee Ramone standing out there. He had a black leather motorcycle jacket on, the one he would later wear on the first album cover. He was just standing there, so I knew what he was doing, because I knew that was the gay-boy hustler spot. Still, I was kind of shocked to see somebody I knew standing there, like, "Holy shit. That's Doug standing there. He's really doing it."

JIM CARROLL: I would actually say, "Listen, you don't have to pay me fifty, because I'm only gonna let you suck my dick, so just give me forty."

If I could get one guy for forty bucks or even thirty, then that was it for me, I was outta there. I didn't wanna hang around. I didn't wanna make a lot of money doing it, you know, thirty bucks is plenty to get straight. I'd done it for as little as ten bucks, but usually it was about twenty-five. Certain times I'd get a hundred.

I could never be with a john for more than one time. You know, go out to lunch after that? It felt too weird, which economically was bad, because the best offers were, "Live with me for a couple of weeks, I'll pay you."

But I was like, "No, no, I'll just shut my eyes."

Unless they had poppers, then I could get into it.

DEE DEE RAMONE: The song "53rd & 3rd" speaks for itself. Everything I write is autobiographical and very real. I can't write any other way.

LEGS McNEIL: "53rd & 3rd" is a chilling song. It's about this guy standing on the corner of Fifty-third and Third trying to hustle guys, but nobody ever picks him. Then when somebody does, he kills the john to prove that he's not a sissy.

DANNY FIELDS: I don't think Dee Dee was a full-time hustler and I know he wanted girls more than he wanted boys. I thought that was very modern. I think everybody should be able to fuck everybody and that gender should be of little consideration. In that way, Dee Dee was very modern. I don't think he was ashamed of having done it.

I mean, I hustled. I hustled people for money. You know, a young poor guy needs a richer older guy to help him get through some difficult moments and if you gotta go to bed with them, so what?

JIM CARROLL: A lot of times it would be in a car, but that made me really uncomfortable, so I'd try to convince the guy to take me to this hotel off Second Avenue that was right across from the synagogue. The other guys thought I was asking too much because it was asking them to put out another fifteen or twenty bucks for a room. But I convinced the guy that it'd be much more comfortable than a car, and then we wouldn't have to worry about the law.

There was also the nighttime scene during the summer—on Central Park West, right across from the Museum of Natural History. That was pretty good. I mean, the park was much better than a car, I always thought.

DEE DEE RAMONE: When I was fifteen I started buying dope at the fountain in Central Park and bringing it back to my neighborhood in Queens and selling it. I would buy a half load from my dealer, which was fifteen two-dollar bags. I could get three dollars a bag for them in Queens, so if I sold ten of them, I'd make my money and still have five left over.

You could snort one two-dollar bag and get loaded. Three two-dollar bags would keep me nice for the day. That was when the dope in New York was coming from France and it was strong stuff that would make you itch and nod. Real dope.

I was making out pretty good selling dope in Queens, until one day I got caught short and started withdrawing. I went back to my mom's apartment and was shaking and in a lot of pain. My mom was so pissed off she picked a pot off the stove and threw it at me. Then she broke my records and threw my guitar out the window. Since my dad wasn't around, I wasn't afraid of her anymore, so I started screaming, "Get the fuck out of here, you fucking whore cunt!"

And she did.

After my mom found me withdrawing from dope, and we'd had our fight, I couldn't live in the house anymore. And I had nowhere to live in Forest Hills. But I had to go somewhere, so I decided to hitchhike to California.

Some guys from Flint, Michigan, picked me up somewhere in Illinois in their junk car. I don't know much about cars, but it was really a piece of junk. They would drive the car real slow up the hills, then speed down them like a maniac. These guys were like really demented, they were talking all this sick stuff. They kept saying how they wanted to cut someone's head off. They wanted to strangle somebody. They had a thin wire and two hoops, and they wanted to garrote somebody.

Finally they pulled over to a gas station in South Bend, Indiana, and robbed the place and we all got arrested for armed robbery.

No one got away with nuthin. The police caught us because the driver tried to step on the gas in the junk car and it stalled. The cop who caught us tried to give me a break. He gave me ten phone calls to try and get the bail money. He was really nice. So I called everybody. I called my father, my grandmother in Missouri, and everybody said, "Fuck you."

That was the first time I ever asked my father for anything. I was desperate. I was really scared. It was a rough place. My father said, "Fuck you! Rot there, you deserve it!" and hung up. So I was stuck there and sentenced to ninety days because I had a weapon on me. The other guys got off because their parents came and got them.

I was fifteen and locked up. The jail was a bullpen. They had about ten little cells, and then they would open it up in the day and keep us all in one big room. I was in jail for three months and then they let me out.

I had nowhere to go, so after I got back from being in jail and going to California, I went back to Queens. I went back to living with my mom and there was this guy, John Cummings, who became Johnny Ramone, that lived across the street, and who was friendly to me.

He worked for a dry cleaners and I would usually see him around, making deliveries. I thought he was cool because he dressed like he wanted to, even when he was working. He wore his hair long, down to his waist, a tie-dyed headband, jeans, a Levi jacket, and cheap Keds. So we were checking each other out. I didn't know him that well, but one day I met him on the sidewalk by my house—Tommy, Joey, Johnny, and I all lived right next to each other, in those nice apartment buildings in Forest Hills—and Johnny and I spoke to each other and both kind of blurted out that we liked the Stooges.

I couldn't believe it, because at that time, no one was into the Stooges. I was raised in Germany and didn't like the United States. It was too weird. There was just all this awful music around. In the early seventies rock & roll was like America and Yes—and I hated it. That's when I started getting into the New York Dolls.

Then I discovered the Stooges and that all seemed to go together and the Stooges became my ultimate favorite group. I would just die to go see them, but they only came to New York every nine months or so. But anytime they ever played New York, I'd see them.

MICKEY LEIGH: Johnny Ramone was nice to me. He was shooting dope, but he never tried to get me to do it. He was John Cummings then, and I thought he was cool. He was wearing a motorcycle jacket. A black leather jacket. When I first started hanging out with him, Johnny was real nice to me. I don't know why. He liked me for some reason. I guess because he knew I could play guitar.

But Johnny wasn't interested in knowing my brother, Joey Ramone. Joey was calling himself Jeff Starship then and hanging out with weird people from the Village. My brother was a real hippie in those days. He used to walk around with no shoes on, and he went to San Francisco, and he hung out with real hippies. That's why John wasn't interested in knowing my brother at all. Joey was just a weirdo hippie. And John *hated* hippies.

DEE DEE RAMONE: I had to have different guys to hang out with to do my different drugs with, so I started hanging out with Joey because he liked to drink. But Joey couldn't do drugs. He tried them and he couldn't handle them. He would freak out. One time I saw him smoke some pot and start convulsing on the floor in a fetal position, saying, "I'm freaking out! I'm freaking out!"

JOEY RAMONE: I never really sniffed glue or Carbona. I never got really heavy into the paper bag. I did it, but I didn't get into it like Johnny and Dee Dee did.

They used to go up on the roof and sniff Carbona and sniff glue and shit. It was this sensation, like "Bzzzz, bzzz, bzzz."

DEE DEE RAMONE: Besides smoking good pot, I started doing a lot of glue. I'd do glue and Tuinals and Seconals. What a party, you couldn't get your head outta that bag. I used to do it with my friend Egg, because Egg was real sleazy. He didn't go for dope or pot or acid, what he liked was sniffing Carbona, the cleaning fluid, and glue. After we'd sniff glue we used to call up numbers on the phone.

We knew these numbers to dial where you could get these weird sounds. We'd call the numbers and it would go "Beep-beep-beep-beep-beep." We'd listen to that for hours. Then sniff some more glue. Or if we couldn't get any glue, Egg would go to the supermarket, get some cans of whipped cream, and we'd do the gas in it. Anything to get high—cough medicine, glue, Tuinals, and Seconals.

But Joey was a wino. No one else I knew liked to drink, except Joey. So that started our friendship. We used to get a couple bottles of Boone's Farm or Gallo, and sit on the stoop in the afternoons and drink all day.

Joey told me he was an ambulance driver, and maybe he was. I mean, he had a driver's license, but then he couldn't get it together to unlock the garage door, start the car, and get it out before the garage door closed. You know, he couldn't even drive. But then, neither could I.

MICKEY LEIGH: Joey was such a mess that my mother threw him out of the house. My mother owned a little art gallery called the Art Garden. Joey lived there for a little while. When my mother would go away for the weekend, I'd let him come and stay at the house and not tell her.

I felt bad for him. I guess my mother thought she was doing the right thing. She was going out with this guy, Phil, who later became a psychologist. He was kind of short, had a beard, and looked a little like Sigmund Freud. Phil was the one who suggested Joey leave the house, because Joey was like twenty, twenty-one, and he wasn't doing anything. And it didn't seem like he was going to do anything.

JOEY RAMONE: I'd just sit with Dee Dee on the corner off of Queens Boulevard and drink and insult people and stuff. That's when I got kicked out of my house. My mother told me it was for my own good.

So I moved into my mom's art gallery. I had to barricade myself in real fast so the cops wouldn't catch me. The cops would come by, I'd see a flashlight and hear the police radio going, and they'd be banging on the door, like they thought I was a burglar. It was a kind of a tense situation. I was always worried they'd get me. So I'd barricade myself in real fast with the paintings and sleep on the floor. I had a sleeping bag, a pillow, and a blanket and then I'd work there during the day. At night, I used to hang out at the Coventry, the big rock & roll club in Queens. One night I met Dee Dee there and I brought him back to the art gallery to sleep on the floor.

DEE DEE RAMONE: I was living all over the place, but the art gallery on Queens Boulevard was home. No furniture, no nothing. It was just a paint store and we slept on the floor, in the stock room.

Joey was painting then. He would chop up carrots and lettuce and turnips and strawberries and mix it all together and paint with them. His paintings were very good. Then he would try and make tapes of different sounds. One time, we went back to his mother's apartment, which was on the twentieth floor. It was lightning out and he stuck a mike from the tape recorder out on the balcony to tape the lightning. And the lightning struck the mike and burnt everything.

Sometimes he'd have me come over and bounce the basketball for a half hour and he'd tape it. And then listen to it all day in a daze.

I knew Joey had been in a mental hospital. I thought he was clever, because a lot of people go in there and never come out. And Joey had managed to get himself back out on the street. What's more, he always had these girlfriends that he met in the nuthouse. He'd say, "I met her in the bin."

Joey always did alright. He always made the best of a bad situation. I swear, he always set himself up good. He had it better than anyone. He was like a pimp. He even got one of these girls to set him up in an apartment on Union Turnpike. She had a really nice apartment and she got him his own records, like, "Be True to Your School" and "Caroline," the Beach Boy records.

MICKEY LEIGH: I guess being in the nuthouse helped Joey because when he got out, he had made friends with all the people in there, especially with all these chicks.

He'd bring these girls he met in the nuthouse back to my mother's house. He had this one girl who was not bad looking, but she was out of her mind. And she would take my acoustic guitar and start singing. She wrote songs. She was a folkie, a real hippie folkie. Joey and this chick were both into that real introspective psych stuff, and she would write songs like that: "Oh, I'm in need and you're so beautiful." I thought it was real crap. The fucking song made me want to throw up.

So I think Dee Dee and Johnny started liking Joey because they thought he was really sick. Everything with Johnny then was about how sick you could be. Anybody who was really sick was cool. He thought Charles Manson was a cool guy. That was one of the things that started turning me off about Johnny, you know, that he glorified people like Charles Manson. Anybody who was really sick, demented, evil, and violent, they thought were cool. Johnny had become so out there that he was able to accept even associating with my brother, although I don't think he took Joey very seriously.

It was about that time that Joey started getting into glitter and joined his first band. Joey joined the band Sniper and started hitching rides down Queens Boulevard to hang out at this club called the Coventry. I think Joey became the lead singer of Sniper by answering an ad in the *Village Voice*: "Let's dress up and be stars tomorrow."

DEE DEE RAMONE: I saw Sniper play with Suicide one night, and Joey was the lead singer and he was great. He was really sick looking. I thought Joey was the perfect singer because he was so weird looking. And the way he leaned on the mike was really weird. I kept asking myself, How's he balancing himself?

The thing was, all the other singers were copying David Johansen, who was copying Mick Jagger, and I couldn't stand that anymore. But Joey was totally unique.

MICKEY LEIGH: Joey was the one that really got into glitter. I didn't like glitter, it was too affected and pretentious for me. I thought, You're either a homo, or you're not. And since I wasn't a homo, I wasn't gonna start being one just because Lou Reed was doing it.

But Dee Dee and those guys would ridicule me. I was still hanging out every day and Dee Dee would come by with his arm around this guy Michael, acting all fruity. They did it on purpose—to shock and separate themselves from everybody. I guess it made them feel cooler. And whenever I'd see Dee Dee on the street, he'd say, "Oh, you still look like a hippie. Why don't you get hip. You're a faggot."

He would say that stuff because I was still dressing like the Ramones eventually started dressing. I was just wearing jeans and a T-shirt and sneakers. But they were all dressing up in glitter and shit. Even John.

But Joey really got into the glitter thing. He was stealing all my mother's jewelry, her clothes, her makeup, and her scarves, which created even more fights between them. She would flip out when she saw all her clothes were missing. That was another reason I didn't like glitter—it just created more fights at home.

I thought it was great that Joey was in a band, but it was really dangerous to hitchhike down Queens Boulevard looking the way Joey did. Joey's so unusual looking to begin with, so tall—he's about six six naturally, but in platform shoes he stood over seven feet tall. And he wore a jumpsuit. At that time, you really couldn't be doing that safely. You were taking a chance hitchhiking down Queens Boulevard looking like that.

JOEY RAMONE: When I was hitching I'd be completely decked out. I used to wear this custom-made black jumpsuit, these like pink, knee-high platform boots—all kinds of rhinestones—lots of dangling belts and gloves. I got rides, but that was my first time experiencing queers. All of a sudden, you'd be halfway there and they'd say, "What do you think about going under the bridge?" Usually, if I was close enough, I'd just jump out of the car.

MICKEY LEIGH: He eventually got beat up. He got his nose bashed in. We had to go pick him up and bring him to the Elmhurst hospital. I felt bad.

Then Sniper became regulars at the Coventry—playing a couple of times a month—so I wanted to check them out, see what was going on. When I got there it was a real glitter crowd—everyone was into that band the Harlots of 42nd Street. So I thought it was going to be lame.

I was shocked when the band came out. Joey was the lead singer and I couldn't believe how good he was. Because he'd been sitting in my house with my acoustic guitar, writing these songs like "I Don't Care," fucking up my guitar, and suddenly he's this guy onstage who you can't take your eyes off of.

I was blown away. I was shocked.

I didn't think the band Sniper was too good, but I was real impressed with my brother. He moved like he would in the early Ramones days. I told him, "I can't believe it. I can't believe how you're coming off, how you're performing."

JOEY RAMONE: It was the glitter days and the New York Dolls and Kiss would come play at the Coventry, all those bands would come in from Manhattan. Then Sniper started playing Max's so they let me in for free and I'd go see the Dolls and hang out there.

DEE DEE RAMONE: I finally found a job working as a mail clerk in an office building. I'd pick up the mail in the morning and sort it out, and I had my cart, and I'd have it lined up according to how the desks in the office were organized. Then I'd drop off the mail and I'd gossip with the people a little bit. Then do it all over again ten times a day, then go home and get drunk.

John Cummings was a construction worker at 1633 Broadway. I got transferred there and me and Johnny would meet every day for lunch. Usually we'd go to the Metropole, a go-go club, and have a few beers. After we got a little tipsy, we'd go over to Manny's Guitar Store on Forty-eighth Street, which was next door, and look at the guitars.

Then one day, it was a Friday, it was a payday, and we both bought a guitar each and decided to start a band. He bought a Mosrite and I bought a Danelectro.

JOEY RAMONE: One day I got a phone call and Johnny and Dee Dee asked me if I wanted to join their band. I said, "Yeah."

DEE DEE RAMONE: Monte Melnick did us a favor by sneaking us into a rehearsal space called Performance Studios. That's when the Ramones really, somehow, got started. We tried to figure out some songs from records, but couldn't. I had no idea how to tune a guitar and only knew the E chord. No one else was any better. Joey started off by playing drums at the first rehearsal. It took him two hours to get the drum set ready. We waited and waited for Joey to put the drum kit together. I couldn't take it anymore so we started playing. We stopped after the first song and I looked over at Joey and he didn't have the stool on the drum stand. He was just sitting on the point. That was our first rehearsal.

JOEY RAMONE: It was just the three of us. I was drumming. Dee Dee was playing rhythm guitar and singing lead. When Dee Dee would start singing, he would stop playing the guitar, because he couldn't sing and play at the same time.

DEE DEE RAMONE: Finally we just started cranking it out. No one was really ready. I was so drunk I fell right over backwards and whacked my amps. They started fizzing and stopped working. Monte was fed up. He had done us a favor sneaking us in and we had messed up. But when we came back the next week, he let us in anyway. Joey had written a few songs, one called "What's Your Game?" and another one called "Suck You Buss." Since Joey knew the words, he sang them while he kept the beat and right then we knew he had to be the singer. I switched to bass. I told Johnny I wanted Joey to be the lead singer and he said okay.

JOEY RAMONE: What happened was, they just kept playing faster and faster, and I couldn't keep up on drums. It was too fast. Every day in rehearsal it was a little faster. So they asked me to sing, actually it was Dee

Dee because he had seen me in Sniper and thought I wasn't like anybody else. Everybody else was doing an Iggy or a Mick Jagger.

DEE DEE RAMONE: Joey became lead singer, Johnny on guitar, and Tommy Ramone, who was managing us, finally had to sit down behind the drums, because nobody else wanted to. That completed the original Ramones lineup. But we didn't know what to do when we started playing. We'd try some Bay City Rollers songs and we absolutely couldn't do that. We didn't know how. So we just started writing our own stuff and put it together the best we could.

We wrote "I Don't Wanna Walk Around with You" and "Today Your Love (Tomorrow the World)." A couple of days later we wrote "I Don't Wanna Go Down in the Basement" and "Loudmouth." I think Joey wrote "Beat on the Brat" then. It was a true story. Joey saw some mother going after a kid with a bat in his lobby and he wrote a song about it.

JOEY RAMONE: Forest Hills was a middle-class neighborhood filled with snobby rich people and their screaming brats. It was filled with these fucking little kids running around who were really annoying. And it wasn't like the parents were beating them, it was just that you wanted to beat them, they were just such spoiled brats. They were so out of control and got away with murder, that you just felt like killing them.

That was about the time I also got the song "Judy Is a Punk." I was walking down the street by this place called Thorny Croft. It was an apartment house where all the kids in the neighborhood hung out on the rooftop and drank. And I remember walking by it and I got the first line. Then I was on another street and the second line came.

DEE DEE RAMONE: After one of the early rehearsals, Tommy and I went into the studio office because he said he wanted to talk to me. He said, "What do you think we should call the group?"

"Oh, I don't know," I said. "How about the Ramones?" Then, somehow, everybody took the name Ramone and added it to their other name, and we became the Ramones.

DEBBIE HARRY: Chris Stein and I ran into Tommy Ramone on the street and he said, "Oh, I've got this band. We're doing a showcase, you should come by."

So we went by Performance Studios. It was great. It was hilarious. Joey kept falling over. He's just so tall and ungainly. Joey couldn't see very well, plus he had his shades on, and he just was standing there singing, then all of a sudden, WHHHOMP, and he was like lying facedown on this flight of stairs that led up to the stage.

Then the rest of the Ramones pushed him back up and kept on going.

DAVID JOHANSEN: I'm terrible. One time, me and Syl were coming out of Performance Studios, and Monte used to have the Ramones there, rehearsing in the back. We were leaving and we saw the Ramones rehearsing, and we said, "Oh forget it! Give up!"

I'm really terrible. I can't pick 'em. I also remember telling Chris Frantz, the Talking Heads drummer, "You're such a nice kid. What do you want to do this for? You don't stand a chance."

Yeah, I was a real inspiration.

Chapter 20

■ So You Wanna Be (A Rock 'n' Roll Star)

PENNY ARCADE: I was living in Maine and I had come down to the city to visit some people, and Robert Mapplethorpe said, "Look, you can't leave without seeing Patti perform tonight. *Horses* just came out and she's gonna be really big."

He told me she was playing at the Lower Manhattan Ocean Club. So I said, "Okay, I'll go." I knew the Ocean Club was owned by Mickey Ruskin, who had owned Max's, and I knew that I could always walk into Max's, right?

Well I get there, at one o'clock, and there's three thousand people trying to get in. I kinda work my way up to the door, and I get the attention of the door guy, and I go, "Excuse me, I wanna come in." He goes, "Yeah, so do three thousand other people."

I said, "No, you don't understand. I'm an old friend of Patti's. Patti wants me to be here."

He goes, "Yeah, everybody's an old friend of Patti's."

Eventually Mickey Ruskin let me into the Ocean Club. The place was really crowded, and we muscled our way to the front. So I see Lenny Kaye, standing onstage, looking just like he always looks, and there's Patti—she's on her knees, scratching at the guitar, you know, whatever she was doing. I was so excited to see her that I ran to the front and I was going, "Patti Lee! Patti Lee!"

That's what I always called her at that time when I was friends with her. People didn't call her "Patti Lee," so I figured she would know that it was me. But right alongside of me were all these seventeen-year-old kids, and they're all going, "Patti Lee! Patti Lee!"

I was like, "I don't get it."

I was playing music at the time, and I had just bought these new tambourines, that I had with me. The band went into one of these long instrumentals, and Patti was underneath the drums, you know, crawling around in between the drum set and the keyboard player—completely oblivious.

So I jumped up and sat on the back of one of the booths. I started playing my new tambourine, a Turkish metal thing, and it had a really incredible sound. The artist Larry Rivers was sitting in the booth across from me, and this woman who was sitting with him leans over and she goes, "Will you stop doing that? It makes Patti nervous."

I looked at her—Patti was like facedown in the drums—and I said, "It makes Patti nervous? How can you tell?"

But I didn't wanna bug anybody and I hated this bitch, you know? But Lenny Kaye sees me, and he says, into the mike, "I can't believe it, Penny Arcade is back!"

Right, so now I'm somebody. Larry Rivers has turned to me, going, "Whoa!" The set ends, and Patti leaves the stage.

But I don't know if Patti heard Lenny or not, or if she was coked up, but I think she was really flipped out. At any rate, she didn't acknowledge that I was there. The next thing I know, Leee Childers comes up, and he says, "Man, you just show up, and you never say anything to anybody," and blah, blah, blah.

So Leee says to me, "Look, is there anything I can do for you? Is there anything you want?"

I said, "I want to see Patti, but I don't wanna go through any bullshit."

He says, "It's done." So he takes me downstairs, and he's just pushing people out of the way, saying, "This is Penny Arcade, she's a friend of Patti's."

We get to the last door and there's the chick who'd been with Larry Rivers, and she's stretched out across the door and she looks at me—I have my hair in two braids, I'm wearing a flannel shirt and jeans, you know, I live in Maine. And the chick says, "Who are you supposed to be?"

I just went, "I wanna see Patti." Really flat, no emotions—"I wanna see Patti." And Leee goes, "Get the fuck out of the way!" He pushes her out of the way, and we go into this room. It's this cellar, a bare lightbulb hanging down, and there's a table with food on it. And there's clouds of people like mosquitoes. A lot of people down there.

Lenny Kaye says, "Penny!" He comes over, hugs me, and gives me a kiss. He introduces me to his girlfriend and he's going, "Penny introduced me to Patti!"

He was being really nice, and we talked for a few minutes. Then the drummer, Jay Dee Daugherty, comes over and he goes, "Hey, you were the girl playing the tambourine. Man, those tambourines are something, I could hear them over my kit." And he was really nice to me.

As soon as he moved away, this swarm of like seventeen-, eighteen-, nineteen-, and twenty-year-olds, who knows what age—they were young to me, because I was twenty-six—and they're all like, "Who are you?"

I said, "I'm nobody."

They kept saying, "Who are you? You were talking to Lenny Kaye and Jay Dee. Like, who are you? You're somebody, we know you're somebody."

I just said, "No, man, I'm nobody." I said, "Really, you should go talk to somebody else, cause I'm nobody." And they went, "Okay, thanks, man," and they actually went. I couldn't believe it. It was so mercenary, like, "You're not anybody, you can't do anything for us, we're outta here."

I couldn't stand it anymore. I kept looking at this fruit that was on this table of food, and all I could think was, All night long there were rats down here, rats running around and this food has been sitting here. The rats have been crawling on this food.

Finally I see Patti and she's talking to Tom Verlaine. Patti had written me about Tom Verlaine, so I knew about him. So she's talking to him, and she's like talk, talk, talk. I'm standing there, and she knows I'm there.

Finally she walks over, and I think she's come over to talk to me, but this twenty-two-year-old guy grabs her and says, "Listen, Patti, man, I gotta tell you, man, my girlfriend wanted to get in here, man, she's a real fucking star, you know, she's a real star and they wouldn't let her in because she's a star, they know she's a star, and they fucking wouldn't let her in."

And Patti started having a serious conversation with this guy. I couldn't believe it. I'm standing there and she's not talking to me. I couldn't stand it, so I just stepped up and I said, "Patti."

I put my hand out, doing our old thing, which was like the boy handshake. She goes, "Wow, Penny, man, wow man, you look exactly the same, man, you look the same."

I said, "Yeah, so do you."

But I didn't feel any connection. I felt there was a Plexiglas screen up. And she goes, "Man, I gotta get a cigarette, I'll be right back."

So she goes back to talking to Tom Verlaine, and she doesn't come back. She's not coming back. I'm standing there thinking, What the fuck am I doing here? I don't wanna be here.

As soon as I heard it in my head, I went over to Patti and said, "Patti, I'm sorry, I'm gonna split. I really don't want to be here. I just came down to see you."

She said, "Wait a minute, where you going, man? Where you going?"

I said, "Well, I'm gonna split." So Patti goes, "Well, where are you living, man? Are you living in Spain? Or are you living in Maine? Where are you living, man?"

I said, "I'm living in Maine," and she goes, "Aw, Penn, Penny, man, I don't feel so good, I don't feel so good, my stomach hurts."

I put my hand on her stomach, and I said, "What's the matter, Patti?" She was going, "Man, you know . . ."

I looked at her and I suddenly realized who Patti had been—like who she'd been to her friends—she was now using that in this public way. So she couldn't be that to me anymore, because it was now for everyone. And I realized that Patti had sixteen people around her telling her that she was the best thing since sliced bread, and for her to see someone like me, who knew her, she just couldn't see me. And I felt really bad for her. But I still didn't wanna be there.

So I stumble out onto the street and I have no money. I have eight dollars in my pocket, but I've got to use that to get back to Maine, so I flag down a cab, and I say to the cabdriver, "I've gotta go to Fourteenth Street and Seventh Avenue, how much is it gonna cost me?"

He says, "It's gonna cost you like ten dollars." I said, "Well, man, I can't do it. I need the money."

So I'm walking, it's four o'clock in the morning, and all of a sudden this yellow cab swings around, and there's Leee Childers yelling, "Penny, where are you going? Get in."

And I went, "Whoa, man!" You know, like my rescuer, right? So I get in, and there's this girl in the cab—this skinny girl, with this Patti Smith T-shirt on. And she's hysterical, she's like ranting: "I can't believe it, man, I, I, I fucking met Patti, man. I MET PATTI!"

I'm like looking at her, and she won't get out of herself, right? Leee introduces me to her, and he says, "This is Patti and she makes these T-shirts of Patti Smith."

I said, "Oh cool. Great, it's a photo of Patti on a T-shirt."

So Leee says to the girl, "I want you to meet Penny. Penny is a very good friend of Patti Smith's. You want to meet Penny, because she's an old and close friend of Patti's."

I'm thinking, I don't wanna meet this girl. I have no interest in this girl.

And the girl looks at me, and she goes, "Wow, you know Patti? I mean, like, you really *know* her? Like, you know, tell me about her."

I said, "What? Uh, I don't know. What do you want to know, I don't know nothing."

She says, "Man, I met Patti, man, like I *met* Patti!" Now she's crying, right—"I met Patti, and, like, I *met* her, and she, she, she asked *me* what *my* name was, and I, I, I couldn't tell her that *my name* is Patti too, so I just said, 'X.' "

I went, "STOP THE FUCKING CAB! STOP THE CAB!"

Leee was saying, "Where you going?"

I said, "I'm outta here." And I got out and I walked, and I was just like, "Man, what the fuck is going on?"

Chapter 21

■ The Death of the Dolls

DEBBIE HARRY: One day I was over at someone's apartment on Thirteenth Street, and all of a sudden this station wagon pulls up in front of the building, and Malcolm McLaren opens the back tailgate and starts pulling out these rubber dresses and platform shoes and selling them on the street.

And everybody was running down to the street to buy this stuff. Malcolm knew Janice, Johnny Thunders' girlfriend, and she arranged for him to show up. So I guess he knew we were going to be there and we would want to buy this shit, because there was a very limited market in those days for rubber dresses.

I loved his clothes, but I couldn't afford to buy anything. Malcolm was just standing around, muttering, selling his clothes from the tailgate of the car. We didn't know who Malcolm was, but that's the day we found out.

MALCOLM McLAREN: The Dolls had come into my shop several times when they were in London, and they were quite staggered and shocked by the store at that time because it was nothing quite like anything in New York. Nobody in New York was selling rock & roll culture in the form of dress and music, in one particular place.

And the store, Sex, had a definite ideology, it wasn't about selling anything, it was about creating attitude. It wasn't some fucking middle-of-the-road golden oldies shop; far from it.

Maybe about two years after the time they came to England, I started managing the Dolls. It was my raison d'être to exist in New York. I mean, I didn't have a reason to even be there. I went to New York to run away from London. I was just bored, I was just absolutely bored—you know, my eyes were getting wider. I mean, we all escape, half the reason one is bothered to delve into pop culture was in order to get out of England, ha ha ha.

The New York Dolls were an adventure I wanted to have, and see the world through. It was a means of travel. But I caught venereal disease quite early on, which was pretty disgusting, and I thought, "Ooh, New York's a bit dirty."

I carried on and carried on, but all the girls around the New York Dolls were all bloody disease-ridden, and so the naïve fun level suddenly went out. I suddenly got terribly paranoid, and I had to look at them with a different kind of eye. You know, like some sort of clean foreigner thinking, "Fuck me, these people are filthy."

BOB GRUEN: Malcolm made these sets of clothes for everybody in the New York Dolls. David got this gabardine suit, and some of the others wanted patent leather. But everything was in bright red—the whole band was in red.

So Malcolm wanted to have a red party. And he made this big communist flag to put behind the band. And it wasn't really a communist party, it was a red party. But the significance of that was kinda lost on people, because Americans got really excited when you talked about communists.

Malcolm and the band didn't really hit it off in that sense, because Malcolm really wanted to get political, and get people excited on a political level.

MALCOLM MCLAREN: The New York Dolls were fun because they were a fucking bunch of vain bastards, and being such vain bastards, I suppose they clung to that notion of narcissism which was so apparent in the sixties generation—of never ever wanting to grow up. And that very notion of never wanting to grow old—the Dolls emulated that in the form of their transsexual clothing, and their general notion of remaining a doll, a little doll.

So I tried to throw politics into the mill. There was the whole notion of the "politics of boredom," and this whole idea of dressing the Dolls up in red vinyl and throwing them Mao's Red Book—I just loved fucking with that kind of pop-trash culture of Warhol, which was so goddamn Catholic, and so boring, and so pretentiously American, where everything had to be a product, everything had to be disposable.

I thought, Fuck it. I'm gonna try and make the Dolls totally the opposite. I'm not going to make them disposable. I'm going to give them a serious political point of view.

TERRY ORK: I knew that I wanted Television to play with the New York Dolls, and Malcolm McLaren had just signed on as their manager, so we began to look for a venue outside of CBGB's where both bands could play together. Someone suggested the Hippodrome. So then Tom Verlaine and I went to see David Johansen to set up the terms for us playing together, and when we left his loft, Verlaine just said, "Man, did you see him?"

I said, "What?"

Tom said, "He's scared, man. It's all over for them."

I said, "Oh, no. I didn't see that."

But I did see it at the Hippodrome. It was pretty bad—wearing the little red plastic outfits and the hammer and sickle flag behind them. I said, "Uh oh, this is nothing like how I remember the Dolls."

It was just wrong. They just didn't have any energy. They felt embarrassed in their little outfits. They knew they were just trying to do a fad. So I said to Malcolm, "That might work in London, on the King's Road, but not here."

GAIL HIGGINS: We HATED Malcolm. He was putting the Dolls in those red commie-inspired suits and doing the whole political thing, and the Dolls had nothing to do with politics. None of them knew anything about politics. We just thought it was ridiculous.

We went to the show at the Hippodrome and Malcolm was at the door, and Janice and I weren't on the guest list. I yelled at him, "I think you better find out who the Dolls' real friends are!" Then he let us in.

JERRY NOLAN: This fucking around with Malcolm was too artsy-fartsy. He had us dressing up in matching red leather suits and playing in front of a giant communist flag. It was so stupid!

Malcolm caught us at a very vulnerable moment. The limos were long gone. Then Malcolm had booked this horrible string of gigs for us in Florida, in these terrible out-of-the-way clubs, and we weren't happy about it.

EILEEN POLK: The show at the Hippodrome was a success and they decided to do the Red Patent Leather tour of the East Coast. The first date on the tour was in Florida and just before they were going to leave, Malcolm told me, "You know, we're going to have to put Arthur into detox before we go on tour, because we can't go on tour with him like this."

I think Malcolm was happy that Arthur was with me instead of Connie. So they put him in detox for like a month and I talked to him every day, and he was telling me how nice it was to meet all these guys who were sober and how things had changed for him and blah, blah, blah.

BOB GRUEN: I credit Malcolm with saving their lives. He got Johnny and Jerry into rehab programs and he got Arthur into the hospital, because he was alcoholic to the point of falling down in the gutter. Everyone always refers to Malcolm as the manager of the New York Dolls, but it was really just the last few shows that he organized. Because nobody else was doing anything for them.

MALCOLM McLAREN: I was a "Yellow Pages" manager in those days. I really just tried to do my job. Here I am, I'm English, this is the way we do it—"Okay, chap, you've had too much to drink, we'd better get you into this clinic. Okay, Arthur, you report at nine o'clock, I'll be round your house, please be ready, pack a little bag, I'm sending you off for a few weeks, don't worry, it's gonna be fine, I'll visit you every three days and yes, of course I'll send Johnny and David, I'll come personally with them, no problem. Yes, you will have some money, you're only allowed to have a boiled egg a day, and I absolutely want you, from thereafter, dating librarians."

EILEEN POLK: Arthur gets out of the detox, and they're getting ready to leave for the Florida tour, and an hour before Malcolm is going to pick him up, Arthur shows up at my house with a bottle of whiskey. It was really sad because he had just gotten out of the hospital and I just thought, They're going to think I gave it to him and I didn't.

SYL SYLVAIN: We were staying at Jerry Nolan's mother's house in Florida. She had a trailer park that was like a motel. She had six trailers that she rented out like motel rooms. Malcolm brought the Dolls down to stay there and she let us use three of the trailers.

Every night, before the gig, we'd have dinner in Jerry's mom's house, which wasn't a trailer, but a real house. At first it was fun, those first dinners, and during the days we'd go to the army-navy store and all get fucking army gear and shit. We were like little kids, you know, wearing our blue jean jackets, like real short, showing off our belly buttons, with army pants and driving around in the Fury III station wagon that the promoter had rented for us.

But then, after we'd been there a week, it started to drag and drag and drag. It was no longer cool.

JIM MARSHALL: When I was fifteen, the New York Dolls ended up doing a two-week stint in Florida, near where I grew up. It was kind of weird for them to end up down there, because we hadn't heard anything from them for a while. Their second album, *Too Much Too Soon,* came and went. I don't think it sold very much, and it certainly didn't get played on the radio there.

So when they came to Florida, a bunch of us were hanging around them all the time—cause they were from New York and the Stooges never played

Florida and the MC5 were long gone, so they were definitely the only game in town.

But it was obvious that Johnny Thunders and Jerry Nolan had a real dope habit at that point, because they were getting kids in my little crowd to go down to Miami to cop dope for them. Johnny Thunders was just like, "Where do I get drugs?"

Obviously, we all totally worshiped the Dolls. In Florida, if you liked rock & roll, there was only the Allman Brothers and Lynyrd Skynyrd, and I hated that shit. So having the New York Dolls down there was kind of cool, and we were willing to drive to Miami to get them drugs.

They didn't go with us to get the dope, they just kind of sat around the hotel room and waited for us to get back. They'd give us money if they had it—at first they didn't—but when it became obvious that they had to come up with a little bit of money, they were always trying to weasel out of it. The one thing that impressed me was that they were always asking people for their clothes, especially girls. They were like, "I like your shirt. Can I have it?"

PETER JORDAN: Malcolm was goofy. He would say things like, "Oh my gosh!" We went to the beach one time and seeing Malcolm at the beach was HILARIOUS! He was all peachy, all dressed up in these fucking clothes! I said, "Malcolm, you're wearing fucking shoes and socks? We're in Florida on the beach!

Malcolm said, "Oh, Pete, you're gonna burn, son. You're gonna burn."

I said, "Malcolm, it's the fucking beach, you come out here, you put on this fucking cream and you don't get fucking burned."

He said, "Oh no, oh no."

SYL SYLVAIN: Then we'd have to drive in the station wagon into the country to the gig, to some wooden shack—more like a barn than a shack—and there'd be like twenty people there yelling, "Play the Rolling Stones!" So we knew we were not doing too good.

Another problem was that Jerry and Johnny didn't like Malcolm. Jerry used to say, "Oh he's so goofy. He's so goofy!" Malcolm was always goofing around. He was always making jokes with that sort of English humor that no one can understand—let alone two guys on heroin.

Plus Malcolm had that goofy kind of look—sometimes he would wake up with his curly hair all sticking up, with his tasseled pants and shit.

So Jerry and Johnny never took Malcolm seriously, especially Jerry. Jerry could hit Johnny with more sense in those days. Jerry would say to him, "Johnny, look at this guy. This is how we're gonna become like the Beatles, with this schmuck?" And Johnny would think, He's right. This guy's an idiot. They didn't take Malcolm seriously, which was a mistake.

JIM MARSHALL: At first David Johansen was nice to us, but then David and Syl didn't want us around, because we were obviously the source of where the drugs were coming from. Then our friend, the one that used to go into Overtown, in Miami, to get the dope for Johnny and Jerry, got busted. He had to spend two nights in jail, in Miami, which was pretty rough on him. He was, like, fifteen at the time and I think the cops roughed him up. So then nobody wanted to go down to Miami to get dope for Johnny and Jerry, so they quit the band.

JERRY NOLAN: We were having dinner one night, talking about it, when David said, "Anyone in this band can be replaced." That did it. I got up and said, "I'm out." Then Johnny got up and said, "If Jerry's leaving, I am too."

SYL SYLVAIN: Jerry made all the arrangements right then and there, and didn't give a shit about leaving us in his mom's house. Which was kind of screwed up, but fuck it. So Johnny and Jerry walked out.

I didn't realize what was happening. David went to his trailer and crashed out, not even interested in what was going on. Malcolm was saying all this inspirational stuff like, "Come on, boys, let's go! Listen, don't forget who you are!" And Arthur was just coming out of his fog from being in the detox, it was just nice to have him there at all.

So I said, "Okay, they're going. Let's put everything in the car." So Malcolm and I drove Johnny and Jerry to the airport in that station wagon. I gave Johnny his bag and they were walking away, and it finally hit me what was happening, and I turned around and said, "What about the Dolls?"

The only guy that turned around was Jerry Nolan, who said, "Fuck the Dolls."

MALCOLM MCLAREN: I thought they were leaving because they hated the group and thought there was no genuine likelihood of them having success in Tampa.

This, of course, wasn't true at all. They really wanted to get back to New York because it was easier for them to score heroin. I was so naïve.

JERRY NOLAN: Johnny Thunders and I got on a plane and flew back to New York. Even on the plane, Johnny thought it was just one of those threat-type things. I told him, "Johnny, this isn't one of those night fights, and then we wake up in the morning and forget about it. This is definitely serious."

ELIOT KIDD: I knew that the New York Dolls were supposed to be in Florida for another week, so when I saw Johnny and Jerry, I said to them, "What the fuck are you guys doing back?"

They said, "We quit the band."

I thought they were kidding.

I said, "No, really, what happened?" They had to say it three or four times before I started to realize that they were serious.

Then I said, "Oh, you'll make up with those guys!"

They said, "No. We're going to start our own band. We got Richard Hell leaving Television and he's going to play with us."

RICHARD LLOYD: Tom Verlaine kept saying to Richard Hell, "You don't rehearse, all you do is show up at rehearsal and drink, you don't practice at home, I keep telling you I'll come by and help you, but you're not interested, you're just not interested in this!"

Richard didn't have much of a leg to stand on with respect to this and would just sort of look at the floor. Tom had a demo tape of us playing, and said to Hell, "Listen to it, it's not any good, just listen to it." It was pretty obvious that Richard's bass playing was just a mess.

DUNCAN HANNAH: I think Tom was mad because Richard would get too high, you know, show up drunk and stuff. But Richard Hell's thinking was, That's rock & roll. So they just had a very different idea of things. I mean, Hell wasn't a great bass player, plus he was goofy—the way he jumped around and made faces, like he was like something out of a revival show sometimes. I think Tom just thought it was too farcical. And Tom wanted to be cold, cool, right? No jokes.

Verlaine wanted to be Bob Dylan. When they first got together I remember Terry Ork said to me, "Why don't you make a Television fan club?"

And I said, "For what? Thirty people?"

Terry said, "Well, it'll be conceptual. Make it an art project or something."

So I wrote this thing. It was gonna be a newsletter, and Richard Hell came over to my place and read it. He said, "Ah, it's cool, yeah. But now Verlaine wants to meet you in a booth at Max's tonight to talk about it."

So I was thinking, Oh great. I'm like the fifth Television guy now, right? Like the fifth Beatle.

Then Verlaine shows up at Max's and says, "Yeah, I read your thing."

He looks at me and says, "What are you? You get up in the morning and you look in the mirror and go, 'I'm Duncan Hannah, and I'm cute.' Is that what you do?"

I said, "What!?"

Verlaine was just hateful, he just started saying all this hateful stuff. It was real personal, he just kept going on and on about me.

Finally I said, "Didn't you like the thing I wrote?"

He said, "You've got us all wrong. You don't *know* me. Okay? Just remember that: You don't *know* me. You'll never *know* me. You'll never *understand* me."

I said, "Hey, look, I'm not getting paid for this or anything. I mean, Richard Hell liked it."

He said, "Yeah? Well, I'm not Richard."

It went on like this, and then I realized what he was doing. He was practicing his Bob Dylan cruelty, like in the documentary on Dylan, *Don't Look Back*. You know how Dylan is in that, he's just like a killer, right? And Verlaine was grooming himself to be the new Dylan.

Richard Hell apologized. He said, "Oh, I'm sorry. He's an asshole."

I left the booth and went over to Danny Fields, at his booth, with this long face. Danny said, "What's the matter?" I told him and he said, "Musicians are assholes. I told you that. From day one. You should never have done that. He's an asshole."

RICHARD HELL: Verlaine withdrew himself more and more until he saw himself as being superior all the time to everybody and everything—so that he couldn't possibly lose. Tom got horrible, man. He gradually decided that he lived by separate rules from everybody else. And if anything fell apart for him, Tom would just say that he was a misunderstood genius, and that nobody else understood him.

ROBERTA BAYLEY: I was living with Richard Hell when he left Television. Tom Verlaine was just cutting all of Richard's songs out, one by one. Richard used to sing maybe half of the songs in Television; then he was only singing one song, which was "Blank Generation."

Then I believe that Tom suggested, "Let's cut 'Blank Generation.'"

Richard was just like, "What's the point?"

RICHARD LLOYD: Eventually Richard Hell announced he was leaving the band. And Tom Verlaine asked Fred Smith, who was the bass player in Blondie, if he would like to join us, and Fred said yes.

DEBBIE HARRY: Fred Smith fucking quit Blondie. I was pissed. I was pissed at all of them—all of Television, all of the Patti Smith Group, and Patti and Fred. I was pissed at Patti because she talked Fred into joining Television.

Boy, did he make a mistake. Ha ha ha.

RICHARD HELL: I left Television the same week the New York Dolls broke up. Johnny Thunders called me and said, "Me and Jerry have just left the Dolls, do you wanna make a band?"

I didn't know Johnny Thunders very well. I was actually surprised that he'd call me. We'd hung out in the bar, they'd come to see Television, but . . .

So I was surprised when he called, but it was perfect, you know? Because part of the reason I was fed up with Television was because it was getting so pretentious, and going so far from that drive that we had originally. So I thought, This is perfect—we'll make a really good rock & roll band that's dealing with interesting subjects, figuring I would bring in the interesting subjects. Turned out Johnny wanted to sing "Going Steady."

BOB GRUEN: David Johansen came back from Florida and said the band had broken up because John Thunders and Jerry Nolan had to come back to New York to cop dope, and David said to them, "If you have to go home to get drugs in between every show, then I'm not going to do this band." And that was the end of it.

Johnny and Jerry were always trying to get the band back together after that, and never quite understood that David didn't want to travel on the road with people who were addicted to drugs. And that never changed, so the band never got back together.

EILEEN POLK: Arthur Kane called me from Florida and said that Connie had followed him down there and that the only way he could get away from her was to move to L.A. So I said, "Well, if that's what you have to do, then that's what you have to do."

SYL SYLVAIN: On the drive back from the airport, Malcolm started telling me, "Sylvain, don't worry about it. Don't worry, don't worry, don't worry."

So here we had this big Fury III station wagon, and Malcolm and I decided to go to New Orleans. Neither of us had driver's licenses, so we got these girls to drive for us. Malcolm and I sat in the backseat, and his conversations went from "Don't worry about the Dolls" to "Look, I've got these guys that hang out in front of my wife's shop in London, and you know, they'd love to be in a band, and we could put a band together."

At first it was just talk, but then he got more serious about it. "Oh, well, this guy can actually be the singer, I once saw him sing, and this guy could be the . . ."

MALCOLM MCLAREN: Traveling around Louisiana was fun—though I caught more venereal disease, which pissed me off again. I thought this whole fucking country was venereal-ridden, so here I was—lost—with a few bits remaining of the New York Dolls and another dose of venereal disease, trying to get back to New York.

SYL SYLVAIN: Malcolm had crabs. We bought like two bottles of that shit, A-200, and it didn't work. Malcolm was whispering, "I gotta do this before I go home to Vivienne"—you know, Vivienne Westwood, his wife.

I'm going, "Alright, I'll help you, but I got to know exactly what's wrong." Malcolm told me, "Crabs." So we had to put the A-200 on him again. Then he told me, "The clap."

After Malcolm and I got back from New Orleans, we went to CBGB's almost every night. Malcolm would go to see anyone that was anybody, but the person that he loved the most was Richard Hell.

He loved Richard. I mean, right before Malcolm left for England, he gave me a suit to give to Richard. He kept saying, "Now, you won't forget to give that suit to Richard, will you? I love Richard. I think Richard has a lot of talent. Now, don't forget to give Richard . . ."

Malcolm's inspiration from Richard seemed less about ripped clothes and more about poetry and politics.

As a matter of fact, that's why he was so intent on giving Richard that suit. Malcolm thought it would help him improve his image.

MALCOLM MCLAREN: I just thought Richard Hell was incredible. Again, I was sold another fashion victim's idea. This was not someone dressed up in red vinyl, wearing bloody orange lips and high heels. Here was a guy all deconstructed, torn down, looking like he'd just crawled out of a drain hole, looking like he was covered in slime, looking like he hadn't slept in years, looking like he hadn't washed in years, and looking like no one gave a fuck about him.

And looking like he didn't really give a fuck about you! He was this wonderful, bored, drained, scarred, dirty guy with a torn T-shirt.

I don't think there was a safety pin there, though there may have been, but it was certainly a torn and ripped T-shirt. And this look, this image of this guy, this spiky hair, everything about it—there was no question that I'd take it back to London. By being inspired by it, I was going to imitate it and transform it into something more English.

RICHARD HELL: I liked Malcolm because he liked me. I didn't know much about him, but he seemed to be really interested in me. There weren't that many people who gave us any respect, you know?

But I was pretty pissed off when I first heard the Sex Pistols' "Pretty Vacant." Malcolm had stolen that whole attitude from "Blank Generation."

But ideas are free property. I stole shit too.

MALCOLM MCLAREN: Richard Hell was a definite, 100 percent inspiration, and, in fact, I remember telling the Sex Pistols, "Write a song like 'Blank Generation,' but write your own bloody version," and their own version was "Pretty Vacant."

ELIOT KIDD: Frenchie gave Malcolm McLaren two months' rent up front to sublet Malcolm's apartment, and he beat Frenchie for the money.

A bunch of us went looking for Malcolm, but he wasn't home. He was told that a bunch of angry guys had been looking for him, so he left for London the next day.

MALCOLM MCLAREN: I came back to England determined. I had these images that I came back with, it was like Marco Polo, or Walter Raleigh. These are the things I brought back: the image of this distressed, strange thing called Richard Hell. And this phrase, "the blank generation."

Chapter 22

■ Why Don't We Call It Punk?

DEE DEE RAMONE: One night, as I was leaving CBGB's at four in the morning, I walked outside and saw Connie sitting on the hood of a car, filing her nails.

I liked her right away. She was wearing a black evening dress and spiked, high-heel shoes, and she had a bottle of blackberry brandy in her purse. She looked like an ancient vampire countess who was definitely on a mission to capture my soul.

In the morning, I acted like everything was normal. Connie was in a bad mood though and wanted to cop. So did I. So we took a cab to Norfolk Street and bought some dope. She was a prostitute, I was a Ramone, and we were both junkies.

EILEEN POLK: I was with Anya Phillips one of the first nights I went to CBGB's, and Dee Dee Ramone and Joey Ramone and Connie walked in together. Arthur Kane had already fled to California, so Anya said to me, "There's Connie with her new boyfriend. He's in this new band called the Ramones." She was saying it like, "Let's check these guys out."

I hadn't seen the Ramones yet. So like an idiot, I think Joey Ramone is Connie's new boyfriend, because Joey looked like Frankenstein, and Arthur looked like Frankenstein. So I figured that Joey must be Connie's new boyfriend.

A few nights later I was at Ashley's, the bar owned by Alice Cooper's tour manager, and Dee Dee walked in by himself. He was getting drunk, and I was getting drunk, so we just started talking. We'd met at CBGB's, but we hadn't talked. So I said, "What's the story here? I saw you with Connie. Are you going out with her or what?"

Dee Dee said, "Well, you know, she likes me, but you know, she's really with Joey." He was stirring up trouble already. So he said, "I'm going to Mother's, this new bar on Twenty-third Street, to see Blondie. Why don't you meet me there?"

So I meet him at Mother's a few nights later. We had a really good time, and after the night was over, I was walking out, and there was . . . Connie!

I had on one of those seventies halter dresses—there's nothing holding it on but a button in the back of the neck. Connie comes up to me, puts her fingernails in my hair, and rips my dress off. It was the end of the night, so there was like twenty-seven people outside the bar, waiting for taxis. And I'm being mauled by Connie, my dress is ripped off, and I'm naked from the waist up, everything's hanging out, and I can't get her fingers out of my hair.

Her fighting technique was to get her fingernails tied into your hair, then do something, like rip your dress off. She had me. I couldn't move, unless I ripped my hair out. Let me tell you, hair is a very important thing to a young girl. It was a dilemma. I guess I figured it was better to be half-naked than have your hair ripped out.

Anya was going, "Connie, cut it out! Connie, cut it out!" And everybody else was going, "Go for it!"

Of course, Dee Dee was standing there doing nothing, being totally useless. I finally got Connie out of my hair and ran. Anya ran with me and we got a cab. Once we were inside, Anya said, "Oh, that Connie, she's such an asshole!" And then she told me the whole story of how Dee Dee was really living with Connie and that he had bullshitted me.

Of course, then I was really pissed at Connie—she'd already tried to beat me up when I was with Arthur—and now she'd really done it. She'd ripped my dress off in front of everybody, so now it was war—total war—and I decided I was going to steal her boyfriend.

LEEE CHILDERS: The first time I went to CBGB's was with Wayne County. There were six people in the audience. We ate the chili, which, years later, Bebe Buell was horrified to learn. She said, "You ate the chili? Stiv told me the Dead Boys used to go back in the kitchen and jerk off in it."

I said to her, "So what? I've had worse in my mouth."

So the first time I went to CBGB's, we ate chili, which tasted horrible. The whole place stunk of urine. The whole place smelled like a bathroom. And there were literally six people in the audience and then the Ramones went onstage, and I went, "Oh . . . my . . . God!"

And I knew it, in a minute. The first song. The first song. I knew that I was home and happy and secure and free and rock & roll. I knew it from that first song the first time I went to see them. I was the one who called Lisa Robinson and said, "You won't believe what's going on!" and she said, "Oh, what are you talking about? Oh, the Bowery, UGGGGHHHHH!!!"

I said, "Just come."

DANNY FIELDS: I was editing *16* magazine and writing a column in the *SoHo Weekly News*, and I was always gushing about the wonderfulness of Television and how exciting their performances were.

I rarely wrote about the Ramones. I hadn't seen them, I didn't know who they were. I was always writing about Television and Patti Smith. They came first, chronologically, of that bunch. And Johnny Ramone would say to Tommy, "You're supposed to be in charge of publicity. Why doesn't Danny Fields write about us?"

I could just hear it happening. I wasn't there, but I can just imagine the conversations. So Tommy would call me at *16* magazine and say, "Please, why don't you ever write about us?" I always had the feeling that someone was prodding in the background, like he better deliver on this or else. And the Ramones were doing the same thing to Lisa Robinson as they were doing to me. That's when Lisa and I decided to divide up. There was some other band who was harassing both of us at that time and we decided to kill two birds in one night. I would go see the other band and Lisa would see the Ramones. I don't remember the other band, they must have left me cold. The next day Lisa called me up all excited about the Ramones, saying, "Oh, you'll love them. They do songs one minute long and it's very fast and it's all over in less than a quarter of an hour. And it's everything you like and you'll love it. And it's just the funniest thing I've ever seen."

And she was right. I went down to see them at CBGB's, and I got this seat up front with no problems. In those days I don't think anybody packed it in. And they came on and I fell in love with them. I just thought they were doing everything right. They were the perfect band. They were fast and I liked fast. Beethoven quartets are supposed to be slow. Rock & roll is supposed to be fast. I loved it.

I introduced myself to them afterwards and I said, "I love you so much, I'll be your manager."

And they said, "Oh good, we need a new drum set. Do you have money?" I said I was going down to see my mother in Miami. When I got to Miami, I asked my mother for three thousand dollars and she gave it to me. That's how I started managing the Ramones. I bought myself into being their manager.

LEGS McNEIL: When I was eighteen, I was living in New York, working at some hippie film commune on Fourteenth Street, making this horrible movie about a stupid advertising executive who takes acid and drops out and becomes sexually, emotionally, and spiritually liberated. It was just crap.

This was 1975, and the idea of taking acid and dropping out was just so lame—like ten years too late. And the hippie film commune was just as lame. I hated hippies.

Anyway, summer came, and I went back to Cheshire, Connecticut, where I grew up, and made this Three Stooges comedy—sixteen millimeter, black and white film—with two high school friends of mine, John Holmström and Ged Dunn.

John Holmstrom was a cartoonist, and Ged Dunn was a business guy, so at the end of the summer we decided we were going to work together. We had all worked together before when we were in high school—Holmstrom had put together this theater group called the Apocalypse Players, which was Eugène Ionesco meets Alice Cooper. We even had the police close down one of our shows when I missed throwing a pie and hit somebody in the audience.

But when John and Ged and I regrouped, it was kind of undetermined just what we were going to do—films, comics, some sort of media thing.

Then one day we were riding in the car, and John said, "I think we should start a magazine."

All summer we had been listening to this album Go Girl Crazy by this unknown group called the Dictators, and it changed our lives. We'd just get drunk every night and lip-sync to it. Holmstrom had found the record. He was the one who really followed rock & roll. He was the one who turned Ged and I on to the Velvet Underground, Iggy and the Stooges, and the New York Dolls. Up until then I just listened to Chuck Berry and the first two Beatles records, and Alice Cooper.

But I hated most rock & roll, because it was about lame hippie stuff, and there really wasn't anyone describing our lives—which was McDonald's, beer, and TV reruns. Then John found the Dictators, and we all got excited that something was happening.

But I didn't understand why Holmstrom wanted to start a magazine. I thought it was a stupid idea.

John said, "But if we have a magazine, people will think we're cool and stuff and want to hang out with us."

I didn't get it. Then he said, "If we had a magazine, we could drink for free. People will give us free drinks."

That got me. I said, "Okay, then let's do it."

Holmstrom wanted the magazine to be a combination of everything we were into—television reruns, drinking beer, getting laid, cheeseburgers, comics, grade-B movies, and this weird rock & roll that nobody but us seemed to like: the Velvets, the Stooges, the New York Dolls, and now the Dictators.

So John said he wanted to call our magazine *Teenage News,* after an unreleased New York Dolls song. I thought it was a stupid title, so I told him that. And he said, "Well, what do you think we should call it?"

I saw the magazine Holmstrom wanted to start as a Dictators album come to life. On the inside sleeve of the record was a picture of the Dictators hanging out in a White Castle hamburger stand and they were dressed in black leather jackets. Even though we didn't have black leather jackets, the picture seemed to describe us perfectly—wise guys. So I thought the magazine should be for other fuck-ups like us. Kids who grew up believing only in the Three Stooges. Kids that had parties when their parents were away and destroyed the house. You know, kids that stole cars and had fun.

So I said, "Why don't we call it *Punk?*"

The word "punk" seemed to sum up the thread that connected everything we liked—drunk, obnoxious, smart but not pretentious, absurd, funny, ironic, and things that appealed to the darker side.

So John Holmstrom said, "Okay. Well, I'm gonna be the editor." Ged said, "I'm gonna be the publisher." They both looked at me and said, "What are you gonna do?" I said, "I don't know." I had no skills.

Then Holmstrom said, "You can be the resident punk!" And they both started laughing hysterically. Ged and John were both like four years older than me. And I think half the reason they hung out with me was because I was always getting drunk and into trouble and Holmstrom found it constantly amusing. So it was decided I would be a living cartoon character, like Alfred E. Neuman was to *Mad* magazine. And Holmstrom changed my name from Eddie to Legs.

It's funny, but we had no idea if anybody besides the Dictators were out there. We had no idea about CBGB's and what was going on, but I don't think we cared. We just liked the idea of *Punk* magazine. And that was all that really mattered.

MARY HARRON: I met Legs when I was working as the cook for Total Impact, the hippie film commune on Fourteenth Street. Legs came in and was the only one who said this movie sucks and these people are crazy. So I asked him what he was doing. Legs said he was just doing some part-time work on the movie, and he asked me what I did. I said I wanted to be a writer and he said, "We're starting a magazine. It's called *Punk.*"

I thought, What a brilliant title! I don't know why it seemed so brilliant, because this was before there was punk, but it was obviously so ironic.

I mean there was something in it, you know, because if somebody said that they're starting a magazine, you think, Oh, a literary magazine. But

The poetess: Patti Smith waiting for the Lexington Avenue subway, 1971.
© *Gerard Malanga.*

From out of the ruins of the Dolls and Television: The Heartbreakers onstage at CBGB's, 1975. Left to right: Walter Lure, Jerry Nolan, Richard Hell, Johnny Thunders. *Photo by Bob Gruen.*

The original Ramones on the subway. Left to right: Dee Dee, Joey, Tommy, and Johnny, 1975. *Photo by Bob Gruen.*

Free hamburgers: Iggy relaxes at the house on Torrenson Drive, Hollywood Hills, California. *Photo by Leee Black Childers.*

Outside the "Punk Dump": *Punk* magazine founders, from left to right: John Holmstrom, Legs McNeil, and Ged Dunn. *Photo by Tom Hearn.*

Iggy Pop and Debbie Harry.
Photo by Bob Gruen.

Impresario in training:
Malcolm McLaren.
Photo by Bob Gruen.

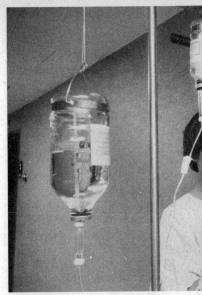
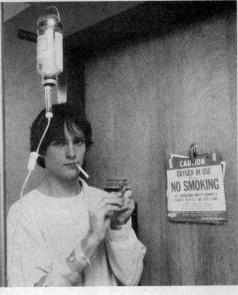

Richard Lloyd, Beth Israel
Hospital, 1978. © *Photo by
Godlis.*

Terry Ork, New York City,
1970. © *Gerard Malanga.*

Boys' night out: Iggy Pop and David Bowie at a Patti Smith concert at the Lower Manhattan Ocean Club. From left to right: Nancy Spungen, Iggy Pop, David Bowie, and Lisa Robinson. *Photo by Bob Gruen.*

Ex-boyfriends on a bad night: Sable Starr with Johnny Thunders and Iggy Pop at CBGB's. *Photo by Bob Gruen.*

"He looked like he didn't care": Richard Hell. © *Stephanie Chernikowski.*

Gyda Gash at the Johnny Blitz Benefit. © *Stephanie Chernikowski.*

John Cale, Patti Smith, and Lou Reed at the Bottom Line, after Patti's show, December 1975. (Note Rachel and Richard Sohl in the background.) *Kate Simon/Sygma.*

Patti Smith and William Burroughs, December 30, 1975. *Kate Simon/Sygma.*

Portrait of the artist as an Amos Poe movie star: Duncan Hannah. *Kate Simon/Sygma.*

Lester Bangs: Last of the white niggers. At William Burroughs's apartment, 77 Franklin Street, December 30, 1975. *Kate Simon/Sygma.*

Punk, it was so funny, bratty—it was so unexpected—and I thought, Well, that's really great. So I said, "Oh, I'll write for you," even though I didn't know what it was about.

A few nights later I was in the kitchen of the horrible film commune, I was washing the floor, being a Cinderella, and doing the dishes. Legs and John came in and said they were going to go to CBGB's and I thought, Okay.

We all went to CBGB's to hear the Ramones and that was the night everything happened.

LEGS MCNEIL: We talked our way into CBGB's, and then we were walking down the length of the bar, when I saw this guy with really short hair and sunglasses sitting at a table and I recognized him as Lou Reed. Holmstrom had been playing Lou Reed's *Metal Machine Music* for weeks. That was Lou's two-album set of nothing but feedback. It was awful, just noise, which Holmstrom loved and proclaimed the ultimate punk album. We were always having big fights about John playing the record: "Come on, take off that shit!" That's how I knew who Lou Reed was.

So when I spotted Lou at the table, I went up to Holmstrom and said, "Hey, there's that guy you're always talking about. Maybe we should interview him too?" I was thinking, you know, as long as we were there. So I went up to Lou and I said, "Hey, we're gonna interview you for our magazine!" You know like, "Aren't you thrilled?" I had no idea of what we were doing. Then Holmstrom said to Lou, "Yeah, we'll even put you on the cover!" Lou just turned around, real deadpan, and said, "Oh, your circulation must be fabulous."

MARY HARRON: I was horrified when Legs and John went up to Lou Reed and told him they wanted to interview him. I thought, Oh my god, what are they doing?

Because Lou was a famous person and I thought, Oh that's so rude. What do they think is going to happen?

I think I was in awe of Lou much more than John or Legs were. I knew quite a lot about Andy Warhol, because I'd had a complete Warhol obsession, and I was a fan of the Velvet Underground. So I was cringing.

LEGS MCNEIL: Just as we were talking to Lou Reed the Ramones hit the stage and it was an amazing sight. Four really pissed-off guys in black leather jackets. It was like the Gestapo had just walked into the room. These guys were definitely not hippies.

Then they counted off a song—"ONE, TWO, THREE, FOUR!"—and we were hit with this blast of noise, you physically recoiled from the shock of it, like this huge wind, and before I could even get into it, they stopped.

Apparently they were all playing a different song. The Ramones had a mini-fight onstage. They were just so thoroughly disgusted with each other that they threw down their guitars and stomped off the stage.

It was amazing. It was like actually seeing something come together. Lou Reed was sitting at the table laughing.

JOEY RAMONE: That was the first night we met Lou Reed. Lou kept telling Johnny Ramone that he wasn't playing the right kind of guitar, that he should play a different kind of guitar. It didn't go over so favorably with Johnny. I mean when John found his guitar he didn't have much money—he bought his guitar for fifty dollars. And Johnny liked the idea of the Mosrite because nobody else used a Mosrite—so this would be his sort of trademark. So Johnny thought Lou was a real jerk.

LEGS McNEIL: Then the Ramones came back, counted off again, and played the best eighteen minutes of rock & roll that I had ever heard. You could hear the Chuck Berry in it, which was all I listened to, that and the Beatles second album with all the Chuck Berry covers on it. When the Ramones came offstage we interviewed them, and they were like us. They talked about comic books and sixties bubble-gum music and were really deadpan and sarcastic.

I really thought I was at the Cavern Club in 1963 and we had just met the Beatles. Only it wasn't a fantasy, it wasn't the Beatles, it was *our* band—the Ramones. But we couldn't hang out with them that long, because we had to go interview Lou Reed, who was old, and snotty, and like someone's cranky old drunken father.

MARY HARRON: We all went off to the Locale and none of us had any money and we couldn't order food. I remember Lou Reed ordered a cheeseburger because I was so hungry. Lou was with Rachel, who was the first transvestite I'd ever met. Very beautiful, but frightening. But I mean definitely a guy: Rachel had stubble.

Legs and John were chatting with Lou so I sat next to Rachel, and I asked her what her name was—him, what his name was—and he said, "Rachel."

I thought, Right. That kind of shut me up for a bit. I think I actually sort of tried to make conversation with him, but Rachel wasn't talkative. I think that was the sum total of our conversation.

I was quite startled because of the way Legs and John would ask the questions. It was quite amateurish. They would ask, "What kind of hamburgers do you like?" Like student journalism, and I thought, Oh god, who are these guys? What are they doing? What are you asking these stupid questions for?

Then Lou Reed started showing some of his famous nastiness. He was mean to Legs. Very mean. And I was very upset by that, actually. I thought he was quite devastating really. But Legs and John didn't seem to mind.

But the night was very exciting, you know—seeing the Ramones, meeting Lou Reed . . . I remember thinking, Oh my god, wait till I tell people back home I've met Lou Reed! That was really going through my head—Wait until I tell people . . .

But then, somehow, because of Lou lashing out or getting bored or whatever, it had ended on this rather sour note. Lou started getting so hostile. I can't remember why. He got very mad at Legs, he just hated him.

But when we got out in the street, John Holmstrom was jumping around being ecstatic and I was thinking, I don't really understand this. Why he's so happy?

I couldn't understand why he was so excited, ecstatic. Because what did we get? Lou Reed being rude to us really.

LEGS MCNEIL: Holmstrom kept jumping up and down, saying, "We got Lou Reed for the cover! We got Lou Reed for the cover!" I didn't know what he was so excited about. I just said, "Yeah, but did you see that chick he was with?"

MARY HARRON: When I finished writing the Ramones article it was late and I still had no money, so I walked that night all the way across town to deliver the article to the "Punk Dump," the *Punk* magazine office on Tenth Avenue. It must have been ten avenues—you know, one side of the city to the other.

It was *Taxi Driver* time, you know, steam coming out of the manholes. It was really a beautiful kind of weird New York night—and the Punk Dump was an incredible place. It looked like something out of *Batman*. It was a storefront under the train tracks on Tenth Avenue with the windows painted black—like a cave. So I found the door and the light was on and John Holmstrom was there at his desk, his glasses on, and he was doing the artwork for the cover, for the Lou Reed interview—the first issue of *Punk*.

He showed it to me, and it was a *cartoon!* I read the Lou Reed interview quickly, and I could see that everything that was humiliating, embarrassing, and stupid had been turned to an advantage. And that's when I knew that *Punk* was going to work.

LEGS MCNEIL: The next thing we did was go out and plaster the city with these little posters that said, "WATCH OUT! PUNK IS COMING!" Everyone who saw them said, "Punk? What's punk?" John and I were laughing. We were like, "Ohhh, you'll find out."

DEBBIE HARRY: John Holmstrom and his living cartoon creature, Legs McNeil, were two maniacs running around town putting up signs that said, "Punk is coming! Punk is coming!" We thought, Here comes another shitty group with an even shittier name.

JAMES GRAUERHOLZ: I was living at the Bunker, John Giorno's loft at 222 Bowery, which became William Burroughs' home in New York City. I'd had an affair with William, and when that ended I started working for him. But at that time William was not as well known. I mean, he was the world-famous William Burroughs, but only a tiny minority knew anything about who that was. William was kind of considered to be a little bit of a has-been in some ways. He was revered, but his works had gone out of print. So I began to see myself as the impresario of William and we began to see ourselves as kind of a symbiotic partnership.

In late 1975, I used to go to Phoebe's a lot. Phoebe's was the off-off-Broadway theater hangout, a restaurant up the street from the Bunker. Phoebe's was a real mainstay. So on my little route from the Bunker to Phoebe's, I would pass these street poles, right outside my house, with posters glued up: "PUNK IS COMING!"

And I loved it, from the first moment I saw that sign I thought, PUNK IS COMING! I thought, What is this gonna be? A band or what?

But "PUNK!"—I loved it, because it meant to me a derisory word for a young, no-count piece a shit. And then from Burrough's *Junky*—you know, there's that great scene where William and Roy, the sailor, are rolling the lushes in the subway and there's two young punks. They cross over and they give Roy a lot of shit and Roy says, "Fucking punks think it's a joke. They won't think it's so funny when they're doing five twenty-nine on the island." You know, five months and twenty-nine days.

"Fucking punks think it's a joke."

So I knew that punk was a direct descendant of William Burroughs' life and work. And I said, "We've gotta put these two things together for the benefit of all parties." And that's what I did.

WILLIAM BURROUGHS: I always thought a punk was someone who took it up the ass.

Chapter 23

■ Chinese Rocks

PHILIPPE MARCADE: Some girl walked up to me at Mother's, and I was wearing one of those Indian scarves, and she said, "Wow, that's just like Keith Richards'!"

She took my scarf and put it around her neck. After a while I was asking for it back, and then she introduced herself. She told me, "I have some dope, but I don't really know how to shoot up, so if you shoot me up, I'll turn you on." So we went to her house on Twenty-third Street, and it turned out that she only had like a half a dime bag. There was no way I was gonna get high on that, so I said, "No point in me doing it."

But I did shoot her up and that's how I became friends with Nancy Spungen.

ELIOT KIDD: The first two times I met Nancy Spungen, I slept with her. She started talking to me at Max's and I said to myself, This is not going to happen.

But you couldn't shake her. I mean, Nancy was a fucking pain in the ass. I think our scene was probably the first scene where guys and girls hung out as friends, equally. Even so, Nancy was a whiner. I mean, it was hard to like her. We used to sit up and make jokes about her. She'd always come over to my apartment, she wanted to cop, and she'd just keep bugging me until I said yes.

RICHARD LLOYD: About that time, it was getting very, very popular to be a junkie on the Lower East Side. In the morning you would see people lined up, like for a hit movie—in a line fifty feet deep—with people that sold the dope running up and down the line saying, "Have your money ready, we'll be open in ten minutes." You know, "No singles, you gotta have fives or tens."

And they would have a menu, like, "Today we have brown dope, white dope, and cocaine." You know, "Got somethin' special today, you're all gonna be real happy."

I mean, you'd be talking to your neighbor, like reading the newspaper, waiting for the dope house to open. It wasn't sleazy, drooling, sick people—it was sculptors, painters, mailmen, dishwashers, waiters, waitresses, and musicians. Totally normal. And I used to like to go between sets—run out and do dope and come back.

PHILIPPE MARCADE: Sometimes it was very scary copping at the dope house—you'd go to these abandoned buildings, you'd go in, it was completely dark, and you'd climb a stairway where half the steps were missing. You can't see ANYTHING at all, complete darkness, then you'd get to the landing and there'd be one candle on each floor.

You'd climb two or three stories, then suddenly, BAAM, you'd run into someone—there's all these people—there's now a line of two hundred people going up the stairs. So you'd wait in line in complete darkness, while some motherfucker would say, "Stay in line!"

Everybody would be real quiet, because they wanted their dope. When you finally got to the top of the stairs, there would be a guy behind the door. There'd just be a little hole in the door. You'd put your money in the hole, and say the initial, C or D, if you wanted either coke or dope.

Then you'd get a little bag back, and get the fuck outta there, hoping they'd say, "Green light." That meant you could walk out, there was no cops on the street. If they said, "Red light," then you had to stay in there and that was really scary, but it wasn't until years later I realized that was a big part of the rush.

RICHARD LLOYD: Richard Hell and I went to cop once and got caught by the police, who pushed us into a building and wanted to strip-search us. They found a needle on Hell and said, "Where'd this come from?"

Richard said, "I'm an antique-needle collector."

Then he proceeded to tell them he was a masochist and all the holes in his arms were there because he liked them. He was like, "You got a problem with that? I stick things into myself. I know I'm sick."

So they just took our heroin and let us go. After the cops left, Hell was like, "Goddamn those fucking cops, they only wanted our dope, now we have to cop again—and we don't even have a syringe!"

RICHARD HELL: The junk scene was just like the sex, it was all a lark. I mean, it still had this "nice" taint of the forbidden, yet at the same time nobody really thought of it as dangerous.

You knew that technically, even if you got a habit, all you had to do was stop using for two weeks, and it would be gone. That's the way you looked at it. And you thought you could maintain that kind of approach to it for four or five years before you were in too deep. It was just like fun, but you know, it was *so* much fun that it definitely accelerated. Things go better with dope!

ARTURO VEGA: I didn't like dope. I didn't like it at all, but I did it a couple times with Dee Dee. The first time he shot me up, I couldn't move. I couldn't get up. And I felt like throwing up. I was so drowsy and sick and I was talking like you hear junkies talk in the street.

Dee Dee said to me, "Oh, I can tell you're really high, I can tell by your voice, I wish I was talking like you're talking, that means you're really feeling good."

I said, "Oooh dear, oh no, I caaan't, oh, I can't get up, Dee Dee."

Dee Dee was like, "Oh great!" Ha ha ha.

I was like, "No, I wanna vomit."

Another time we did it, he did me first and then he did himself, and then he started turning blue. I got really scared. Dee Dee asked me, "Do you think that something is happening to me?"

I said, "I don't *know*, Dee Dee. *You* should know better than *me!*"

He wasn't unconscious or anything, but I could see his skin turning rubbery and getting bluish and I freaked. I was like, "Oh my god!"

PAM BROWN: The first time I saw the Ramones at CBGB's and saw Joey Ramone, I said, "This is the guy for me!" I fell madly in love with Joey. I just packed my bags and moved right in with him. Dee Dee and Connie lived in the bed by the window, and Joey and I would be in bed every night with the covers over our heads hoping nothing hit us, because Dee Dee and Connie would be fighting.

Connie was really nuts. I would walk over to CBGB's with Connie and the next thing I knew she'd be dragging me out of there, hailing a cab, and she'd have ripped off three pocketbooks from poor punk girls! Hops in a cab, goes through the purses—you know, she was really nuts.

ARTURO VEGA: I let Connie and Dee Dee and Joey Ramone move in my loft on Second Street. Joey wasn't a problem. Joey was great. We got along real well. And I liked Connie. She used to call me "Oh Arturo, my hate" instead of "Oh Arturo, my love." She would say, "I could hate you, but I can't."

She'd say that because I used to tell Connie the truth. I'd say, "Connie, you're too old. You know if Dee Dee has any success, he's gonna leave you." Ha ha ha. I'd say, "You should stop doing drugs, maybe then you'll have a chance. Maybe that would create a real bond between the two of you. But even so, he'll probably dump you anyway, you know, because you're too old."

But Dee Dee didn't last here very long because Connie and him were fighting a lot. I couldn't take any of that. I came back from a show one night and Connie had freaked out, they had had a fight, and they had thrown my jars of paint at each other. There was paint all over the place, and they had burned the floor with candles, so I told Dee Dee he had to move.

RICHARD HELL: Me and Dee Dee hung out for a year or two, mostly to cop dope. You could get a bag of dope for three bucks. That's what the standard price was. We'd cop on the corner of Twelfth Street and Avenue A. There was a crowd of about ten or twenty Puerto Rican children, about the age of thirteen, who were the runners. So we'd give them three bucks and they'd bring back a bag.

I felt an immediate affinity with the Ramones. I dug them and didn't have any reservations about them. They were just the way they always were. Lisa Robinson hired me to write about them in *Hit Parader*—the first article about them that was ever published nationally. All their songs were two minutes long, and I asked them the names of all their songs. They had maybe five or six at the time: "I Don't Wanna Go Down in the Basement," "I Don't Wanna Walk Around with You," "I Don't Wanna Be Learned, I Don't Wanna Be Tamed," and "I Don't Wanna" something else.

And Dee Dee said, "We didn't write a positive song until 'Now I Wanna Sniff Some Glue.'"

They were just perfect, you know?

But Dee Dee was the only one of the Ramones that I could ever hang out with. I didn't ever become good enough friends with any of the other ones to know much about what they were like. Except that Johnny was serious about his baseball cards, and Joey was into his English singers, and Tommy was a serious producer guy.

It was pretty obvious that Dee Dee was madcap. He was so funny. Dee Dee was one of these guys who was really wide-eyed dumb. But his dumbness was so smart that you never really knew how much of it was his style of dealing with the world. He played it. Everything he said was really on the money and funny.

EILEEN POLK: I was really attracted to Dee Dee Ramone because he was in a band, and I liked going out with guys in bands. I mean, he was really cute. He was adorable, but I'm sure there was a part of me that just wanted to create chaos—to steal Dee Dee away from Connie.

It was a good drama, and I had the perfect excuse for doing it. Because if Connie had come to me and said, "That's my boyfriend," I might have stayed away from him.

But because she beat me up, I felt like I had full license to ruin her life. She ripped my dress off and she embarrassed me. So the next time we ran into Connie, I beat the shit out of her.

Dorian Zero, Dee Dee, and I were all getting drunk at this bar on the corner of Eleventh Street and Sixth Avenue. Dorian left. It was just me and Dee Dee—and then Connie showed up!

I don't know how the fuck she knew where we were; she just had this radar and could just find Dee Dee wherever he was. So she came into the bar and she said, "Oh, Dee Dee, I just wanted to tell you that I'm really happy that you two are together and I still love you, but we can be friends and blah blah blah." Then she left.

So I said, "Dee Dee, she's waiting for us outside." And he said, "No, no, no, she wouldn't do that."

And of course she was. We came walking out of the bar, Connie came running over and started cursing at Dee Dee. He was drunk out of his mind, and Connie pushed him. He hit his head against the grille of a big old car, a Cadillac, and then hit his head again on the pavement. He was knocked out cold.

So I thought, I'm going to have to win this fight, or I'm going to get really hurt. So I didn't hold back, because the first fights we had, I held back because there were other people around who I thought would protect me. But this time there was nobody. Dee Dee was knocked out on the ground.

So I beat the shit out of Connie.

I just got her down on the ground and started punching and kicking her. I wouldn't let her get up. Once she was down, I made sure she was down. And I made sure she didn't touch my hair. Once I got her down, I knew if I just kept kicking her and punching her, if I just kept her from getting up, I'd be okay. So I beat her up, and I was really happy I did—and Dee Dee and I managed to get away.

The only thing Dee Dee ever said about it, the next day, was, "It's really bad to get knocked out like that when you're drinking. You can lose the oxygen supply to your head." I said, "Yeah, right, Dee Dee."

RICHARD HELL: Dee Dee called me one day and said, "I wrote a song that the Ramones won't do." He said, "It's not finished. How about I come over and show it to you and we can finish it if you like it?" So I believe he brought an acoustic guitar over. And I had my bass. Basically the song was done, but he just didn't have another verse. I wrote two lines. That's all. It was basically Dee Dee's song, though I think the lyrics, the verses I wrote, were good.

DEE DEE RAMONE: The reason I wrote that song was out of spite for Richard Hell, because he told me he was gonna write a song better than Lou Reed's "Heroin," so I went home and wrote "Chinese Rocks."

I wrote it by myself, in Debbie Harry's apartment on First Avenue and First Street. Then Richard Hell put that line in it, so I gave him some credit.

ARTURO VEGA: The Ramones talked about "Chinese Rocks" and didn't want to play it because Tommy Ramone said, "No drugs. Nothing about drugs. That's not a Ramones song. Give it to somebody else."

RICHARD HELL: The controversy about that song comes from the fact that we played it in the Heartbreakers. I brought it to the next rehearsal, exactly as it was done by the Heartbreakers for all those years. I would sing it because it was a song I brought in, and it became famous in New York.

But after I left the Heartbreakers, they kept playing "Chinese Rocks" and then ended up recording it. And they put all of their names on it, though nothing had changed about the song—they just added their names to it. Johnny Thunders did have great songwriting instincts. He always had the greatest touches and the most catchy kind of ideas, but he had nothing to do with "Chinese Rocks" at all.

JERRY NOLAN: The Heartbreakers were still trying to get it together. But then Richard Hell started getting unhappy. In the beginning, Richard thought he would be the front man. He had a special style, but he just couldn't overpower Johnny. It got so that Richard actually had the nerve and really thought that we would get rid of Johnny. I just fucking laughed. I said, "Richard, I'm sorry, buddy, but do you really think I would leave Johnny for you? You're the one who will have to leave."

RICHARD HELL: It did start chafing at me, how moronic the songs the Heartbreakers wrote were. They sounded good, but you know, it's like "Goin' steady, can't keep my eyes off you—Can't keep my eyes ON you." I couldn't figure out what it meant.

ROBERTA BAYLEY: It didn't help the Heartbreakers that Richard was going out with Sable, who was Johnny Thunders' big girlfriend from the New York Dolls days. I'm sure it was no accident on Sable's part that Johnny breaks up with her and then she starts going out with the guy in his band. And I think Richard was into having this "rock star girlfriend."

SABLE STARR: I was really still fucked-up over Johnny Thunders. It took me a long time to get it together. I met Keith Richards and it was really weird. It took a great person like him to show me what a great person I was. He's such a beautiful person.

I was in Atlanta with Keith and I had money and I wanted to come to New York to see what was going on. I was also curious about Johnny—I hadn't seen him for a year. He called me the first night I was here and said, "Do you wanna go out with me?"

It could have been heavy, but I was in such a neat place. I knew who I was—I was with Keith Richards, not him.

So I went out with Johnny, and he introduced me to Richard Hell—and I fell in love with Richard and moved in with him.

EILEEN POLK: I really didn't want Dee Dee doing dope because of Connie, because I just figured that was her way back into his life. And I wasn't going to tell him he couldn't do it, but every once in a while he'd try to stop. And he did stop a few times, but he always went back to it. He'd stay off it a couple of weeks, but Connie would always be waiting for him with a big pile of dope in her pocket. That's how she'd get him.

DEE DEE RAMONE: Connie was very naughty, she had a thing about knives and broken bottles and she'd just go at anyone if she was in the wrong mood, and one night she went after me.

Nancy Spungen used to live on Twenty-third street. I was with her one night, and Connie came there and found me in bed with Nancy. So Connie stabbed me because I was fucking Nancy.

But Connie didn't give a shit cause she just stole Nancy's collection of silver dollars and sold them to get some dope. Connie just said, "Lets go get high."

I said, "Alright."

So we left Nancy there.

DANNY FIELDS: I loved the drama between Dee Dee and Connie. That's what boys and girls are supposed to do; stab each other, sure. I mean, you're not supposed to die, but short of dying—or missing a gig—it's alright.

DEE DEE RAMONE: Connie might have brought me close to death a lot of times, but in a way, she kept me alive. No one else did. I had all that responsibility—I had to play every night—and no one gave a damn if I had a place to live, or if I had any dope, or if I had anything to eat.

Connie did. She was all I had.

Chapter 24

■ Metallic KO

WAYNE KRAMER: When the MC5 broke up in 1972, we all lost each other. It was like losing your brothers—we were schoolboys together, we started out together, and we'd all been through the fire together. In the end, when the band broke up it was so painful and so ugly that nobody talked to one another. Nobody was friends anymore.

So I just packed up my guitar and went to the dope house, because the dope kills the pain, and I didn't have to deal with anything. Of course, when you got that kind of pain, it opens the door for all kinds of funky behavior.

I became a criminal after the band broke up. I was doing burglaries, dealing, and fencing TVs, guns, and drugs. I mean, in seventy-two, seventy-three, and seventy-four, there was really no music scene in Detroit to speak of. It was brutal. The automobile industry started to go downhill, so there wasn't any clubs, so if I went out and robbed two or three houses a night, I was a star again.

I had this hole that had to get filled, from the loss of my band, so I filled it up with dope and crime. But if you're putting the money in a hole in your arm, there's never enough money, so you always gotta find a new scam, you know?

Around this time, Iggy came to town, and I remembered he owed me a couple hundred bucks from our failed dope business. So I went backstage at one of his gigs in Ann Arbor and said, "Look, you owe me this money, you know?"

Iggy said, "What, what do you mean?"

I said, "You remember, from our business deal?"

So he says, "Oh, yeah, right, but you wanna cop?"

I said, "Yeah, sure, tomorrow, when you play in Detroit, man. I'll get the dope, and I'll meet you at the hotel afterwards."

The next night I went to the hotel and I brought this dude with me, because I was worried about Scotty Asheton—you know, I thought I might need to neutralize Scotty when I took the money from Iggy.

Iggy collected all this money from the band—it was about two hundred bucks—so they could get the dope, and he said, "Okay, you wanna do it here?"

I said, "No, let's go down in the street," and we went down in the street. He gave me the money and I counted it, then said, "Well, this means we're even."

He said, "We're even?"

I said, "Yeah, you owe me this, man."

He said, "You mean there's no dope?"

I said, "No, man."

Iggy started crying, and my backup guy saw Iggy crying and went over and gave him a hug, saying, "It's alright, man. Don't worry, it's just drugs. Don't worry about it, brother." I'm certainly not proud of it, but I needed the money.

BEBE BUELL: The last time Iggy and I were together I went with him to Washington, on the train, where he was playing at Constitution Hall. It was really a prestigious date and I brought this girl with me, and she brought some of that drug that almost killed me—that PCP stuff, elephant tranquilizer. She gave me a line of it once and told me it was coke and I almost died. It was really horrible—I saw angels coming to get me, and they all had guitars. No, I'm telling the truth, it was a hallucination and the angels all had guitars. I really thought I was dying.

So I did not like this girl. I didn't want her to come, but she came anyway. I found out later it was because she had arranged to bring some of that drug—she kept it from me because she knew I would flush it down the toilet.

Iggy and the Stooges were all hanging out in the hotel room and this girl breaks out the drug. I knew immediaely that it was *that* drug, so I got really, really upset. I went down to James Willimson's room and said, "Man, she brought that shit and if Iggy does that he's never gonna be able to do the show."

My mother was even coming to see him that night, because he was great then, he was his best—when he wasn't stoned. But I knew if he did some of this drug, that there'd be no way there'd be a performance. I knew it. I was really scared.

The first thing James Williamson said to me was, "You should have called me—you shouldn't have left him alone in the room with her, because no doubt he's done it already."

I went back to the room, and sure enough, Iggy had done an elephant line—you know, a line for seventy-five people. Sure enough. We get over to

Chapter 28

■ London Calling

LEEE CHILDERS: I started managing the Heartbreakers after Richard Hell left. Johnny Thunders called me and said, "Do you want to help us out? We need to find a bass player, we need to get a gig, we need to get rolling again very quickly."

So I called my friend Tony Zanetta, who was a huge fan, and I said, "Will you be my partner in managing the Heartbreakers?"

Tony said, "Are you crazy? It's one thing to sit in the audience and say how fabulous they are, and how they're the most brilliant rock & roll band ever, but it's a whole other thing to get involved with them. They're junkies! Are you nuts?!"

And I thought, Well, that takes care of that. I'm gonna do it.

JERRY NOLAN: After Richard Hell left, the Heartbreakers stuck it out. We got Walter Lure in on guitar and Billy Rath on bass. Johnny and I were heavy into drugs then. After the Dolls, we went at it all the way. Everything we did was based around drugs. There would be no rehearsal without drugs. Everything we did, we had to do drugs first.

LEEE CHILDERS: The phone rang. It was Malcolm McLaren. He said, "Do you want to come and do a tour with my band, the Sex Pistols?"

I'd never heard of them, so I said, "Well, yes. But I'll have to call you back."

Then I called Johnny Thunders and I said, "You want to go to England and do a tour with Malcolm McLaren and some band called the Sex Pistols?"

He hadn't heard of the Sex Pistols either, but he said, "Well, you remember Malcolm, he was that weird guy who managed the Dolls for a few months and made us all dress like Russians? It should be fun. It's a trip to England. Let's go!"

JERRY NOLAN: Malcolm said, "Fuck it, two Dolls are better than none." And he booked the Heartbreakers. We were second billing to the Pistols.

We had no record, we had jack shit, but me and Johnny knew the English would fucking love the Heartbreakers.

LEEE CHILDERS: The night we arrived, Malcolm and the Sex Pistols met us at the airport. They were saying things like, "We just did this weird TV show. It was really funny. It was really stupid. This guy was really a jerk and so we just told him where he could get off."

We're jet-lagged, we couldn't care less. They took us to the Great American Disaster for hamburgers, that's all we cared about. And then we went to this little bed and breakfast in South Kensington.

The next morning at dawn, Jerry Nolan, who never slept, who was a vampire, came into my room with all these tabloid newspapers. He threw them on the bed, and every headline said "The Sex Pistols: The Day the Air Turned Blue!" and "The Horror and the Scandal of the Sex Pistols!"

Jerry said, "Well, look what you've gotten us into!"

I thought, Oh my god, here we go!

MALCOLM MCLAREN: I knew the Bill Grundy show was going to create a huge scandal. I genuinely believed it would be history in the making and in many regards it was, because that night was the real beginning—from the media's and from the general public's point of view—of what became known as "punk rock."

That was also the day that the Heartbreakers arrived to go on a tour with this so-called phenomenon that the media were labeling "punk rock." But, basically, the Heartbreakers and Sex Pistols were going for a ride around the country together and would never get to play a show.

LEEE CHILDERS: As Americans, we didn't realize how much power the British tabloids carry, and how intensely they can work the populace into a frenzy. On the Anarchy in the U.K. tour, we would be met at town borders by the mayor and the entire constabulary refusing to even let our bus enter the town!

In freezing-cold, blazing-winter blizzard weather, they would not even let us go to our hotel, much less let us play our show. I think we probably ended up doing six dates out of the eighteen or so that we booked.

And with the press it was cover your head and run—photographers chasing you, flashes going off.

JERRY NOLAN: The Clash were on the Anarchy tour, and so were the Damned. But the Damned got thrown off after a couple of gigs, because they were such sissies. The drummer, Rat Scabies, and the guitarist, Captain Sensible, they were tough kids, but the others were a bunch of poufs. They wanted to ride in their own bus. The Pistols were a little afraid of us too, but they tried hard not to show it.

ELIOT KIDD: As soon as Johnny Thunders met the Pistols he called me back in New York to tell me about them. We had heard of them. We knew Malcolm was involved and the Pistols were getting some kind of a notoriety. But we didn't know what they sounded like, we didn't know what they looked like, or what their names were.

So when Johnny called, I said, "So what's the deal?" And he said, "Forget about it. These guys are awesome."

He was really impressed. I said to myself, Well, if Johnny thinks they're that great, I guess they're worth meeting.

When I first got to England, I went right to where the Heartbreakers were staying. I'm asking them what the Pistols are like, and since I was a lead singer, I asked Walter, "What's Johnny Rotten like?"

He said, "He's an asshole."

And he was an asshole, a total asshole, a jerk-off. It wasn't like I just didn't like him; *no one* liked him. And it wasn't like he was sitting by himself on the tour bus. He was an in-your-face type of guy.

I mean, these little fucking skinny fags, like trying to put on leather jackets and sticking fucking safety pins in their ear, trying to like tell me they're tough guys?

I used to tell them, "I'll fight your whole fucking band. Not me and my band, me myself."

LEEE CHILDERS: The Heartbreakers blew everyone away, for no more reason than that they were just more experienced—they had their roots in rhythm and blues and rock & roll. They were able to go onstage and draw on all of that, whereas these kids couldn't draw on anything yet.

At that point, the audiences would watch the Clash or the Damned just kind of blathering about to their songs. Suddenly the Heartbreakers would come out and it would be like "VVVVRRRMMMMMM!"

Real rock & roll would start to happen, and there's no fighting that, there's no getting around that. No matter how anarchic an audience thinks it is, if the bass player can actually play bass, and the drummer is Jerry Nolan, then suddenly they're going, "THIS IS GREAT!"

ELIOT KIDD: The Heartbreakers were better, but the Pistols were more outrageous. The English bands were basically doing their impression of what they thought was going on in New York, and it was over exaggerated.

Like punk, punk, punk—I mean, were the Talking Heads tough? Was Television tough? Was Blondie tough?

I mean, basically punk rock was just rock & roll. We weren't taking music anywhere new. What a lot of people would have to understand is we were all at the age where we had grown up with pop radio: Buddy Holly, the Everly Brothers, Little Richard, and Chuck Berry. So it wasn't that the music was new, it was a return to the three-minute song.

NANCY SPUNGEN: Punk started in the sixties with garage bands like the Seeds and Question Mark and the Mysterians. Punk is just real good basic rock & roll, with really good riffs—it's not like boogie rock. It's not very embellished, intricate music—it's not with the synthesizers, it's just real basic fifties and early sixties rock.

ELIOT KIDD: The only thing that made the music different was that we were taking lyrics to places they had never been before. The thing that makes art interesting is when an artist has incredible pain or incredible rage. The New York bands were much more into their pain, while the English bands were much more into their rage. The Sex Pistols songs were written out of anger, whereas Johnny was writing songs because he was broken hearted over Sable . . .

MALCOLM MCLAREN: The Sex Pistols were identical to the New York Dolls. David Johansen was like Johnny Rotten, Johnny Thunders was exactly like Steve Jones, Arthur Kane was exactly like Sid Vicious, and in a way, Paul Cook was like Jerry Nolan, except he wasn't a drug taker.

So after Johnny Thunders, I knew exactly where Steve Jones stood, and after David Johansen I knew exactly where Johnny Rotten was gonna stand, and they *were absolutely identical* in terms of their actions.

Johnny Rotten was the person who, if anybody offered him anything he'd be over there, but if there was somebody who'd love him more than the person next to him, he'd be over *there*. He would suffer less criticism than everybody else, same as David Johansen.

JERRY NOLAN: I'd always see John Rotten, Steve Jones, and the drummer, Paul Cook, standing offstage studying us. They'd watch the combinations between Thunders and me, how fast we played. Then they'd put the combinations in their act, which they openly admitted. When we would get offstage, they'd come in our dressing rooms and say, "Oh you bastards. Oh you fucking scumbags."

The Pistols loved us. Johnny Rotten would just stare at me and say, "Nigs"—my nickname—"you are the fucking greatest drummer I've ever seen. I hate you for it." I was kind of tickled.

But I couldn't really enjoy myself on the Anarchy tour. Two weeks before we had left New York, I'd gone on a methadone program to try to clean up. But I didn't know how heavy methadone was. They started me on thirty milligrams, got me up to fifty, taking it for two or three weeks. And I was still shooting heroin.

PHILIPPE MARCADE: Nancy Spungen was always telling me how she was in love with Jerry Nolan. One night she called me up in tears and said, "Philippe, I just slashed my wrist, I'm gonna die, I just called to say good-bye."

I ran over there, and I'm like completely out of breath once I got there, and there was no blood, there's no cut, there's nothing. She's got a Band-Aid on.

I said, "You fuck! You had me so worried that I ran here. You didn't slash your wrist!"

She goes, "Yes I did."

I said, "Let me see under the bandage."

Like no she didn't want to, so after going back and forth for a while I grabbed her hand and I just pulled off the Band-Aid. What a gash. It was like, oohh, oooh holy shit man, this is *really* bad. It was a huge fucking cut. It didn't hit an artery by luck. I couldn't believe she did that to herself.

Right after that, she called me and she was crying her head off. She said, "Ain't no fucking guy wanna go out with me, no fucking guy . . ."

I told her, "Listen, no fucking guy will go out with you because you're a junkie and it's kinda gross, you know, especially on a girl. What you should do is clean up your act, like maybe go for a vacation. Don't stay here, it's too easy to cop."

She said, "I don't wanna go anywhere, don't know where to go."

I said, "Go to England. They have all this great shit happening over there. I mean, you speak English, so you'll be fine."

LEEE CHILDERS: The Heartbreakers and I were at Caroline Coon's house for Christmas dinner. She was a journalist and she had money. And we were rock performers and we had none. On Christmas Day in London, everything shuts down. There are no buses, there are no subways. How are poor people supposed to go visit their relatives? It really is cruel. There's only taxis, and they're double fare. So we scraped our pences together and got a taxi to Caroline Coon's house because then she would at least feed us.

But once we were there, we were trapped. Along with every other punk rock band in London at the time. The Clash were all there, the Damned were all there, the Sex Pistols were all there. Everyone was at Caroline Coon's house. She was trying to make herself the queen of punk. She was an awful woman.

The whole Christmas dinner was set up to seduce Paul Simonon from the Clash. Which she got away with. She got laid. So that's fine. I've done worse.

Oh, everyone was very well behaved. They literally behaved just the same as other people all over England were behaving on Christmas. They just looked weird, that's all. Caroline was having the Christmas pudding in her basement, the ground floor in her language, and so they had just set it on fire and everyone was standing around waiting for it to burn before they served it. And I heard Jim Reeves drifting down through the stairwell singing . . . Jim Reeves' songs.

Who's Jim Reeves? Oh you little rock & roll neophytes! Jim Reeves was one of the great country singers of all time, killed in a plane crash in 1964. He sang, "Put your sweet lips a little closer to the phone./Tell your friend you've got there with you, you've got to go."

And I began to cry, like I'm crying now, because I'm a real pushover for memory. So I walk up the stairs to the second floor, which is the third floor in American language, and there was this little guy, just sitting there crying. So I sat down opposite him. And I cried too.

And when the song was over, I said, "I can't tell you what that meant to me, because I'm from Kentucky, and I know my family is listening to Jim Reeves right now. Hi. I'm Leee Childers."

And he said, "Hi. I'm Sid Vicious."

JERRY NOLAN: I used to hang out a lot with Nancy in New York, but I basically used her. She had money for drugs, and I didn't. She was a stripper and a prostitute and very much in love with me. I mean she followed me everywhere, and told everybody stories about us that were all lies. Pertaining to sex, which we never had, trying to convince them that I was her boyfriend. Then when I confronted her, she would deny saying anything.

Nancy Spungen came to England after the Anarchy tour, to follow me. She brought a guitar I had hocked. I don't know how the hell she got that guitar, but she did it. I'd never seen anything like it, and I have hocked many things. She might have given the pawnbroker a blow job, who knows? But she got that fucking guitar.

ARTURO VEGA: I ran into Nancy in London. I was just walking around the King's Road and I bumped into her. She started telling me how easy it was to be a drug addict in England because the government would give you all the drugs and how great it was. We were walking down the King's Road, it was a Saturday, and those were the days when they used to have all those fights between punks and mods on Saturdays. But I didn't know anything about it, and I was wearing a leather jacket. So we see all these mods coming our way and Nancy goes, "Oh my god!"

I said, "What?" She thought that I knew, and she said, "The mods are coming!" And I said, "Good." Ha ha ha, you know? I didn't know anything.

And Nancy goes, "No, get in here." And she pushes me into a doorway and she stands in front of me. I said, "What's the matter? Why do they wanna kill me?"

She said, "Oh you don't understand. They're mean!"

I'm thinking, What's going on here?

And the mods come and try to get me out of there and beat me up. They tried to hit me, but Nancy stood there. She stood in front of me and she saved me. Yeah, Nancy saved me.

LEEE CHILDERS: One day I was walking down Carnaby Street, and all of a sudden this hand tapped me on the shoulder. It was Nancy Spungen.

I just said, "What are you doing here?"

She said, "I wanted to come over and see Jerry."

I said, "Go away."

She said, "I wanna see Jerry."

I said, "No, no, no, you can't, no."

I was terrified. I couldn't imagine anything more horrible than Nancy Spungen showing up. It was like the devil arrived on Carnaby Street.

She said, "Jerry's my friend . . ."

I said, "No, you can't, no, you can't see him. No. Go away, now."

I actually liked Nancy, but she was a junkie, a drug supplier, and an all around lowlife. And I was doing all I could to keep my band, the Heartbreakers, alive. The last thing I needed was Nancy Spungen to complicate things further. She was a very, very, very, very, very, very bad influence on people who were already a mess. She was a troublemaker and a stirrer-upper.

So I told the band she was in town and I said, "And I do not expect any of you to have anything to do with her!"

Jerry Nolan laughed. He thought it was funny that she was in town, but basically, they all did the old junkie two-step: "Oh, don't worry, man. We won't have anything to do with her, man." But they were probably thinking, Where is she?

MALCOLM McLAREN: When Nancy Spungen came into my shop it was as if Dr. Strangelove had sent us this dreaded disease specifically to England, and specifically to my store.

I thought, They've sent this on purpose from one of those creepy dark festering dirty little clubs in New York! It's to pay me back, I'm sure of it.

I was ready to fucking fumigate the place.

I said to the band, "This doesn't bode well, guys. This is a bad omen." Of course, the Pistols thought I was absolutely mad.

But I tried in every single way possible either to get her run over, poisoned, kidnapped, or shipped back to New York.

LEEE CHILDERS: As it turns out, Nancy sidestepped the Heartbreakers and went straight to Sid Vicious. The next time I saw her was about four days later, at a party, and she was on Sid's arm. I thought, Oh, shit, oh no, what's happened? Oh no.

There she was, draped on Sid's arm like Miss Queen Bee.

When I first got to London, Sid was playing bass and singing in this band, the Flowers of Romance, that I tried to manage. I felt very protective of Sid. He would sleep with me, cuddled in my arms. Sid didn't live with me, but he more or less did. He'd come by, get drunk on beer, and sleep over. We never had sex. But he would curl up in my arms like a little baby and sleep all night.

I wish I had sex with him because I was attracted to him. But I didn't, because at the time, he was so vulnerable that even an old reprobate like me drew the line. Sid didn't know what his sexuality was—we talked about that a lot. I thought that he would have sex with me, but the next morning he'd freak out: "What have I done, am I a queer?"

At that time, the Flowers of Romance weren't performing much, they were just getting themselves together. Then Glen Matlock either left or was booted out of the Sex Pistols and Malcolm asked Sid to join. Sid came to me and he said, "What do you want me to do?"

I said, "It's outta my hands, you pick whatever you want to do."

The Sex Pistols by that time were really rolling, so I said, "I'll understand if you don't want to beat it out with the Flowers of Romance, if you want to go straight into a band that's already established."

So that's what he did. And Nancy didn't especially want Jerry Nolan, she just wanted a rock star that she could fuck and give drugs to and take drugs with. That's all she wanted. So when she got Sid, her goal was complete. She didn't need to continue her search.

PHILIPPE MARCADE: Nancy called me up a month or two after, and she had a British accent which was like, "Hey Philiiiippe, it's Nancy."

I was like, "WHAT?" And she's like, "You won't BELIEVE who I'm going out with—I'm going out with SID VICIOUS!"

LEEE CHILDERS: After the Anarchy tour the Sex Pistols stopped playing. That was Malcolm's strategy, so they only played two or three free, unannounced gigs. It paid off; Malcolm was right. But Malcolm had the financial backup, so he could do that kind of strategy. We couldn't. We had to play or die.

We needed drugs, we needed food, we needed to live. There was no record company yet at that time, so we played two or three gigs a week, and every single one of them was absolutely packed. We were the sensation in London at that time.

But the Heartbreakers were junkies, and that was what they were most famous for. Record companies don't want to sign junkies and then have them die on them.

GAIL HIGGINS: When Chris Stamp signed them to Track Records, that's when Johnny Thunders had the brilliant idea of changing their name to the Junkies.

I said, "That will really help when you're crossing borders!" They used to get per diems and they'd go to the methadone clinic, and of course they couldn't get to the methadone clinic by themselves. They had to have a car take them and bring them back. That's the only time I ever saw Johnny withdraw or get sick—on methadone, not from heroin. Because he used to save his doses, so he was constantly drinking more than his dose, and withdrawing from that was just much, much harder . . . He'd get REALLY sick when he ran out of methadone.

One day Walter called up and went, "Get in a cab, get in a cab—Johnny's turning blue, Johnny's turning blue." We had no money or anything, so we had to scrape together the cab fare.

That's when things started getting really bad. Then of course it was, "Who we gonna blame everything on?" So then it was, "Let's blame it on Leee!"

LEEE CHILDERS: Track Records put us in this really nice little studio in SoHo, with a really nice little recording engineer. I had told Chris Stamp, "Don't let Johnny have anything—no heroin, no pot, no cocaine, no booze. Don't let him have *anything* because it's not just that he's a heroin addict, he's an addict-addict."

Later I walk into the recording session and there's a bottle of Johnny Walker sitting there, a present from the record company. Of course Johnny drank the whole bloody thing and became totally useless. I freaked out and beat him up.

I just beat the shit out of him, though I should have been beating the shit out of Chris Stamp. I just slapped him till Johnny said, "Please don't hit me anymore."

I thought, Oh my god, what am I doing? For as long as we knew each other, I never, ever, hit him again.

So that day was a loss. But the recordings over the next few days were brilliant—one of the ten best rock & roll records ever made.

GAIL HIGGINS: I knew that Johnny was a junkie waaay before they left for that tour. After thousands of all-night talks of, "I don't wanna be like this, Gail, I wanna stop, I wanna . . ."

Johnny would wear you out, not just John, but every junkie. I could write the junkie book. They're all exactly, EXACTLY the same. They wear out one person with "I DON'T WANNA BE LIKE THIS, CAN'T YOU HELP ME?"

Then when that person gives up, they go on to the next person who is going to feel sorry for them. So I spent THOUSANDS of nights talking to Johnny about being a junkie, THOUSANDS of nights over all the years.

So it was really difficult being on the road with them because Johnny, Walter, and Jerry were all junkies. Billy Rath was just plain weird, but I think he was taking speed and junk, too. It was like baby-sitting—constantly rounding them up, constantly listening to them whine about the money for the day. They couldn't do ANYTHING by themselves, and because Johnny couldn't, or wouldn't, then the rest of them wouldn't because if Johnny was having everything being done for him, then they had to have it too.

And they'd always be running off to cop five minutes before the show was going to start, and I'd be biting my nails, wondering if they were going to make the show. I mean, when we got to Amsterdam, before the bus even STOPPED they were out the door . . .

Johnny's line was, "Keith Richards made it and he's a junkie." And I used to go, "But John, Keith Richards made it *first*, then he became a junkie, not the other way around."

JERRY NOLAN: We hung out a lot with the Sex Pistols. I was the first guy to turn Johnny Rotten on to heroin, the first guy to shoot him up. I'm not proud of that. I didn't like the feeling I got from it and I changed my mind about turning people on to drugs. I didn't do it anymore after that. Nancy, who I introduced to Sid, was the first to turn Sid on. One time, I shot Sid up backwards, pointing the needle down the vein rather than up, and he didn't know you could do that. Scared the shit out of him, but he didn't want to say nothing.

That was the whole trip about the Pistols. It was all an act. Everything was a fucking act. They were young. They were kids. We were a lot older. When it came down to the real nitty-gritty shit, throwing works on the table and cooking up some junk, they got scared.

LEEE CHILDERS: Johnny Thunders and Johnny Rotten didn't like each other at all. That was mutual. I know from talking to each one of them separately that neither one of them liked the other one at all.

Thunders thought Rotten was an awful little poseur—phony, social-climbing—you know, just a little twerp. I think Johnny Thunders was right. Not to take anything away from Johnny Rotten's talent. Johnny Rotten had fabulous talent and could hold an audience in the palm of his hand. But he just had no soul. He just didn't get it. He wasn't rock & roll at all. He was just an opportunist.

That's how Johnny Thunders looked at Johnny Rotten—as an opportunist. And I agree. Rotten saw his chance and he grabbed it. Nothing wrong with that, god knows. The public are the great mass of suckers, so they might as well be suckered in by one person as another. But there was nothing real, nothing musical about Johnny Rotten.

Chapter 29

Fun with Dick and Jayne

LEGS MCNEIL: The whole idea for *Punk* magazine came from two inspirations: John Holmstrom's teacher at the School of Visual Arts, Harvey Kurtzman, who was the cartoonist who had started *Mad* magazine, and the Dictators' *Go Girl Crazy!*

HANDSOME DICK MANITOBA: I was so drunk during the making of *Go Girl Crazy!*, I laid down on the bathroom floor between the two stalls in the men's room because the floor was tiled and it was cold. I fell asleep between the two stalls and they found me there hours later.

I was always the kind of guy if you throw food at me, I have to throw ten times the food at you—I have to one-up you all the time. I was always the most excessive.

During the recording of *Go Girl Crazy!* I remember taking a fire extinguisher off the wall. It made this white foam and I sprayed it all over the twenty-four-track console and almost ruined the tape. I almost destroyed a hundred thousand dollars' worth of machinery, but somehow things were okay. By a miracle. I felt bad, but then I felt good cause I didn't ruin it. But what are they going to do? Sue me for a million dollars? I had no idea what we were doing.

LEGS MCNEIL: It wasn't until I heard *Go Girl Crazy!* that I thought someone else shared the same sensibilities that we did. After we heard that record, John and Ged and I kept saying, "We got to find these guys! We got to meet these guys!" My only ambition in life became to meet Handsome Dick Manitoba. That's why we started *Punk* magazine, so we could hang out with the Dictators.

But when we started hanging out at CBGB's, the Dictators were nowhere to be found.

HANDSOME DICK MANITOBA: The Dictators were late comers compared to the guys who were living downtown and hanging out in downtown

Manhattan, even though we had the first record out. *Go Girl Crazy!* was released in 1974. But we were from the Bronx and never felt part of it. Somehow we were never accepted—I get the feeling that we were perceived as these Bronx bullies. Boorish rednecks. It's not true, but maybe, to some degree, we came off like that.

ANDY SHERNOFF: After *Go Girl Crazy!* I was discouraged because we got dropped from Epic. I thought, Gee, this is my fault. I'm not good enough.

To be honest, the first record wasn't the record I wanted to make. I mean, the songs were there. The spirits were there, but the sound . . . You were supposed to have a sense of humor about it, but it wasn't supposed to be a joke. It came across as a joke.

I mean, I don't know what in the world we were thinking. When we first started the Dictators, we would bring Handsome Dick out in his bathrobe for the last song and he would sing "Wild Thing." And since the audience was usually composed of all our friends, they would just go crazy! And why not? It was the loudest guy they knew, onstage, being louder.

HANDSOME DICK MANITOBA: I had a reputation for destroying people's houses and being like the maniac party guy. I don't know why I got invited to people's houses. I was like the loudest, noisiest, most destructive guy. One time my parents went on vacation to Florida, and as soon as they left, I went around to all the playgrounds in the Bronx and told everyone we knew that I was having a big party at my house.

We started off with ten cases of beer and a bag of one hundred real 714 Quaaludes. Quaaludes were great, the Love Drug, they made you real horny. You just wanted to rip off your clothes and scream, "Suck my dick!"

So everyone was eating 'ludes and drinking and it was crazy. I remember sleeping with a friend's sister, I remember two girls in bed with each other, I remember shopping carts flying off the twenty-sixth-floor terrace, I remember the Co-op City security police raiding it twice and the regular cops once, I remember cooking eggs with the shells in them and eating them. I don't remember this, but at the end of the party all of my sister's and mother's jewelry got robbed.

I was so stoned that I was walking around in a red jockstrap and nothing else, except red lipstick swastikas drawn all over my body. My friend Cliffie got locked out with nothing on and had to hide in the stairwell when the cops came. My friend Alex was so stoned that he fell over, couldn't figure how to put his hands out in front of his face, and broke his nose. It was like a Fellini movie and it went on all night. All the furniture flying off the terrace, and cops coming up. People wrote "Fuck You" with lead pencils and put shaving cream all over it, which makes it impossible to get out of the walls.

The next morning it was like you were watching a war movie and it had been dark for fifteen minutes and the camera is panning the battlefield as the sun is rising . . . The smoke is clearing . . . And then you see the destruction . . .

All my motor senses were gone from the 'ludes and I was moaning to Scott Kempner, "Come over here and help clean up . . ." But I couldn't talk.

It took six of us eight hours to get the apartment back to disgusting. That's how bad it was. My parents came home and found the place a wreck and all their jewelry gone, so it was the last party I ever had in that house. I still hear about it. My mother still says things like, "Your fucking friends! It was those friends of yours!"

JAYNE COUNTY: I was born and raised in Dallas, Georgia, and the best way I can describe the place is eleven thousand people and one red light. It was very rural, a rural southern town with dirt roads, so if it rained you couldn't even drive on them.

We were Methodists, but then my mother started listening to this guy on the radio and joined this religious cult. It was one of these right-wing Christian religions where earthquakes are coming and it's the Second Coming, and all the evildoers will be thrown into this lake of fire.

It alienated the whole family. My father started having an affair with a sixteen-year-old hairdresser. I mean, we couldn't even keep Christmas anymore. Every Christmas my daddy would drag a Christmas tree inside and say, "Decorate the tree, kids."

We'd start decorating it and my mother would come running into the room screaming, "THIS TREE IS A SYMBOL OF NIMROD. NIMROD FUCKED HIS MOTHER"—no, she didn't say "fucked," she said, "NIMROD MARRIED HIS MOTHER TO KEEP THE BABYLONIAN BLOODLINE PURE, AND THE CHRISTMAS TREE IS THE EVERYTHING TREE! IT'S A SYMBOL OF THE BABYLONIAN BLOODLINE! IT'S PAGAN! IT'S AN ABOMINATION!"

And we'd scream and she'd drag it out and my daddy would drag it back in and say, "DECORATE THE TREE!"

And we'd say, "Please, we don't wanna decorate the Babylonian symbol of evil."

It was horrible. So I left home, because I couldn't stand it anymore. So I moved to Atlanta, was working for this optical company, and one day I bought the book *City of Night,* by John Rechy. It was a revelation, because in Atlanta I started coming into contact with these really freaky, crazy drag queens that I noticed walking down the street one night. They had like long, long hair, like bangs down to their heels. And when I saw these drag queens, I said, "Huh, those are real drag queens just like in *City of Night* by John Rechy!"

I became really good friends with one of the drag queens, Miss Cox, and she's the one who talked me into bleaching my hair. In Atlanta there was a really big drag scene. They had clubs that I started going to in drag. You could actually go in drag, but it was funny because you could really be arrested, because there was this law in Atlanta, where if your hair touched the top of your ears you could be arrested for being homosexual.

We got chased all the time. I never got caught, I was a good runner, but we used to take two pair of shoes out with us, a pair of high heels and a pair of sneakers.

I mean, I was walking down the street one day with these two queens, we were dressed really over the top, high-heeled boots, bell-bottoms—and we got shot at.

We heard bullets—I was walking, I turned to Daisy and said, "They're shooting at us! They're shooting us!"

These fucking rednecks just came out of a truck and started shooting at us. All the time, they would yell things out: "Are you queer? Are you a man? Are you a boy or girl?"

But I was considered strange, even by the other drag queens, because I was into rock & roll. We had this party one time, and the drag queens came out and did Supremes songs. I said, "I don't want to go to one more fucking party where one more fucking queen comes out and does a fucking Supremes imitation, and if they do I'm gonna fucking strangle her!"

Every party you'd go to, some queen would come out and go, "Ooooh, baaaby love, my baaby love . . ."

So I came out and did Janis Joplin.

Eventually I left Atlanta and got a Greyhound bus to New York City.

JIMMY ZHIVAGO: The first out-of-town gig I did with Wayne County was also my last gig with Wayne. We played this Catholic college upstate somewhere, god knows where.

And I assume that nobody in the band knew that this was a Catholic college, and I assume that nobody at the college knew that Wayne was a drag queen. These people were in total shock. They did not know what the fuck to make of it.

We were up there just pie-eyed, and not giving a fuck, because we didn't realize there was any danger involved. But when Wayne took out the statue of Christ and started spitting chicken blood from his mouth, singing "Storm the Gates of Heaven," and then smashed this statue of Christ as the finale, that was it.

They had had it. You know, there was Wayne up there killing their god. So they started to storm the stage, and Peter Crowley, who was Wayne's manager, got up onstage and broke a bottle, no, I think he pulled a gun, and the whole place just froze. I was hiding under the piano, just going, "This is it, I'm a dead man."

We had to get the fuck outta there really quick.

SCOTT KEMPNER: Handsome Dick was at CBGB's for two nights in a row because Wayne County was playing. He liked Wayne County. He thought Wayne County was really funny. I hated Wayne County. I thought he was camp. I thought he was a totally talentless piece of shit.

Anyway, Handsome Dick went to the show, and part of his thing was— we considered it a real rock & roll thing to have an interaction between the audience and the performer, a lesson we learned from the Stooges.

Like Wayne County would yell something out, and Handsome Dick would yell something back to engage him, not to like heckle him. To engage him, to take part in it.

JAYNE COUNTY: When Handsome Dick Manitoba came down to CBGB's that night, it didn't click in my head that he was the singer of the band the Dictators. I'd seen them at the Coventry and I liked them. But I didn't put two and two together, particularly onstage with the lights and the band and the music and four black beauties.

All I kept hearing was, "Queer!" That was the one word that used to get me going bad. He had to pick the one word that would get me all riled up. "Queer!" Yeah, he knew how to do it.

I mean, I was from Atlanta and was used to being chased down the streets and people shooting at me and stuff. So my first reaction to something like that is, you know, look for the nearest thing to hit them with.

ANDY SHERNOFF: Richard was heckling, sort of loud, and sort of out of the blue. Wayne County picked up his microphone stand and smashed it down on Richard's shoulder. There was no violent move from Richard, outside of verbal aggression. Wayne said that there was an attack, but there was none.

JAYNE COUNTY: I kept hearing, "Drag queen, fucking queer!" I yelled something back like, "Stupid fucking asshole!" So then when I saw him come up on the stage, well, on five black beauties, and him screaming, "Queer!" at me, I didn't wait.

HANDSOME DICK MANITOBA: I remember not having any sort of feeling of anything but verbal aggression, I had no feeling of physical aggression. But in those days at CBGB's, you had to step up on the stage, literally, to get to the bathroom. So the taunting was going on back and forth, and then he interpreted a move that I made as a violent move.

JAYNE COUNTY: Just as I grabbed the microphone stand, it ran through my mind, Do not hit him in the head, do not hit him in the head, hit him down there somewhere where it'll just get rid of him but not kill him.

At least I was thinking that much on four or five black beauties. So when I swung it, I made it go low, on purpose, so it hit him on the shoulder. I could very well have killed him if I'd hit him on the head. Oh god, I don't want to think about it.

He went first into tables and after that, he jumped up back on the stage and grabbed me. We rolled around the stage. I tried to get him to go off, I was kicking him off, he wouldn't go off again. It was horrible. It shocked everyone. David Johansen was standing on the left of stage, he couldn't believe it. And then, after that, I was drenched in the blood, and I was totally freaked out. Yeah, totally freaked out.

BOB GRUEN: I was standing in the back of CBGB's, there was all this commotion, we didn't quite know what was going on, except there was some chaos. It seemed like a fight—people screaming and yelling. Next thing I knew, they dragged Handsome Dick Manitoba out—literally, two guys were dragging him, he was like limp in between their shoulders, with blood pouring out of the side of his head. They dragged him out the door and Wayne stood up on the stage and said, "Do you want me to quit or do you wanna rock & roll?"

Everybody started screaming, "Rock & roll! Go Wayne! On with the show!" So Wayne kept playing and finished the set.

JAYNE COUNTY: I was sprayed with his blood from top to bottom, covered in his blood, and the next song was "Rock Me Jesus, Roll Me Lord, Wash Me in the Blood of Rock and Roll."

And my friends were all standing up going, "Finish him off, finish him off, man, finish him off!" They were standing up going, "Finish him off," with their thumbs down.

ANDY SHERNOFF: I had to take Richard to St. Vincent's Hospital emergency room.

SCOTT KEMPNER: He broke his collarbone with the base of a microphone stand. If he'd hit him in the head, he would be dead, and there isn't that much distance when you're swinging something that's this long. To me, Wayne's never had to pay for that. I mean, Richard's still got an outstanding debt.

We went to get Wayne County, and his manager and anyone else that decided to stand up for him, and couldn't find them. He was hiding, like a little fucking pussy. Then reality set in and we were talked out of beating up Wayne County.

JAYNE COUNTY: I heard that the Dictators were out to get me. I was deejaying at Max's, so I dyed my hair black and got a fake mustache. I went into work one night and you could hear people going, "Doesn't that person look a lot like Wayne?"

The next night the police came in. They took me away and put me in jail with a raving queen with painted eyebrows up to here. Well, I wasn't in drag, but they must have sussed me out. I mean, I didn't have any eyebrows, I had my hair dyed black, but I'd taken the false mustache off. Anyway, I looked weird. So the cops asked me, "Do you wish to be in a special cell?" Because all the other criminals were going, "Hey look at you, you're a faggot!"

So they put me in one of those special cells with the raving queen, to protect us from all those other people who wished to do us harm. I mean, how was I to know that Handsome Dick Manitoba wasn't like one of those guys? I thought he wanted to kill a faggot, a queer, a drag queen, you know what I mean?

TERRY ORK: Everybody knows that drag queens are the most vicious butch dykes in the world. They'll clobber you. They have to be strong—if you dress like that, you gotta be strong to take all that shit.

BOB GRUEN: It became kind of a dividing point between the Max's crowd and the CB's crowd, because Manitoba had been hurt, had been injured, and had some serious medical bills. I think Handsome Dick was suing Wayne and Wayne had to get a lawyer and had serious lawyer bills to be paid. So they had a benefit for Wayne County. And all the bands—Patti

Smith, Blondie, New York Dolls, Suicide—everybody played for Wayne. They had a benefit to support him.

It was a kind of an interesting thing, because although there were a lot of gay people on the scene, it wasn't spoken of that much. I mean, certainly Wayne was not in the closet, but most of the other guys who were around rock & roll were kinda heterosexual, macho males.

For me, I felt that it was kind of a turning point, that all these guys had to 'fess up and say that Wayne's our friend. And we stand up for him and it's not okay to come into a club and call a guy a queer. It's not okay.

LEGS MCNEIL: Gay liberation had really exploded. Homosexual culture had really taken over—Donna Summer, disco, it was so boring. Suddenly in New York, it was cool to be gay, but it just seemed to be about suburbanites who sucked cock and went to discos. I mean, come on, "Disco, Disco Duck"? I don't think so.

So we said, "No, being gay doesn't make you cool. Being cool makes you cool, whether you're gay or straight." People didn't like that too much. So they called us homophobic. And of course, being the obnoxious people we were, we said, "Fuck you, you faggots."

Mass movements are always so un-hip. That's what was great about punk. It was an antimovement, because there was knowledge there from the very beginning that with mass appeal comes all those tedious folks who need to be told what to think. Hip can never be a mass movement. And culturally, the gay liberation movement and all the rest of the movements were the beginning of political correctness, which was just fascism to us. Real fascism. More rules.

But as far as us being homophobic, that was ludicrous, because everyone we hung out with was gay. No one had a problem with that, you know, fine, fuck whoever you want. I mean Arturo would regale me with these great sex stories. I'd be going, "Wow, what happened then?"

What was great about the scene was that people's curiosity seemed stronger than their fear. The time was rife with genuine exploration, but not in a trendy mass-movement way. And I was always fascinated by how anyone made it through the day, what they really did when the lights were out, to keep their sanity, or lose it.

SCOTT KEMPNER: Danny Fields wrote shit about us, all kinds of people wrote really hateful things about us, everywhere you looked, we were the most hated people in New York, over Wayne County almost killing Richard.

There was a Wayne County defense party, a benefit at Max's. Debbie Harry took part in it, and later apologized. Dee Dee apologized, everyone apologized when they realized how completely duped they were. Nobody knew the real story, no one knew what the truth was about that incident—that it wasn't Richard attacking Wayne County, getting beat up, and then crying about it. That was the furthest thing from the fucking truth.

ANDY SHERNOFF: The backlash was that there was more publicity. Good publicity is good publicity and bad publicity is good publicity and no publicity is bad publicity. There was a bunch of people that went, "Yeah, Manitoba kicked Wayne County's ass!" Some stupid stuff like that, so the story is now legend.

JOHN HOLMSTROM: When Lester Bangs was still editing *Creem* in Detroit, he had called us at the Punk Dump and told us *Punk* was the greatest magazine he'd ever seen and that it made him want to quit *Creem* and work for us immediately.

But I think he'd had it in his mind for a while to leave Detroit and come to New York. Nothing was happening in Detroit anymore. Detroit was a big city for rock & roll in the late sixties, early seventies. And then by the time seventy-four, seventy-five rolled around, nothing was happening, so any time *Creem* writers had to do a story, they'd have to go out of town. And Lester wanted to quit *Creem* because he couldn't stand the publisher and he wanted to freelance.

So Lester moved to New York. It was just about the time that the Wayne County–Handsome Dick Manitoba fight went down and Lester was championing the Dictators' cause. He wrote this thing, "Who Are the Real Dictators?" He was all like hyped-up on drugs or something when he was writing the piece at the Dump. The whole time he was writing it, he kept playing the dialogue from *Taxi Driver*.

So he read "Who Are the Real Dictators?" out loud at a Dictators rehearsal, which is where we took the pictures of Lester and Handsome Dick wrestling. Then a story started going around the entire New York underground that we were gonna run this article exposing the gay mafia.

So everybody started telling us, "You better not do that if you know what's good for you!"

Then Lester refused to let us print the article.

Lester chickened out because he didn't want to screw up his reputation—but it was just a rambling, stupid, harmless little thing, you know? Everybody read more into it than there was. We would have been better off printing it just so people would have left us alone. That was one of the things that really helped to put us out of business. A lot of places would not touch us after that. Nobody wanted to talk to us, nobody wanted anything to do with us.

"*Punk* magazine is gonna expose the gay mafia," that's what Lester was telling people. And the scene was so small, everybody heard about it. Everybody was scared. I guess people were more in the closet back then.

I didn't even know what the gay mafia was supposed to *be*. It was like a joke somebody made up. The gay mafia? There was no gay mafia! It was Lester's idea. And *Punk* magazine took the rap for it.

BOB GRUEN: This was in the very early days of gay liberation, when being homosexual wasn't just wrong or bad, it was illegal, and gay-bashing and putting down queers was accepted. It was a real turning point. Everybody had taken it for granted that you could rank out a queer. Then all of a sudden it did matter, you realized this was a real person who was being insulted, that this was a friend of yours.

JAYNE COUNTY: I'm sorry it happened, I'm sorry Handsome Dick got hurt, but he really pushed it too far that night. I was on speed, I was paranoid, I reacted, a spur-of-the-moment reaction, adrenaline. And five black beauties. Do you remember what those black beauties were like?

SCOTT KEMPNER: We were blackballed from the clubs, and any band that played on a bill with the Dictators was told they wouldn't be allowed to play Max's, which was a big thing. Richard couldn't move, he was in a wheelchair. It was serious. Then we started playing little by little. Club 82 took us in. Then Hilly said, "Blackballed? Well, no one tells me who I can hire or can't hire, I don't care about none of that."

So he gave us a Monday night and we broke the house attendance record. Then we were just kind of off and running, and then we were back, we were accepted. Then Karin Berg from Elektra Records signed Television and the Dictators at the same time. So then I got really friendly with Joey Ramone and Debbie Harry, and Richard Lloyd and Willy DeVille, and Tina Weymouth and Chris Frantz. CBGB's became very communal and it was great. It felt so good to be a part of that whole thing, even then I was aware of how much fun it was.

JOHN HOLMSTROM: After the gay mafia fiasco, I realized Lester Bangs was not to be trusted. And then, later, he wrote that article, "The White Noise Supremacists," calling us racists. He pretty much tar-and-feathered us in that article. I don't know why he did it. I tried to talk to him about it. But he would just, like, blow it off. He just said, "What are you getting upset for?"

I didn't speak to him for a long time after that. Lou Reed had warned me about Lester. Lou said, "Don't get involved with Lester. He'll fuck you over."

But I thought, "Aww, Lester's a great guy. Lester's a cool guy. He'd never do anything like that."

And Lou was like, "No, he's trouble. Stay away from him."

Lou was right.

I mean, we weren't racists. But we were unashamedly saying, "We're white, and we're proud." Like, they're black and they're proud. That's fine. We were totally into that, you know? I always thought, if you're black and you want to be hip you're a Black Panther, and you tell whitey to go fuck off. And you carry a gun.

That's what I thought was cool. And if you're white, you're like us. You don't try to be black. What I thought was stupid was white people trying to act black. Like Lester. His use of the word "nigger" was his way of trying to act black. He was trying to be the "white nigger." The "white nigger" idea was Norman Mailer's fifties lesson in how to be cool. And we were really rejecting that. We were rejecting the fifties and sixties instructions on how to be hip.

Chapter 30

■ Who Said It's Good to Be Alive?

RICHARD HELL: I wasn't really suited for being a professional rock & roll musician. I mean, I believed I was intrinsically a rock star, ha ha ha. I thought I'd been a rock star my whole life, ha ha ha.

When I first started, I got kind of a thrill out of it. I had exactly what I wanted. There were mornings when I felt like the king of the world. I'd imagined myself into my life.

But that wore off pretty quickly. My aims for the music and stuff were pretty unconventional, so it made it hard. Also, I don't like being on the road. And I don't understand what goes on between a performer and his audience, at least when I'm the performer in question.

I never liked going to concerts. I don't understand what audiences are at concerts for. I really don't. I'm not into that communal thing that I hear people describe. I've felt it at a Knicks game; I liked that cheering and getting all excited during the fourth quarter, but I don't have it at rock & roll gigs. I don't like being there with all those people, when they were looking at me when I was onstage—I was very suspicious of that. I was pretty scornful of the whole apparatus. It was just so clear how hollow it all fucking was.

BOB QUINE: I had seen the Heartbreakers when they opened at CBGB's. They started playing and Hell's gum flew out of his mouth, right in the middle of the phrase "Going steady, going steady." I said, "That guy's a star."

After Richard left the Heartbreakers, him and Terry Ork were over at my house. I was pretty down, my girlfriend and I had split up. I was quite drunk and they were high on whatever. I went from playing records to being drunk enough to play Hell some tapes of a band I was in in 1969—some outdoor gig where I'm doing "Johnny B. Goode" and "Eight Miles High." Those were the days of long, excessive solos and I guess Hell suddenly realized that I had what he was looking for.

So after playing him this tape, Hell asks me, "Oh, you wanna be in this band?"

"Hey what?" I was really surprised. I'd been treated like a leper in the rock world for years, because I refused to change my appearance.

But Hell had problems with my appearance, too. Instead of wearing these button-down shirts that I always wear, to accommodate Richard I would wear a T-shirt under my sport coat, but he'd shred it. Once we were in a cab going to CBGB's, and he set my T-shirt on fire. It was one of those flammable materials and it went quite out of control. It was a major thing to put it out. I grew the beard for him. I let him give me a haircut, but that never happened again. He took what little hair I had, and created bald spots all over, which I didn't appreciate. I'd never been treated in such a way at grocery stores in my life.

He'd launch into all of us about our appearances. On the one hand, he said, "I don't want you to all look like me, but I wanna create a statement."

I said, "Well you have a statement here—look you got this hippie stupid-looking guy Marc Bell here, you got this rastaed-out black guy over here, and you got me, this guy who looks like a deranged insurance salesman."

He said, "Yeah, you do look like a professor or an insurance salesman or something."

I said, "Yeah, well there's nobody who looks like that in CBGB's is there? For better or worse."

He said, "Everything you do—it seems like you strive for anonymity. Did you ever have a car, Bob?"

I said, "Yeah."

He said, "I bet it was brown or gray."

I said, "You're absolutely right. It was brown."

But to the extent he tolerated me at all in that regard, he had more faith in me than I did at the time. I like to think because of my unlimited talent I would've risen to the top and been recognized sooner or later anyway, but that's not necessarily true. As much as he would criticize me, he had more faith in myself than I did. My self-confidence was at an all-time low. By then I was thirty-three years old, and I'd been playing since 1958 . . .

IVAN JULIAN: I went down to the rehearsal space on Thirtieth Street, the Daily Planet, and I really didn't know what to expect. I walked into the studio, and there was Marc Bell in the corner guzzling vodka. Marc had these two chicks with him, one was blond and one had red hair, and they were both like seven feet tall, with ripped-up fishnet stockings, and they were passing the bottle around and cursing each other out. The two chicks were fighting over Marc, ha ha ha.

I couldn't really figure out who Richard Hell was, because Bob Quine was more or less running the show. Quine was talking to me, and Richard was just sitting there. Richard was the bass player, and Quine was the lead guitar player, so I thought Bob Quine must be Richard Hell.

TERRY ORK: The first time I met Lester Bangs I told him that I had gone to bed with Lou Reed and that really impressed him. I hadn't gone to bed with Lou Reed. But every time he saw me he'd say, "There's the guy that fucked Lou Reed!"

Lester stayed at my loft for a while and he responded most intimately to Richard Hell's vision of the world; also his vision musically and lyrically — he liked what Hell had to offer.

LESTER BANGS: I had been looking forward to interviewing Richard for a long time. Through hanging out at CBGB's I'd become fairly close friends with him and everybody in his band, close enough to be gratified that when their album *Blank Generation* finally appeared it turned out to be one of the wildest rock & roll onslaughts of the year.

But there were also things in his music and his persona that bothered me: the feeling that when he was onstage he was singing not so much for the sake of communicating with his audience but somehow almost totally for himself, and the unsettling sense that he didn't have to cut his flesh like Iggy or the Dead Boys' Stiv Bators to give off an aura of pain or simple unpleasantness. It's the same thing that comes across on his album's terrible cover, where he intentionally reduces the most fanatically penetrating eyes in rock & roll to the level of a drugged toad.

RICHARD HELL (FROM A *PUNK* MAGAZINE INTERVIEW WITH LEGS McNEIL): Basically, I have one feeling . . . the desire to get out of here. And any other feelings I have come from trying to analyze, you know, why I want to go away . . . See, I always feel uncomfortable and I just want to . . . walk out of the room. It's not going to any other place or any other sensation, or anything like that, it's just to get out of "here."

L.M.: Where do you feel comfortable?

R.H.: When I'm asleep . . .

L.M.: Are you glad you were born?

R.H.: I have my doubts . . . Did you ever read Nietzsche?

L.M.: Ha ha ha.

R.H.: Legs, listen to me, he said that anything that makes you laugh, anything that's funny indicates an emotion that's died. Every time you laugh that's an emotion, a serious emotion that doesn't exist with you anymore . . . and that's why I think you and everything else is so funny.

L.M.: Yeah, I do too, but that's not funny.

R.H.: That's cause you don't have any emotions [hysterical laughter].

LESTER BANGS: Just for the record, I would like it known by anybody who cares that I don't think life is a perpetual dive. And even though it's genuinely frightening, I don't think Richard Hell's fascination with death is anything but stupid . . . And all the Richard Hells are chickenshits who trash the precious gift too blithely, and they deserve to be given no credence, but shocked awake in some violent manner.

Either that or spanked and put to bed.

RICHARD HELL: I always thought that all that stuff I was doing was trying to be truthful and honest, whatever that means. I did have this whole feeling of—the root of an attitude I'd noticed in myself—that once all the discussion was done, basically, I don't care.

When anything got into the final analysis, I didn't care. That's what that song "Blank Generation" was about. I would always take the opposite view of the person who was trying to analyze it, so I was deliberately giving as much latitude as possible: "I belong to the —— generation."

The idea is that it's supposed to be blank. I mean how can you misinterpret that? Anything you think is correct, ha ha ha.

MARY HARRON: We really didn't have anything to be idealistic about, and I was so sick of hippie culture. People were trying to keep up those peace and love ideals, but it was so devalued. That was the era of real hip capitalism too, and you just didn't buy it anymore. It was exhausted, but, because what hippies stood for was good, no one could let go and say "this is over."

It was like you were forced to be optimistic and caring and good. And believe in peace and love. And, even though I probably did, I resented everyone telling me what to believe. I disliked the hippie culture, I found it nauseating and prissy and sentimental, and smiley-faced. So Richard Hell just came over and said, "This is what we are, we're the blank generation. It's over."

It was very exciting. What was so thrilling about it was that we were moving forward into the future and I had no idea what that future was. I felt like everything was new—there were no definitions, or boundaries, it was just moving forward into the light, it was just the future, everything new, no rules, no nothings, no definitions. "What are we? We don't know."

It wasn't for years that I realized it was nihilism. Or whatever.

RICHARD HELL: I got labeled being a nihilist and a solipsist, which I had to look up in the dictionary. It means somebody that's just totally self-involved, ha ha ha. That's fair.

BEBE BUELL: *Blank Generation* is one of my favorite albums of all time. And I thought Richard Hell was just—please, I mean, he was like the male ideal. But I was always just way too afraid to talk to him because he was too cool. He was Bob Dylan, man. He was like from another planet to me. He was so damn good looking; I mean, let's face it, he was a big hunk a man and a good-looking guy. He was really hot, totally crazy, like onstage too, forget it.

I would just sort of walk by him and hope he would talk to me and sometimes he would go, "Hi, Bebe," and I would go, "Hi."

Oh, no way, it was like too much. And people would say, "How can Richard Hell do this to you? You've hung out with Mick Jagger, you've lived with Todd Rundgren, you know everybody in the universe, and you're intimidated by Richard Hell?"

I'd say, "I don't know. I don't know."

IVAN JULIAN: Basically Richard had a lot of girls around because he used them to get high, you know? They would get him high and have sex with him. And when those two things weren't happening, then I guess Richard thought the girls were annoying.

EILEEN POLK: Anya Phillips was really obsessed with Richard Hell. She would like cut her wrists over him, but never enough to really do anything, just like, "I'm going to kill myself."

But it never really worked with him. Richard Hell didn't care that much. He would hang out with her and she would pay for the dope—and then he'd go and hang out with someone else. That would really piss her off. But she was in love with him. Neon Leon said to me one night at Max's how he couldn't stand to see Anya destroying herself over Richard Hell. Because she would just cry and slit her wrists and do all this stuff to get him to pay attention to her and it just never worked. He was really the only person I ever saw her degrade herself for. She was always into being on top, but with Richard Hell it was the other way around.

DEBBIE HARRY: I met Anya as soon as she appeared in New York, because there were no other girls to hang out with, believe me. It was mostly guys, and the few women that were there didn't really know that they were women.

But Anya was great—very sarcastic, a great dry sense of humor, very pretty, and a terrific dresser. She dressed like a whore. I mean, we were all sort of dressing like that, we always wore the stilettos. But Anya had more of an overview. She saw things from another point of view entirely. She was very organized—she wasn't an emotional wreck, let's put it that way, ha ha ha.

DAMITA: I was at CBGB's and Anya Phillips was staring at me.
She said, "What are you doing?"
I said, "Nothing."
She said, "You want to come over and get tied up and have coffee?"
I said, "Yes. You got any cigarettes?"
She said, "I got to buy a pack."
We bought a pack of cigarettes and went to her house and heated up some sake and got drunk. She pulled out all these chains that went around my waist and had leather cuffs for my neck and ankles and put leather underwear on me and a little leather vest. I told her I was a stripper and she said, "Dance for us."

I danced around the apartment for them, her and her friend, Diego Cortez. They just sat on the couch and smoked cigarettes and watched me. Then Anya said, "How would you like to come to bed with me?" I said, "Sure." Then she said, "You have to sleep in that." She kept me chained up for a few days and Diego came over and spent the night and jumped on me and fucked me, which I thought was a lot of fun because I couldn't do nothing about it if I wanted to. It was sort of romantic. I thought, Gee, decadent New York.

SYLVIA REED: Anya and I met in Taiwan. We were actually real oddities in high school, because Anya was very fashion conscious and I was this sort of intellectual, bookwormish type. So people really didn't know what to make of us. We were a strange combination, and we were always together. Inseparable.

After high school, my dad was in the service and was stationed in Hawaii, so Anya came to live with us there. That's where she and I had made a plan—she was going to come to New York and become famous as a fashion designer, and I was going to be her assistant. It was a very "Cosmo Girl" type of fantasy, like, "I'm going to marry a rich rock star, I'm going to know everybody, we'll have all these famous friends who will make records and I'll design the record covers and we'll go on tours and I'll just do everything and I'll design the whole look." That was her plan. She had it all figured out.

EILEEN POLK: Anya got into dope. I'm not sure if Richard Hell turned her on to dope, but I know she got into it with him. I liked Richard Hell, but

Richard would always tell me a sob story. He was always like, "I'm so depressed. Life is just a mess. I just can't get it together. Look at me, I've got a ripped shirt."

I would say, "You just ripped your shirt to look like a punk." But all those guys—Richard Hell, Johnny Thunders, and Dee Dee—were all the same in that James-Dean-tortured-soul kind of way. Johnny, Richard, and Dee Dee all had that tortured "I need to be saved by a woman" look. And all the women fell for it. They'd start out buying them drinks, and then they'd take them to buy dope, and that would be the way it went. And then they'd get dumped and then they'd go on to the next guy.

SYLVIA REED: Anya and I met Lou Reed at the same time in this bar on Eighth Avenue. We walked in, Anya saw him and said, "That's him! I'm gonna go and meet Lou Reed."

She went up to Lou, which really surprised me, because I thought, No, not even Anya's gonna be able to do this. But she did. She started talking to him, and then I wasn't really paying attention. But later on, Lou had seen me from across the room and so Anya said, "Oh, I want you to come over." So he came over and we spent all that night talking and started arguing right away.

Lou's very, very, very smart and I fancied myself to be very, very, very smart and Lou made some remark that I was not as bright as he was. He would always do that, but not in such a warm way, but then it was done in fun. But I was not gonna let this guy think that he was some rich famous rock star that was impressing me.

But Anya was getting madder and madder that Lou was talking to me. Then, after that first night that we met Lou, I decided to try to get his address and write him a letter—not his phone number, a letter. That night we met Lou, I had been talking about writing and books and stuff, so I wanted to write him a letter and see him again. Anya was like, "Don't do that. He'll think you're really stupid."

So against Anya's advice, I got Lou's address from Diego Cortez and I wrote him a letter. Lou called me and then we started seeing each other.

EILEEN POLK: Anya had a diary that she kept in the bathroom by the toilet, so if you went in her bathroom, instead of picking up a magazine, you could read her diary. Every guy she had sex with was rated in the diary. And she would write the worst insults about them. She would rate people with four stars or, you know, three thumbs-down. Every single person she slept with she would write about in her diary in a very detailed way: "He couldn't get it up, his dick was this big . . ."

SYLVIA REED: The first time Lou came over to the place we were living, unbeknownst to me he stole two of Anya's diaries because he thought that they were mine. I demanded them back and he gave them back and I gave them back to Anya—she was really mad about that.

But Anya wanted people to get to know her, which is why she left her diaries in the bathroom. I mean, her approach was usually to go up to a guy, she would be dressed outrageously, she'd be very forward, and put herself right in his face and say, "Well, I'm Anya, what do you think of me?"

I tried to emulate her as best I could, but I was not even in the same league. Which was why she was pissed that I started seeing Lou. Then we got evicted and I went to Denver to visit my parents. Anya was really, really mad at me that whole time. She really couldn't get over that I was seeing Lou. She never really got over it.

So I came back to New York from Denver and I totally didn't have any idea what I was going to do. So I went to CBGB's and Richard Hell said, "Oh, come over and rent an apartment in my building."

When I had accomplished that move I had no phone, and I went over to Anya's and I asked her if I could use the phone to call Lou. She was mad, but I called Lou anyway. He was very happy to hear from me and said that we would meet at Phoebe's.

But he stood me up that night and I was very angry about it. I called him back and Lou said, "Oh well, I was going to come, but the guys came over and we had to jam."

I was really furious and told him off and hung up.

The next morning there was a knock on my door and it was Lou. He'd been waiting outside for hours to get into my building, I don't know if you remember the building, but you couldn't get in because there was no buzzer, you had to call from the street. Since I didn't have a phone yet, Lou had been waiting outside for a couple of hours for someone to come out the door, so that he could get in.

So Lou said, "Do you want to go to Montreal?" Which is, like, much cooler than saying, "Do you want to go to the movies?" or something. So I said, "Sure." And we pretty much stayed together after that.

BOB QUINE: Sylvia took Lou Reed to CBGB's to see the Voidoids. When I came offstage, he grabbed me and said, "You're a fucking great guitar player." He didn't remember me from previously when I had hung around with him when he was in the late Velvets.

I said, "Well, I really appreciate your saying these nice things about my guitar playing because you were a big influence on me."

He said, "I don't give a shit about that, you're fucking great, you're blah, blah, blah." But he was downright nasty.

He said, "I hope you know that this is by no means a band you're playing with. Music is about power and domination and you should just go over there and take the whole band over. You should go over to the other side of the stage and put the guitar player out of his misery."

I'm sitting at the table with him, and for a second somebody passed and I looked away, and he said, "God damn it, you look me in the eye when I'm talking to you or so help me god I'll smash you in the face."

I started laughing.

He said, "Don't laugh for a second, I'm deadly serious. You look away from me again, I'll smash you in the face."

This is while he's telling me how great I am. I did keep my eyes on him from then on.

IVAN JULIAN: I was a new kid in his band and Richard Hell was just kind of aloof at first, but then he would take me around, he'd take me to Max's and we'd eat there for free, and then I'd sit there and watch him burn his hair with his cigarette while he passed out. I was like twenty years old and one night Richard left me with Terry Ork, who started feeding me drinks. Then Terry said, "Hey, you want to come down to my place and listen to some music?" And I thought, Wow, what a nice guy.

We get down to his loft in Chinatown, he puts on some music, then brings out some more alcohol and whatnot, so all of a sudden I just pass out, BOOM, on the bed. And all of a sudden this hairy ball like collapses on top of me. BMMPH. I'm like, "Oh man, what's going on?"

He tried to get my pants off. I was saying, "Terry, I'm going to be sick. Get me outta here." Then he dragged me to the toilet. But while I'm throwing up over the toilet, Terry's still trying to take my pants down. I'm like, "Man, no. I'm really not into this."

I literally ran outta there with my pants half down. It was like freezing cold, I had no shoes on, just a shirt or something. I just ran back to Richard's house at like five in the morning. I told Richard the story and he said, "Well, that's very Terry." I said to him, "Why did you leave me with him?" He goes, "What do you mean?"

He was oblivious.

But eventually Richard said, "Well, come and live at my place." He had an extra room and everything, so I did, and then everybody thought we were lovers for a while, ha ha. But the scariest thing about living with Richard is that I'd walk in the door and Richard would be lying in the bathtub, high on dope, and the corner of his mouth would be just slipping underwater. I'd just grab him under his arms and pull him up. He'd kind of wake up and go, "Ugghh." And I'd be like, " 'Scuse me, but you're drowning."

Luckily, the Clash heard the Voidoids, liked us, and asked us to open for them in England.

RICHARD HELL: The first time we toured England was with the Clash in 1977. I was going into it with an open mind but I didn't know what to expect, and it turned out to be totally miserable. Not only was I like strung out and not knowing how to cop, but the British audiences were just horrific. Just vile. You know, it was at the peak of gobbing. And I tried to look on the bright side—that it's the British way of saying "We love you"— but it got tired quick.

BOB QUINE: It was a horrible experience, being covered with spit every night from the audience, and not necessarily out of admiration. In the beginning of the set, at least they'd have beer to spit on you. But then they'd run out of beer and they'd just hawk up whatever they could. Meanwhile I'm singing background vocals, and spit's flying in my mouth. Every night I'd go back to my hotel room and rinse my clothes out, wipe my guitar off, and hope my clothes would be dry the next morning when we had to leave.

It was pretty demoralizing being hit in the head with unopened cans of beer. Those cans were like mortar shells and I was touched by the dedication with which they would willingly sacrifice a full beer in order to really harm members of the band, which they did. If Ivan was hit by something, he'd just throw it right back in the audience, but the problem is you could hit a nine-year-old girl or something who had nothing to do with it, and I would try to keep my eye out to see who did what.

There was one night in Derby—Lester was there, he was so drunk that when I talked to him about it later he didn't even remember it and he was right in the middle of it. We were being soundly abused. The guy had a pitcher of beer by the front of the stage, just threw it on me like I was a fire hydrant, completely soaked me. I was being hit with stuff, and spit on, and I see this kid with this heavy-duty plastic glass. And we had just finished a song and for once I could see the person who was getting ready to throw something at me, so I said, "Don't do it." He bounces it off my head and I just unplugged my guitar—it's a Fender, they're like baseball bats. I went out in the audience and smashed about seven or eight of 'em. I'm a coward, I'm a total coward, I'm not a strong guy, I was just flipped, I had had it, and they loved it. They absolutely loved it.

It was a horrible experience.

RICHARD HELL: Quine is very obsessive about the care he gives his guitars. He would just move to the back of the stage as far as he could get, you know, to get out of range of people gobbing on him. But somebody got his guitar with a huge, really thick gob of mucus. And he saw who did it, so he split this guy's skull with his guitar.

Yeah, and the guy came backstage afterwards, asking him to autograph it! They were nuts, those crowds, it was just like British soccer crowds, they were headbangers, you know, par excellence. They just wanted to get fucked-up and violent and obnoxious and go berserk, you know?

Then there was another part that was really annoying—which was that the Clash's first number would be "I'm So Bored with the USA." And we couldn't help but take that personally. Even though we didn't exactly identify ourselves with the USA, you know?

BOB QUINE: Nobody was there to see us. They were from England, they'd invented rock & roll, and they wanted no part of us. They'd be chanting, "We're so bored with the USA."

I thought the Clash were nice guys personally, but they had as much musical interest as the Ramones. Plus they tried to put a socially redeeming value about social issues in their fucking songs but I don't think they had the slightest idea what they were talking about. And I found their music just abominable. It was only because of Lester Bangs' worship of them that I bought their albums to try to like their stuff, but I can't think of anything I liked.

IVAN JULIAN: Can you imagine waking up everyday at eight o'clock to get into this crammed little car, knowing that by seven o'clock that night you were going to be covered by spit? Plus Richard was dope sick . . .

RICHARD HELL: Oh man, I'd be so sick, I didn't want to see anybody. I'd be lying in bed sweating and vomiting.

I'd go in drugstores and get this stuff they told you had, like, codeine in it—this horrible, thick brown stuff that looked like vomit. I'd try to get down a few bottles of it.

Also, the traveling conditions were really squalid. We were really disgusted with Sire because they had the road manager driving and then the four of us squeezed into a minicar—not a minivan, but a minicar, the kind where the guy in the back had the hump of the drive shaft pushing his knees into his forehead. We drove for three weeks all over England squeezed together like that. It was really miserable.

BOB QUINE: I'd never become a junkie, because I was always watching "Dragnet"—and I knew that if you smoked a stick of marijuana you'd be robbing banks in two to three weeks.

The first English tour was extra nightmarish, because we'd be traveling around England, and whenever we had a day off, we'd have to go back to London because Richard's little pals, the Heartbreakers, were there. We'd always have to fucking go back to London so Richard could hang out with them. Once, Richard couldn't even wait to get to the hotel, he was so frantic. He said, "I'll get out here." Then he jumped out at a light and we took his bags to the hotel for him.

RICHARD HELL: I was strung out and sick the whole trip. And all the stuff that was going on in England just was really alien. I knew we couldn't reach those kids being who we were because I'd been where the Clash and the Sex Pistols were four years before. It was just like, there's no way these kids are gonna be into what I'm doing because the whole thrust of what was going on there was to be as moronic as possible. You know, like strictly to be as shocking and obnoxious and moronic as you possibly could, and I'd already kind of played that out for myself.

I mean, I could certainly still be moronic and obnoxious, but it was pretty tired by then.

Chapter 31

■ The Fall

JIM MARSHALL: I used to call Lester Bangs up at *Creem* magazine in the middle of the night. Like two in the morning. I'd always been a really bad insomniac, even when I was a kid, so I would call up Lester because he would be in the office all night. So one night when I called, he played me a test pressing of Patti Smith's first album, *Horses*, over the phone—all the way through, from beginning to end.

So I bought *Horses* the day it came out. I was really into it. I had sent away for Patti's single, "Piss Factory," in the mail, and I really liked that. But I was a little disappointed with her second album, *Radio Ethiopia*. It was a little more commercial and a little more avant-garde, both directions at the same time. I didn't quite understand it. I didn't know what to make of it.

LEGS McNEIL: When Patti Smith was in the studio doing *Radio Ethiopia*, I was sent to interview her for a cover story in *Punk*. After the Lou Reed interview, our style of getting people to talk was to hang out, get as drunk as possible, and let the whole thing deteriorate into a stupor.

Basically the *Punk* interview was a good excuse to get smashed. Then I'd just keep asking the same dumb questions over and over: "What kind of hamburgers do you like to eat? Are Blimpies better than McDonald's?"

Everyone would get so pissed off that I was asking them these stupid questions that they'd start yelling at me and then something would happen. And if it was funny enough, Holmstrom would make it into a comic strip. I think more than listening to what anybody had to say, the idea was to make something happen.

Patti was expecting to sit down and do a serious interview. Then I showed up. I didn't have any questions and hadn't done any homework, and I didn't want to hear about art or poetry. I was like, "Hey! Is it true Aerosmith is playing on your record?"

Patti was pissed. She started yelling at me right off, "That was a stupid question, and whoever gave it to you wanted to see you abused, because if I was in a bad mood, if I was feeling like tombstone teeth, you'd be out on yer ass! But yer lucky I like ya."

Then Patti gave me a big lecture on the importance of the underground press, and professionalism, and getting the message out to the people, and how art would save everyone, and then she went off on this sermon about Italian Renaissance frescas. I had no idea what she was talking about.

I was like, "I'm sorry, Patti. I won't do it again, I promise. So, do you think I could have a beer?"

JIM MARSHALL: I was still in high school in Florida, and I was trying to get a Xeroxed fanzine together. I knew a lot of drug dealers and people who had money, so I knew I could get somebody to publish this thing. So when I heard Patti was coming to play Tampa, I just called up her management company in New York and they set up an interview for me. You know, I was just a sixteen-year-old kid with a tape recorder who showed up thinking, I'm gonna get thrown outta their hotel room.

But Patti and Lenny and the band were really, really nice. I ended up interviewing her for four ninety-minute cassettes and hanging out with them for two days. They weren't big drinkers so they gave me almost all their beer. They were all smoking pot and I brought them a bunch of pot, so of course they liked that. Patti was absolutely like the nicest, most inspiring person. She was the first person who put the idea in my head of moving to New York City. She said, "Oh, you should move to New York. There's more people up there that like that kind of music. You might be able to like figure out what to do with your life if you got outta where you are."

The Patti Smith Group was playing at this sports arena in Tampa, Florida. The place was like something out of *Spinal Tap*. It was this horrible arena where Ted Nugent, Aerosmith, and Kiss used to play.

Patti was opening for Bob Seger, and they went over like a lead balloon. It was classic: Patti and the band did their first song, and there was, like, no applause. The audience just stared at them. So they started playing their second song, "Ain't It Strange," and Patti was twirling around. The stage there was really high, like ten or twelve feet off the ground, and below it was this pit filled with these two by fours that were all nailed together to make a barrier.

JAY DEE DAUGHERTY: We were opening for Bob Seger and they wouldn't let us use all their lights. Patti had ventured over to the edge of the stage during "Ain't It Strange," which is a confrontation with God. It's like, "Come on, gimme your best shot, I can take it, motherfucker," sort of very defiant—like, "I'll meet you on your terms."

JAMES GRAUERHOLZ: Patti told me that she considered every performance to be a life and death encounter with ecstasy. She had a "whirling dervish" philosophy about her performance, and felt that her obligation to the audience was to put herself into a trance. So she told me that she used to masturbate onstage.

LENNY KAYE: Patti and I would always do a little ballet in the middle of "Ain't It Strange." Then she would sing the part in the song where she'd challenge God—"C'mon, God, make a move"—and she would start spinning.

We're playing it, and we're really locked at this point, we're riding this thing, we start wobbling the beat, so Patti's twirling and she twirls and she reaches for the microphone—and misses.

JAY DEE DAUGHERTY: It was dark, and there was a monitor on the floor, which she didn't see because it was painted black. She fell over backwards. I saw her go over, and my first thought was, Oh my god, she's either dead or she's gonna jump back up onstage, and then my second thought was, Oh fuck, I'm out of a gig. You know, it was a very human thing, but I always felt extremely guilty about that.

JIM MARSHALL: Patti literally twirled right off the stage—backwards. I was standing three feet away, literally, when she was going down. I tried to catch her, like put my arms up. Her brother, Todd, was a roadie—he was on the other side, and he tried to catch her too.

Patti hit the base of her neck on these two by fours in the pit—BANG. Then flopped up and hit the back of her head—a second shot on the floor. There was blood everywhere. I don't know if I imagined it or not, but it sounded like a very loud crack, like on the level of Joe Theismann's leg breaking—CRACK!

It was obvious she's really fucked-up. She was twitching and there was blood everywhere, and it looked like she had broken her neck. They had to strap her into one of those big stretchers with the wheels on it and took her to the hospital. No visitors. I think they thought she'd broke her neck, and then they flew her back to New York the next day or so.

LENNY KAYE: The stage shows had been getting crazier and crazier. It seemed like there was no place for them to go but total chaos. When Patti spun off the stage in Tampa and cracked a vertebra in her neck, it seemed like *there* was the moment.

At that point, the universe began contracting. We'd ridden our challenge as far as it could go. It was "Jesus died for somebody's sins, but not mine" up to that point.

After the fall, "reconciliation" is what we were about. We got off the road. We had to cancel the European tour. We stayed home for a year, the year punk rock took over the world. And we were there on the sidelines, really frustrated.

JAY DEE DAUGHERTY: We never performed "Gloria" again after that. I think Patti changed and came to grips with her own spirituality and some sort of a spiritual system. I think she didn't feel that way anymore. This is something I've not talked to her about, this is my own observation. She was working out some theme of resurrection and coming to a different place, but I was working on the crucifixion at that point, my own personal Golgotha. We went back to New York and all went on unemployment. That's when I thought maybe this drinking during the day wasn't such a bad concept.

LEGS McNEIL: Patti sent me a note thanking me for the interview and said to call her. So I did. I had heard that she had fallen off the stage in Florida, but I didn't know how bad she was hurt. It didn't seem like a big deal, because you'd heard stories of Iggy falling off the stage for years and never thought about him getting hurt.

At that time, people still seemed indestructible. There was a cartoon quality to everyone's life. For all the sex and drugs and falling down everyone did, people didn't seem to get hurt. But Patti was hurt, she was really in pain. She told me not to make her laugh because it hurt too much.

JIM CARROLL: I always found Patti to be very Christian; very, very Christian. I mean, we didn't go to church or anything, but she would read stuff from the Bible. People talk about "Jesus died for somebody's sins but not mine," but to me she was always Christian.

I don't know, maybe she knew I was this Catholic kid and I never really lost that. I mean, I love the rituals of Catholicism. I hate the fucking politics, and the pope and shit, but the rituals of it are magic. I mean, the mass is a magic ritual for God's sake, it's a transubstantiation, and the stations of the cross—I mean a crown of thorns? Getting whipped? It's punk rock. I remember saying that on the Tom Snyder show one night and he said, "Some people would—not me, but some people might think that's a blasphemous statement."

I said, "Not so, Tom, because I'm coming from a very reverential place." Ha ha ha. Boy, did I get letters after that.

Part Five

■ Search and Destroy
1978–1980

Chapter 32

■ Because the Night

Legs McNeil: Punk was like, this is new, this is now, the apotheosis, powerful. But it wasn't political. I mean, maybe that is political. I mean the great thing about punk was that it had no political agenda. It was about real freedom, personal freedom. It was also about doing anything that's gonna offend a grown-up. Just being as offensive as possible. Which seemed delightful, just euphoric. Be the real people we are. You know? I just loved it.

I remember my favorite nights were just getting drunk and walking around the East Village kicking over garbage cans. Just the night. Just the night. Just that it would be night again. And you could go out, you know? It just seemed glorious. And you'd be humming these great songs and anything could happen, and it was usually pretty good. You'd pick up some chick. You'd have an adventure. You'd go to some fantasy where you'd never been before.

Mary Harron: When I'd walk to CBGB's, I'd get so excited—there was that block where you'd walk past the Amato Opera House and then past the Palace Hotel—ironic title to see on the Bowery, but everything was ironic—and then, after the Palace Hotel, would be CBGB's.

My heart would just be racing every time I did that block. And then the doors would open and I'd be there. I was so excited every night I went. Everything was new, and it was so exciting because I knew I was walking into the future.

It was too good to be true. And of course I was feeling guilty about it, because I'd been on a really hot career track back when I left college and I didn't know if I wanted a hot career track—I wasn't sure whether I should be writing a novel or something. I would have my puritanical guilt about what I was doing with my mind, and should I, you know, be more serious.

So I was sitting there with Legs at Max's, saying, "What are we doing?"

I was doing some ridiculous job during the day, then sitting up until four in the morning every night, thinking, What am I doing with my life?

And Legs said something I never forgot. He just looked at me and said, "Mary, we're young. We hang out."

And I said, "Okay." You know, "Yeah, he's completely right, so shut up." And I'm so glad I did.

DAMITA: On the eve of my twenty-first birthday, we went to CBGB's and Anya introduced me to former New York Doll Sylvain Sylvain. He said to me, "Well, I'm going home. You coming?"

So I went out with him and I had a really good time and the next night we were going to see the Talking Heads at the Ocean Club. Anya talked me into taking acid. I said, "No, no, no." She said, "Yes, come on. It's your twenty-first birthday, you've got to take acid."

So I did. She dressed me up in skintight purple satin pedal pushers, black stiletto high-heel boots with maribou feathers around the top, and a really tight angora sweater and we went out.

They were videotaping at the Ocean Club that night and we were at a very fun table trying to share a shrimp salad. It looked really horrible. The lights were so bright I could not stand to look at anybody.

Then Joey Ramone came in. So I told him, "Look, I don't have any money and I am just coming down off acid. Can you help me out? Buy me a couple of beers or something?"

There was this girl following him around and she kept saying, "You're talking to him too much. I want to be with him. Please go away and let me have a chance!"

I said, "I'm just drinking with him."

I didn't plan on going home with him or anything but it ended up Joey was trying to, like, ditch the girl. So he says to me, "Come on, let's go to CBGB's and drink there."

It was well after five in the morning. I go, "But it's closed now."

Joey goes, "It's not closed to me."

PATTI GIORDANO: I had a '66 Mustang convertible and that made it easier to go from Max's Kansas City to CBGB's. We would do that run back and forth—Max's to CBGB's—depending on which bands were playing. If there were five different bands playing and we could swing it, and if it was boring at one place, we'd say, "All right, let's leave." Then jump in the car, go back, and see another band.

So one night I was parked in front of CBGB's. Dee Dee was inside, I had been talking to him, and he was having problems with Connie. Apparently she was really fucked-up and fighting with him. It was very intense that particular night. Connie had rage in her.

Quiet, genius at work: John Holmstrom, founder of *Punk* magazine, talks to Harvey Kurtzman, founder of *Mad* magazine, 1976. *Photo by Roberta Bayley.*

Typical night out number 1. From left to right: David Johansen, Lenny Kaye, Dee Dee Ramone, Patti Smith, Jay Dee Daugherty, Tom Verlaine, and John Cale. Basement of the Lower Manhattan Ocean Club at Patti's show, 1976. *Photo by Bob Gruen.*

We're a happy family: Connie Ramone, Arturo Vega, and Dee Dee Ramone, 1976. *Photo by Roberta Bayley.*

Girls in training. Clockwise from top: Syl Sylvain, unidentified, Nancy Spungen (before she dyed her hair), Peter Jordan (below Syl), Anya Phillips, Rita, and Cindy. *Photo by Eileen Polk.*

Typical night out number 2. From left to right: David Johansen, Danny Fields (sitting), Earl McGrath, Joey Ramone, and Arturo Vega. Also shows James Sliman (with back to camera) and, second to last, Jimmy Destri, keyboard player for Blondie (in black shirt). *Photo by Bob Gruen.*

The first girl: Anya Phillips. *Photo by Bobby Grossman.*

First night in town: The Dead Boys at their CBGB's Monday night audition, 1976. From left to right: Cheetah Chrome, Jimmy Zero, Stiv Bators, and Johnny Blitz. (Note the "WATCH OUT, PUNK IS COMING!" poster behind them.) *Photo by Roberta Bayley.*

Cross-pollination: Johnny Thunders in Malcolm McLaren's T-shirt that introduced punk to Britain. *Photo by Bob Gruen.*

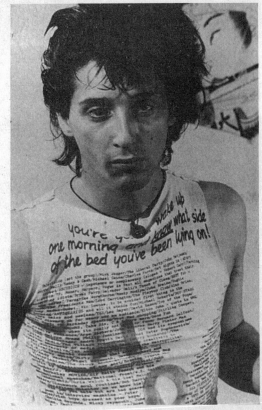

Typical night out number 3: The Ramones meet Iggy Pop at CBGB's, 1976. From left to right: Joey, Tommy, Iggy, Danny Fields, Seymour Stein, Linda Stein, Dee Dee and Johnny. *Photo by Roberta Bayley.*

Punk interviews David Johansen at Max's: Legs McNeil, David, and John Holmstrom. *Photo by Roberta Bayley.*

Dead Boys sign to Sire Records! Top row: Unidentified, Cheetah Chrome, Stiv Bators, Seymour Stein, Johnny Blitz, and Jeff Magnum. Second row: Jonathan Paley, James Sliman, Jimmy Zero, and Hilly Kristal (with beard). *Photo by Roberta Bayley.*

Blondie roadie and Rikers Island survivor Michael Sticca. © *Photo by Godlis.*

Genya Ravan performing at Max's Kansas City. © *Stephanie Chernikowski.*

Sid Vicious out on bail! From left: Richard Hell, Johnny Thunders, and Sid Vicious backstage at Iggy Pop/Blondie show at the Palladium, 1978. *Photo by Eileen Polk.*

Wouldn't it be nice: Lou Reed and Sylvia Morales Reed cut their wedding cake. *Photo by Roberta Bayley.*

In memorium: Jerry Nolan and Johnny Thunders. *Photo by Eileen Polk.*

Dee Dee was like, "I don't know what to do, I don't know where to go, because I live with this person and she's going to kill me."

I fell right into, "Oh, I'll help you."

I think the reason why Dee Dee talked to me was because he needed somebody who was stable, and I looked sane. I looked like some conservative, mellow-type girl from Jersey. I had a look about me that wasn't your average wild-and-crazy type of slut.

So when I was leaving, I said to Dee Dee, "If you wanna come with us, I got a car, it's out front, and we can take off and go to Max's or whatever."

So Dee Dee came out and jumped in the car with us. And Connie proceeded to run out the front door of CBGB's, like a total lunatic, in a raving rage, screaming, "What's he doing in your car? What're you doing? Where're you going? Who's that?" You know, very ranting and raving, like, "I'll kill you!"

Then Connie jumps on the hood of the car and starts trying to smash the windshield with a beer bottle. My friend Laura was yelling, "Patti, Patti, quick! Put it in drive!"

So I peeled out with Connie on the hood of my car. She hung on until she fell off. We went to Max's and laughed about it. When it was time to go home, I had offered Dee Dee a place to stay, and he came home with me and stayed a couple of months.

DAMITA: On the way to CBGB'S, I held my coat so nobody could see Joey Ramone take a piss, and this girl was still following us. She was w..ining, "Joey!" like practically crying.

So I told her to come into CBGB's with us. The rest of the Ramones were there and Hilly and a bunch of people like Legs and Roberta Bayley and we were playing pinball. I was sitting on the pool table and Joey jumped on top of me and spilled beer all over my pants. And then he started kissing me. And I was like going, "Oh my god, this is really exciting. I got Syl last night, who I always wanted to fuck, and now I'm getting Joey!"

And the girl was like crying, "Oh, that's right! Why don't you just drag me all over town and then just ignore me!"

Joey said to me, "Oh, are we going home now?"

This girl was following us right to his door and Joey goes, "Well, we're going to bed."

She goes, "Oh, that's it! And I took the train all the way in from the Bronx!"

So we said, "Okay, come on up."

We were sitting on his bed giggling and kissing and she was sitting on the corner of the bed crying.

Joey said to her, "Hey, do you want to watch TV? Just keep it low, so Arturo don't wake up."

The girl went off and we heard her fumbling around in the dark. She knocked a bunch of stuff over and Arturo jumped up screaming and threw her out. Me and Joey were just laughing our heads off, but trying to be quiet so Arturo didn't scream at us.

I ended up fucking Joey, but it was like really awkward the next morning. He was looking for his glasses. I couldn't find my bra.

PAM BROWN: One night after the Ramones played the 82 Club, I was walking back to the Ramones' loft at four in the morning, and this Cadillac pulls up next to me and this guy says, "I'll give you fifty dollars for a blow job."

I thought, Wow, *fifty* dollars!

I was so desperate for money all the time. I was living with Joey Ramone at Arturo's and we were living on cereal and cream cheese and tomato sandwiches—that was pretty much what we lived on. So when the guy propositioned me—it was something I'd always wanted to do, a lot of women have that fantasy—I was just drunk enough to do it.

So I said, "Okay." Then I hopped in the car.

It was so EASY. The guy liked it so much he called me afterwards, and he was my one customer.

A while after that I started hanging out with this real pimp. He was so scary to me. I'd get in his car—he had these girlfriends and heroin—and we'd go up to the scariest places and hang around. To me that was the ultimate—I was so scared to go to Harlem, but it was so cool, and I could snort heroin and coke all night for free. It was the greatest.

DAVID GODLIS: I started to figure out that what I wanted to photograph at CBGB's was the way things looked at night. I was transfixed on this book by Brassaï, *The Secret Paris of the Thirties*. The book was about certain evenings he had in Paris, mixed with his photographs, all taken at night. I devoured it.

Since I was at CBGB's every night, I thought, Wait a minute, I'm in this place, it's nighttime, and I'm here all fucking night. It may not be the thirties—it's the seventies—but I can do it here.

You know Robert Frank? He was a really big influence on me, too. Some of my pictures were inspired by his book *The Americans*—like when he's got kids sitting around jukeboxes, I wanted to get a picture like that in CBGB's.

Then Robert Frank came in one night—he lives on the Bowery, across from CBGB's—and he asked me, "What's going on here?"

I said, "Well, it's kind of a music scene . . ."

He goes, "It looks like the way people dress is very important."

I was tongue-tied because my idol had just walked into the place where I was like trying to do what he had done. I'd somehow crossed between these two cool worlds.

After Robert Frank left, everybody said to me, "Who was that old guy you were talking to?"

They didn't know who he was—they didn't have any idea about this other world. Then it finally occurred to me. I said, "You know the pictures on the cover of *Exile on Main Street?* He did them. That was Robert Frank. He did the film *Cocksucker Blues!*" Then he was a cool guy. Then it was, "Yeah. Okay, we get it."

RICHARD LLOYD: I met this woman named Susan. She was in cahoots with this guy who was importing dope from Thailand. They would hire fat women to fly over there on vacation and bring back a pound of dope strapped to their asses. Susan kind of fell for me and she became my free supplier of pure heroin.

I don't think human beings are allowed to do as much heroin as we did. I mean, language fails me here. We were doing so much dope that no amount of dope was doing it anymore.

Somehow I got the name of this doctor who was the doctor to the Rolling Stones. I went to him and I got a black box that was a trans-electronic catalyst that you put behind your ear. It doesn't take away the dope craving, but it takes away the withdrawal symptoms. It's a temporary thing, a stopgap. You're still ten seconds away from the withdrawal, but it's like hovering around you and over you and near you but it can't get you. You're still sick, but you're not the kind of sick that you would be without it, let's put it that way.

That's where I met Anita Pallenberg. She was trying to get off drugs, sorta. I think Keith Richards was straight, whatever straight constitutes for Keith. He wasn't doing heroin at least.

I fell in with Anita and we started buying dope together. Our relationship was platonic and drug-related. She would pawn some of her jewelry and we would go down to the Lower East Side in a limo. The dealers were like, "GET THAT FUCKING LIMO OFF MY BLOCK! WHAT ARE YOU, CRAZY?"

But one time that limo saved my ass. We were down at Ninth Street and Avenue C. I had just copped and I heard, "STOP."

I kept walking—the limo was parked across the street—and then I heard, "STOP, POLICE!"

I ran and jumped in the limo and I'm like shitting my pants, and I've got the dope, and I'm like, "What do I do? Anita, what do I do?"

The cops came to the limousine and they demanded that the driver let them in, and he said, "No."

Anita and me were both in the back, shaking and quivering. The limo driver said, "This is a private vehicle and you need a search warrant. This vehicle is on hire and I'm not even allowed to tell you who's in the back."

Eventually the cops gave up. So that limousine helped us.

SYLVIA REED: Even though I was obsessed with Lou Reed, I continued to see other people. In those days, we didn't see people or date people, we just went home with them. It was my strategy for preserving myself and my identity from this incredible obsession with Lou.

Anya actually sat me down and gave me a talking to because she felt—and this was a real compliment coming from Anya—that I was getting a reputation as being a loose woman. I felt, in my own small way, that I'd achieved something if *Anya* was warning me about the evils of promiscuity. You see, for Anya, it didn't count if it was someone famous—then it was understandable. What she objected to was that I was going home with some guy from some lousy band.

I was just so bad—I wasn't even seeing the lead guy, it was the drummer, the drummer of a horrible band. It was embarrassing, but he was a nice guy.

Anya claimed that people were talking about me. I said, "Well, who?" She was like, "Oh, I'm not going to tell you." It was that whole trip.

I think my response to Anya's talk was to go home with somebody. We were at CBGB's, and I was kind of proud of it in a strange way, because even *I* knew I was totally obsessed with Lou—so my going home with someone else sort of said that I wasn't. It allowed me enough distance to maintain some sort of breathing room, which quickly evaporated as soon as I moved in with Lou.

GYDA GASH: One night I tried to take Iggy home. Cheetah was oblivious because he was so drunk. I thought, Oh, it's Iggy Pop. My hero.

We were both way drunk and I maneuvered Iggy out of the club, and as we were getting into the cab all the Dead Boys surrounded him and said, "No way, man. That's Cheetah's old lady."

Iggy burped and went back inside. I was pissed.

DUNCAN HANNAH: I was sitting at Max's with my French cigarettes and my François Truffaut hairdo, dirty shirt and tie—you know, the French gangster look—and Amos Poe came up to me and said, "Hey! You wanna be in my next movie?"

I'd seen *Blank Generation*, his documentary on CBGB's, which was crap. He's got the zoom lens and he keeps on jerking it back and forth—it drives you nuts, you wanna strangle him. Just keep the camera steady. But when he asked me to be in his next film, I said, "Sure."

Then I thought, Oh, I get it. This is never gonna happen, right? You know, somebody's goofy idea.

So I said, "Oh, when do ya start shooting?" You know, thinking he'd say, "Oh, in about a year and a half."

He said, "Two weeks."

I said, "Two weeks! Whoa! You better let me see a script then."

He said, "Actually I haven't written it yet." I was like, "Oh, great. This is really lame." I said, "So you're making a feature with no script, starring a nonactor, and you're starting in two weeks? Great."

Amos was a cabdriver at the time, but somehow he'd saved up six thousand bucks. He was gonna make this feature film as an homage to the French new wave—this Jean-Luc Godard kind of thing.

It was called *Unmade Beds*, and Debbie Harry played my girlfriend. I met her on the set and we had this sort of love scene together. She had her boyfriend, Chris Stein, with her. We didn't actually touch, unfortunately. We were clothed and then my reflection was in a mirror and she kissed my reflection. Then it went black.

Next scene, we're both in our underwear. Smoking. I'm being cool and French and expressionless. She's being cool and sultry. She sings a little song. It was very stiff. And I'm not talking about woodies.

Basically, I was just supposed to be this . . . "image." That smoked. And had all this stupid dialogue. It was awful.

At one point during filming, I said, "We need, you know, some existentialism."

Amos said, "Right." But I don't think he knew the difference between surrealism and existentialism. So he gives me this thing to read about "How a hamburger is a cow"—this kind of surrealistic thing about eating meat. You know, this is not "God is dead." We're talking diet here.

RICHARD LLOYD: Anita and I went to Jamaica and stayed at this fabulous beach villa with maids. We only took a two-week supply of heroin with us, and of course we ended up using it all in three days. We had tons of Percodans but they don't work. I went to a Jamaican doctor, literally SHAKING, and told him, "I'm a narcotics addict, and

I'm stuck on your crummy little island without any heroin. PUHLEESE help me."

He said, "I'd be glad to prescribe something but the pharmacy has no syringes. You'll have to go to Kingston . . ." Kingston was eighty miles away.

We were like, "But you don't understand . . ."

BEBE BUELL: I was giving L.A. a try—I was meeting directors, you know, doing the whole movie thing.

One night my girlfriend Pam says to me, "Listen, I wanna go to Hollywood High tonight because there's a really cool show—Mink DeVille, Nick Lowe, and Elvis Costello."

So we get there, and we watched all night from the seats, and then right before Elvis comes on, Pam goes, "We've really gotta go to the front for this because this'll be the most intense thing you've ever seen."

I went, "Are you kidding? He's really that good?"

So we're pressed up against the stage, and there was a really hot buzz in the air, because everybody was really excited, and Pam and I were like two excited little kids.

All of a sudden these really intense lights start and the next thing I know this bottom light comes up on this figure. He's standing there with his legs spread, with his toes locked in, wearing horn-rims. I looked up and I went, "Oh my god. There's that fucking guy again. I can't believe it."

Two years before I was at a photo shoot in London, when this computer operator from Elizabeth Arden dropped by to deliver something. I fell in love with him the second I saw him. I never expected to ever see him again. I didn't know even what his name was. I didn't know anything about him. I had thought about him all this time.

I think once or twice in your life you have moments that are just totally magical and you really feel like God is at work. I just couldn't believe that this was the same guy. And it was just like an Elvis Presley movie— he looked right at me and sang to me the whole night. It was just too much, I thought I was gonna die. It was just too good, it was truly pure. It was just brilliant.

So afterward Pam says, "Let's go back and say hello," and I was like, "No fucking way, man."

I was too scared to meet him. I said, "We're outta here. We're going to see the Runaways."

So the whole way to the Whiskey, Pam was like, "Why wouldn't you go back? I want you to meet Jake Riviera. You'll love him."

She was trying to get me a nice respectable manager for a boyfriend and she thought I would like Jake. You know, "He's really cool, he combs his hair like a gangster, and he wears shiny suits just like Johnny Thunders."

So we get to the Whiskey and we're sitting there and I felt it. You know when somebody's staring at you and you can feel it? So I turned around and there was Elvis with this really beautiful black girl. She was staring at me, and he was staring at me, and I was looking at them but pretending that I wasn't, and this went on for such a long time that it was getting ridiculous.

I had had a couple of vodka and orange juices, so I just walked over and said to both of them, "Look, what are you staring at?"

The girl said, "Oh, I just think you're really pretty and my friend would really like to meet you. This is Elvis Costello."

I turned and immediately knocked his glasses off by mistake. I apologized—he had a great sense of humor about it, he told me he didn't need his face anyway—and we were sweating and shaking and totally scared to death of each other.

It was so cute—you don't feel that kind of purity too often in your life. I mean, we were in love. It was just, forget it, that was that.

DUNCAN HANNAH: They reviewed *Unmade Beds* in the *New York Times.* Like it was a real movie, right? And Amos got it in these European film festivals. It went to the Berlin Film Festival. David Bowie saw it there and somehow tracked Amos down.

Bowie said, "Hey, I'm really interested in working with you." When Amos told me that, I just went, "Wha-aat? Are you kidding?"

Godard saw it and like took it seriously.

He said, "Well, maybe in zee future veee'll vork togezer . . ."

It was like, I couldn't believe it. Frankly, I thought the movie was stupid.

Then Amos raised money for the next one, *The Foreigner,* which starred Eric Mitchell, Anya Phillips, and Terence Sellars.

I played the psychopathic killer. The first one, I'm this French guy. This time, I'm this punk guy. I got an Egon Schiele haircut, skinny tie, and all that stuff.

The Foreigner got reviewed in the *New York Times,* like the other one, and this time I went to the Deauville Film Festival with it. Amos was a very disorganized guy; it was amazing he got these things done.

He said, "Yeah, we've got a room for you in Deauville if you wanna come. It's a week long, everything's paid for, so if you wanna show up, do."

I said, "That's it? You mean I just say yes?"

He said, "Just go to Deauville."

"Yeah, but where? And what's the date?"

"I don't know, sometime in October."

So somehow I get myself to Deauville. You know, I flew to London and then took a train to—I don't know, wherever you go—and by the time I got there I'm all jet-lagged and drunk and weird, and finally I knock on this room and Amos opened the door.

I went, "Amos!"

He went, "Duncan! What are you doing here?"

I thought, Oh no!

But then he said, "You're just in time. We're supposed to go to this reception right now in the auditorium."

So we go there. It's like ten in the morning. Pierre Salinger, who was President Kennedy's press secretary, was at the podium.

He announced, "Welcome to the fifth annual Deauville Film Festival. Our guest of honor this year is Gloria Swanson! Gloria, come up!"

Gloria Swanson went up onstage, and I'm going, "What's going on?"

Then it's, "John Travolta!"

"Olivia Newton-John!"

"George Peppard!"

"John Waters!"

"Françoise Sagan!" She's one of my heroes, right?

Then he goes, "Amos Poe!"

I'm like, "Amos Poe? What is wrong with this picture?"

Then he goes, "Duncan Hannah!"

I was like, "WHAT?"

So I go up onstage, and you're supposed to shake everyone's hands. "Hi, Gloria! *Sunset Boulevard*—that was wild! Wild film!" And Travolta? I can dig it: "John—*Grease*, good work!"

I felt like we were gonna get caught. That all of a sudden they were gonna go, "Excuse me, there's been a big mistake. Your film is a piece of shit. We're deporting you. You guys aren't movie stars. You're just, like, drunks."

Then we went to a party for King Vidor. I was really, really drunk. I was kind of being a punk unintentionally, right? I got all spiffed up—I was wearing an ascot and I had slicked my hair back. I wanted to be F. Scott Fitzgerald, but I was so fucking wasted that I'm just lurching around this party, not pulling it off. Everybody was like, "Oh, punks from New York," right?

So I wound up hanging out with these kids from Paris—I wanted to know all about Alain Delon and Jean-Paul Belmondo, and they wanted to know all about Johnny Thunders. They'd been reading about all this punk stuff, right?

I said, "No, I wanna know about, you know, Godard."

They said, "Godard? Who cares about Godard? We wanna know about Blondie!"

Like, I'm on this European trip and they're on this New York trip, and I'm their representative punk—along with Amos. It was wild.

But that was the great thing. You could make this crummy little homage to the French new wave, and David Bowie and Jean-Luc Godard became *your* fans. And then you're getting drunk with King Vidor.

The time was with you, you know?

BEBE BUELL: I was so freaked out by Elvis Costello. Pam said to me, "How are you ever going to get together with him if you keep running away?" So the next day Pam said, "Look, I have to drop something off for Jake Riviera today, so I want you to come with me and just stay in the car and blah, blah, blah."

So we go over to the Tropicana Hotel and I went with her to take this package to Jake, and I guess Elvis saw us through the window, because when we came back outside he was leaning against the car . . . waiting. He was in a powder blue suit and it was ninety-eight degrees—a tie, the whole bit. It was hysterical—but he looked great.

So I dropped Pam off at work and she gave Elvis and I her car for the day. At that time, he had never used any drugs and I got him to smoke pot with me. So all we did was drive around all day, you know, laughing. We were driving down Sunset and we look over at the bus stop and one of the Bay City Rollers was sitting there.

Elvis goes, "We've gotta give the guy in the Bay City Rollers one of my records." So we drove to Tower Records, bought *This Year's Model*, came back, pulled the car up to the bus stop, Elvis frisbeed his record to the guy in the Bay City Rollers, and then we drove off. It was hysterical.

We went to see somebody record and Elvis didn't like them, so we crawled out of the recording session on our hands and knees—and we ran right into the president of Columbia, which was Elvis's label at the time. I'm sure they thought I was a horrible influence on him, because at that point there was only one person badder than me and that was Anita Pallenberg.

I think they really saw trouble when they saw Elvis and me together. They thought, Oh god, how are we gonna explain this one? Immediately it was sort of like the Punk and the Model—Beauty and the Beast. And the press pulverized us.

HOWIE PYRO: It was so retarded. I was like running drugs to Cleveland, and on the way there they'd be half done, and then I'd stay in a hotel for a few days and do more. The Dead Boys came into town so I was hanging out with them and they were really funny, just out of their minds. They were playing at this club and it was like packed, and in the middle of their show they just go, "We have a very special guest here," and I'm looking around like, Wow, who's here? Stiv's making this whole long introduction, and suddenly he points right at me, and goes, "Johnny Thunders!"

Everyone's saying "HUUUUHHHH," and I'm like, "FUCKING ASSHOLE!"

Everyone's going, "COME ON! COME ON!"

People were thinking that I was just being modest, so they were pushing me up to the stage, I was like, "Uh, no, you don't understand." But they were just like, "COME ON!"

Of course the Dead Boys are laughing hysterically. They're pulling me up on the stage and I'm like freaking out. And they're like, "Just take this guitar, don't play good or anything, just pretend to play."

After that nobody would believe that I *wasn't* Johnny Thunders. So everybody just started giving me lots of drugs. And so everybody thought I *am* Johnny Thunders after all. You know, I was like, "Yeah, okay."

It was just like this endless ridiculous worship-drug thing. I felt weird doing it, but what the hell, ha ha ha. Of course I didn't go back to New York, I stayed in Cleveland and had this whole thing sewn up for like a week and a half.

And then some girl was gonna give us a *ton* of drugs. But she was talking to Chrissie Hynde on the phone the night before and she was like, "Johnny Thunders da da da" and Chrissie goes, "Really? I just saw Johnny."

So I got totally busted by the rock/punk community of Cleveland. And I had nothing to do with it really, you know what I mean? That's the kind of Dead Boys joke that you wind up in—it's like complete hell and everyone hates me. I've never been back to Cleveland since.

Chapter 33

■ Young, Loud, and Snotty

JAMES SLIMAN: After the first Dead Boys album came out it was decided that the Dead Boys were going to open for Iggy Pop on a couple of his Midwest dates. Iggy had put out *The Idiot* and *Lust for Life* and was making a comeback. Blondie opened the Idiot tour, for Iggy Pop, and David Bowie was playing keyboards, unannounced. I went to four or five cities with Blondie and I just loved it. That was just the greatest show—Blondie and Iggy Pop, with David Bowie playing keyboards. So we were all pretty excited when we found out the Dead Boys would be opening for Iggy.

The first show was in Cleveland and it was decided we should all have dinner with Iggy, since we're going to be doing these shows with him, right? So I arranged this dinner at Chung Wa's, a Chinese restaurant downtown, because it's a restaurant that we all used to go to when the clubs would close, when we all lived in Cleveland.

So Stiv, me, Jimmy Zero, and Iggy and his girlfriend all go to Chung Wa's for dinner. But Stiv could not deal with the fact that he's meeting his idol for the first time—so he's done a couple of Quaaludes, before we even get to the restaurant. But I'm thinking, Stiv will be okay, because he's going to eat something, so that will sober him up.

Then dinner comes and Stiv literally passes out in his soup. BAM, right into the bowl. Stiv was sitting right next to me, so I had to pull his head out of the soup.

Iggy and his girlfriend kept their composure, but I knew Iggy just wanted to crack up. He probably thought, What an asshole!

So I picked Stiv's head up, wiped him off a bit, and leaned him over. When he started to come to, I dragged him into the bathroom and splashed some water on his face. He was conscious, but he couldn't have a conversation—he couldn't even get out a sentence.

So we finish our dinner, and in the cab back to the hotel, Iggy said that Stiv promised to give him some Quaaludes. We get to the hotel—Stiv was out like a light, so I threw him on the bed, and when I turned around, Iggy was going through Stiv's suitcases.

I said, "What are you doing?"

Iggy said, "Stiv promised me the Quaaludes, he told me he had 'em here in his room, he promised me, it's okay, you don't have to worry, it's okay, it's alright."

I felt like, "Here's Stiv, he wants to meet his idol, gets too fucked-up, and Iggy can't even be a little compassionate, instead, he just says, 'Throw him on the bed, I want my Quaaludes.' "

So I said, "Don't go through his stuff, get your hands out of his stuff. Come to my room, I have some 'ludes, I'll give you a couple of mine—fucking here, take these, and fucking get lost."

It really pissed me off. Iggy was just making fun of him, saying what an idiot he was—"Oh, this guy's gonna open for me? Is this what he's gonna do onstage?"

I mean, Iggy should talk. And you know, Stiv based his whole career on Iggy Pop. He worshiped Iggy, and Iggy just made fun of him.

JEFF MAGNUM: The only reason we recorded the second Dead Boys album in Florida was because Hilly said, "If they stay in New York they're gonna get too drunk. They can't create in New York."

Like good, send us to Florida, that's a REAL good idea, where white port just flows down Biscayne Boulevard. Yeah, nobody has a drinking problem in Florida.

Cheetah and the drinking stuff in the studio didn't work. Eventually that was stopped. I drank Gatorade in the studio a lot—we can't bring beer, so I'm gonna drink this. God, Gatorade is horrible.

All I wanted to do was play my electric bass real loud. Cheetah and Johnny would both be having star fits. Those guys didn't wanna play. We would be playing these songs and gee, if you had to do it more than three times Johnny just didn't have anything left in the tank, he didn't wanna play that song no more. He used to say, "Isn't that good enough?" It's like, "What do you mean isn't that good enough? Maybe if you'd start playing!"

JAMES SLIMAN: We were getting to know the Bee Gees and Andy Gibb. They were recording in the next studio, and they wanted to be part of the gang. They had heard all about this New York music, which was like totally foreign to them, but they thought we were great. I think the Dead Boys were like a novelty act to the Bee Gees.

JEFF MAGNUM: Stiv gave Andy Gibb his leather jacket to wear, and then somebody took pictures, and Andy said, "Oh, I hope Mr. Stigwood doesn't see this." Like Robert Stigwood's gonna have a coronary if he sees one of his Bee Gees wearing some black leather motorcycle jacket.

CHEETAH CHROME: Lou Reed wanted to fucking produce the album but the other guys were scared to death of him. So they got Felix Pappalardi, who clearly did not know what the fuck to do with the Dead Boys. He produced Cream, so I figured if this guy can go back and listen to some Cream records . . . because he just didn't understand what I wanted, which was basically a half stack of Marshalls.

GYDA GASH: During the recording of the second Dead Boys album in Miami, Cheetah was out of his mind. I really didn't understand, because I wasn't involved in the creative process, but Cheetah was getting way drunk and just crying. He'd be on the phone to James Williamson from the Stooges, like, "Please, will you come here and rescue this album? They're destroying the Dead Boys!"

I don't know what James Williamson thought of this; I don't even know how the fuck Cheetah got his number. But at two o'clock in the morning, from a pay phone on some boulevard in Miami, Cheetah would be on the phone with James Williamson, begging him to come to Miami.

JEFF MAGNUM: We had a big listening party at the Criteria studios. Felix was wearing this suit that had marijuana leaves all over it that he called his "listening party suit." It was just the goofiest suit I had ever seen in my life. Hopefully he was buried in it. I'm pretending that he was, in my own mind.

Oh, the record was awful. No bass, and you couldn't hear the guitars. That's how he got back at Cheetah, he neutered him, just didn't put any electric guitar in there at all. And the recording just didn't sound very loud at all.

I screamed in Felix's face. I said, "I can't believe you did this to us!" It had no effect at all.

I had to scream at Felix because nobody else was going to. I was pissed that I couldn't hear my bass, that's all I wanted to hear was *bass, bass, bass.*

Things shouldn't have been so dramatic all the goddamn time about the tiniest little insignificant little speck stupid thing, but when you're high and drunk everything gets enlarged and enhanced and you know, it becomes, I'M GONNA KILL YOU.

GYDA GASH: That whole period—from the end of 1977 on—was like a death period. It was the beginning of the end, and you could just feel it. I mean they were fierce days—some nights we would walk into CBGB's and I'd have a bottle thrown at me. One time I had to get three stitches. There was a lot of fucking violence. There was all kinds of shit going down. The glory days were over.

GENYA RAVAN: I knew that something had to give with the Dead Boys. You can't walk around with a chip on your shoulder in New York City. You just don't. The Dead Boys, as tough as they thought they were, knew nothing about the streets of New York City. It's alright to swagger in front of CBGB's. But don't be walking on First Avenue doing that. Because someone's going to know you're not from this town and they'll fucking kill you.

MICHAEL STICCA: I was roadieing for Blondie and I had just come off their fucking world tour. I had bought this bitching switchblade in Bordeaux. It was so cool. It was like CLICK, and it would come out; no wobble on the blade.

Johnny Blitz had this shitty fucking knife that he bought in Times Square. It was like those shitty switchblades from Mexico, the crappy knives that wobble. One of those pieces of shit with the wobbly blades.

But mine was really good, a very good blade. I carried knives all the time, but I knew you don't pull a knife out, because if you pull a knife out, you gotta use it.

JAMES SLIMAN: I was back at the Paramount Hotel. I'm in bed, sleeping. It's five in the morning, and Michael Sticca calls and says, "Listen, we just got in a fight, me and Johnny Blitz, and Johnny's on his way to the hospital. I don't know what to do!"

He was ranting and raving, so I said, "Just get here. Get in a cab." He says, "I don't have any money, they took my money." So I said, "I'll meet you downstairs. Get in a cab right now and come over here." He said, "I think Johnny's dead. They put him in an ambulance. I think he's dead. There was so much blood . . ."

I told him to get to the hotel, which he did, and I sat him down and he calmly told me what happened.

MICHAEL STICCA: We had just come from CBGB's, me and Marsha, Billy Rath's girlfriend, and Johnny Blitz and Danielle. We were very drunk and we went to the Deli Stop on Fifth Street to get something to eat.

I walked out of the Deli Stop with Marsha, and we were standing on Second Avenue, hailing a cab. This fucking car comes along and swerves towards us, like it's going to hit us.

Then the car stops at the light. We're still trying to hail a cab. All of a sudden like these fucking guys just get out of the car. There were five of them . . .

One of the guys yells, "Hey, what the fuck are you doing?"

I said, "What the fuck are you doing? I'm just standing here hailing a cab, asshole."

They started to surround me, so I shoved Marsha through the fucking circle—I got her away from the guys. But some girl comes out of the car and goes after Marsha and starts beating up on her.

I had the switchblade in my pocket, and I was thinking, Don't let them get around you—if they get around you, out of your peripheral vision . . . Keep everybody in sight.

I got my back up and I said to one guy, not the driver, "Listen, you swerved. You fucked up. I'll give your friend a break."

One guy pulled out a fucking chain, and the other guy pulled out a fucking baseball bat. They were getting around me, saying, "Hey, asshole. You trying to fuck with us?"

I had the knife in my pocket, but I was thinking, God, if I pull the fucking knife out, then I gotta do something.

But they're completely around me—but at least Marsha's out of it—so I took the fucking knife out of my pocket. I opened it up behind my leg, you know, CLICK.

They heard the noise, and they looked down, and they go, "He's got a knife."

This one guy was in front of me—he was wearing an army fatigue jacket, and he was saying, "Yeah, he's got a knife."

So it was between a baseball bat and a chain. I still had the knife behind my leg.

The guy in the army jacket kept getting closer, so I just swiped him with the knife—like I figured he was gonna back up, right? That's normal. But they weren't normal. So I swiped him with the fucking knife and he came on.

I swiped him again and it cut the fucking jacket. It was a very good blade; I mean, you could shave with it.

I sliced his fucking jacket, and it sliced through into his fucking chest. But when I did it, he didn't see it.

And he obviously didn't feel it.

But when he went to raise the fucking chain up over his head to fucking hit me, his fucking chest opened up.

I didn't feel it and he didn't feel it, and he was like, "Oh, shit!" and then we were on.

Marsha goes scrambling across the street into the fucking Deli Stop, screaming, "They're killing Michael! They're killing Sticca!"

Johnny was still in there with Danielle.

But when Marsha went in screaming, the guy with the chest pulled up, realized he was really fucked-up, and I saw my opening. I got out of their little fucking circle.

They were fucked-up—the guy was cut open, and they started running away. That was the end of it for them. It was over, right?

Then Johnny Blitz comes running out.

He sees those guys running and he says, "They fucked with you—I'll kill 'em!"

I said, "No, no, no. It's over. It's done already. It's done. It's a done deal."

But Johnny chased them down Fifth Street, towards Third. You know that block, right, it's got trees and everything? There was a streetlight that was out—about halfway down the block—and everything just became silhouettes.

The lights were shining behind them and Johnny's chasing after them and I'm yelling, "Johnny, it's over! It's over!"

Johnny yells back, "Fuck them, I'll kill 'em."

Two guys faded back. I see somebody hit somebody and somebody go down. So I run down the fucking street after them.

Then I see the guy is punching the guy on the ground, but as I get closer I see the punching isn't punching—it was stabbing. The guy knocked down the other guy, took his knife, and was stabbing him in the chest.

When I get down there, the guy on the ground is like . . . open. Just open. He was like open shirt, open guts, just this mess.

Johnny had on this Conan T-shirt. It said CONAN in big, orange Day-Glo letters. So I see the Conan T-shirt and realized it was Johnny on the ground. He was just lying there; I thought he was dead. He was cut from like his fucking groin to his neck. And he was open across his chest. It was like open—He was . . . opened.

When I saw it was Johnny, I fucking freaked. I was screaming, "YOU MOTHERFUCKING ASSHOLES!"

Everything got real sketchy. The guy who was stabbing him stood up, and in his hand he still had the knife.

I still had my switchblade and I just charged him from the back and stuck him. I got him from the thigh up to the rib cage. And he just went down.

Then I heard someone say, "Get the gun." Then "Hogan's Heroes" came into my head, and I thought, Oh, if you're running zigzag, they can't shoot ya.

So I started running. I'm telling you, it was a fucking circus. I'm halfway up Fifth Street, I know the girls are behind me, as far as I'm concerned my friend is dead, and now these guys are gonna shoot me.

So I run back the way I came, but I'm going two steps this way, three steps that way—I looked like a total asshole: "Oh, oh, I'll run zigzag."

I got back to Second Avenue. I got the girls with me, then things started happening, sirens and everything. I got a cab and just threw a twenty-dollar bill at the cabdriver.

I said, "Get us the fuck outta here."

I pulled Marsha and Danielle into the fucking cab, and a cop stopped us right away. The cabdriver already had the twenty dollars, and he was looking at us, and I said, "We were from uptown, right?"

So the cop comes over and asks the driver, "Where'd you get them?"

The driver said, "They were from uptown. I picked them up on Fifty-seventh Street."

So the cop said, "Okay, go ahead."

So they let us go.

I had blood all over me, and we went back to Marsha's place, and I called James Sliman and said, "They fucking killed Johnny. They fucking killed Blitz."

JAMES SLIMAN: I called Hilly and told him what happened. Hilly called St. Vincent's Hospital to check on Johnny's arrival and condition. It was too soon to get any information about how he was doing. So Hilly said, "Alright, we're all gonna have to meet at the police station."

JEFF MAGNUM: I was like, "Johnny got cut? What, shaving?"

I just couldn't imagine it was as bad as it was. I mean these guys got in fights in Cleveland bars where they'd be beating the shit out of some guy with pool cues. Johnny was like a bulldog. I wouldn't have fucked with him. You had to be an idiot to fuck with him.

I don't know about you, but I also wouldn't yell at a car filled with Puerto Ricans. I think my mom told me one day, "Don't cross the street without looking both ways and don't ever yell at a car filled with Puerto Ricans."

They wouldn't let us see Johnny when we went to the hospital. They told us he was in surgery. They had some trauma team working on him— and they mentioned that he might not make it.

GYDA GASH: Cheetah and I were living at the Irving Hotel on Gramercy Park when we got the phone call. We didn't believe it at first. I don't remember the details. We were getting pretty high at that time.

JAMES SLIMAN: I woke up Jimmy Zero, who was with Suzy Headbanger. They came with us. And Stiv met us down there too. We all went down to the police station at nine in the morning.

MICHAEL STICCA: I went down to the Ninth Precinct two or three hours after I'd cleaned up and spoke to everybody. When I got to the police station, they already had those stupid magazines out. They had the fucking Dead Boys layouts and all this Dead Boys stuff—they already knew Johnny Blitz was a punk rock guy.

I said, "I'm reporting a murder. These guys murdered my friend."

So they busted me. For stabbing Johnny.

The cops took me to this "Barney Miller" kind of room. I mean, I split the guy—I knew I did the guy, so I'm not saying anything. But when they gave me the papers to sign, it said "Mr. Sticca stabbed Mr. Madansky."

Johnny Blitz's real name is John Madansky.

So I was like, "Oh, no, that's not the guy I stabbed. Madansky was with me."

So they said, "Oh, let's just cross his name out and put the other name in."

What happened was, after I split the guy who stabbed Johnny, he disappeared. The police found a trail of blood that went from the crime scene into a bar—I guess they dragged him somewhere and he just like disappeared. Totally disappeared. They never found the body even. Never.

So I thought the cops are talking about the guy that disappeared, but it was the name of the fucking guy in the army fatigue jacket that I slashed at the beginning of the whole incident. Because the other guy was just like totally gone. So I ended up going to Rikers Island.

JAMES SLIMAN: The next day, I had to leave on a two-week vacation from the Dead Boys, and Hilly, and all that crap, to go to Los Angeles. Blondie was leaving on the same day to play L.A., but I was not going to work for them.

Michael Sticca said that I deserted him when I went out there and tried to take his job away. See, they kept Michael at the Ninth Precinct for one night, and the next day he was off to Rikers Island, because nobody posted bail for him.

Michael was working for Blondie as a roadie. But I didn't want his job. I didn't roadie for them. I didn't do anything. I just hung around with them.

But Michael says that I deserted him and that I left it to Hilly and Suzanne to bail him out. Suzanne told me it would be taken care of. And it wasn't. For whatever reason, it wasn't.

Big success had just kicked in for Blondie. I think this was right before "Heart of Glass." But everyone could see Blondie was starting to make it big. I mean Blondie was adapting and Michael Sticca couldn't grow with the band. When you grow like that you have to make compromises. The Blondies compromised their own artistic integrity or whatever to make more commercial music. Right?

But Michael couldn't do that. He just couldn't conform with the procedures of more business-like, big money procedures. You know, being more prompt, trying not to drink so much, being more responsible. The fact is that the roadies have to be more responsible than the band members do. When you're on the road, you can get fucked up all you want as long as you're onstage doing your show for a couple hours. Right? And also when the level of success gets higher, the band members are separated from the crew more. So Michael can't pal around with them as much as he did before because they're surrounded by record-company people and press people and kids wanting autographs and stuff like that. So there begins to be a bit of a class system there. Sometimes the crew even stays in a separate hotel. Michael was just the pal of the band who was a roadie.

MICHAEL STICCA: I told the stupid-ass public defender guy what happened, but then he told some fucking ridiculous story that he made up for the fucking judge, and I said, "That's not what I said!"

The fucking judge was banging away: "Order! Order!"

They sent me to Rikers Island right away. I was wearing all black—you know, the black fucking sweater, the black fucking corduroy Levi's, the black fucking Beatle boots with the Cuban heels—and I was like scared to fucking death.

After I did the whole physical and all that shit, they were leading us out into the cellblock. I'm chained, and there's two Puerto Ricans and blacks in front of me and two Puerto Ricans and blacks behind me—I'm like Mr. White Boy in the middle.

All these guys are looking out of their cells at me. All I see are eyes. It was four in the morning, and this one guy says, "Hey! Juan! *Que pasa?*"

Another guy goes, "Ramon! Where the fuck were you, man? Oh, shit, I was looking for you six months ago . . . I've been in here for eight months!"

I'm going, "I'm in hell. Here we go. They know everybody. I know nobody."

Somebody says, "Hey, who's the white kid?"

I'm like, "Oh god."

So the guys I was chained to were put two and three to a cell, but they put me up on the fucking top tier. Little fucking Mr. Homicide Boy. I had my own cell.

JAMES SLIMAN: Johnny was all fucked-up, his whole midsection was all stabbed and cut up and everything. He was in the hospital, St. Vincent's, for a month or so. He was hooked up to all kinds of tubes and he had blood transfusions. He was really, really, really bad—and he had no health insurance, with major medical bills. That's when Hilly decided that we should do a benefit for him, the Blitz Benefit.

GYDA GASH: I put together the fucking benefit, it wasn't Cheetah. I was the one sitting in the fucking pay phone at CBGB's with the phone numbers, making the calls, arguing with people about their positions—you know, what time they were going to go on.

JAMES SLIMAN: We did the big benefit, which was a three-day weekend here in New York at CBGB's, and we did a smaller one in Cleveland. I had a blast at the Blitz Benefit in New York. It was the funnest weekend. Divine got up there with the Dead Boys, John Belushi played drums with the Dead Boys, and all the New York bands played.

MICHAEL STICCA: The Blitz Benefit? Totally ripped off. Hilly told me I was supposed to get money, that's why I had Blondie show up there. Blondie was gonna do two gigs in Long Island and give me the money from those shows.

Debbie Harry was very cool: "Michael, I know you're in trouble. I know you need money. We're just gonna give you these gigs. We're gonna give you the money from them."

I said, "Do that Hilly thing. Do that CBGB's Blitz Benefit thing."

Debbie said, "No, Hilly sucks. We don't wanna do that fucking thing. No."

I said, "No, no. It'll be okay."

Debbie said, "Are you sure you're gonna get half the money?"

I said, "Yeah, I'm gonna get half the money."

Divine was there, John Belushi, and I got nothing from it.

JAMES SLIMAN: I think Blondie thought Michael Sticca's bail was under control, that Hilly was taking care of it. Which is what I was told, so I didn't tell them any differently. I said, "Hilly and the other people who work for him are taking care of it."

But Michael thought they deserted him. Michael thought that everybody just left him there. Which I guess everyone really did, but not intentionally, you know? I mean, Blondie was becoming one of the biggest bands in the world. So they were getting pretty wrapped up in their own stuff.

I mean, it was getting crazy for Blondie. I had a party at that time and Debbie Harry and Chris Stein showed up with a guy from the record company. Debbie grabbed me, and said, "Come here, I gotta talk to you."

Her and Chris pulled me into the bathroom and opened up a big sandwich bag full of blow. The guy from the record company or the radio interview had given it to them. Debbie said, "We have tons of it back at the hotel. This is nothing."

Debbie was very freaked, she was very nervous. She didn't know what to make about all of this, people all over her, pulling her from all directions, everyone's telling her she's gonna be the next Farrah Fawcett, and she was saying that she didn't want to be Farrah Fawcett. All she wanted to do was sing. I mean, she was on every magazine cover in Europe, in this country, Japan, Australia, all over the world. She didn't understand it, and she didn't know what to make of it.

LEGS McNEIL: I felt really sorry for Debbie and Chris when they started to make it. Debbie and Chris hung out all the time. They were really mainstays of the scene; you know Debbie had her car parked out in front of CBGB's and would give everyone a ride home. And though Debbie was gorgeous, she was more than that, she was hysterically funny.

Then one day I was walking to CBGB's and there was this film trailer parked out front and a line of about five hundred people waiting to get inside. I thought, What's this?

So I went into the trailer and it was Debbie. She was all dressed up, surrounded by asshole record-company people, and she told me they were doing a live television show. Not long after that she couldn't hang out anymore because people would follow her and bother her. She had to wear scarves and dark glasses. Being famous is everyone's dream, but the reality for Debbie looked really ugly. I felt sorry for her—she had been this really hilarious chick, and after success, she just seemed so lonely.

JAMES SLIMAN: Debbie didn't want to go back out to the party where the record-company guy was waiting for her. She said, "They give this stuff to us just to keep us stoned, I don't even want it. You fucking take it. They just keep giving it to us! That's all these fucking guys give us! They want, they want, they want, and for that they give us this shit! James, this is for you, I don't even want it, my hotel room is full of it."

So I kept it. It was like a couple thousand dollars' worth of cocaine.

MICHAEL STICCA: I didn't find out that Johnny Blitz was alive until after I got out of Rikers.

The punching that I saw was them stabbing him in the chest. There were five puncture wounds around his heart. He had the fucking cut here, the cut this way and then he had these five holes, but they all missed his heart.

But what happened was, when I heard the sirens coming and we were in the cab, the cops came, saw Johnny lying there with all his organs out—the cops are not supposed to move you, they're supposed to wait for an ambulance, but they just freaked out. They picked him up and put him in the back of the squad car and drove him to Bellevue. If the cops would have waited for an ambulance Johnny would have been dead.

The doctors started working on Johnny immediately. But when the surgeon saw Johnny's swastika, he just stopped working on him. The surgeon was Jewish.

A black doctor came over and said, "We can't stop doing this, man."

So the black doctor worked on him for eight hours. The black doctor saved Johnny's life. He was cool.

CHEETAH CHROME: We had a lot of time on our hands while Johnny was gone. We didn't think the band would have to break up. I mean we knew Johnny was gonna be alright, so we were just waiting for him to get better. That was it, and so we went down to CBGB's and hung out.

Oh man, it was like hell, you know, that was when I started getting into dope and shit, just a lot of extra time.

JEFF MAGNUM: Of course I got blamed for Johnny getting stabbed. When Johnny got better, we played at someplace in Queens and we didn't do very good. I think we only did two or three songs, and the others threw everything up in the air and got offstage.

After the show everybody had a fight. That's when Jimmy Zero said to me, "You know, the reason Johnny got knifed is because you weren't there!"

I said, "I wasn't even gonna go out with the guy. We had no plan to go out together, why are you telling me this? This is all bullshit. You're making this up!"

Jimmy Zero said that I might've created something in Johnny's mind where he needed to be more macho or something. I never did it, it's all bull—I can't wind people up.

I started crying. I got real emotional about it, like, "I didn't do this, it's not my fault, I wasn't even there, how dare you accuse me of this?"

I told Johnny, "They musta stepped on the air hose to your brain if you believe this. This is stupid! How can you believe this?"

So we had this fight and then we had to get in the car and drive back to Manhattan. We had to pile into the back of this fucking station wagon and I'm sitting in the way back with Cheetah and Gyda, you know the way backseat? Looking out the back window like we're eight years old?

So then Cheetah and Gyda start duking it out. And Cheetah's hitting Gyda and missing her and hitting me. He punched me. I said, "Hey, will you watch it? You're getting me!"

He was making me spill my drink. I mean, how can you sit in the back of a station wagon and stare out that back window? I mean, that's where they put the dog. And he kept hitting me.

MICHAEL STICCA: Anyway, the thing goes in front of the grand jury; I'm the last person to go in. And I tell my story to the grand jury. Suddenly I'm free, like what the fuck happened?

What happened was that the grand jury called the girl up, the one that was in the car that tried to hit us, the girl that knocked down Marsha. She was the one. They called her to testify, and their argument was that I said, "You Puerto Rican thugs, you all should die, you spic this, yabbada yabbada ya." They said that I was a racist and said all this fucking racial shit, and that's why they got out of the fucking car.

But when they called the girl up—their own witness—and asked her, "What exactly did Mr. Sticca say to make you come out of the car?"

She said, "I couldn't hear anything. It was cold that night, and the windows were all rolled up. He was just waving his hands, and then they piled out of the car."

So that blew their whole case. I did nothing. They provoked the whole thing, and they threw the fucking case outta court because of that chick's testimony. It cost me eight thousand dollars and a fucking year of bullshit.

JEFF MAGNUM: All I wanted to do was play the bass real loud. I didn't want to have to hang out with these maniacs. Jesus, what is this? I can't even drink my drink, cause Cheetah can't aim? And they didn't even put seat belts in the back, you know—they want you to die, it's a death seat.

Finally Gyda decides she's gonna go for a walk. We're at a red light, and Gyda decided she wasn't gonna sleep at the hotel. So she got out and got a big pout on and said, "I'm leaving. I'm getting outta here."

So we get back to the hotel—me and my girlfriend shared a room with Cheetah and Gyda—and Cheetah decides that he's mental. So he threw a bunch of shit out the window and called the cops. He did, Cheetah called the cops on himself. He said, "Come and get me, I'm mental. Please come now and arrest me."

You know, he's standing there in his leopard-skin spandex pants, no shirt on, telling the police, "Come here and arrest me because I'm not fit to live."

I was like, "Gimme the phone, let me talk to them, they won't believe you, I can be *way* more convincing than you."

So finally the cops show up. They're big, fat, slobby cops and they say, "Hey, what's going on? Living the commune life, huh? Are you guys hippies or what?"

But the cops wouldn't take Cheetah. They wouldn't take him away; they refused to arrest him. They said he wasn't psycho enough. You know, "We're sorry, you don't get taken away, our limit is filled."

So the cops left, and before they reached their car—we were on the third floor, and before they could get back to their police car, Cheetah threw an electric fan out the window, one of those big window fans, and it bounced off their cop car. It almost hit one of the cops in the head.

Cheetah made the cut then.

All of a sudden the cops were up those stairs a whole lot faster than when they first came. They *flew* up those stairs. That's when they took him and bounced him around the room. They closed the door to the other room and we heard "BOOM! BOOM! BOOM!"

I was like, "God, I wish I could hit him. Can I hold his arms? Let me hit him once, come on, you cops are used to this. Let me hit him. I'll deny everything."

Then we hear the cops yelling, "AND PUT ON SOME PANTS!"

Cheetah says, "I GOT PANTS ON!"

They're dragging him out to the hallway, and of course he's got his leopard-skin spandex things on. The cops are saying, "YOU GOT PANTS?"

Cheetah's saying, "YEAH, I'M WEARING 'EM. I GOT PANTS ON!" Then they took him away.

I mean, what the fuck was I doing with these guys? I just wanted to play the bass real loud.

Then Hilly calls up and says, "Well, red-haired people are more ready to snap than normal-colored-hair people. They're crazier than all of us."

And I'm listening to THIS? I don't know, I was like, "Naaaaahhhh, this can't be, this can't be right, I'm on Mars. I mean this can't be right. This can't be the way you're supposed to be in a band."

Chapter 34

■ Anarchy in the USA

BOB GRUEN: When the Sex Pistols came to America I went down to the first show in Atlanta on my own as a freelance photographer. I had photographed them in London before they became notorious and had gotten along with them. So when it was announced that Atlanta would be the first date on their American tour, I decided to go to the show.

My plan was to go down for the day, see the show, stay overnight, and come back home. So I went down, and saw the show. I was amazed by the amount of press that was in Atlanta. I would say that the opening-show audience was about 60 to 75 percent press. It wasn't like the record company had paid for anybody. Everybody was there totally on their own money or their company's money. I was thinking, How are we all going to make our money back?

As the Pistols were getting on the bus, getting ready to pull out that night, I went over to say good-bye to Malcolm. Malcolm said, "Well, too bad you can't come with us, Bob."

I said, "Yeah, I'd love to come along. I'm sure you're gonna have a great trip."

Malcolm went, "Yeah, well, we can't take you because we can only take twelve people on the bus and there's the band and the bodyguards and there's the secretary and there's me and the driver and uh, well, that only makes eleven . . . Why don't you come with us, Bob?"

I said, "Say what?"

He said, "Well, why don't you come along?"

I said, "Yeah, okay, what the hell. I'm not busy. It's only a couple of days."

We were in the parking lot of the hotel. I just ran in and got my bag. I didn't have a suitcase because I wasn't planning to stay. I had the clothes I was wearing and my camera bag and I just ran in, checked out, and ran back to the bus and off we went. That was it. I was on the bus with the band. It was like, "Hi guys, what's happening?"

DANNY FIELDS: I was following the Sex Pistols in the press, thinking, This is trouble. They interfered with our Ramones agenda all over the place, not rightly or wrongly. They were just diverting attention and energy from what we were doing.

But then again, what am I going to do, wish them out of existence? They were real and they were inspired into existence by Iggy and the Stooges. The first song that the Sex Pistols played was "I Wanna Be Your Dog," the greatest punk song ever written to this day. The one and only true punk song if there had to be one. And Malcolm McLaren was inspired into existence by the New York Dolls, whom he managed.

But Malcolm's strategy for the Pistols was the theory of chaos. It was out of control and it had nothing to do with anything musical. It had to do with this phenomenon of terror that was coming over from England. They put safety pins in the queen's nose and they would vomit and curse and say it's the end of the world. I always say when the music moves from the music section to the front page of the newspaper, you're in trouble.

BOB GRUEN: Traveling with the band was a real contrast compared to just seeing their concerts. Their shows were complete chaos but the bus was actually mellow. Mostly we drank beer, passed joints, and listened to dub reggae music.

But then the bus would pull up, the doors would snap open, and there would be three television cameras pointing up from the bottom of the stairs. The fans would be gathered around and the madness would start.

At one stop, Johnny Rotten opened a window in the back and leaned out. The fans came running over and a kid held up an album and begged, "Would you autograph this for me?"

Johnny just leaned over and spit on it.

The kid said, "Wow, man, thank you! I can't believe it! Thank you so much!"

That's when I started thinking, There's something wrong here. This is not normal.

It wasn't only the band who were crazy—the people who were supporting them were worse. The Sex Pistols weren't violent people, but by shouting their boredom and rage with everything, they attracted the most bizarre reactions from every side.

One night Noel Monk, the Sex Pistols' road manager, was asleep. We pulled into a truck stop like two or three in the morning and Sid and I were sitting up front talking. We pulled into this place, so we jumped off to get a hamburger. We were sitting down at the counter and we ordered. I got a hamburger and Sid got some eggs. Noel came running in—"What are you doing? What's going on? What's happening here?"

I said, "We're getting something to eat. Nothing's happening, you know?"

Noel said, "Okay, well come right back on the bus." Everything was very normal, but then this big cowboy walked in with his family and took a seat at a table right next to us. The cowboy recognized Sid and started talking to him, and then invited Sid to join him at the table and eat with his family. Everything was fine, until I heard the cowboy say, "Oh, you're Vicious, can you do this?"

I looked over just in time to see the cowboy putting a cigarette out on his own hand. Sid was just sitting there eating his eggs with his knife and fork. He looked up, unfazed, and said, "Well, I can, you know, hurt myself."

Then Sid hit his hand with his knife and it made a small cut in the skin. Not very deep, but the blood started seeping out, slowly working its way down until it reached the plate of eggs. But Sid didn't care, he was hungry and just kept gobbling them up.

And the more Sid ate, the more horrified the cowboy became, until he completely freaked out, jumped up, gathered up his family, and started running for the door.

Then we pulled into a truck stop in Oklahoma. Some Okie had a really cute daughter. They recognized the band. They saw this big flashy bus. It was kind of outrageous.

He said, "Take my daughter with you."

I was like, "*Yes.* This girl is gorgeous."

Noel said, "Nobody can go on the bus."

We were like, "Noel, take her! Her father is saying it's okay."

And Noel's saying, "No. Nobody can come on the bus."

So we left her standing in the hail.

LEGS McNEIL: After four years of doing *Punk* magazine, and basically getting laughed at, suddenly everything was "PUNK!"

I was in Los Angeles, staying at the Tropicana and hanging out with the Ramones and Alice Cooper, when the Sex Pistols landed in Atlanta. It was very bizarre, because as the Pistols made their way across America, and the hysteria was broadcast on the news every night, kids in Los Angeles, and I imagine the rest of the country, were suddenly transforming themselves with safety pins, spiked haircuts, and ugliness.

I was like, "Hey, wait a minute! This isn't punk—a spiked haircut and a safety pin? What is this shit?"

I mean, after all, we were *Punk* magazine. We had come up with the name and had defined punk as this underground American rock & roll culture that had existed for almost fifteen years with the Velvet Underground, the Stooges, the MC5, etc., etc.

So it was like, "Hey, if you want to go start your own youth movement, fine, but this one's already taken."

But the answer that came back was, "Oh, you wouldn't understand. Punk started in England. You know, everyone is on the dole there, they really have something to complain about. Punk is really about class warfare and economic blah, blah, blah."

So I'd say, "Yeah, well, what the fuck was Malcolm McLaren doing hanging out, managing the New York Dolls, and watching Richard Hell at CBGB's?"

But you couldn't compete with those images of safety pins and spiked hair.

BOB GRUEN: John Holmstrom showed up and we had a birthday party for him after the show in Tulsa or Oklahoma City. Everybody came down to my room, we had a whole bunch of booze, and a couple of local people showed up who had been at the show. There was this one really gorgeous blond woman, but a couple of the other locals came over and said, "By the way, that girl Laurie—used to be Larry."

This gorgeous blonde was a guy that had his dick cut off. Everybody in Tulsa knew him, but we didn't. He looked like a good-looking girl to us.

Sid ended up going off to his room with her, and everybody at the party was going, "Wow, Sid's with the transsexual."

So when he came back, we're all going, "Hey, Sid, what was it like?"

He said, "Oh, she was okay."

Sid wasn't looking for anything, everything found him, you know? He was sort of like he was a magnet, like zoom! Everything would come to him. Weird things seemed to happen around Sid. That very same night, this Vietnam vet asked Sid to make it with his girlfriend while he watched.

After a while, Sid came back and he said, "I just shit in her mouth."

I said, "What? Are you kidding? Why'd you do that?"

He said, "Well, her boyfriend said he wanted her to have an experience she wouldn't forget."

It seemed to make sense at the time. After you've had a few drinks, you can say to yourself, "Well, it's okay. It wasn't *my* mouth."

People came to get bitten. They didn't really come to get petted. They came to see if the Sex Pistols really were wild, and if they were, so much the better. Because the people that were showing up were pretty off-the-wall. I mean, a guy who cuts his dick off is not your average person, you know?

The division between Malcolm and Noel started because Noel was trying to keep the band under wraps and keep things under control. He started putting us in different hotels. Nobody from the press could find us.

Malcolm was really upset about this. His concept of the tour was to be constantly mixed with the press. He constantly let incidents happen. Malcolm loved it when it got out of control. He didn't have *fun* unless it went out of control. That's why everyone liked him so much. Because rock & roll is about losing control. You're not supposed to sit in your seat and be aware of everything that happens. You're supposed to have a chaotic experience.

The Sex Pistols weren't making it on musicianship. I mean, what kind of bands were big at that time? Bad Company and Led Zeppelin. And the Sex Pistols managed to make it without playing music like that.

DANNY FIELDS: The Sex Pistols were on Walter Cronkite every night! I mean, can you imagine the marketing, the hype! He would say, "They're now arriving in America."

I mean, who was this news for? It was news for the wrong reasons. It was like, here's the Pistols making front-page news in England every time they burp and fart, which they did a lot. So it was reported in America, and it couldn't help but define punk rock, because as soon as something is on the seven o'clock news and on the front page of the newspapers, then *that* is punk rock.

It's the Sex Pistols and what does it do? It burps and farts and curses. Does it make music? Maybe, maybe not. Who can be bothered to listen to the music? Do you think Walter Cronkite was going to listen to twenty seconds of the music? There was no music on the network coverage of the Sex Pistols. It was simply that this sociological phenomenon from England that happened to play music was playing here.

But they never did anything outrageous. I mean, they didn't really do anything radical in terms of getting on the CBS seven o'clock news. What they did radical was in terms of music, which no one really appreciated. They were famous for the wrong reasons.

BOB GRUEN: When we finally made it to San Francisco, the band was feeling the strain. So Noel Monk took the guys out to buy leather jackets for behaving themselves. We went to this gay store in San Francisco, a giant supermarket of leather stuff, so that the band could buy their leather jackets. But they also had all of these dildos and K-Y jelly. So Sid bought all of these leather bracelets, leather belts, and then he bought some K-Y jelly, or some lubricant, some butt-fucker's lubricant, and put it in his hair. It was like Crisco and Sid shoved it all in his hair and his hair was sticking up and Johnny Rotten said, "Great, Sid. Now you can stick your head up somebody's ass."

LEGS MCNEIL: When Holmstrom called me from the road and told me to meet him in San Francisco for the last show of the tour, I had no interest in going. But John told me it was my job, that I was Resident Punk and I had to show up, it would be good for the story he was writing. Also, Tom Forcade was making a movie, and he had given us a lot of money and I owed it to Tom and him to show up.

So I picked up the receptionist from *Playboy* magazine and we drove up to San Francisco.

BOB GRUEN: After the Winterland show all the fans were cheering. Sid came back out, looked down at the audience, and picked out four pretty girls near the front. He grabbed them by the hand and said, "Come with me."

Bill Graham was standing there, shocked. I mean, lots of band members come out and talk to a girl or two, and maybe pull a chick, but they never actually physically pull four of them up and say, "Come with me."

I didn't see Johnny with a girl until the last night. He left the last show with some girl who was backstage. It was kind of a surprise, because from the first minute I met him, Johnny didn't seem to ever like anything.

He just seemed to be in a really bad mood from day one. You know, everything sucked. He was so cynical and sarcastic about everything that he would always point out the derogatory aspect of everything. That's why I was so surprised when I saw him leave the Winterland gig with a girl on his arm and half a smile on his face. It was the most human thing I ever saw, because it was something so out of character to see him enjoy a moment of life.

LEGS MCNEIL: The Pistols sucked at Winterland. The show was awful, but it didn't seem to matter. Everyone was just thrilled to be there in the presence of the Sex Pistols. After the show, Holmstrom handed me a backstage pass and said, "Go talk to Sid. You'll like him, he's just like you."

I thought, Fuck you, Sid's a fucking moron. You know, "Thanks a lot."

I went backstage, and Bob Gruen was there, and he got me a beer and introduced me to the band. Every one of them looked miserable. Sid sat in a chair with his shirt off. Johnny was alone on a couch muttering to himself.

Steve and Paul were lounging next to a plastic garbage pail filled with Heinekens. They were all just sitting around griping to each other. What was funny was that Sid had pulled four chicks from the audience, and the four girls were just standing around, everyone was ignoring them, and then Sid turned to them and said, "So who's gonna fuck me tonight?"

"Don't we even get a kiss first?" one of the girls asked. She wasn't kidding.

Just then Annie Leibovitz, the *Rolling Stone* photographer, and an assistant carrying flash boxes, cables, and white umbrellas came barging in. She paraded through the dressing room and began setting up all the equipment in the bathroom at the end.

She said, "Ah, excuse me . . . Johnny, could we get you in here for a shot with Sid?"

"Fuck him," Johnny said. "Why should I have to go over to that bastard. Tell the wanker to come over here!"

"Ah, Sid, do you think you could join Johnny on the couch so I can get a shot of the two—"

Sid said, "Fuck off!"

"Okay, then, Johnny can I get you in the bathroom alone?"

"Piss off!"

"But it's for the cover of *Rolling Stone* magazine . . . ," Leibovitz said.

"WELL THEN, IS MY HAIR ALRIGHT?" Johnny shrieked as he pulled on his greasy, matted hair, so that it formed two little horns. It was pretty funny, but over all the whole scene was pretty depressing. The Sex Pistols didn't seem to be having any fun. I just wanted to get out of there.

So I loaded up my jacket with Heinekens and split.

I didn't know it at the time, but that was the last few moments of the Sex Pistols' existence. That was the last few moments of them together as a band.

I came out of the dressing room, and Damita just happened to be walking by wearing a Ramones T-shirt. She was eight months pregnant and had a hole cut out in the T-shirt, so that her bulging stomach popped through. I peeled off my backstage pass and slapped it on Damita's pregnant belly, and said, "Go for it, Damita!"

She said, "Wow, a backstage pass! Cool."

Then she waddled away to the dressing room.

BOB GRUEN: I woke up the next morning and there was Damita, eight months pregnant, sleeping in the bathtub. I said to myself, "What the fuck am I doing in San Francisco?"

I hadn't been home in ten days, I hadn't changed my clothes in ten days, and because there was so much competition, I was under a lot of pressure to get back to New York and develop my film.

So I made one of my favorite phone calls and said, "What time is the next flight to New York?"

When I was leaving the room, I saw Joe Stevens, the photographer, in the hallway. He said, "The band is planning to go to Brazil. They're gonna record and do some filming down there with Ronald Biggs, the Great Train Robber. You wanna come with us?"

I looked at him and I said, "Brazil! What, are you kidding? Who's gonna pay for that?"

He said, "Well, I'm going to get my newspaper to pay for the airfare." I thought, You lucky bastard.

I said, "I'd love to go to Brazil, but nobody's paying for it for me and I'm not putting another two thousand dollars into this."

So I went to the airport and took the first flight out. When I got back to New York it was snowing. It snowed for two days. I stayed in the house and worked in the darkroom day and night, during the entire blizzard. I felt pressured because tons of magazines were going to be doing big features on the Sex Pistols.

I finally took a break in the middle of one of those nights and went over to CBGB's. I walked in and Johnny Rotten was there. He had flown in from San Francisco.

He said, "Did you hear the news?"

I said, "What news?"

He showed me his T-shirt that said "I survived the Sex Pistols tour." Johnny had written on his shirt "But the band didn't."

I said, "Well, what does that mean?"

He said, "What do you think? This is it. We broke up."

I said, "What do you mean, you broke up?"

I had just invested two weeks and a lot of money into these pictures.

He said, "That's it. Malcolm and the rest of the guys went off to Brazil and I'm here. We're not doing it anymore."

They were the biggest band in the world and they just broke up. Everything just seemed to be the opposite with that band all the time.

DANNY FIELDS: When the Sex Pistols broke up in San Francisco, it showed everyone that this punk thing wasn't viable. That they were meant to self-destruct and so what's the point in investing in any of them?

Why build an audience for the Ramones or the Pistols or the Clash? Why institutionalize them if they're just going to be destroyed, if it's their nature to destroy others and to destroy themselves?

The whole thing just got out of control and whatever chance the Ramones had to get on the radio based on the merit of the music was then wiped out by the Sex Pistols because it became too hot to handle. American radio, then as now, doesn't like to participate in anything that is dangerous or revolutionary or radical. So the whole thing became a great pile of shit that no one wanted to go near.

LEGS MCNEIL: It's funny, but now "punk" was being used to describe something the world thought of as English. When we first started the magazine, we had subscribed to a newspaper clipping service that sent us a clipping every time the term "punk" was used in an article or newspaper story—so we had watched as the name had grown into this phenomenon. Four years earlier, we had pasted the Bowery with bumper stickers that said "WATCH OUT! PUNK IS COMING!"

Now that it was here, I didn't want any part of it.

Overnight, punk had become as stupid as everything else. This wonderful vital force that was articulated by the music was really about corrupting every form—it was about advocating kids to not wait to be told what to do, but make life up for themselves, it was about trying to get people to use their imaginations again, it was about not being perfect, it was about saying it was okay to be amateurish and funny, that real creativity came out of making a mess, it was about working with what you got in front of you and turning everything embarrassing, awful, and stupid in your life to your advantage.

But after the Sex Pistols tour, I had no interest in doing *Punk* magazine. It just felt like this phony media thing. Punk wasn't ours anymore. It had become everything we hated. It seemed like it had become everything we had started the magazine to rage against. So Holmstrom found a new resident punk.

I was replaced. But I didn't care. It was over.

ARTURO VEGA: I was shocked when the Pistols broke up. I thought it was so stupid. Fucking young people—it's like Oscar Wilde said—"Youth, it's wasted on the young."

Assholes.

Chapter 35

■ Sonic Reducer

CHEETAH CHROME: They called us back off tour, they called us into Seymour Stein's office. The whole band, Hilly, everybody, right? Seymour said, "I bet a lot of money on punk rock. I was wrong. Now, if you wanna continue your relationship with the label, we want you to change your image, change your style of music, and change the name of the band."

At that point Jimmy and Johnny said to Seymour, "What do you mean, Seymour?"

I just flipped out, just the fact they expressed interest at all. I just thought to myself, Well, these aren't the same guys that I used to be with. This is over.

JEFF MAGNUM: We always brought tallboys of beer to the meetings with Seymour Stein at Sire Records. It was like, "Let's get our beers and go to the tallboy meeting." We would ask Hilly, "How many tallboys is this meeting going to be? How long is Seymour gonna yell at us? Through one tallboy or two?"

Oh man, the last time was the worst—Seymour said, "You gotta stop this!"

We were like, "Well, we thought you wanted this."

Seymour was saying, "You guys gotta clean up your act. This punk stuff can't go on. You're bustin' up everything and it's not happening. There's no money and people ain't buying your stupid records."

Hilly was there too. I don't think he had a tallboy that day, but he looked like he needed a crate of tallboys. He just sat behind us going, "Grrrrrrrr, how did I get into this? Why do I do these things?"

This was the black cloud of tallboy meetings.

I was so astounded by the whole thing. I thought, You sign the chimpanzees, you tell them to go out on the road and *be* chimpanzees, and now you're telling us *not* to be chimpanzees? What are we supposed to be now? Considering half of the band *are* chimpanzees and we've learned how to walk dragging our wrists, *I am* part chimpanzee now! Now you're telling us to stop—well, can I have another tallboy?

CHEETAH CHROME: Seymour said, "Well, this punk rock thing is just a flash in the pan, you'd better get more pop." Stiv was buying into that shit, because he was totally career-minded. I got my guitar, got up, and walked out.

Stiv came out into the hallway and said, "Come on back in."

I said, "No, you stay and tell me what happened later."

JEFF MAGNUM: I could have told Seymour, "You're having a hard time with this band now? Guess what? No songs in the tank for these songwriters. Plus we have drummer bee who has one wing instead of two."

We all went home on the train and we were dragging our tails, and we were like, "Gosh, this must be kinda like the end, huh? Is this the beginning or the end, or what?"

DUNCAN HANNAH: Then the scene got polluted by the press. Suddenly, people from uptown were coming downtown and it was really a shame to me. Suddenly, CBGB's was packed. And the more people you got, the more you got clones, right?

So what used to be individuals, like James Chance and Anya Phillips and Richard Hell, suddenly you were getting twenty-five versions of each of them, milling about. I remember punk was in *Vogue*, and when that issue came out, I saw Diana Vreeland at CBGB's, and all these tourists, right? Slumming—in the Bowery. And I just thought, "Ah, forget it. You know, if they're gonna do this, I quit."

But of course I couldn't quit, because it was my home.

PHILIPPE MARCADE: Things were getting crazy. Around that time, I was hanging out at Max's with Jerry Nolan. We were there one night and Jerry and I walked into the downstairs bar. There used to be a bench by the window, and there was this big dude standing there. A big guy in a polyester suit that looked like he was in the mafia. You know, a really sleazy fuck. And he had his drink on the arm of the bench. Jerry's pants brushed against it and spilled the drink.

The guy turned around and said, "Motherfucker, you spilled my drink!"

I think if he had said, "You spilled my drink," Jerry probably would have gotten him another one, you know, would've said, "What were you drinking?" But the guy was looking for a fight, he played it like Mr. Macho.

Then I saw what I could not believe. Jerry is a real tough motherfucker, he nailed that guy with about five or six punches right to the face. Jerry was like Mike Tyson, bam bam bam, left, right, left, right, left, right, and this guy just went down. Jerry turned around, looked at me and said, "The fucker, shouldn't have fucked with me, man."

MARIAH ACQUIAR: Connie caught Dee Dee getting a blow job in the parking lot of the Amato Opera House, around the corner from CBGB's. When Connie saw Dee Dee with this blond girl, she started screaming and running towards them. Of course they ran away.

Dee Dee ran in one direction, the chick ran in the other, and Connie lost them. So Connie came back into CBGB's looking for the blonde. She saw my blond hair, went up to the bar, grabbed a beer mug, smashed it sideways, making this weapon—two cutting edges with a handle.

Connie came up to me from behind, and just as she was bringing the thing down on the back of my head—she was so much taller than I was, especially with her high heels on—but just as she was bringing this thing down on my skull—somebody grabbed me.

It was Helen Wheels. Helen grabbed me with her arm around my waist, pulled me back behind her, and as she did, my body swung around and the glass went right past my face. Within an inch or two. I was cross-eyed looking at it, I could feel the air, I could smell the beer.

Connie immediately tried to get me again. She pulled her arm up, and Helen Wheels barked right in her face. Helen said, "Look, you don't wanna fuck with me, Connie. If I was you, I would not fuck with me."

Helen was a tough chick.

Connie's eyes were really blurred, she was very strung-out. She still had her arm up in the air, but she teetered a few times back and forth on her heels, thought about it, and then went, "I guess it's just not worth the trouble."

Connie dropped the beer mug and walked off. Helen just said that I looked like a nice kid and shouldn't get mixed up in things like that, then walked away. I was left standing there, shaking and holding on to the railing going, "Oh my god, what just happened?"

I had no clue, I had no clue.

PHILIPPE MARCADE: The guy was still on the floor, but not unconscious. Jerry was standing right on top of him, and the guy picked up the broken glass and went for Jerry's balls. He missed his balls by an inch, but got Jerry in an artery in the upper thigh.

Jerry went AHHHAAH and fell into my friend Bruce's arms, who was saying, "What's happening? What's happening?"

I saw a spot of blood on Jerry's crotch, but then I look at his feet, and man I couldn't believe it. It was like a shower, blood was just *pooouring* onto his shoes.

We tried to get an ambulance, but Jerry was bleeding so bad that we just took him outside, put him in a cab and took him to the hospital. Jerry had bled so much that the entire entrance of Max's was just blood. They were cleaning off the sidewalk with buckets of water.

I was on the sidewalk and suddenly the fucking guy in the suit is stepping out, he's just walking out onto the street. I didn't know what to do, but I put my arm out and said, "Look man, you ain't going anywhere!"

Then I said to myself, "Philippe, what are you doing man? This guy's gonna kill you, you don't want to be doing this!"

But I'd already done it. But then Michael Sticca appeared, you know, he's way tougher than me. Michael said, "Is this the fucker?"

I said, "Yeah."

Sticca grabbed him by the collar, and dragged him back upstairs. Tommy Dean, who owned Max's, he bought the place from Mickey Ruskin, said, "Look, don't call the cops, this guy's part of the mafia. I'm gonna take care of this my way."

RICHARD HELL: After we recorded *Blank Generation*, I felt like I had shot my wad as far as music was concerned. My heart just wasn't in it anymore.

That was the whole period when we basically sued to get off of Sire. I didn't know where Seymour was coming from, but I also never gave him a chance. I was both arrogant and out of it at that time. I had a lot of attitude and behaviors that weren't grounded in any reality except this eccentric little world I'd invented for myself.

IVAN JULIAN: One time Richard invited Seymour Stein down to the apartment. He was showing him around like, "Look how we live!" And then he opened the door to my tiny room with the crumbling ceiling and goes, "Look!"

Seymour turned different shades of red and kind of put his eyes down, and said, "Richard, the record will be released soon. You'll just have to wait."

RICHARD HELL: I just was not comfortable in an office with a business-man talking to me from the seat behind the big desk. I had so many assumptions about a person like that. I wouldn't trust a business person on that basis alone, I wouldn't have any respect for them at all. I just wouldn't give 'em any benefit, only doubt.

And then to have hashed that out with Sire, and getting a couple of nibbles from other labels, there was one offer we coulda taken but we didn't because we felt we could do better. But we ended up not getting our major record deal. I was just shocked—we were clearly miles ahead of everybody else—but when I think back, and think of the condition I was in, and how or why these guys in suits and ties didn't try to talk to me—it's not too surprising.

I was kind of losing interest, but I had nowhere else to go and I was strung out, so I sort of limped along, did just enough gigs to pay the rent.

IVAN JULIAN: Richard decided that we're only going to play punk venues, okay. Now, at that time, there's like, what, three of them in the country, right?

RICHARD HELL: I doubt that I was really ever cut out to perform, to make it my life's work. The only practice I ever get on the bass is either when I'm in rehearsal or writing songs. I've always thought of myself as a writer. I don't know, rock & roll is for when you're a kid anyway. Rock & roll is like a kid's game, you know? A lot of it is based on that kick out the jams thing—this release of all this pent up energy and frustration and anger and desire for attention that you have when you're that age.

I was strung out. I was just very tired.

BOB QUINE: Marc Bell came to a rehearsal and threw his bills down on the floor—his electric bill, his gas bill, his rent bill—and said, "Who's gonna pay this shit for me? I'm eating dog food! What you gonna do about this?"

Then he made it clear that he had an offer from the Ramones. My reaction was, "Let him go, drummers are a dime a dozen."

I was wrong. I had no idea how rare good drummers were, and although Bell wasn't a perfect drummer, he was a great drummer, he had power. We never did get a really good drummer again.

IVAN JULIAN: I talked to Quine about it and he was like, "Well, I'll stop if you stop," but he didn't want to quit himself. And then he's going, "Well, why don't you do it?" And I said, "Okay, I'm not that scared of Richard."

I went over to his house one day and said, "Richard, I don't think I can do it anymore."

He said, "That's cool."

So I got my stuff and left. But Richard was pissed at me—but, I mean, he was totally disinterested.

RICHARD LLOYD: In the middle of recording Television's second album, *Adventure,* I came down with a medical problem that threw me into the hospital. I had endocarditis, which is a heart ailment from shooting drugs. It's the same bacteria as strep throat only it gets into your bloodstream, and in the pause between the heartbeats it sits on the heart tissue and begins multiplying and eating away at the tissue.

DAVID GODLIS: I got a call from Terry Ork saying that there was some kind of delay on the Television album and that they needed publicity pictures to illustrate the reason for the delay. He told me that Richard Lloyd had some disease with a really, really long name. The big rumor going around was that Keith Richards was having his blood changed so maybe that was what Lloyd was doing.

So we went to Beth Israel Hospital and I took pictures of Richard Lloyd all day. Pictures of Lloyd smoking cigarettes next to NO SMOKING signs; pictures of Lloyd playing dead, pictures of him sitting with all the old men on the floor and their IV units.

When I went back to show him the proof sheets—so he could decide which pictures to send to *Rock Scene* or wherever—he was lying in bed behind the curtains, and he was weighing out pot on a scale. He was selling pot behind the curtains, from his hospital room. And enough people were coming by that the seventy-five-year-old guy in the next bed was cranky about it, because he was going, "What's going on in there?"

And Lloyd was going, "Shut up. I told you, this is private business, so shut up."

RICHARD LLOYD: Television was going pretty good until we went on tour with Peter Gabriel. We would go into record stores and not be able to find our record, which is aggravating to any artist.

Then Elektra sent over a bunch of tapes while we were on tour. When we heard the first Cars record we said, "Uh oh. This is like our music only right down the commercial alley. This is gonna take our place." You know, they're gonna sell a million of these Cars records, and they're gonna tell us that we should be like them, which is almost what happened. They never told us to be like them—they didn't give us the chance.

We'd always been quirky. Tom writes lyrics that are like triple entendres, and he didn't have a singer's voice. I think if you slit a goat's throat it would sound like that. Anyway, he never would take singing lessons, so what are you gonna do? It's not a radio-ready voice, that's for sure.

BEBE BUELL: I finally met Stiv Bators at a party for Kiss upstairs at Max's. He was there with Cynthia from the B Girls, his fiancée. Liz Derringer goes, "There's that fucking guy, there's that weasel guy."

I walked up to him; he had on a pink jacket with bright black stripes and he looked great. He'd quiffed that night, sometimes he would grease his hair out and do a Brian Setzer. He had like a curl here, and he looked very cute.

Since it was a Kiss party, we'd been drinking champagne, the champagne was like endless. So I just walked up to Stiv and said, "I love you."

He looked at me and said, "You do?"

I said, "Uh huh, Liz and I love you."

And he said, "Well, how about if you just love me and not Liz."

It was really funny. So he was standing there with his fiancée, Cynthia, who I thought was a little goody-two-shoes, a little prissy boots, and I just said, "Cynthia, I'm stealing him."

And I took his hand and took him away. I couldn't believe I did that. It's amazing what a few glasses of champagne will do, right? Turn you right into a little dog, but I kind of wish I hadn't done that. It was kind of mean. Anyway, Stiv broke up with Cynthia the next day and I took him to Liz's, fed him, and gave him a bath.

GYDA GASH: Stiv was always very smart. He was a little bit older than everybody else and he was willing to do whatever it took for success. I was very disappointed when he put on his fucking little pink suit and did the pop thing.

At that time Cheetah really started shutting down. The Dead Boys tried to kick him out of the band when Stiv was with Bebe. We were doing a lot of dope and Bebe became like holier than thou. But we were pretty fucked-up at the time.

Then Keith Richards had a birthday party at a roller rink. Cheetah and Richard Lloyd were racing and Cheetah fell on his face and broke his arm.

CHEETAH CHROME: I was racing with Mick Jagger and Richard Lloyd on roller skates and I fell and broke my wrist. It was the stupidest thing to do . . .

GYDA GASH: So the band wanted to get rid of Cheetah. Stiv was like, "I'm gonna make money, I don't give a fuck what I do to anybody." We finally got hip to the idea that Cheetah was going to get canned. So we started doing more dope.

BEBE BUELL: I loved Stiv, he was a great guy, but he was getting a little too crazy, as far as his ingestion of substances. He started doing a lot of coke and alcohol, and he started to change. He became violent when he drank. Yeah, he would hurt himself and people and objects. But I was bigger than him so he never fucked with me.

I was a good four inches taller, and I outweighed him by about fifteen pounds. So he would never strike me, but he would strike anybody that was around me. So sometimes I would have to tie him up, to get him to calm down. Stiv would get crazy, he would be bouncing off the walls like a maniac, he would get insane.

So I'd have to get him down on his stomach, put my knee into his back, and I would take his belt and tie it around his wrists. Then I'd sit on his legs, until he calmed down. I likened it to epilepsy. That's what I used to say to him, "You had one of those fucking psycho epileptic fits last night."

So then I started fooling around with Jack Nicholson, and that's what ended the relationship. It hurt Stiv, but I was in control of my life. I wasn't some victim, I knew what I was doing, and I wanted to hang out with Jack Nicholson. I mean Stiv had gotten too crazy.

But I didn't stay with Jack because I really didn't want to be riding around in somebody's Rolls-Royce, listening to Pat Benatar. It was just not my idea of a good time. And whenever I tried to put on the records I liked, everybody thought I was so adolescent. You know, immature and freaky.

But I was thinking, "Why? Just because I like good music? Just because I'm trying to turn you on to good rock & roll? I'm trying to get through to you, and you think I'm flaky? Well, I think you're bourgeois, and I don't like you. Bye."

WAYNE KRAMER: After I got out of jail, I was living in a halfway house, and I heard that Patti Smith was playing in Ann Arbor, so I thought, "I should go thank her for putting my name on her record." Patti had put "Free Wayne Kramer" on the record sleeve of the *Radio Ethiopia* album, which was a brotherly kind of revolutionary thing to do.

After the show, it was really hard to get backstage. I felt uncomfortable, because you know how icky those backstage situations can be. I saw Fred Smith, and he was being weird with me, and then I saw he was with Patti.

I said, "Hi, Patti. I'm Wayne Kramer. I just thought I'd come by and say hello, and thank you for mentioning me on your record." She kind of went, "Oh," and space-cadetted away from me. I felt like, "She doesn't know who I am. She doesn't care who I am."

Then I realized that putting my name on the back of her record didn't have anything to do with solidarity with me, or to keep my name in front of the public. It had to do with lending credibility to her. It was her aligning herself with me as opposed to me being aligned with her.

I mean, I wasn't being a jerk to her, I was simply trying to say hello and thank her. And she just shined me on. So I never bothered with her after that.

My relationship with Fred also kind of disintegrated around that time, because he was going through a divorce and I sided with his wife. I'd been locked up and I was really into holding on to whatever you had, especially in terms of relationships. So I thought he was being an asshole. I mean, Patti was in town and he was fawning all over her in front of his wife, and I thought, Jeez, do that on your own time, man. This is really embarrassing— it's bad form.

LENNY KAYE: The Patti Smith Group met Jimmy Iovine right at the time we were finishing *Radio Ethiopia*. He'd been an engineer on John Lennon's record, an engineer on Bruce Springsteen's *Born to Run*, so he was kind of hip. He was a Record Plant engineer and became our friend, you know, like started bringing Patti up clams from Umberto's and coming up with projects.

He always kept bugging us to write songs, because he was looking for a hit. One time I was playing in the studio, he came in and said, "That's a great riff!" I worked on it some more and brought it to Patti and it became "Ghostdance."

But that wasn't the song he was looking for. Then one day, while we're making a record, Bruce Springsteen was in the next studio making *Darkness on the Edge of Town*. Jimmy kept saying, "Oh man, wouldn't it be great if we could get Patti and Bruce together? No FM radio station in America would be able to resist that!"

Bruce Springsteen and Patti Smith were intrigued with each other. There had been some rivalry, because they're both from South Jersey. Bruce is a friendly guy, and Patti thought he was kind of cool, and they started getting along. So Bruce wrote a couple of songs for Patti. He kind of tried to write them in her style and they just weren't happening. He sent them over, we listened to them, and we were like, "Hmm, he's trying to write like us, isn't he?"

We just thought, Oh, this is cute.

But Jimmy had heard this song, "Because the Night," that he had done. And he'd done a complete demo of it with the band. It had a kind of Latin feel and Patti changed a lot of the words. But it had the hook.

Jimmy would say, "Oh god, what a chorus! How could you miss it? It hits you over the head!"

So we did it. It almost hit the Top Ten. It was definitely the hit of that summer.

We did a very different version of Bruce's version. We rocked it up considerably. It's not typical of who we are, but that's what happens when you write with somebody outside your little home. But it's a really cool song.

There was some odd blood between Patti and Bruce after that, because I think Patti got a little frustrated when people thought of it as a total Bruce Springsteen song.

But you can't take away from the fact that it was instantaneous. When the record came out, they sent it to WNEW for the first time, and Vin Scelsa played it three times in a row. That was in the days when you could do that on radio. We really went into making that record; we'd been off the road for a year, we wanted to make as clear a statement as we could, we didn't want to be misunderstood.

JAMES GRAUERHOLZ: The Nova Convention was held at the Intermedia Theater in December of 1978. It was considered a summit meeting of the New York avant-garde, in William Burroughs' honor. It made a lot of artists look to where their leaders were pointing, namely back to William.

Keith Richards had been an early promised appearance, and John Giorno had leaked that to Howard Smith at the *Village Voice*, so the next day the Intermedia Theater was like a mob scene for tickets. We broke even, but of course I don't think Keith was ever really committed to come—he was probably talked out of it by advisers who said, "Hey, you're facing charges on this Toronto drug bust. Don't go hang out with Burroughs and those people, it's too downtown."

So anyway, he bailed, and after the first night of the Nova Convention, I was at the Ukrainian Theater, where Blondie was playing as part of our No-Wave Music lineup, and Jane Friedman, Patti Smith's former manager, was there with Frank Zappa. By then she was his publicist. So Jane introduced us and I said, "Frank, I'm missing like a superstar for the big night. Keith Richards bailed out. Would you read something?" He said, "Yeah. I'll read 'The Talking Asshole' piece from *Naked Lunch*."

So Patti Smith is one of my stars, right? The big night comes around, and Patti is very sick, supposedly with a flu. Her voice was shot. It was definitely like the lemon-hot-towel-around-the-neck scene in the dressing room—the whole Turkish-bath trip there, and she was milling around with her clarinet. Who knew what she was gonna do?

It was a nightmare. Pandemonium backstage. Marcia Resnick was snapping photographs, and either she or Victor Bockris knocked over a glass of wine on William's suit, and they were all just boincing around like nutcakes. Somebody came to me and said, "There's some rich bitch at the back door demanding to be let in, and she says she's Tim Leary's wife." It was crazy.

Then Frank Zappa shows up and he needs to go on and then get out of there quickly . . . and I'm getting worried that Patti's not going to go on, so I go to her dressing room to check out the situation and she says, "What is this? I'm not gonna go on after Frank Zappa. I'm not gonna do this."

I pleaded with her. I said, "Patti, we need you."

Meanwhile the audience are screaming, "KEITH! KEITH! KEITH!" through everything—even through Philip Glass, "KEITH! KEITH! KEITH!"

I said, "Patti, I really need you. I don't know what it is with you and Frank, but Frank is really helping us out. He came through for us, and he's making the whole thing a bigger deal, so forget about Frank. Please go on . . ."

So she does. She goes onstage and she says, "Well, if you people think you're gonna see Keith, you aren't, because he's in an airplane somewhere between here and L.A. So anybody that wants their money back can come up and get it from me right here and now."

Then she reached into her pocket and pulled out a ten-dollar bill and waved it at the audience. "Who wants their money back?"

Nobody knew how to deal with that, so she kind of diffused the "no Keith" thing once and for all.

Then Patti noodled around. She was in her own world. She was wearing her new fur coat, which was very odd—one of those things where punks get money and then they revert to type. I mean, she was from where? Bergen, New Jersey?

She said, "This coat cost ten thousand dollars. I sleep in it. I live in it. I haven't taken this off in . . ."

So she was showing off this fur coat, and I don't know for a fact, but I believe that her hands were in her pockets, and she was like doing something funny down there. I don't know what. She was gyrating around.

ANDI OSTROWE: That whole period after Patti falling off the stage and having the hit record was the beginning of her thinking that there are other things in life, you know? That rock & roll is not worth giving your life for.

That time reminded me of the movie *Still Moving* that she made with Robert Mapplethorpe. Very early on, Patti had gone over to Robert's house one day, and she had a little bag of props and clothes and feathers and bells and her family Bible. And he had this big statue of Mephistopheles— big and black.

Patti opened up the Bible in front of Robert's devil statue. She's blindfolded as the film starts, and she starts talking about being in the darkness, and about going into the light. She starts reading from the Bible, and at the end she says, "I choose life."

I think her whole premise is that you can't be stopped by the darkness, you have to take the light force, and go with that because that's the force of life, that's the force of God, that's the force of art and creation, not degeneration and self-degradation—like all that Sid Vicious stuff.

Chapter 36

■ Tuinals from Hell

JEFF MAGNUM: The Dead Boys started to get to me. I was starting to wonder about my own mental health.

Cheetah and Gyda had two guinea pigs, Ace and Winkle. Winkle was a long-haired white guinea pig that was there when I moved in, and then they got Ace, a little red-haired thing.

One day the guinea pigs got on Cheetah's nerves and he says to Winkle, the white one, "You shall live," like Moses. "You will live to prosper. And you, Ace, must die, because you have a brain the same size as me."

And he flung Ace out the window like a big old football. He fired the guinea pig just like an old quarterback, he didn't even look.

I just hoped nobody was walking by. Can you imagine? "Oh dear, a guinea pig just hit me in the head!"

What kind of psycho would throw out an animal?

I mean, I was thinking, What am I doing here with these assholes? I should be back being a keypunch operator in Cleveland. I can't believe I'm here doing this, there's gotta be something wrong here. This is not a rational working band.

It had gone beyond that. They're killing animals, birds, and guinea pigs—I gotta be next. You know, stabbings, dead animals, here come the drug dealers, when does it end?

And then Sid Vicious shows up.

Me and my girlfriend were sleeping one night at the hotel, and Cheetah and Gyda come in and turn on the lights and Cheetah says, "Look everybody, look who I have. Look who I brought home."

And, oh god, it's Sid Vicious. So we get up and the only thing Sid said was, "So you're Jeff Magnum, you think you can beat me up?"

It was just pathetic. It's like, "God, you're such a little wimp. How could you be beating up all these guys in England? You're just so pathetic."

So Sid and Cheetah decided we were gonna play with Sid at Max's. We were gonna back Sid up at Max's, but the rehearsals were ridiculous. We went to Max's, and Sid's face was in a bowl of salad. He was gone.

I said, "Oh well, I guess our star for the evening is not shining too brightly."

It never happened. I don't even think we played two notes with this guy, then I got the word that he told Cheetah that we played too good and he didn't want us.

CHEETAH CHROME: When Stiv Bators was with Sid Vicious, it was like the blind guy trying to talk to Frankenstein's monster, that's about the only thing I can compare it to. Stiv would be there, showing Sid something, and Sid would be nodding, "Oh . . . o . . . k . . . yeah . . . that's . . . great, oh . . . Stiv . . . that's . . . really . . . neat."

And Nancy would be, "WAKE UP, SID! WAKE UP, SID! COME ON, YOU'RE BEING AN ASSHOLE, SID. QUIT DROOLING, SID, NA NAA NAA NAA!"

Poor Sid believed his own press. He totally bought it lock, stock, and barrel.

TERRY ORK: After the Sex Pistols broke up, I was booking the groups at Max's for a while. Sid and Nancy were living at the Chelsea Hotel and Nancy became Sid's manager. They'd come by Max's, Sid wanted to do a gig, they needed money, they were on heroin.

I dealt with Nancy. She would come by and say, "Ork, we need some Tuinals. Sid's sick. He can't sing." So I'd go out and get some Tuinals for him.

Sid and Nancy were great. They had a genuine affection for each other. I mean, there was that "punk love" where they would put each other down, like Connie and Dee Dee, but it was real. You could tell there was a deep run of affection there. And you could also tell that Sid was like a fish out of water. He didn't have a clue about the big bad world really. He was like a child that depended on Nancy.

IGGY POP: I knew Nancy Spungen. Yeah, I knew her, ha ha ha. I spent the night with her once. She wasn't a beauty, but I liked her. There was something really spunky there. But I was a big boy by then. So my thought was, Trouble.

ARTURO VEGA: I had already been through Connie and Dee Dee, so Sid and Nancy were just a continuation. You know, different characters— same play.

CHEETAH CHROME: Dee Dee Ramone had given Stiv Bators a 007 knife at one of our first gigs. Stiv carried it all the time, and one time, we were up were up at the Chelsea Hotel and the 007 was just lying there on a nightstand or something. Stiv just picked it up and mentioned that Dee Dee had given it to him.

Sid Vicious was infatuated with Dee Dee Ramone. Dee Dee was Sid's hero and as soon as Sid found out Dee Dee had given the knife to Stiv, Sid wanted one too. So a couple days later we all went up to Times Square so that Sid could buy one.

It was really funny because Nancy had all this cash, and they were so out of it—they had taken a bunch of Tuinals—so she was dropping hundred-dollar bills on the ground. We had all of Times Square following us, a crowd following us waiting for the next bundle to fall out.

Nancy liked the knife. She was into it. I think she even bought one for herself. She wanted to have a knife because she was getting hassled by people and wanted to have some protection.

You see, they didn't know how to cop dope. Sid got beat a lot. He got sold a lot of crap because he was a born victim.

Sid was a mess. He'd draw attention, he'd draw heat. And that's not something you wanna do when you're copping dope. It's a serious thing. You wanna get in and get out quick.

But fucking Sid and Nancy were a pain in the ass—you know, everybody would be laughing at Sid, he would be bumping into telephone poles, Nancy would be bitching at him, and then she never wanted to pay full price for the stuff. I mean, these were not people you fucking bicker and bargain with.

And fucking Sid would be asking all these dumb questions: "Can you give me a deal?"

You know, buying heroin is not negotiable. You don't bargain with dope dealers. It's a fixed price. Like William Burroughs said, "It's the ultimate merchandise, and a customer will crawl through a sewer and beg to buy it."

And fucking Nancy, if someone you knew was selling dope, she'd sneak off and try and buy up all the dope, before you got there. So I'd just as soon go cop by myself.

Fucking Nancy. If Sid hadn't killed her, I woulda, ha ha ha. Nancy was probably the most miserable person I've ever met in my life.

ELIOT KIDD: We were out at some places and I heard there was a party going on over at Sid's place, at the Chelsea Hotel. I was with a couple of girls and we arrived at Sid's room about four in the morning. I know Nancy was still alive then, because it was Nancy who let us in.

She was running the show. Everybody was stoned and people were just floating around. Neon Leon was there with Kathy. There was at least a half a dozen people there, probably no more than a dozen. If I said nine I could be exactly right, if I said ten I might be exactly right. I don't know. It was crowded for a small room.

Nancy was stoned. She was stoned and she was bragging. She's talking in that fucking cockney accent, you know, being Mrs. Sid Vicious. But it wasn't much of a party because Sid was passed out. Sid did not look like he was going to get up. He wasn't moving.

I said, "What's wrong with Sid?"

Someone said, "Oh, he just ate about thirty Tuinals."

I said, "Oh, he's going to be fun tonight."

It was more crowded with Sid fucking out on the bed—you know, it was a hotel room, so besides the bed, how much more furniture was there? That's another reason why I didn't want to stay. There was no place to sit.

So we left. I mean, I didn't know it was going to be an important night when I was there.

NEW YORK POST, OCTOBER 13, 1978: SID VICIOUS SEIZED AT CHELSEA HOTEL—PUNK ROCK STAR ACCUSED OF SLAYING GIRLFRIEND. "Sid Vicious, bass guitarist of Britain's spitting and stomping Sex Pistols punk rock band, yesterday was arrested and charged with stabbing his sultry blond girlfriend to death in their room at Manhattan's famed Chelsea Hotel. His face pale and scratched, the dazed looking Vicious muttered curses and, 'I'll smash your cameras,' as he was led from the hotel, where the body of Nancy Laura Spungen, 20, clad in blood-soaked black lace bra and panties, was found crumpled under the bathroom sink. Miss Spungen . . . had been stabbed deep in the abdomen."

NANCY SPUNGEN: *I could have been a ward of the state. I had like a lotta problems. I was just real different from everybody else. I was a lot smarter than them. So I just started to really rebel against my parents, I hated them a lot. They got real worried and sent me to a shrink. They just couldn't handle it, I hated them so badly. I just couldn't stand them.*

My parents didn't like me at all. They just weren't into what I was into. So I just came to New York like all the time. Then I got a job as a dancer. I was a professional dancer for about a year when I first moved to New York. Then I met a lot of people through other people. A lot of my really good friends are musicians who are in the top bands right now in New York.

It's just that ever since I've gone out with guys, I've gone out with musicians. I don't know, my life was going so slow for a while and then suddenly, it started to go so fast . . . The most exciting things started to happen in 1975. But I wasn't really concentrating on the punk scene. I was concentrating on big rock & roll stars, like Ron Wood. Mick Jagger—I know him, but I never fucked him. I was with Keith Richards. I toured around with Aerosmith for a while. One of the first nights I was with them was in Washington, D.C. We drove out there in the limousine. I was sitting in the backseat with Tom Hamilton on one side of me and Brad Whitford on the other. I had one hand on one prick and one hand on the other . . .

I had a good time, and I got treated nice, you know? It was the fun of it. It was exciting. I'm friends with just about everybody. I know everybody. A lot of my really good friends are in the top bands. Musicians—a lot of them are really nice, you know?

But sometimes they are really terrible.

BOB GRUEN: I don't believe that Sid killed Nancy. I don't think he had it in him. He wasn't vicious. It was kind of like a reverse name. I mean Sid was such a wimp that they called him Vicious.

Sid loved Nancy. On the Pistols' American tour, he wanted to talk to me about her all the time, because I had known Nancy before he did. Sid would ask me questions about her like, "Was she really a prostitute?"

I said, "Yeah."

I told him about the time in New York when my friend Dave, Nancy, and I were driving around. And Nancy was describing the whorehouse she worked in. It was this uptown brothel where they had theme rooms and they had various girls—little girls, teachers, nurses . . .

Nancy was in the S&M room. She would wear black leather garters and beat German bankers for money. They would pay her a lot of money and she would whip them and make them crawl around and suck on her boots.

She ended up by saying, "You guys come up anytime you want; it's on the house." She was like, "We'd love to have you. You'd have a great time, and you could do anything you wanted."

And so from then on, whenever we were driving around late at night and there was nothing to do, we'd say, "We can always go get beaten up by Nancy."

Somehow we never took her up on it. But on the tour Sid kept asking me about her: "Was she really like that?"

I said, "Yeah, she was."

And Sid loved her.

ELIOT KIDD: I talked to Neon Leon the next day. He said when he left Sid and Nancy, that fucking guy was still there.

I said, "Who was that?"

He said, "You know, that Tuinal dealer."

Neon Leon told me that when everybody had left, the Tuinal dealer was the only person that stayed. All he knew about the guy was that he lived in Hell's Kitchen.

Sid was in jail two or three weeks before he made bail. I think Malcolm and the other guys in the Sex Pistols chipped in to bail him out. I talked to Sid the day he got out of jail. He told me that all he knew is that he woke up, he went into the bathroom—which most people do the first thing when they wake up—and Nancy was under the sink, blood everywhere, and she was dead.

I think he kept his knife on the wall. Sid had a big knife, and in the morning, that was laying on the floor next to Nancy.

Sid told me they had eighty bucks between them. And the drawer that they kept the money in was open and the money was missing.

If you knew Nancy, you could see her going to the bathroom, coming out, seeing the guy going through the drawers and catching him taking the money—and going after the guy.

It wasn't like she thought she was tough. But she didn't take shit from anybody. She would have flipped out if she caught somebody trying to steal from them. And if this guy had it in him—if you corner a rat, you're going to get bit, you know?

NEW YORK POST, OCTOBER 17 AND 18, 1978: VICIOUS SPRUNG ON $50,000 BAIL—SID SAYS HE'S IN A FOG. "Punk rocker and accused murderer Sid Vicious claims he doesn't know how his girlfriend, former go-go dancer Nancy Laura Spungen, was stabbed to death in their Chelsea Hotel room. 'I don't know what happened,' Vicious said in an interview after he was released on $50,000 bail Monday night from Rikers Island. 'I'm really going to miss her. She was a great woman, a great help to me. I want to get in touch with Nancy's parents and talk to them.'"

EILEEN POLK: I was at Max's with Joe Stevens when Sid met Michelle Robinson. I didn't think that they were together. I wasn't expecting that they'd end up together.

Joe told me the next day, "Guess what happened? Sid and Michelle ended up together. You know, they seem like a pretty good couple."

I thought it was kind of strange that right after Nancy died he hooked up with someone new, but then maybe it wasn't. Sid liked to be led around by women.

JIM MARSHALL: Everybody knew Sid Vicious was at Hurrah's that night. When somebody as famous as Sid is in the room, you know they're there, you like keep glancing over your shoulder looking, just to keep an eye on him to see if he's going to do anything wild, and sure enough, I saw Sid hit Todd Smith, Patti Smith's brother, with a bottle.

Sid hit him with a beer bottle across the side of the head. Yeah, classic bang with a beer bottle.

Some people carried Todd out. He was definitely bleeding. But he was on his feet; he wasn't out cold, so it couldn't have been that bad. But they took him to the hospital.

LENNY KAYE: We were in Woodstock, recording the last Patti Smith album, when we got the phone call that Sid had slashed Toddy. We were all pissed off. Maybe there was a discussion of busting his head open. You know, there's that gang mentality—"Hey, you fuck with one of our guys, we're going to fuck you up."

But we were a girls' band. We didn't get into fights. Maybe we wanted to . . . cook him dinner. No, only kidding.

Todd went to the hospital. He wasn't there that long. He wasn't mortally wounded. His face was cut up. He got some stitches.

But when things start to fall apart, you look at situations like Sid—as I'm sure the hippies must have looked at Altamont—as "Here's our symbol."

And it ain't too pleasant—it just proves we fucked up this time. Maybe we'll get it right next go-around. And I think it tended to sour Patti even more on this brave new world of rock & roll. The Sex Pistols rode the punk force right off the edge of the cliff, and then it was time for something new.

NEW YORK POST, DECEMBER 9, 1978: SID IS BERATED IN COURT, SENT BACK TO JAIL. "A prosecutor called him vicious and dangerous, the judge pronounced him unstable and unreliable, and today Sid Vicious is back in the Rikers Island lockup. The $50,000 bail the punk rocker posted for freedom after his sweetheart's murder was revoked yesterday in Manhattan Supreme Court when he was arrested anew in a Broadway discotheque ruckus . . . His latest bind with the law came after the *Post's* Page Six item on Thursday, chronicling Vicious' late hours encounter in Hurrah's with rock star Patti Smith's brother, Todd. As disco manager Henry Schlisser described it, Vicious pinched Tarrah, Todd's girlfriend. Then, 'Todd said something protective and then Sid did it. With a broken Heineken's bottle.' "

EILEEN POLK: After Sid smashed Todd Smith with the beer bottle, he had to go back to jail. Sid's mother snuck him heroin while he was in jail. She had this great trick—she would put the heroin in her shoe, and she would wear boots that had a lot of metal clips on them, and then when she went through the metal detector, it would go off. Then she'd say, "Oh, it must be my shoes!"

Then, while she was taking off her shoes, she'd put the dope in the cuff of her pants. Then she'd walk through the metal detector again. The alarm wouldn't go off, and they wouldn't search her for the dope.

Since they were expecting her to have a weapon or a piece of metal on her, they didn't check her pant legs, because they'd already checked them. And when she took her boots off, she'd switch it to a different spot, and they wouldn't check that spot again.

Then Sid would come to the visiting room with his butt greased and stick it up his ass and he'd have some dope.

Ann did it because Sid was complaining about being sick. She didn't do it every day. She did it like twice or something while he was in jail. Just for withdrawing, because Sid was really clean when he got out of jail. He looked really healthy and he was talking very positively about everything.

We went to pick Sid up at the courthouse when he got out of jail again. It was really quick. I mean, we went in and the judge said a few words to Sid and then we left with Sid. He came out of jail wearing this white T-shirt, because he had to appear in court. So the first thing he did when he got home was put on the swastika T-shirt.

We ended up having a party that night. So I went over to the Jefferson Market, where my mother had an account, and I got these two big six-packs of Bud. I said to one of the owners of the shop, "My friend's just out of jail and we're having a party!"

So we went back to Michelle's at 63 Bank Street and we made spaghetti. It was all very normal.

Then Jerry Nolan came over with Esther, and Sid said, "Ma, can I have some money? Can I have some money? I just want to go get some coke."

Ann said, "You're sure you're just going to get cocaine, right?"

Sid said, "Yeah, Mom, don't worry, I won't get any dope." So Ann gave him a hundred dollars.

I said, "Ann . . ."

She said, "Look, he's going to get it from somewhere, at least if I give it to him, he's going to come home."

So she gave him the money and Sid and Jerry Nolan went out for a while. Maybe they actually did get coke, because they came back pretty quickly. So then we just had a nice dinner party. We drank beer. It started getting late and the atmosphere of the party changed, you know? Like I always hated that about the scene. That's why I never got into shooting dope a lot, because you'll be having a good time, and all of a sudden, everyone will start running off to the bathroom. If you're going to do drugs, just do them in front of everybody. Don't be running off into the bathroom. It's rude.

ELIOT KIDD: I OD'd the same night that Sid died. We were all sitting at a table at Max's, and this English guy I was friendly with came over to our table and said he had some really, really good shit. We weren't really planning on doing dope that night. I think we'd done Quaaludes.

Anyway, this friend said he had some dope. We went back to Sheila's apartment, and this guy who brought the dope in from London said he would turn me on in the bathroom. We went into Sheila's bathroom, and I got off. I knew it immediately, as soon as I got off—I knew I was going out.

I walked out of the fucking bathroom and I said, "I think this is it."

I just heard Sheila start to scream, "You're not going to die in my apartment!"

The last thing I said was, "Sheila, just shut up!" And the next thing I knew it was four hours later.

EILEEN POLK: More people started coming over and I knew that it was the English guy that came later on in the evening that brought Sid the dope. The English guy had really good dope. They started going in the bathroom, and then Sid went in the bathroom. When he came out, he turned all blue and white. We had to take blankets and wrap him up in them. Then he passed out on the bed and everybody was massaging him and shaking him.

It was really kind of scary, and then he woke up and said, "Oh, wow, I'm sorry I scared you all."

Howie Pyro and Jerry Only and I were like, "This is getting bad. Let's just leave."

I just didn't want to be part of a drug party because we really didn't want Sid doing drugs. We just wanted him to stay clean, because he looked so much better after he'd been in jail. He looked so much better than he ever had before.

ELIOT KIDD: It was obvious that I was going to live. I could actually, like, walk, but I felt more like laying down. Sean said to me, "If you lay down, make sure you lay on your stomach. Because if you pass out and vomit, if you're on your back, you'll choke yourself to death."

Debbie took me up to her apartment. Sheila lived on the sixth floor, and Debbie lived on the eleventh. Now it's morning, almost nine o'clock.

Debbie says, "I'm going out to get some breakfast for us."

She leaves and all of a sudden I'm alone. I was so scared of passing out. I was thinking about what Sean said. So I go into the bathroom and run my wrists under the freezing cold water and splash it on my face; anything I could do to stop myself from passing out, because I thought if I passed out, I might not wake up.

Then the phone rings. It was Pam Brown. She says, "Did you see the news?"

I said, "No. I've seen very little since last night."

She said, "Sid died."

Fucking hell. It went through me like an electric shock. Sid must have gotten the same dope. I couldn't see where he would have gotten dope from anywhere else that night.

EILEEN POLK: The next day Michelle called me at noon. She was crying. She said, "Sid's dead."

The first thing I thought was, She's just hysterical. He's probably just sleeping.

But I got dressed and I ran over there, and saw the crowd of reporters outside the apartment. When they saw me, they said, "There's that girl from the courthouse!"

And then they all started taking my picture. I ran up to the door and the police let me in and then I realized it was true.

Ann, Sid's mother, and Michelle were sitting on the couch, crying. But Ann always acted like she knew it was going to happen, she just didn't know when.

Michelle was just hysterical. Everyone was getting real annoyed with her because she was so hysterical. She'd only known Sid for two weeks at the most. So everybody was like, "Michelle, please, you're going to drive his mother crazy. The poor woman's been through enough. Do you have to cause a scene?"

Then Ann told me what happened. She went to sleep on the couch in the living room. Sid had to show up for something the next morning, bail bond, I don't know, something court related. She went in the bedroom around seven o'clock in the morning, tapped his shoulder, and realized he was dead. Michelle was lying next to Sid in the bed, and then Ann woke Michelle up.

It's possible he shot up more of the dope. But after overdosing, just falling asleep is enough to kill you. If you overdose, you have to drink lots of coffee and keep walking around to make sure it's out of your system, because just falling asleep can slow your body down enough for your heart to fail. So it's possible that Sid might have taken one of Michelle's pills. He might have done more dope. He might have just fallen asleep. Apparently, the heroin that he had done was really pure, like 99 percent pure. That's what the cops told me.

The police came back to the apartment and said, "Now we need to take Ann and Michelle down. Do you mind staying here with the body and answering the telephone?"

I was like, "Oh, okay."

But the phone was in the bedroom.

And the body was in the bedroom.

So I was just sitting there on the bed, with Sid's body. I was in the bedroom for three hours with Sid, dead. And no one else was in the apartment.

They sent for the body bag and everything, but it took a long time for them to come. I arrived there at eight in the morning and it was dark by the time they removed the body. When Michelle and Ann went down to the police station, it was about six o'clock at night. And then I was left there from like six until nine and I answered the phone. And it was so disgusting because people would call up with these fake British accents and say they were a relative and, "Oh, we just heard," and it would be the *Daily News*.

I'd always catch them because I knew Sid's relatives' names. So I would say something like, "Oh, did you talk to his sister Susie?" and they would say, "Oh, yes. We just talked to Susie," and then I'd hang up on them.

NEW YORK POST, FEBRUARY 2, 1979: SID VICIOUS FOUND DEAD. "Punk rock star Sid Vicious was found dead in a Greenwich Village apartment in an apparent suicide, police said today. Police said that Vicious, 21, apparently died of a heroin overdose and was found face-up in the bed of a friend's apartment at 63 Bank street. Police said the apartment belonged to Michelle Robinson. The former Sex Pistol was released from jail yesterday on $50,000 cash bail. He had been jailed since December 8th when his bail on the charges he murdered his girlfriend Nancy Spungen was revoked after he assaulted Patti Smith's brother in a Manhattan disco."

ELIOT KIDD: I think it's just a shame that when Sid died, they closed the book on Nancy. Somebody got away with murder.

I don't think Sid really knew what happened. I mean he wasn't a witness to Nancy dying. What he told me is he got up, went to the bathroom, and she was lying there dead. The drawer was open where their money was and the money was gone. That's all he knew.

I imagine the cops could create a scenario where he woke up, found out that she spent the money on dope, so he killed her. I assume that's what the cops were going on, because they charged Sid with second-degree murder. I don't think they would have won the case. I think he would have been found not guilty.

But I don't think the police were interested in finding out who killed Nancy.

EILEEN POLK: Ann started staying at my mom's house because she didn't want the press to know where she was and I figured it was the best place for her to go because they didn't know anything about me. All they knew was that I was a punk girl with blond hair and they thought I was from England. So it was perfect.

So after Sid died Ann stayed at my house for two weeks and just drank the whole time and cried.

We couldn't get a place to give us a funeral in New York without charging us like a zillion dollars because it was Sid Vicious. It was hard because we wanted to find a nice burial place so people could visit his grave.

Instead, we ended up getting a place in New Jersey that cremated Sid, then we took the ashes down to Philadelphia because Ann wanted to put them on Nancy's grave.

When Sid was alive, he was always saying, "When I die, bury me next to Nancy." We wanted them to be together so we called up Nancy's parents and we asked if we could get a burial plot next to Nancy. They said no.

Ann talked to them. She told Mrs. Spungen how much she really wanted to make friends with her because she felt that they were both in the same boat, and that she felt really bad about the whole thing, and that there were no hard feelings. But Mrs. Spungen was just like, "Okay, I'm not going to blame you, but just leave me alone."

So me and Howie Pyro and Jerry Only and Ann, and Ann's sister, Renee, drove down to Philadelphia to put Sid's ashes on Nancy's grave. On the way to the cemetery we stopped because we wanted to see what the ashes were like before we got there. So we opened it up in the restroom of a mall we stopped in to get lunch, and it was really weird because I'm in this women's bathroom with Ann and her sister and we're prying open Sid's ashes.

We'd never seen ashes before. And they're really hard. It's like they compress them in this can, like an oil can, and you have to pry it open like one of those vacuum-packed cans. They're packed solid. It's more like gravel than ashes. It was like a vacuum-packed can of gravel, but it's bone and stuff like that.

So we drove to Philadelphia and we went to the graveyard. We were escorted by two people who worked there, and we said to them, "We just want to pay our last respects," but they wouldn't leave us.

We had the ashes with us, but we didn't want to tell them that we had the ashes with us, because it's like a Jewish sanctified ground. Nancy was Jewish and you can't have like non-Jews buried in your Jewish cemetery. That's what they told us, but they really didn't want to have anything to do with Sid Vicious.

We're standing at the gravesite and it was snowing. We were all crying. We just said some prayers and left some flowers.

Then we drove around to the other edge of the cemetery. We parked the car and Ann took the ashes, went over the fence, back to the gravesite, and dumped Sid's ashes on Nancy's grave. Then she came back and got in the car and said, "Well, they're finally together."

And that was that.

Chapter 37

■ Too Tough to Die

MATT LOLYA: The Ramones were in L.A. making the movie *Rock 'n' Roll High School* and doing the album with Phil Spector, when Dee Dee sent me to the airport to go pick up his new girlfriend. I think he sent me saying, "Go look for a girl that looks like Connie."

So I took the van to the airport, picked up this girl that looked like Connie, and brought her back to the hotel. That was Vera, and we were all amazed at how much she looked like Connie. But Vera was really nice.

With a lot of people, myself included, I know that a girlfriend sometimes can keep you calmer. So we thought Dee Dee being with Vera was a good thing, because Dee Dee had just gotten arrested.

We were staying at the Tropicana Motel and everyone was there. There was some room up there in the corner of the motel and everyone was in there; the Dead Boys, the Dictators, the Sic Fucks—all these New York people—and there was lots of vodka and pills. So me and Monte Melnick left to go get food, and when we came back, there was a police car in front of the Tropicana.

And there's Dee Dee being dragged by handcuffs on his butt into the patrol car. En route to the jail, Dee Dee went into a coma, went unconscious. So he never made it to jail. They took him a Cedars-Sinai, and they had to pump his stomach. He spent a day or two in the hospital.

DEE DEE RAMONE: I just know I woke up at Mt. Sinai and I had so many tubes in me. The cops beat me up when I was drunk in jail. I can't remember why I was arrested.

Then Vera came out and we had Christmas in that hotel. We had a lamp in the hotel room and she cut out like a paper star and put it on there and that was our Christmas tree. We had nothing to give each other. That was Christmas.

At that time the Ramones had been touring for three or four years and we were flat broke. I only had enough money to buy two damn Tuinals and a beer every day.

So we started working with Phil Spector because the idea was that the record company thought they could get a hit out of punk rock. Punk rock was getting big, and someone thought we could have a hit record if Phil Spector produced us. But it was a nightmare.

Phil was totally out of his mind. I hadn't met anyone crazier than him, but he liked me a lot. He used to carry a gun all the time. He had two guys with him that were fully armed.

JOEY RAMONE: While we were in L.A., Phil Spector would always come to our shows and say, "Do you guys wanna be great or good? Cause I'll make you great."

ARTURO VEGA: Phil Spector came to the Whiskey to see the Ramones, I guess to check them out, and that's when I met him. He came with the twin bodyguards and I thought, This weirdo is Phil Spector? This little weasel?

I was a little disappointed and impressed at the same time, because the guy was so weird. Phil didn't talk to me until I was in his house once, because I used to wear this German machine gun pin on my leather jacket and he asked me if I was a Nazi.

I said, "No."

He said, "Then why do you wear that?"

I said, "I like machine guns."

I guess he liked that, because he let me off the hook. He could torture you if he didn't like you. Phil would start picking on you, insult you and call you names and everything.

DEE DEE RAMONE: One night Phil pulled out his gun and wouldn't let us leave. John took care of it. He told him, "Cut it out, Phil, or we're gonna leave."

Phil said, "Alright, you guys just try and leave. I'm not letting you leave."

We had to sit there for a day and he just held us with these guns. We had to sit there in the living room and listen to him play "Baby, I Love You" over and over again.

I didn't know what he was drinking. I couldn't figure it out, because he had this big gold goblet with all these jewels on it. He looked like Dracula drinking blood. So I said, "Phil, let me have some of that."

He said, "Okay, Dee Dee," and it was Manichewitz wine, ha ha ha.

ARTURO VEGA: I heard that Phil Spector had taken Dee Dee hostage the day after it happened. Dee Dee was really scared. Sometimes

Dee Dee doesn't have a real good grasp on reality, so he couldn't see the joke in it. He thought that Phil could get seriously dangerous. But I guess Phil could.

JOEY RAMONE: If a stranger would ever come into the room—everything in the studio would stop. Phil would get all freaked out. Nobody could come in that he didn't know. And he'd have some hooker hanging out in the studio, and he'd just like insult her. I guess that's what she was paid for, to take this abuse. And the control room would be like a fucking icebox.

ARTURO VEGA: Phil Spector was fucking nuts. The house was like a museum—he had all this stupid paraphernalia everywhere. You know, little cheap promotional paraphernalia things that record companies and radio stations make to promote the band? Cheap stuff. I'm sure everything had its meaning and it must've meant something to somebody, but I remember thinking, This guy must have money, why does he have all this junk here? What's wrong with these rich people, why don't they know how to live? Ha ha ha.

DEE DEE RAMONE: We started making the Roger Corman movie *Rock 'n' Roll High School* at the same time we were making the Phil Spector record, *End of the Century*.

I never read the script to *Rock 'n' Roll High School*. I was so out of it. If you'll notice, I don't say a word in the movie. They had lines for me and things for me to do, but I just couldn't function. I couldn't do anything. So they just did their best with what they could.

LINDA STEIN: Dee Dee was supposed to have one line in the movie, something like, "Is there any pizza?" or "Can we get pizza?" or "Order pizza"—something about pizza. He had one line, he couldn't get it. Did about forty takes. And we were all so nervous that Dee Dee wouldn't get it. And he didn't get it! We tried to rehearse Dee Dee and everything, but we knew it was going to be a problem and it was a problem.

DEE DEE RAMONE: They got us outta bed no matter what. They would get us up at 2:00 A.M. to be there at 10:00 A.M. That's one thing about the Ramones, they were very organized. During the movie, we'd film in the day and write for the *End of the Century* album at night.

The director, Alan Arkush, was a nice guy. He performed a miracle with what he had to work with. I think the movie brought the group down one level, to stupidity. It made the group look very stupid and the Ramones weren't a stupid group. But that movie was the kiss of death. After he made the movie, Alan had to be hospitalized. He had a heart attack and he was only thirty-eight.

JOEY RAMONE: In the end the album cost like $700,000 to make because Phil just kept remixing and remixing. Finally Seymour just told him, "Look, Phil . . ." you know, that he wanted it as it was, because Phil, he was just never satisfied. He wanted to remix the whole record all over again. It's like he'd mix it and send it song by song. It was crazy.

DEE DEE RAMONE: Phil Spector couldn't mix the album. He collapsed with a nervous breakdown after the album was recorded. I just remember I was driving home with the band from the record company in New York and they put on something from the album—I think "I'm Affected" or something—and I couldn't believe how awful it sounded. It was horrible. I hated "Baby, I Love You." I think that some of the worst crap I ever wrote went on that album. That was me at my worst, but we had two hits with the album in Europe—"Baby, I Love You" and "Rock 'n' Roll Radio."

ARTURO VEGA: When Dee Dee married Vera, I thought it was a good idea—anything that would help keep Dee Dee under control. Plus I liked Vera; I think she was good for Dee Dee, and you always hope for the best with people who get married. I think that love is a great medicine for many illnesses. I believe in the power of love, so I thought the marriage could be good for Dee Dee.

LINDA STEIN: The great thing about Dee Dee is that he slept with everybody. Dee Dee slept with me, Dee Dee slept with Seymour, I think he slept with Danny—I mean Dee Dee slept with everybody and anybody. And he made you feel good. I mean, he was a professional hooker! So everybody fell in love with Dee Dee.

So Dee Dee and I had like an affair. I mean, I remember one Thanksgiving—Seymour was always out of the country when it was an American holiday cause he was a workaholic—and it was Thanksgiving and Dee Dee and I went to dinner and then checked into this hotel on Sixty-fourth Street and Park Avenue, and spent the night—Thanksgiving with Dee Dee Ramone and his leather jacket. And I'm the mother of two!

So when I found out that Dee Dee was getting married I couldn't believe it. Danny Fields and I always thought Dee Dee should have an affair with Farrah Fawcett or somebody very famous. We thought he could be like Cher and just keep having continual affairs with famous people.

But he chose to be completely domesticated and settle down in College Point, in Whitestone, Queens—with his cutlery and all his porcelain and his dinette set and his living-room sofa and his color TV. We wanted to buy him a very practical gift, but he already had everything. They had this real wedding, they had this real dinette set, they had everything, except the honeymoon—because he left the next morning for Helsinki to tour with the band.

DEE DEE RAMONE: When I wasn't touring with the Ramones, I went home to my little basement apartment in Whitestone, Queens. Whitestone is a boring, middle-class neighborhood where Vera and I lived for ten years. I never felt at home there. I just felt paranoid.

If I wanted a tattoo, I would have to see the shrink with Vera and hassle. Vera would get totally insane about me and tattoos. I fought her for every one I got when we were together. I'd sit there and Vera and the psychiatrist would try to brainwash me out of my integrity.

DANIEL REY: When I was writing songs with Dee Dee, he would go back and forth to these various doctors—psychologists, analysts, therapists—and we would arrange our writing schedule around his doctor appointments.

He'd say, "I gotta see Dr. Blahblahblah, so I'll be over at four, then I gotta see Dr. Blahblahblah."

Vera would give him five dollars, just enough for cab fare home or cab fare there. But not enough to buy anything in the street, just enough to get here and back. It was really sad.

When he was really medicated, he was on a lot of mind-altering drugs that the doctors prescribed, he was really kind of a walking zombie. Which was a trade-off. Everyone—his wife, Monte, and the doctors—seemed to want him to take them because it made him easier to control. It was like someone in a mental hospital—you pump them up with Thorazine so they're not breaking the walls down, but they might as well be dead.

So it was sad. Dee Dee smelled of prescription drugs.

BOB GRUEN: I knew Vera because she was friends with my assistant, the girl that was my photo assistant at the time. I had broken up with my wife, and since I was single, my assistant introduced me to Vera and we went out a couple times. Then I brought her down to Max's and introduced her to Dee Dee. And she took an immediate liking to him, it was like love at first sight. They only had eyes for each other.

Dee Dee had been with Connie, and she was really on his case, being a real terror, and her psycho energy was driving him crazy. I remember Vera seeing that and feeling kinda sorry for Dee Dee. She said that he didn't really deserve to be treated like that.

ARTURO VEGA: After Dee Dee was with Vera, I started seeing Connie a lot on Third Avenue, working as a prostitute. I remember seeing her looking *so* bad. So I thought it was only a matter of time. I had tried talking to her. I used to tell her everything that I thought would help her, but by then she was too far gone. And we were touring all the time, so I would only see her when I was passing by in a taxi and she would be standing on the street, turning tricks.

LAURA ALLEN: It was really sad. Dee Dee told me that they found Connie dead in a doorway somewhere. She had overdosed on methadone and Valium and nobody claimed her. I guess she wasn't in touch with her relatives, and they didn't find any numbers or ID, so they buried her in Potter's Field in Staten Island.

What was so sad was that right before she died, Dee Dee would see her working as a prostitute on Eleventh Street and Second Avenue. He would try to give her money, but she always ran away because she was really ashamed. She looked really bad, like she wasn't doing too well.

DEE DEE RAMONE: Johnny Ramone told me that Connie had died. He called me up. He said, "Connie's dead."

I said, "Oh?"

I couldn't really say anything because Vera was there. I couldn't mourn because I was with Vera. I couldn't show any emotion about it because Vera was jealous.

The last time I saw Connie she was turning tricks. I used to go in the van and wait for them to pick up Joey in front of his apartment building and Connie was always working that area. I tried to give her some money so she could cop and stuff. She looked pretty bad. I don't know why anybody would love her, but I did.

Later, I heard that this girl was trying to raise money to get Connie a casket and all the girls pitched in, but then the other girl took the money and spent it on dope. A few years later I broke down over it.

LAURA ALLEN: It's funny, I was talking to Vera once, and she said, "I really hated Connie, but later I realized that whatever Connie did or whatever she was about, she always tried to give Dee Dee a home. I at least have to give her that much."

Then Vera told me this story about how Connie had bought a couch. She'd worked and made some money and bought this couch for Dee Dee.

But Dee Dee went into a rage and sliced up the couch. He just ruined the couch; all the stuffing was out. And Vera said, "Oh it's really sad because poor Connie worked so hard to get the couch and Dee Dee destroyed it. She was trying to make a home for him, trying to make something stable, but with all those drugs and all that craziness . . ."

I always felt very bad for Connie. Her ending was so sad, and I know Dee Dee definitely loved her. He really loved her. I think that was probably his first love. He told me that the times with Connie were the happiest times in his life.

Chapter 38

■ Frederick

KATHY ASHETON: After my brother Scotty came back from L.A. and detoxed himself, he was living at our mom's house. One day he told me that Fred Smith and Scott Morgan were after him to play drums for this band they were starting.

I hadn't seen Fred for several years, but when they started the Sonic Rendezvous Band, I ended up hanging out quite a bit, because I thought the band was really good. Then Fred and I started up a relationship again.

I spent the next couple of years hanging out with him, going to the gigs, and having a good time. But also, those were pretty alcoholic days, too. Not myself, but those guys were drinking a lot.

I was attracted to Fred physically, because it was still sort of left over from when I first met him, plus I was pretty crazy about him. But I didn't think about it in terms of being in love, like this is the man for me, we're gonna settle down and get that white picket fence—there was never any of that kind of thing. It was just hanging out—you know, buddies.

When Patti came into the picture around '78, at first I thought to myself that it was kinda cool that she was into the Sonic Rendezvous Band, but not so cool that she was moving in on my territory, ha ha ha.

Fred and I had been involved for a couple of years at that point, and although it was pretty casual, it was apparent to anybody around us that we were an item. But when Patti started coming here to play, and then the Rendezvous started opening for her, then she started moving in on Fred.

BEBE BUELL: When Patti Smith decided to quit—when she decided she was going to get married and become a housewife—the only person that knew was Todd Rundgren. He was producing *Wave*, and he was the only person who knew it was her last record. She didn't even tell the band. Then Todd told me but I was sworn to secrecy—I was never allowed to let on to Patti that I knew—but one time I went into the studio and just started crying, and Patti went, "What the fuck is wrong with you?" I was just bawling, and Todd took me outside.

I was like, "I don't want this to be her last record." I was much more adolescent about my feelings about rock & roll. To me it was an incredible loss; I considered it a death in the family. Maybe they thought it was just the last record—"Big deal, I'm gonna go be a housewife now"—but I took it very seriously.

Patti told me she was in love with Fred Smith and that she wanted to get married and have babies, and how cool it was that Fred had the same last name as hers, because she didn't have to change her name.

She'd met God—it was as simple as that.

JAMES GRAUERHOLZ: Patti said to me, "I've found the man I love, and all I've been looking for all my life was a man to love. I want to have children and I want to be a good mother and a good wife, and that's all I wanna do."

That really rang true to me. I said, "Right on." I mean, a lot of people were really shocked and surprised, but I wasn't surprised. Because through all of the revolutionary I AM RIMBAUD, I AM BAUDELAIRE, I AM BURROUGHS, there was a very strong torch-singer type—a Billie Holiday. I mean, the art was there, but in principle she'd give it all up for a good man.

I remember I rode with her and Lenny in a limo out to a show in New Jersey one night. It was a long car ride, and Patti was reading a biography of Rodin, the sculptor. And her preoccupation was with this woman who was Rodin's mistress, who had done everything for Rodin's career. You know, behind every successful man . . .

All Patti's heroes were usually heroic men, but her women heroes tended not to be the Joan of Arcs—the strong leader women—but the kind of uncredited, passed-over-by-history supporter women.

JAY DEE DAUGHERTY: The last two concerts that the Patti Smith Group played were in Bologna and Florence. Patti was in a very frightening situation in Bologna. It was a large soccer stadium and they had lost control of the crowd. A good number of the audience had gotten in for free—sort of broken down the gates. Part of the deal the promoter had to make with the local communist party was that they were to provide the security.

The concert went on without too much event, but afterward we got locked in backstage because the clowns that were the security guards had shut this iron gate and nobody had a key.

So there's 80,000 people chanting, "Patti, Patti," you know, going nuts, and the band were starting to panic, like, "What the fuck's going on? We want to get back onstage! Who's got the fucking key?"

All of a sudden these security guys started getting heavy. They pushed the rest of the band out of the way and surrounded Patti—they were going to spirit her off in a car. Patti was really frightened for her life—she thought she was going to be kidnapped and get her ears cut off or whatever. That was the night that Patti got down on her knees and prayed. It sort of worked, but finding the key helped, too.

So the next night her manager Ina said, "This absolutely cannot happen again—we'll only play under such and such conditions."

But the next gig was a carbon copy of the night before—same kind of stadium, and a long tiled corridor backstage. And so I'm wearing my stage costume—a white T-shirt, white see-through parachute pants, with a white jockstrap on underneath so you could see my ass . . . I know, it seemed like a good idea at the time, okay? So I'm coming around the corner and there's the *carabinieri* standing there with submachine guns and I was like, "Oh, shit." They were our guards for the evening.

There was a riot. The audience went nuts. Patti will probably kill me for my interpretation of this, but she was very much into making her own statement without much thought of how it would be perceived. I'm not saying that's particularly selfish, but it was like, "This is what I'm doing and if people don't like it, including you, Jay, tough shit." In America, we would raise a very large American flag for a backdrop during the last song. I had mentioned previously that I thought that when we were in Europe we might want to eighty-six that. You know, lose the flag. It might be perceived imperialistically perhaps. And what I got back was, "What's the matter? Aren't you a patriot? Don't you like America?" I was kind of like, "Whoa, never mind."

That night, Patti did a long piano improvisation, over which an address by the pope was played over the sound system. This did not go over well with the youth of Florence. People were upset. Maybe they thought it was sacrilegious or maybe they just didn't want to hear that shit anymore.

So the American flag went up and then the barricades started getting broken. Big pieces of wood with nails in them started getting thrown on the stage. Then I started to remember all the horror stories about Lou Reed's concerts in Italy being firebombed. So as soon as I saw those things coming, I ran over to this gigantic road case for the B-3 organ and got inside of it, and then when it stopped raining debris, I came out, and we started to play again.

LENNY KAYE: All the kids in the audience came up on the stage, and you'd think they would have trashed it, but they just sat down on the stage.

It was the ultimate in respect and honor. It was like these kids were the metaphor—we were turning the stage over to them, and now it was their time, to go off and become who they were going to become.

JAY DEE DAUGHERTY: All the security had left. There was nobody. No promoters, no nothing, no cops. People just started getting up onstage and they were carrying off the instruments and playing them. And we were being very nice, trying to avoid a very explosive situation, so I said, "I'm sorry, but I'm not finished with these drums yet."

That was our blast of glory that we went out in. It was very scary.

LENNY KAYE: We started out playing in front of 250 people at St. Mark's Church, and finished up in front of 70,000 in a Florence soccer stadium. You can't invent a better narrative than that.

JAY DEE DAUGHERTY: The official end of the band came when we were in our accountant's office. . . . Patti basically said, "The group is no more. We're going to go out gracefully—we're not going to announce that the group is breaking up."

I know that it was very hard for her, and I know that she probably thinks that we think badly of her. Deep down inside, I hope she knows that I don't.

I wasn't angry, but I was devastated. I mean, for like the last year of the Patti Smith Group she was living in Detroit with Fred, so it was something I had feared might happen, on a purely selfish kind of level. But I didn't realize at the time that the group was my identity. That's who I was—I was the drummer of the Patti Smith Group. I wasn't anything, I wasn't me, I was a thing. So it was just like, "Wow. Now what?"

After that I drank a lot, ha ha ha, took a lot of drugs, ha ha ha, and spent money as fast as I could, ha ha ha. I also started becoming a freelance drummer, so I kept pretty busy.

LENNY KAYE: When Fred sealed their love, Patti moved to Detroit and it was very hard to keep the communication going when the arrowhead of the band is not there. I mean, it was our job to support Patti—she was the aesthetic direction—so without that, we slowed considerably. If you listen to *Wave*, she was saying good-bye during the entire record—no odd mystery in there.

We could see it coming because we'd done everything. We'd had a top-ten hit, we'd gotten rock & roll to its next incarnation, we'd lived out our dreams, and the only thing left would have been to make money out of it, and what more rock & roll thing can you do than not make money out of it, ha ha ha. That was never in the cards, we didn't want to grow up and become a human jukebox, and in some ways we had become a prisoner of our success because the stadiums weren't really conducive to our type of show. I mean, you can't play Wembley Arena in front of tens of thousands of people and diddle around improvising on something for twenty minutes.

I mean, *Don't Look Back* was Patti's inspirational movie. She didn't wanna become her own oldies act, she didn't want to go out there and sing "Gloria," she didn't feel like Jesus had died for somebody's sins but not hers anymore. She had solved the question that she'd opened up, her artistic question, and now she was on to her next art.

Art is sometimes incompatible with relationships, and I think that's also one of the reasons why Patti made her relationship her art. I think that it was important for her to devote herself full-time to loving another person, because when you're making art, there's a certain selfishness involved. I sometimes think that musicians or artists shouldn't even think about having a permanent relationship until they're in their late thirties, because until then their relationship will always take second place to their art. Artists don't make the best in-laws.

JAY DEE DAUGHERTY: Patti wanted to do something different. She wanted to make beautiful music with Fred, and I think like any sane man he probably wanted her all to himself—a trick I would've tried to pull off if I thought I could have gotten away with it, ha ha ha.

Fred was just Patti's type: a tall, brooding, silent guy. When I met him I thought, Oh, a Detroit rock & roller, this guy's heavy. Might kick the shit outta me. Ha ha ha.

It was personal chemistry, and the MC5 factor was just the icing on the cake. She loved tall guys with crooked teeth. It was like love at first sight for Patti.

LENNY KAYE: Sometimes I think of us as the last of the sixties bands. We liked those long rambling songs, we liked twenty minutes of improvisation. We weren't the Ramones, we weren't ironic like Blondie, we were like the White Panther party, New York Division.

We had a lot of that revolutionary kick out the jams, motherfucker, fervor, plus there's a direct link with the Velvet Underground and their urban noire music. We had the Stooges' sense of destructiveness, but we also had a lot of literary things like Rocking Rimbaud.

KATHY ASHETON: I was pissed at Patti, ha ha ha. I never confronted her. I felt left out, but on the other hand I never really visualized any permanence between Fred and I, though I felt like my fun was being taken away.

I remember thinking to myself, Well, I'm not quite through with this. It pissed me off, but I was saddened by it too, because it was just one of those things that you couldn't do anything about.

One time I was going to my mom's house, and Patti and Fred were in the car in front of me, going to my mom's house to see Scotty. Somehow I had ended up driving behind them, and there they were together, going to *my* mother's house, ha ha ha. I mean, the nerve!

I mean, Fred didn't flaunt her, Patti stayed in the car, but still, my reaction was, "How dare he bring her into my mother's house!" I did a little glare at both of them, but I'm not really the confrontational type, and so for me it was just my own private glare and FUCK YOU.

Fred and I would still talk on the phone. But eventually, obviously, my calls stopped completely.

JAMES GRAUERHOLZ: Patti actually managed a pretty canny thing. She managed to be a rock & roll death without having to die.

Epilogue

■ Nevermind
1980–1992

Chapter 39

■ Snatching Defeat from the Jaws of Victory

WAYNE KRAMER: I put a band together as soon as I got out of jail, and after about a year playing around I went to England and cut a single for Radar Records. I was supposed to do an album, but that got fucked-up. When I got back from England was when Johnny Thunders came to Detroit with the Heartbreakers.

The guys in my band knew this drug dealer that was looking after Thunders, and they invited me to meet Johnny. They said, "Man, Johnny wants to meet you. He's a big fan of yours."

So I went down and sat in with the Heartbreakers, and they were all dope-fiending and shit backstage. I just thought, Man, I do not want to get into this. I've starred in this movie a couple of times already.

I held Johnny at arm's length for a while, but then he had a job in Chicago and he didn't want to use the Heartbreakers. He asked if me and my rhythm section would play with him. The money was really good, so I said, "Sure."

The expression on the kids' faces when they were watching Johnny was amazing. They just adored him. I mean, I'd never seen that kind of adoration. Johnny would fuck with them; he'd spit on them and kick them in the head and all that shit, and they just loved him.

I looked at this, and thought, Man, this has potential. Maybe we should talk seriously about this band thing.

Johnny Thunders, as you know, was capable of being real charming, when it was in his interest. So he turned on the charm with me. All that time that he was staying in Detroit, the most we would ever do is drink.

I wasn't gonna use. I'd just gotten out of the penitentiary. I'd seen the error of my ways. And I wouldn't turn Johnny on to my dope connections because I didn't want to be involved in it. I was trying to get my career rolling again and make a living, so everything with Johnny and me was pretty cool in the Midwest. We decided to call our band Gang War.

But when we moved to New York, and Johnny was back in his element, he just turned back into a street-rat dope fiend. And then he crossed me out of a couple deals. He tried to tell me that Tommy Dean at Max's didn't want to hire Gang War anymore, that he just wanted to hire Johnny, but if I would play with him, Johnny would give me a hundred dollars.

I said, "For the hundred dollars, man, I'll stay home, thanks."

MICK FARREN: Gang War was a good band for about ten minutes. When I heard Wayne and Johnny were getting together, I thought, This is gonna be good, until heroin takes over. And within hours, Johnny was back in the bag, and within a few weeks, Wayne was back in the bag. And it all went to hell in a basket.

PHILIPPE MARCADE: Johnny Thunders called me up and said, "Hey, man, I'm starting a group with Wayne Kramer! WHOA, this is gonna be great. Yeah, we're gonna be called Gang War. You wanna come and play the drums?"

I said, "Yeah, great. I'll come right away. Where are you?"

He said, "Ann Arbor."

"So how the fuck am I gonna get to Ann Arbor?"

"We have a manager guy and all that, and we got you a plane ticket. We'll come pick you up at the airport."

So I got on the plane. But the only cheap place the manager could find for us to record was a little studio that was under some guy's house where they did jingles, not rock & roll. So we show up and the owner of the studio sees this bunch of fuckers come out of the car. You know, Johnny in a ripped T-shirt, all fucked-up, and the owner asked to see everybody's ID.

Johnny said, "Fuck this crap, man, let's go somewhere else." The manager said, "Cool, cool it."

So the manager starts negotiating with the owner of the studio. The manager was saying, "Are you crazy? This is Johnny Thunders, from the New York Dolls."

The owner said, "No it's not, and don't try to lie to me, because my son, who is upstairs, is a very big fan of the New York Dolls, so if you're trying to pull some number on me, I'm gonna know right now."

So he tells his son to come down, a big fat kid in his shorts, who comes down, looks around, and then says, "It IS, that's Johnny Thunders!"

So they got their mom, they got the Instamatic camera out, and they're all posing, and Johnny's all fucked-up, ha ha ha.

Then we went into the studio and Johnny was like flat as hell. The owner of the studio, this guy smoking a pipe, dressed in his suit, was looking at Johnny singing, going, "But he can't sing!"

I said, "Oh, it's great, it's fine."

But the guy said, "He just can't sing." Then he kept asking me why Johnny kept making trips to the bathroom.

I said, "He drinks a lot of water."

Then, at the end of the session, the owner came up to me, I could see he was feeling bad about something, and he had a clean T-shirt in his hand. He said to me, "I feel really bad inside because my son's with a big star, but Johnny must be so poor, he's got that T-shirt, it's old and ripped, there's holes in it. Give him that so he can at least have a clean T-shirt to wear."

WAYNE KRAMER: We had an expression that we used to say about Johnny Thunders. We'd say that he was always "snatching defeat from the jaws of victory" because everything would be set up perfectly and Johnny would fuck it up. We had some Dutch labels that were gonna give us forty grand to make a record and keep the change. Johnny went up there and tried to talk the guy into making it a Johnny Thunders record, and do the deal with him direct, but he was fucked-up out of his mind, scared the guy to death, and queered the deal. That was typical with him.

MICK FARREN: Then Wayne married Marcia Resnick. How the fuck did that happen? Didn't I introduce them to each other? I think Wayne was wandering around homeless; it was a confusing time. It seemed like Wayne got married in order to have a place to live. God knows, Marcia's place was big enough, so they went and got married. But that went bad pretty quickly.

Marcia was always screaming at Wayne, "Why don't you practice your guitar?" Wayne would scream back, "I know how to play the guitar. Fuck you." Then he'd come over to my house, and then after a while she'd come around, and Wayne wouldn't let her in, and she'd scream outside in the street.

Oh, it just got completely out of hand. Resnick, oh my god—she could take a good photograph though.

BEBE BUELL: Around 1980, 1981, Marcia Resnick was taking a lot of photographs of Johnny, and she was also taking photographs of me, so I started running into him a lot at her apartment. We started being friends again, and I think Johnny had a little crush on me then. Johnny really reached out to me during that period, and if he hadn't been so scabby and stuff, I might've wanted to, but he scared me.

Johnny was a not a pretty sight, let's get real here. His hands were unbelievably disgusting. They were all plumped up like sausage, and scabby and weird all the time. I don't like talking like that about somebody that I love so much, but he just made me a little scared. You know, sometimes you'd be talking to him, and blood would just start to drip down his hand . . . Not exactly somebody you wanna pounce on.

CYRINDA FOXE: I used to beg Johnny, "Please don't die!" But I knew he was too FAR, man. I'd cry and cry and cry, "Johnny please don't die, because I don't have anyone to love or to be friends with, I have no friends left, so please don't die!"

WAYNE KRAMER: After Gang War broke up, Johnny had this guy from Detroit, they called him Brim, he was a drug dealer, and their deal was that Brim would keep Johnny high, Johnny would play music, and Brim would be the manager.

It was a good deal for Johnny, except somebody did Brim in, one of his business associates. Brim was murdered while managing Johnny, because Brim was still dealing. Brim dealt a lot of weight, and I think somebody just said, "Well, why should I pay you when I can shoot you? Why should I give you twenty thousand dollars for these drugs when all I gotta do is shoot you?"

MICK FARREN: Well, it all broke down, didn't it? It was the eighties. And there was cocaine. Shovels full of cocaine. And ingesting drugs doesn't require a lot of talent, and that's why I think we brought ourselves down to Sid, who, it could be said, was the ultimate product of the entire punk movement. I mean Sid was completely worthless, ha ha ha.

So drugs brought money back and Ronald Reagan was elected president, and you know, shit went on. In fact, that's the sad part: hippies survived Nixon, but punk caved in to Ronald Reagan, know what I'm saying? Punk couldn't actually take a good challenge.

I mean, look at Lester Bangs, the great intellectual of the punk movement, this fucked-up Seventh Day Adventist kid who tacked on to rock & roll but really didn't wanna go the distance. Lester got the madness that he knew, peripheral madness, like the guy who goes to a Chinese restaurant and orders the same meal, because that was the first one he ever had and that will do.

It always pissed me off that the man couldn't do anything outside of this very narrow field of rock & roll writing. He couldn't even write a functional book about Blondie; on the other hand, at some given point, he was a better writer than I am, and I'm a very good writer. I mean, take any given paragraph of Lester Bangs, and it's a piece of fucking brilliant writing, but it's all about the same shit. What I'm saying is that if you don't get a life, that's what happens to you.

I just wondered why Lester didn't sit down and write himself a kind of Jim Thompson novel, because god knows, he was prolific enough—I mean, there's so much Lester on the cutting-room floor. It really started to bother me that he wasn't literally going anywhere, and it seemed like the only thing he could fucking do was die. That's really what struck me about Lester—it seemed like a fucking waste of a brain. Because you sure as shit don't have a lot of fun OD'ing on NyQuil. I mean, there are better things to die from.

BOB QUINE: I used to lecture Lester once in a while because I really thought he was gonna kill himself. The drinking thing was so outta hand that I said, "You know you're an alcoholic. You gotta stop."

Now, allegedly, he never mentioned this to me, I saw Lester the night before he died, but apparently he'd gone to an AA meeting that week, his first AA meeting. What happened was, he'd finished this book, the *Rock-Gomorrah* book, the one that's never come out, and he had a tradition whenever he finished a big long article, or a book, that he'd go on a major binge. And that's what he did. He had just finished this book, he had the flu, and he wanted to binge, but he wasn't gonna drink. Instead he went out and got all kinds of cough syrup, went over to the McDonald's on Sixth Avenue, where the pill pushers had a table, and got handfuls of pills. I think Lester decided he'd binge out on pills and he made a mistake.

He died.

I really loved that guy, you know? He was totally vulnerable and human. He was one of the few people that I could talk with for billions of hours on the phone, and whether he was drunk or sober, what he had to say was of interest. He'd say, "Hey, listen to this piece I just wrote for the *Village Voice*." And he'd read me thirty-five pages of it. I can't say I had anything better to do, it was a privilege. Lester gave a shit about music and that's partly what killed him, because music in the eighties was total shit.

So I'd say to Lester, "Do what I do—just buy these old fucking blues records."

He'd say, "Well, yeah, I like listening to this, but it's just depressing to me. You know, this is all dead music, there's nothing going on now."

I said, "Well, you know it's better to acknowledge it." He was playing me a Lonnie Mack forty-five and it was pretty cool, but then he just said, "Well, you know, it's still . . . There's just nothing happening now."

MICKEY LEIGH: I was in a band with Lester Bangs called Birdland, but I couldn't keep people in the band because Lester kept scaring them away. So finally I left too. A couple of months after we split, maybe half a year, I put out that single, "On the Beach." The B side was "Living Alone," a song that I wrote about Lester.

I wonder if he knew it? "Looking like a farmer in your Sunday best / Walking up the stairs to get a good day's rest. / Hasn't worked a day in quite a while / He's living life his way because that's his style / and he's living alone."

Chapter 40

■ Exile on Main Street

JAMES GRAUERHOLZ: William Burroughs' son, Billy, died in March of 1981. And William had really gotten started back on junk in the summer of 1978, as a result of being in Boulder, and going through Billy's liver transplant surgeries, and hanging out with these Boulder punks, who, like so many of the other people, got off on giving heroin to William Burroughs.

That was a really big kick for them. It was, "I shot up with Burroughs." I mean, what, "Can you top that?" You know, like "The pope gave me mass in his quarters." Right? I mean, isn't it? So that's where they were at. And once William got back to New York, other people brought him heroin. The whole scene was like really creepy. William was just like obviously hiding something from me, and he was just kinda useless. And kinda zonked all the time. And the worst thing is, the worst thing about junkies, is they are SO BORING. They sit around and talk about junk. As if there were anything to say about it.

So I was tired of this whole trip, and I felt that I had done it. I mean, five years, and I had, you know, climbed Everest and it was time to do something else. I wanted to kind of retire. I wanted to do a Patti Smith. So I loaded up a twenty-foot moving truck with all these archives and shit from the Bunker and drove across country to Lawrence, Kansas.

I didn't really want to leave William. I mean ultimately, I cared about him; I loved him; I still do. And so I kind of struck a halfway position. I moved out of New York. But I brought the archives and the bank accounts, and everything else. But he could live where he wanted to, and I'd often go there, and we'd travel together, and I would visit, and he would visit here sometimes. And I also frankly was hoping to lure him here to Lawrence to retire. Because at his age, and with his fame, it would just become intolerable in New York and he would burn out and he would OD or he would drink himself to death, because everyone would come around and everyone would want to get high with the Godfather of Dope, as they saw him. And it was a real dancing bear phenomenon: "We're going to go see *Burroughs*."

JAMES CHANCE: When the Contortions first started playing, one of my main motivations—I think it's a motivation for a lot of people—was just to show everybody that I was as good as they were. By that time, most of the people in the audience were those SoHo people who really bugged me. They would just stand there with a kind of blank attitude like they really thought they were so cool. I just didn't feel any real enthusiasm coming, so I thought, You motherfuckers, I'll get you to pay attention. A lot of it was just coming from my own emotions—my own total rage and hate.

But I never planned to do it onstage. It just came out one night at this gig at the Millennium. This overwhelming thing came over me and I just started running out into the audience and like pushing and shoving people. I just started grabbing people and slapping them around. And I walked through the whole place and people were just like backing up, but there was Anya Phillips giving me this look like, "Don't you dare do that to me!"

I didn't.

SYLVIA REED: I think James is a talented person, but when he came into our life he made it impossible for Anya and I to see each other. She became extremely erratic and whenever I tried to see her when he was around it would always end in a fight—a physical fight—between her and somebody, usually him. There was a night at the Paradise Garage and there was a really sleazy promoter and of course they didn't pay any of the bands. The big bouncers came in and were like, "Okay, everybody out," and everybody was like, "Where's the money?" James' reaction to this was to start screaming in the corner to get their attention. They started coming towards him, because they were gonna throw him out, and James took something and cut himself.

His blood was rushing down his neck and these big bouncers stopped in horror, they didn't want to touch him, they thought he was out of his mind.

That became Anya's life, these incredible scenes.

JAMES CHANCE: Anya and I pretty much thought that punk was over, that it was time for something else. She had been in Germany and she got interested in the terrorists over there—the Bader-Meinhof—and she told me that she had to make a decision whether she was going to become a terrorist or whether she was going to get into something where she could make some money. She was really pretty knocked out by the Contortions, so eventually she became our manager.

When Anya started managing the band I put myself totally in her hands. Not as far as the music, but everything else—as far as my looks, as far as a lot of things, just my life in general. I think a lot of people got the impression that she was like egging me on to be like even crazier and shit, but actually it was the total opposite. She was always trying to calm me down and like knock some of the rough edges off. It was like there was this free-flowing hatred and aggression that was starting to take on a life of its own, and spill over into real life too, especially when I got drunk. It was fun, but it was starting to get to a point where it was getting too crazy.

SYLVIA REED: Anya never really came out and said, "I have cancer." She said that they had found this lump behind her ear, and that they were looking for other lumps . . . I don't think she accepted it for a long, long time. We were out at dinner when she said that, and the really weird thing was that she looked great—she had lost a lot of weight, and she was all dressed up and was really elegant. She was really pleased that she had lost all that weight, and she said, "Don't I look beautiful?" and everyone was like, "Yes."

I didn't see a lot of Anya after Lou and I had gotten married, so it took about a year and a half for it to really dawn on me that she just wasn't dealing with the reality of her illness. She wasn't taking care of herself. She wasn't trying to get medical insurance, and she was doing a lot of drugs. It was a way of not having to think about that it was happening. At some point Anya went to Debbie Harry for help, and Debbie helped her get into the hospital in Westchester. I had gone back to school, at Sarah Lawrence, and I would go to the hospital to visit her quite alot. But then when I would talk with other people, they would be unaware of that.

JAMES CHANCE: Anya's real father was a Taiwanese general, a general in the Chiang Kai-shek army. And Anya's mother was a very aristrocratic woman from Peking who escaped Taiwan when the communists took over. She was very creative—she had been a screenwriter—but when Anya's father abandoned her she married this American serviceman who was a sergeant at the time. And she made him ambitious, I think he ended up a major or something. But he was very straight, a very straight guy.

Anya told me her mother always resented having to get married to this guy. She made it very obvious to Anya that she had married her stepfather to give Anya a home and security but that she had really wanted a more creative life. And that created a lot of problems in Anya's childhood.

SYLVIA REED: One time she did tell me she wasn't afraid to die, and she didn't seem afraid, but I know at the very last she must have been terrified. I got a call when Lou and I were living on Christopher Street, and she was like, "I want you to come with me to London," and I said, "I can't go to London. Should you really be going to London? Shouldn't you really be in the hospital?" She'd checked herself out and went to London, and that's what I recall as the time that led to the last hospitalization.

When she got back, someone had to make arrangements to pick her up from the airport in an ambulance and get her back to the hospital. It could have been another two and a half to three weeks I think, of . . . They tell me she was pretty much out of it at that time. Plus which, none of those people that were around her had the wherewithal to call people, and she created the impression in my mind when she said she was going to London that "Oh, she must be doing much better." I didn't know about the ambulance and that stuff until after it was all over. I didn't know that she was back until I got a message, I think it was from Roberta Bayley, telling me that Anya had died. I was . . . shocked.

There was a sort of gathering, and Lou and I went. Everybody was like, "Oh, what are you doing here?" "What do you mean what am I doing here?"

That was where I found out from Roberta that Anya had given the impression to all these other people that I had just abandoned her. I guess it was a way of controlling people even beyond the grave . . .

By that point I had quickly learned that now no one was going to be awful to me to my face, never again, because of Lou. It was like they were all very excited that Lou was there. There was this heightened dramatic tension in the air, and people were saying all these things about Anya that were not true. I mean, I guess it depends on who you are if it's true or not. Personally, I remember her as incredibly difficult, incredibly talented, and incredibly troubled . . .

And she was also very destructive. Later on, I came to realize in my head what the problem was: I thought she was my best friend, and she was more like an antifriend. She was somebody who was so intensely affecting my life . . . If I can be completely honest I would have to say her death was a release. She could really get to me in a way that nobody else could, except Lou, and she always did, she always took every opportunity to.

JAMES GRAUERHOLZ: Finally the rent on the Bunker was increased from $375 to $750, so William decided to move to Kansas too. It's laughable now, right? But we couldn't afford it. And William was tired of it. And he said, "That's it. I'm getting out of here. I'll move to Kansas."

Shortly after William got here, I started promoting some shows in Lawrence, and I ended up setting up a show for Iggy.

Iggy was great, his eyes were as big as the moon, as always, and blue. He was wild—I mean, he was a pro, he got the show together, but he was really a party monster . . . He fucked all the chickees, he was really drunk, he dragged me into the bathroom to get away from all the groupies and hangers-on. So he drags me into this little teeny bathroom and closes the door and he's hunkered down on the floor by the toilet and saying, "My manager's no fucking good. James, you've done such great things with William, why don't you manage me?" Meanwhile, we're like sniffing coke on the top of the toilet, and I'm thinking, This is really what I need to do with my life, follow this maniac around, and get killed . . . And so I sort of demurred, like, "Oh man, what an honor, thanks, I'd love to do that, and then I could help you blah, blah, blah."

Later that night we went to this shitty rednecky truck driver kind of stripper bar. Iggy was drinking Black Russians, like, bang, another one, bang, another one. Again he drags me out to the parking lot to go talk about stuff, and he was actually doing this kind of Lester Bangs thing of like, "Man, nobody understands me, I'm really sensitive, and everyone thinks that I should be so happy with fucking all these chicks, and all the drugs and being a star but I hurt and I'm lonely and I need someone in my life to stabilize me, James, someone like you." At this point he had stretched out on the ground, up on one elbow, and I'm mirroring him, because I'm with Iggy, right, I'll just do it, so I'm also lying in the parking lot.

I hear the roar of a motor and this car parked right in front of us starts to back over us. So as Iggy's blubbering about his loneliness, I grab him without warning in my arms and roll over like four times, *bump bump bump* in the parking lot out of the way of this pickup truck, VVRRMMM, the guy didn't even see us and backs out, ERRRR . . .

Iggy suddenly wakes up from all the "I'm so lonely, no one understands me" shit and he starts screaming at the driver. He says, "You fucking pig, you asshole, you almost killed me, you know who I am, you could've like stopped the history of rock & roll. You fucking pig, why don't you watch where you're driving?"

The guy says, "Fuck you." I'm saying to Iggy, "Come here, hey, let's go have another drink, buddy." So the truck pulls out and we go inside the Blockhouse and we sit down at our table and two minutes later, the door of the place bursts open, and the big burly asshole redneck charges in. He marches straight to our table and says, "I don't like what you said about my mother, faggot," and punches Iggy right in the face and blood was squirting like in fight videos. Just one hard punch and back across the table and all the glasses fell down and the guy turned around and left—a real Magnum PI in a lumberjack jacket.

We got a cold wet towel from the barman and applied it to Iggy's bleeding nose and he was kind of sniveling. But that's the thing, Iggy's feelings were actually hurt, he was misunderstood, once again, by this big hairy redneck of all things.

We took him to his room. It really deflated his mood quite a bit. There was no more talk of managing.

Chapter 41

■ Born to Lose

DEE DEE RAMONE: Rock & roll on automatic sort of desensitized my rebellion. We just toured all the time, without a break, for fifteen years. I couldn't take the van anymore—me sitting at the back looking out the window. No one ever talked to me. Johnny and Joey didn't talk for years. There was a time when we had a bus that had four separate compartments. John would sit in one with his girlfriend. Mark would sit there with his. Joey would sit there with Linda, and I'd sit in another one. And if we'd see each other, it would get real ugly. We couldn't even walk out of the bus together. We couldn't even get our keys to the hotel room together. We couldn't look at each other.

A lot of things were irritating me about the Ramones. The thing that was driving me crazy was playing that damn "Pinhead" song every night. My teeth are chipped because I used to have to sing the chorus of "Pinhead." We had a roadie who weighed three hundred pounds—his name was Bubbles, and he would dress up in a pinhead dress and pinhead mask. But he was so fat that when he would jump on the stage, the whole stage would shake, and the mike where I was singing would come banging into my mouth. I hated that damn song. I'm so glad I don't have to play it every night. The only good thing about it was that it came at the end of the show. So that cheered me up a little. I would think, Let me play this damn thing so I can get outta here. There was another song, "Glad to See You Go." When that used to come up I'd say, "Oh boy, three-quarters over. I can get off this stage and go to my hotel soon."

I was also sick and tired of the little-boy look, the bowl haircut and the motorcycle jacket. I didn't wanna be a little boy. I wouldn't grow up. Four middle-aged men trying to be teenage juvenile delinquents. I was just getting sick of playing in a revival act. It made me feel like a phony standing there in a leather jacket and torn jeans—like I used to dress when I thought I was a worthless piece of shit.

Bob Gruen: I ran into Dee Dee one night at the Cat Club after he left the Ramones. He said to me, "I have no wife, no girlfriend, and no band. I'm all alone, nobody loves me." I said, "Dee Dee, I love you," because I do like him, but it didn't help him much because he was feeling very alone, and very cut off—he had cut himself off.

Arturo asked me if they should let him back in the band, and I was saying, "Definitely, he's the Ramones, he's Dee Dee Ramone, he's the most Ramone of the Ramones, he is the rock & roll guy!"

Arturo said, "Yeah, but it's so hard with Dee Dee in the band. It's been so much trouble for all of them over the years to take care of Dee Dee." The Ramones felt like they could never throw him out, because he had done so much. He had written all the songs, and he had been such a pilot to them.

But since Dee Dee had left on his own, they didn't have to take him back. And they didn't want to. They just felt that he had dropped them flat, he had left them cold in the middle of a tour and cost them all a lot of money, without seeming to care. And they felt that they really didn't want to go through that again. That's why they wouldn't let him back in the band.

Laura Allen: I was living with Dee Dee Ramone right after he left the Ramones. The first year we were together we bought a gun from some Spanish kid on Tenth Street. Dee Dee would always carry a knife, he always had brass knuckles and all kinds of paraphernalia, but I didn't really worry about the brass knuckles or the knife. But the gun I was kind of scared of, because one time me and Dee Dee went to cop some pot on Tenth Street and this cop followed us.

He went, "Okay, over there, against the wall. Okay, what you got there in the pocket?"

And Dee Dee had the gun on him. Right in his jeans and the cop frisked Dee Dee and I thought, Oh my god, forget it. Dee Dee's gonna go to jail.

I think carrying a gun is like a one-year mandatory prison term. So the cop's searching him, right, and the pot comes out. This cop was an undercover cop, a plainclothes cop, and he said, "Oh, you used to play in that band the Ramones, didn't you? You look familiar. Aren't you Dee Dee Ramone?"

Dee Dee was like, "Yeah, I am." The cop says, "Well, how are you?" And he starts like talking about how he saw the Ramones when he was fifteen at this college. I was dying. I really thought he was gonna find the gun. But thank god the cop did not feel the gun when he frisked Dee Dee. So the cop took the pot and said, "If I catch you down here again, we're gonna have to take you in."

CYRINDA FOXE: I let Johnny Thunders come stay with me when I moved into Jack Douglas's apartment. There was a navy blue sofa there, and of course I put Johnny on the sofa, because man, he can't sleep in my bed. "You're my friend, sleep on my sofa." Cool.

So one night Johnny was sleeping on the sofa, and I came out of my room and the pancake makeup Johnny used to wear had rubbed off, and it looked like there was this dye all over him, all blue-black blotches, big blue blotches on his skin.

It was a dark sofa, so I thought he'd been sweating and it dyed his skin. I mean, that's what I thought, so when he woke up I said, "You'd better go wash up, because I think the dye got all over you."

I put him in the shower and scrubbed him. He was just so bad, he was so bad, I just never saw anybody that bad in my life. He had these big scars, lumps, and bumps, and his feet were filthy; he had big bruises where he'd been shooting up all over his feet, and on his legs, and anywhere he could shoot up. Abscesses everywhere.

He was so gross, and I just wanted to scrub the evil out of him. But I didn't know he had taken some pills. He was fine, and then all of a sudden, once he hit that water . . . Well, I almost drowned with him, I literally almost killed him, because his head hit the tub and I thought he was gonna die. I was so scared, because what was I gonna do with him now?

LAURA ALLEN: Stiv Bators wanted Dee Dee to start a band with him in Paris. Stiv told Dee Dee to come to Paris, that it was going to be great. Stiv was calling the house, saying, "We have a huge apartment. You can stay here."

They were gonna call the band the Whores of Babylon. And Caroline, Stiv's girlfriend, had a gorgeous apartment in Paris. It was a duplex, really nice. She comes from money, her father owned a famous hotel in Paris, and the parents took care of her, you know, supported her. So Stiv wanted us to come stay with them in Paris and put the new band together.

JAMES SLIMAN: After the Dead Boys broke up, Stiv Bators had gone to L.A., where he did some power pop singles with Greg Shaw, and then moved to London and formed the Lords of the New Church.

The Lords of the New Church were signed to IRS Records, and put out, I think, three albums and a whole slew of singles. While they were on IRS, they were managed off and on by Miles Copeland, who really didn't have much patience for them, and from what I've been told didn't want to put up with a lot of Stiv Bators' bullshit, and Brian James's bullshit, you know—always needing money, and fights between the band, and drugs. Miles was a businessman and he didn't want to fuck around with it, and if they didn't keep up what he wanted from them, he had a bunch of other acts; he could care less if they wanted to fall apart.

From what I was told, when the Lords of the New Church finally did break up, Stiv found out he was out of the band when he read an ad in *Melody Maker* that the band placed looking for a new singer. That's how he found out. And he flipped.

MICHAEL STICCA: Stiv was such a fucking weasel. They flew me over to work the crew for Lords of the New Church and I told Stiv, "Take it easy." But Stiv threw himself on the monitor, then was like, "Oh, my back is hurt. My back is hurt." So we all had to go back to London for two or three days off and then continue the tour. Stiv's saying, "Oh, my back is hurt." So I said, "We'll get you a doctor in London. You stay with us." He said, "No, I gotta go back to Paris, I gotta go back to Caroline." Everybody's like totally freaking, because we got this tour, and there's no way we're not doing this tour. Everybody's life was left dangling—we were out on the fucking edge. So we auditioned people. Stiv found out about the ad we placed for a new lead singer, flew from Paris to London, and he did one show with us in London. He did the fucking gig and then said, "Fuck you guys. I'm outta here."

JAMES SLIMAN: When Stiv was living in London, he was with this girl—Angelica? Alexandra? No, wait a minute, I'm sorry, scratch that. Anastasia. Anastasia, because Stiv always called her Stacy. She was British, she was pretty, she had blond hair, and she practiced witchcraft. They supposedly had some kind of a wedding, a witchcraft ceremony, but it was never valid or legal. But he was pretty much in love with her, and her I liked.

But then, when he hooked up with Caroline and moved to Paris after the Lords of the New Church, whenever I would see Stiv, I couldn't have a conversation with him because he was too high. Either on smack or crystal meth, or a little bit of both.

LAURA ALLEN: When Dee Dee and I got to Paris, to Stiv and Caroline's place, for the first couple of days it was okay. We all went out to dinner with some guy who was the head of the MTV of France. He was talking about putting out a Whores of Babylon album in Paris, and the dinner was really nice. Paris is very pretty, very romantic, really nice. But things got ugly real fast.

Johnny Thunders showed up in Paris about a day or so after we did, and after that it was a real nightmare. I think he was gigging around Europe and stuff. Stiv was good friends with Johnny, and Caroline really loved Johnny, but Dee Dee had told Stiv, "As long as Johnny's not going to be there, it's fine. Just don't have Johnny there."

I guess Stiv didn't really know what to do. He didn't really want to take sides and Johnny was in Paris at the time, so the second day we were there, Johnny showed up. At that point Dee Dee was cool, kind of like letting his guard down, like, "Oh, alright, what the hell." And then they started talking about starting a band together. It kind of evolved after we went to Paris, it was going to be Stiv Bators, Johnny Thunders, Dee Dee, and this drummer guy, I think from Mike Monroe's band, or Hanoi Rocks.

So it came time for them to rehearse and they decided to get all glamorous. They got all done up for the rehearsal. It was kinda cute, you know—all of them took two hours looking in the mirror, doing their hair, and changing into really cool clothes. But then the driver of the van showed up two hours late. Dee Dee's a real stickler for time—he told me that the Ramones were really on schedule, everything had to be on schedule, and even though it was a year and a half after he left the Ramones, he was still acting like he was on that Ramones schedule. So Dee Dee got freaked out when the van showed up late.

Stiv was like, "You're not in the Ramones anymore, it's a different city, a different band." Dee Dee was like, "I don't give a fuck. This is really bullshit, man!"

Stiv was trying to explain to us that Paris is different from New York and that people take their time, that if someone says they're gonna hang out at noon, they show up around two o'clock. That it was real laid back. But Dee Dee could not understand that. So when the guy with the van showed up two hours late, Dee Dee was livid. So me, Dee Dee, Stiv, Johnny Thunders, and Caroline got in the van, and then Stiv and Johnny had to get drugs. Johnny wanted to get like pot or hash or something, so we had to wait while he tried to cop drugs.

Dee Dee was saying, "This is really bullshit! Johnny's always pulling this shit!"

Stiv said, "Dee Dee, you're not in the Ramones anymore, you know? Like chill out!" Me and Stiv were trying to calm him down, but Dee Dee jumped out of the van, ran after Johnny, and found him eating a falafel and talking to some guy, who, according to Dee Dee, was a total beat artist and did not have anything on him.

BEBE BUELL: I thought Stiv and Caroline were very destructive for one another. I also thought that they truly loved one another and I definitely felt that they were made for each other. I don't think they were the greatest influence on one another, but that doesn't mean that I didn't like her. Caroline truly loved Stiv. She gave him the best love he ever had. She didn't leave him and she didn't cheat on him, but did they take care of each other? Did they eat well? I don't think so. Did they get sleep? Naaah, I don't think that was really on the agenda.

LAURA ALLEN: Johnny Thunders was sleeping on the couch a lot when we were at Stiv and Caroline's—it was very sad. He was getting high a lot, and soon after we got there, my watch ended up getting stolen, my sunglasses disappeared, and Dee Dee's coat disappeared.

This was January or February, and it was chilly, so when Dee Dee's coat disappeared, he started freaking out. Right away Dee Dee was like, "Okay, Johnny's taking our stuff. This is really bullshit."

So we go through Johnny's suitcase and Dee Dee finds his overcoat.

So Dee Dee snaps. He loses it. At this point, I couldn't control Dee Dee, he was in such a rage. It was like, "Oh boy, he's gonna do what he's gonna do."

Remember Johnny's guitar, I think it was a Gibson Sunburst, 1957 Sunburst? Well, Dee Dee breaks the guitar, and then he takes all this Drāno and dishwashing detergent, and anything he could get his hands on—Windex, whatever—and starts pouring it all over Johnny's clothes, then ripping the clothes up, just shredding them. Oh boy.

Stiv and Caroline had been out, I think they'd been partying at an after-hours club, so they showed up at six o'clock in the morning. When Dee Dee lost it, it was about ten or eleven at night, so I stayed up all night with him trying to calm him down. Dee Dee was furious, so we stayed up, waiting for Stiv and Caroline to show up.

When they finally showed up, Stiv was fine, but Caroline seemed a bit out of it because she immediately ran downstairs and just hid in the bedroom and wouldn't come out. Dee Dee was really flipping out. Freaking. Totally freaking out. Dee Dee was saying, "Laura's watch was stolen, her sunglasses have been stolen, and we found my overcoat in Johnny's suitcase! Why did you have Johnny around when I told you at the beginning, when the original game plan was not to have Johnny around? I knew this would happen! I knew it would happen!"

Dee Dee starts flipping out, grabs a knife, and gets me and Stiv and this guy, Gaba, on the couch. Gaba was a really nice kid, a French guy in his early twenties. Gaba was a dead ringer for Joey Ramone. He was so impressed by the Ramones and obviously idolized Dee Dee and Johnny Thunders—and Dee Dee had Gaba on the couch with a knife. All of us. It was terrifying.

Dee Dee wanted dope. He wanted heroin. He was pointing the knife, being really menacing, saying, "Unless you get it for me, I might fucking kill you. I'll start cutting you, I'm gonna start cutting you. You have to give me drugs, otherwise I'm gonna kill you all."

Then Dee Dee wanted me to stab him. He said, "Here, take the knife, take it, stab me, come on, wanna fight with me?" I was like, "Uh, no." So he says, "Well, Stiv, you wanna fight with me? Come on, come on, let's see if you can do it, fight with me, here, here, take the knife and try to stab me."

Dee Dee was like a ballerina with the knife. And Stiv—thank god—started to calm Dee Dee down, saying, "Dee Dee, we're not your enemy, I'm really sorry about bringing Johnny around, but he's a friend, so calm down. Just calm down."

Eventually Stiv made a phone call, and some guy showed up with dope. Dee Dee got high, and then he calmed down.

By that time, Johnny's stuff had been ruined, and the guitar, which had been Johnny's life, was smashed to bits. And his clothes were all shredded and had Drāno on them. So Stiv and Dee Dee talked about it, and Dee Dee said, "Well, we should really get out of here because Johnny's really gonna be upset about this. This is obviously not working, it's not gonna fly."

So Stiv had to make a phone call to the airline saying that there'd been a death in the family, and that it was an emergency, and Dee Dee and I had to get on the next flight to New York. Stiv ended up calling a cab. He walked us down with our bags. He was really nice, and that was the last time we ever saw him.

CHEETAH CHROME: I first heard about the fight from Dee Dee. He started saying that Johnny Thunders and Caroline were having an affair, which was total bullshit. Then he said he cut up Johnny's clothes, broke his guitar, and spilled Clorox on his clothes.

I didn't know why. And when Johnny came back to New York, he was really, really hurt. And Johnny didn't know why either. I guess Dee Dee felt that Johnny stole "Chinese Rocks."

I talked to Stiv in Paris over the phone about it, and Stiv didn't know why Dee Dee did it either. Stiv was like, "I don't know what the fuck is with Dee Dee, he was working out good and then when Johnny got here it all went to shit."

I don't know, I really don't, but sometimes I really can't stand Dee Dee's mind.

PATTI GIORDANO: When Johnny got back from Paris he started staying with me at my apartment on Twenty-second Street and he was really pissed off about what had happened with Dee Dee. He said that it was totally wrong what Dee Dee did, that Dee Dee was scum, and that Johnny was gonna get even with him. I mean, it was like a real major part of Johnny's life and he had a very big vengeance or anger about it. I even attempted to fix the guitar for him. I brought it to the studio and one of the engineers at the record company where I worked was gonna fix it for me.

Johnny was living with me when that came to pass. Johnny was out one night at the Scrap Bar and he told me that Dee Dee came in there and Dee Dee didn't see him. So Johnny snuck up from behind and clocked him in the back of the head a little with a beer mug. He told me he whaled on Dee Dee's head and then ran out the door.

Johnny came straight home from there, and he was all pumped up, and he said, "I got the fucker back for doing what he did to me! I got him! I got him!" He was like a little kid, you know, "I got back at him!" And that was the end of it.

JAMES SLIMAN: Caroline called me from Paris and told me Stiv had died. I had to call Stiv's parents and tell them. Apparently, Stiv and Caroline were out walking around Paris and he got hit by a car. Supposedly it was a drunk driver.

Now let me get this straight. Caroline said she took Stiv to see a doctor, the doctor said he wasn't injured, they went back home, they went to sleep, and Stiv died in his sleep. It turned out he had a blood clot from the injury and the blood clot went to his brain and under the circumstances you're not supposed to go home and go to sleep, right, but he did.

MICHAEL STICCA: It's funny, because after all Stiv Bators and I had been through, that one time when he left the Lords of the New Church, that one fucking time, I said, "You fucking suck, like you totally fucking blow, you did a fucking shitty thing leaving the tour, go back home in disgrace, blah, blah, blah . . ."

The one time I say that shit to him, Stiv dies, and I never see him again.

Chapter 42

■ No More Junkie Business

BEBE BUELL: The last time I saw Johnny Thunders was at the Limelight, with Leee Childers and some other people. We all went to see this band that Leee was managing, called Rockin Bones or something. Johnny had on a green sharkskin suit and he looked really bad. His cheeks were really hollow and he had these skin blotches, they looked yellowish, I don't know, I'm not a doctor, all I know is that it scared me.

But I still loved him and was actually very affectionate to him that night. I just let it go. I just gave him a big hug, I didn't care, know what I mean? I was very happy, so I just sort of went, "Oh, well, I don't know if those splotches will get on me too, but I just don't care tonight."

That night at the Limelight, Johnny told us he was going to Bangkok, and that he was gonna be getting some suits made at this really great place he had found. And that he was gonna be getting all this money from something that he was doing.

Then Johnny and I talked about the fact that we had never had sex. Ha ha ha, we definitely discussed it. Because I said, "How come we never went out?"

Johnny said, "I don't know. Why didn't we?"

We were laughing about it, and Johnny said, "You know, it's not too late." But I was thinking, Yes it is.

LEEE CHILDERS: Bob Gruen took me and Bebe and my band and Johnny out into the stairwell to do a photo shoot. And Johnny was absolutely patchwork, his face was yellow and white, almost green. He looked awful, just awful. And, I confess, I said to my boyfriend, one of the kids in the band, "Look at him and think about it before you ever take drugs. Just look at him."

BOB GRUEN: The last time I saw Johnny Thunders was when he came back from Japan. He played a tour there and, I think, went to Bangkok afterwards, you know, bought some drugs, bought some suits. When he came back he called me up at like, maybe 8:30 in the morning or something and asked if I wanted to meet for breakfast. And I was surprised that he was up, but I thought maybe it was like the jet lag or something. I was just hoping that he hadn't been up all night.

So we met at David's Potbelly on Christopher Street. Johnny showed up late, I was standing out front, and as he walked up, from a couple of feet away, I could smell the coke just sweating out of him.

He was just wired out. Anyway we had breakfast, he ate I don't remember exactly what, but I do remember he was talking about going to Europe and that he was going to produce a band in Germany. He was going to go to England and get some methadone, a few months' supply of methadone, and then go to Germany, where he had an offer to produce a band that was going to pay him like ten thousand dollars just for being in the studio. And he had like twenty thousand dollars he had brought back from Japan.

His pockets were stuffed with hundred-dollar bills. It was kind of odd. He actually owed me fifty dollars from the nights that we'd been hanging out earlier, which I didn't remember. And he remembered, he payed me back at that breakfast, which I always held to his credit. He was telling me he was going to go to Germany to produce this band. Then the whole point was to take the money and go to New Orleans and set himself up in New Orleans and get some good blues players down there and make an acoustic album. That had been his dream for some time, but now he finally seemed to be able to do it. He'd made some money, he had the time, he was going to get some more money, he was going to get the methadone and get out of New York and clean up and go to New Orleans and make this dream acoustic album.

After breakfast we went back to his house, because I'd lost a watch and I thought maybe it was in his apartment. But on the way he wanted to stop on Twelfth Street, and he was saying, "Is it alright if I get something?"

He knew I had cleaned up, and he was asking, "Would it bug you if I stopped to pick something up?"

I said, "Well, just make it quick."

So we stopped at some Lower East Side drug place and the cab driver got upset because the block was really hot. Lots of cops up on the block and the cab driver doesn't want to wait. I said, "Oh, he's just picking something up from a friend."

Finally Johnny comes back and we go to his place on Twenty-first Street, which is right across from the police station. There's all these cops and police academy recruits walking up and down the block, and Johnny goes to pull the keys out for his apartment, and this huge bag of coke falls out on the sidewalk. He kind of looks up and down the block like, "Is anybody noticing?" Then quickly scoops it up back into his pocket and said, "Sorry, Bob, I ain't got no class."

I said, "No, you got a lot of style, but you got no class."

JERRY NOLAN: Johnny and I still got together for the odd gig but he could still be such a pain. When it came time to play, and he started putting on his little act, I'd have to tell him, "Johnny, you either put that guitar around your neck, or I'm going to wrap it round your head."

And he'd put it on and go out. He loved me for that. He'd be so puppy-eyed and wag his tail when I put my foot down and told him I'd have to kick the shit out of him. He'd get cocky and try to push people around, but if he could push you around he'd hate you. If you pushed him back, he'd love you for it. If you could smack him down, he'd be your best friend. He needed me for that. He was a little bit of a masochist.

Then he was trying to get me to go with him to New Orleans. He wanted to move there and put together a new band. I told him I'd go with him if he was really serious, and he said he was.

BOB GRUEN: That night I went back to Johnny's place to see him off to New Orleans. His cousin, Danny, was going to drive him to the airport. And while Rachel was trying to pack his suitcase, he was sitting on the floor in the bathroom trying to find a vein.

I told him that I hoped things worked out in New Orleans and that he cleaned up because I really wanted to see him again. And he just kind of looked up at me, it was just like a faraway kind of farewell look. Kind of spooky.

The sad thing was that I knew he did want to finally clean up. I was with him when he came back from Hazelden, the drug rehab place, for the second time. We were at the Cat Club having soda waters together, and somebody came over and said, "Hey, Johnny, wanna smoke a joint?"

He said, "No, man, no, I'm not doing that now."

The guy went, "Aww, what fucking good are you then?"

But I used to talk to Johnny; one time I told him that he was the Chuck Berry of his generation. I was trying to say to him that it was his talent that was great, and that he would be greater if he was straight. I tried to tell him that he didn't have to be a drugged-out person to sell tickets, that he was a genius guitar player, and just because some kids came out and said, "Oh, he didn't fall off the stage tonight," that a lot of other people would say, "He played great." I mean, he didn't need to get fucked-up. Johnny Thunders developed a unique style and sound that every guitar player younger than him was trying to copy.

WILLY DEVILLE: New Orleans is a marvelous place, but it really is very strange. If you're not careful, funny things can happen in New Orleans. People come down here from New York and think that because we have trees in the housing projects that nobody's gonna fuck with them. Well, you gotta be real careful. Get too drunk in a bar one night or try to buy drugs from somebody, go with somebody someplace . . . more people have disappeared in New Orleans than you could shake a stick at. There's just something in the ground. There's tragedy here, I think it's left over from the slaves.

It was very weird. I usually sit on my doorstep every day next to the St. Peter's Guest House and play my guitar, but the day Johnny Thunders came to town, I wasn't out there.

Anyway, the next day I was out there again, sitting on my doorstep, playing my guitar. It was about twelve o'clock, twelve-thirty in the afternoon, and we were sitting there, a couple of us guys drinking beer and talking, and all of a sudden all these cops pull up.

Naturally we're checking out what the hell's going on. We thought it was a robbery. Then somebody overheard something and said the coroner's gonna be here. We all started laughing, thinking that some old guy probably died in there with a whore or something.

Then the coroner came, and after that the guy from the St. Peter's Guest House comes running over to me—his daddy owns the hotel—and he said to me, "Er, Willy, did you send that guy?"

Most of the musicians and record company people that stay there, I put them in there, because it's next to my house. So he said to me, "Did you send that musician, some rock star from New York to my hotel?"

I said, "What are you talking about?"

He said, "He's some rock star from New York. His name is Johnny Thunders."

I said, "No." I said, "I didn't even know he was in town."

LEEE CHILDERS: The night before Johnny Thunders died, Bebe Buell had called and said that she was putting on a show of her band at CBGB's. So we all went and it was a great time and then a couple of us went out to dinner and got to talking about Johnny.

We were laughing about Johnny and his money. Bob Gruen was saying that Johnny had just been there a few days before and had ten thousand dollars in his pocket in cash. Gruen told Johnny, "You can't have ten thousand dollars in your pocket. It'll kill you. You'll die from having ten thousand dollars in your pocket."

But Johnny told him, "Don't worry about me. I'm going to New Orleans for the jazz festival, and we're gonna have a fabulous time. Don't worry about me."

I went to work the next day, and about ten o'clock in the morning, Gruen called and said, "They found Johnny dead."

WILLY DEVILLE: I don't know how the word got out that I lived next door, but all of a sudden the phone started ringing and ringing. *Rolling Stone* was calling, the *Village Voice* called, his family called, and then his guitar player called. I felt bad for all of them. It was a tragic end, and I mean, he went out in a blaze of glory, ha ha ha, so I thought I might as well make it look real good, you know, out of respect—so I just told everybody that when Johnny died he was laying down on the floor with his guitar in his hands.

I made that up. When he came out of the St. Peter's Guest House, rigor mortis had set in to such an extent that his body was in a U shape. When you're laying on the floor in a fetal position, doubled over—well, when the body bag came out, it was in a U. It was pretty awful.

CHEETAH CHROME: I was playing at the Continental with that band Lost Generation. A friend of mine came over and asked, "I've just heard that Johnny Thunders died. Is it true?"

I had five minutes before I had to go on, so I went downstairs to get my guitar, and when I came back upstairs, the guy was on the phone. He said to me, "It's true."

I just went onstage and said, "This one's for Johnny."

WILLY DEVILLE: The next day, the little girl who worked at St. Peter's Guest House came over to me and said, "Willy, would you go in that room? I have to gather up his clothes and things to send to his family, and I've never been in a room where somebody died so I'm a little scared to go in there."

I said, "Sure, I don't mind helping."

I went in the room and there was small change all over the floor and a lot of Japanese money and clothes and empty methadone boxes. There was a syringe in the toilet. There was something funny in there, I could really feel it. I don't think he OD'd—somebody dosed him.

Knowing Johnny, he probably checked into the hotel, then I heard that he went across the street to the Pound Sterling. There were these two guys hanging around the French Quarter, real street scum, because I ran into them too. They were selling acid.

Now Johnny didn't take acid, I know that. I'm sure Johnny said something like, "Look, if you get me some cocaine I'll put you in a hotel room there." And some rigs, if he wasn't carrying. You know, syringes. So I think they crushed a tab and Johnny, thinking that it was blow, just went in the bathroom and hit it. All of a sudden it's LSD, and he must have been bouncing off the walls and talking crazy. That's what the girl that was working in St. Peter's told me. I think they dosed him and Johnny took the methadone to come down. And I think that he took so much methadone, that's what killed him. Because there were two empty boxes there and that's enough to kill the entire French Quarter.

DEE DEE RAMONE: My friend Mark Brady was trying to get me back on the scene. He was making a Johnny Thunders movie and gave me a little part in it. After we called it a wrap, we went to our friend Rachel's apartment to relax with some weed. We were sitting there and the phone rang. It was Stevie, Johnny Thunders' guitarist. He had some bad news. Johnny was dead.

I felt cold. I was not really aware of what I had just heard. Six months before Stiv Bators had died, and my friend Phil Smith had just died.

Life seemed pretty cheap at that moment. I got up and left. I was hoping that I would be next.

BEBE BUELL: Bob Gruen and I went to the wake and funeral together. At the wake you could go up to the casket and kneel down and say a prayer. I was sitting there, and one by one, each one of us went up to the casket. I told you what I said to Johnny, didn't I? When I went up to the casket I said to him, "Well, you know what we're gonna discuss, that we never made it. That we never did it."

I was having my little conversation with him and stuff, and as I got up to turn around to go back to my seat, I walked smack into Steven Tyler, my daughter, Liv's, father.

We were crying, we just all were crying, but I didn't know he was there, didn't expect him. I had just finished doing my little prayer to Johnny and I stood up and I don't think Steven knew that it was me either, and you know how you just crash into a person? It was very bizarre.

Steven Tyler is the least public of any relationship I've ever had, because I have never spoken about it, not ever, in any interview I've ever done—anything. I used to just pretend like it didn't happen. I just pretended that Todd Rundgren was Liv's dad, for years.

Steven Tyler was a really important relationship to me. I wanted to marry him, you know? We were cut from the same cloth. We were two peas in a pod. I really cared about him.

CYRINDA FOXE: I was so sorry that it wasn't my ex-husband Steven Tyler lying there instead of Johnny Thunders. Steven just stood there going, "It coulda been ME!"

I said, "How dare you, how dare you! Johnny hated you! He hated you!"

Oh, I was sick, I was foaming, I was so upset. I was like, "Too bad it wasn't you, who cares about you. You never cared about another person, it's HIM lying in that coffin. Jesus Christ, you are so disgusting. You are the most disgusting human being I know. I mean, how could you think of yourself at a time like this?"

Chapter 43

■ The Marble Index

JIM CARROLL: I was at the Mabuhay Gardens, which was like the CBGB's of San Francisco, and I was trying to hit on one of the girls in the Go-Go's. I had this really good coke, so I'm doling out some lines in the manager's office, and we're doing some and then all of a sudden Nico comes in.

She sees the coke and says, "Is that cocaine?" Then she says, "Oh, you are Szhim Carroll. I read about you. You are so skinny. I am so fat."

She was really large and she looked pretty bad. I said, "You sounded great. Here, have some coke."

She was really thankful. She said, "Oh, this is very good coke."

I said, "Thanks. Coming from you that's a real compliment." Ha ha ha.

She claimed that she had literally lost the money that had been paid to her for that night's show, so the manager booked her for another show, but then I heard that she was too fucked-up to make it. She was living in England then, and it was that period when she was really on junk.

PAUL MORRISSEY: Nico was a childlike, infantile person, very sweet, but the drugs made her so awful. All through the fifties, she had been a famous model for that yellow-haired German look. But with all that poison in her system, she wanted to make herself ugly, because if you wanted to be accepted in the drug world, you must be unattractive and make ugly sounds. So she managed to look awful and sound awful, but it was just a self-destructive course she got on when she got on the heroin. It took her a long time to die, but by that time she'd given it up. She was on methadone, but her system was probably debilitated.

ARI DELON: Late one morning on July 17, 1988, my mother told me that she had to go into town to buy some marijuana. She sat at the mirror and wound a black scarf around her head. My mother stared at the mirror and took great care to wind the scarf properly. She rode down the hill on her bicycle: "I won't be long." By the time she left it was the start of the afternoon, say 1:00 P.M., and the hottest day of the year, thirty-five degrees centigrade.

PAUL MORRISSEY: Nico died from not having health insurance in Ibiza. She wore these hateful hippie woolen clothes to disguise her figure, which had deteriorated from the drug addiction. And she was bicycling, wearing these woolen things in the middle of summer in the hottest climate, and she had this little sunstroke, which probably would have been very easy to deal with. But this man who picked her up off the road took her to two or three hospitals in Ibiza, and none of them would take her. Finally the Red Cross took her and she died there.

ARI DELON: When my mother died, Alan Wise took me to the probate registry in order to inherit the royalties, and the debts. When I got my mum's royalties for the first time I spent the money on smack. I was hooked. I was taking a gram a day. So I called my psychiatric doctor in Paris and I spent two weeks in the hospital. I got off heroin. Then I got a check from the Velvet Underground and bought a ticket for Raroia, Tahiti. I was taking Valium, pot, and beer and I got beaten up, then arrested, and someone tried to kill me with a harpoon.

Back in New York I went out of my mind. I spent winter out on the street; rescuers found me in the River Hudson. Then on Staten Island I fell down a chute, fifteen meters, in an old flour mill. I now have steel pins in my feet. Workmen found me and said, "Are you crazy?!" Maybe I was. I had no money, no passport, nothing. Someone told the cops, who took me to a psychiatric hospital. They gave me five brain electric shocks. A friend got me out and took me back to Paris. I had two months of treatment in psychiatric hospitals there and then in the south of France. Now I'm trying to get back into myself. I'm not yet strong enough, but one day, when I am, I will confront my father and I will do it for the sake of my mother.

RONNIE CUTRONE: The Velvet Underground reunion was wonderful. I went to one of their rehearsals in Prague and it was just me and the Velvets. I stayed out of their way, crouched down in the corner like a fan, with the hairs standing up on the back of my neck.

For two hours I just stayed crouched down like a little boy, my knees were like breaking, but I just stayed there, out of their way, with a lot of humility in me, thinking about what had been. And seeing John Cale and Lou Reed in the same room—without tearing each other apart—was just wonderful. And that same old sound, only with better equipment. I was thrilled to death.

MAUREEN TUCKER: The first time my mother saw the Velvet Underground was in Europe in 1993. I brought her and all my kids over because I figured, This is probably going to be it. I said damn the expense—"Get the tickets, I don't even wanna know what it costs." I really wanted her to see us because when I was playing with the Velvets I was living at home, earning ten dollars a week or something, and she could very well have said, "Hey, cut the shit." You know, "Get a job and give me some money." But instead she lent me her car!

She was in heaven. Oh she was just . . . it was so great . . . she really was just . . . I don't even know what word to use. We played Prague first, and she was flabbergasted, not only at the music, but from the response—all these people were just swooning over us.

I had played in Prague with my band years earlier, and after the show Havel had come backstage to introduce himself. We had a translator, and he was trying to describe to me what the Velvets' music and lyrics had meant to him and his cohorts when they were trying to blow up Russian tanks, creeping around the woods, and going to jail. Many people have said, "Oh your music got me through high school," and that's wonderful, but Havel is much more than a fan. It's very hard to describe. He couldn't even describe it.

So when we all had dinner with him, I thought my mother was gonna have a heart attack. There was Havel, the Velvets, my family, Sylvia Reed, and a few of the people who had been in that Chapter 17 thing. One guy had spent eight years in prison for playing rock & roll. Eight years for being in a band.

There was one band who used to go out into the woods and have secret concerts of Velvet songs. They printed up lyrics from our first album, and made about two hundred little booklets, and they passed them out to people they could trust, because it was known that if anyone got caught with this— big damn trouble.

So all these Rasputins are sitting around the dinner table, who are now like the secretary of the interior, ha ha ha. I have five kids and my mother along, and they were thunderstruck, the whole bunch of them. Holy shit.

RONNIE CUTRONE: Everyone had a wonderful time, but then Lou and John went back to the rivalry. Then they went on tour together, and you know, divorced. It was like, "We love each other but we just don't get along."

Chapter 44

■ The End

JERRY NOLAN: I have a rough time getting through the days. I get real lonely, and I miss Johnny terribly. I don't like the idea of living without him. We were so similar. I didn't have to repeat myself. Sometimes we didn't even have to talk and we'd know what to do. He never had a father. I was like a father to him, a brother to him.

It's just not fair. Everywhere I look I see Johnny clones. Poison, Mötley Crüe. I could name a hundred bands that have a Johnny Thunders clone in them.

I bumped into Keith Richards. I was walking down Broadway across the street from the old church, Grace Church, at Tenth Street. I've met him many times, but I'm really just an acquaintance. I had the blues. I was feeling sad. He was just leaning up against a wall, reading or something, smoking a cigarette, and he'd seen me first. He made a sort of motion, showing that he knew we knew each other. It was very early in the morning. There was no one out, me and him, that's it.

Of course he knows all about me and Johnny Thunders. Keith's the kind of guy that keeps up. He gave me the typical limp English handshake and says, "Look, Jerry, I'm sorry. I know what it's like. I don't know what to say. I wish I had a poetic answer. But I will say one thing. Somehow, I don't know how, but somehow, hang in there. Stick to it. Don't give up."

Keith really picked up my spirits.

But I can't sleep, I can't eat, I'm getting headaches again. I'm not getting through my days too well. I feel exhausted. But I don't want things to go to waste. I'm forcing myself to shave.

CYRINDA FOXE: I felt so guilty over Johnny Thunders dying that I went to see Jerry Nolan in the hospital. I just started doing Hail Marys when I saw him.

A month before, I'd seen Jerry at a Bob Gruen photo shoot and he looked big and healthy, with thick hair—but bloated, like an alcoholic. He didn't look sick to me, just bloated and pink.

But when I walked into that hospital room, I saw a 110-year-old man. He was just not the same man I saw one month earlier. Here was this small, emaciated person, like Howard Hughes without the beard. They'd shaved his head back, he was laying there in mucus and crud and stuff caked all over his face, and his head was rocking back and forth.

CHEETAH CHROME: I held Jerry's hand in the hospital and said, "Jerry, listen, man, I don't wanna see you like this, you know? You wouldn't like to see me like this. My prayers are with you."

CYRINDA FOXE: He had tubes, big tubes going down his mouth and he was gumming them constantly, like, "Ngngngngng." He was chewing, chewing, chewing on the tubes and his eyes were just going all over the place, and his girlfriend told me that he didn't know that he was still alive.

I went over and looked at him, and his eyes looked at mine and he had consciousness, he had thoughts going in his head. He looked at me and said, "I remember . . ."

JERRY NOLAN: *My mom remarried a soldier, and we moved to Hawaii. We lived in Pearl City. That's where Pearl Harbor got bombed. My sister Rose and I, we were Brooklyn kids. I was ten, she was about fourteen, a tough chick, really blossoming. Back in Brooklyn, Rose had been in a gang and everything. This was a big switch for us. All we knew was five square blocks in Williamsburg, and all of a sudden we're in Hawaii.*

Every week Rose and I went to this arena to watch roller derby, and they'd also have music shows there. That's where I saw Elvis Presley. We're talking in the fifties, before he got drafted, with Bill Black, Scotty Moore, and D. J. Fontana on drums. I was in the third row, as close as you could get. You could almost touch him.

CYRINDA FOXE: "I remember." I know he said that, and no one can tell me he didn't say that. And it was the most soulful look in a person's eye that you ever saw in your life. I just thought he meant that he remembered his time, The Dolls and everything.

It was so sad and then that heart thing, that machine that they connect to your heart, started going "BEEP BEEP BEEP BEEP!" Everytime he would look at me, that thing would go, "BEEP, BEEP BEEP!" I couldn't leave, but I was getting scared that he was having emotions. His eyes were going back and forth, and he kept gumming the tubes, it was so painful to see. I was just grossed out by this puny little body. I looked at the nurse, and I went, "What is this?" And Jerry looked at me . . . Don't tell me he didn't know what was going on, he knew what was going on. He did remember, he said that to me, he mouthed it. "I remember . . ."

JERRY NOLAN: *Elvis was wearing a white jacket, black baggy peg-leg pants with a pleat — white inside with little white stitching. He had two-tone shoes on, white on the top, black on the sides, rock & roll shoes. I think he had on a silver lamé short-sleeved shirt. And he wore his belt buckle, a skinny little belt, on the side, to be cool.*

I was pretty excited. Everyone was carried away. I had never seen anyone put on a show like that. I was almost embarrassed. It was just shocking. I was even more interested in my sister. She was screaming and jumping around. I was amazed she was doing this.

At one moment, Elvis threw himself on his back, sort of doing the splits, with one leg pointed right at me. I could see that his shoes were worn out. Maybe they were just his favorites and he didn't want to quit wearing them. But I also had a tinge of pity, thinking maybe he was poor. But I dug it. I thought he looked like a real street kid from Williamsburg.

That show, even at ten years old, really changed my life. I was overwhelmed by Elvis. I was overwhelmed by the musicians. I could feel the playing.

But most of all, I remember two things from that show: my sister completely losing her cool, and the hole in Elvis's shoe.

Authors' Note to the Penguin Edition

The "Cast of Characters" for the cloth edition of *Please Kill Me* published by Grove Press was chock-full of mistakes. It shouldn't have been. Our good friend Jim Marshall (co-owner of the Lakeside Lounge, manager of the Prissteens, famed WFMU deejay, and *High Times* magazine columnist) fact-checked and edited the "Cast of Characters" for Gillian and me while we were working on the manuscript's final deadline. In the rush to make our publication date, unfortunately, Jim Marshall's edited copy was misplaced and the rough version, full of mistakes, was published instead. Gillian and I apologize for such a massive error, especially to Jac Holzman, who we listed in the "Cast" as being dead. He isn't. Sorry, Jac.

To atone for our blunder, we are presenting our new, improved "Cast of Characters" (edited by Jim Marshall) and an extra bonus—twenty-two new pages of our favorite stories that were left on the cutting room floor. (We used only a very small percentage of the five hundred hours of original interviews we conducted in order to write *Please Kill Me*. Since there is no narrative to fall back on when doing an oral history, we needed a massive amount of material to cover all bases. Unfortunately, we couldn't use a lot of the good stories because the book was already 423 pages long.)

We hope you enjoy the new stuff and that it makes up for our mistake. If you have any comments, weird thoughts, dirty pictures, favorite recipes, fanzines, books, sick cartoons, bad poetry, grand schemes for taking over the world, or money you want to send us, you can reach us at:

Legs & Gillian
Suite H
151 First Avenue
New York, NY 10003

Cast of Characters

Mariah Acquiar: Former CBGB's employee.

John Adams (a.k.a. The Fellow): Former Stooges road manager and roadie.

Dave Alexander (a.k.a. Zander): Musician. Bass player: the Stooges (1967–1970). (Deceased: 1975)

Laura Allen: Runway model. Former girlfriend of Dee Dee Ramone.

Penny Arcade (a.k.a. Susana Ventura): Performance artist. Actress. Writer and star of BITCH! DYKE! FAGHAG! WHORE! Star of Andy Warhol's *Women in Revolt*.

Al Aronowitz: Writer. Former columnist for the *New York Post*. First manager of the Velvet Underground. The man who introduced Bob Dylan to the Beatles.

Kathy Asheton: Singer. Younger sister of Stooges members Ron and Scott Asheton.

Ron Asheton: Musician. Lead guitarist (1967–1971) and bass player (1972–1974): the Stooges. Lead guitarist: New Order, Destroy All Monsters, and Dark Carnival. Costarred with Gunnar Hansen (Leatherface) in the film *Mosquito*. Older brother of Kathy and Scott Asheton.

Scott Asheton: (a.k.a. Rock Action): Musician. Drummer: the Stooges, the Sonic Rendezvous Band. Younger brother of Ron Asheton.

Tom Baker: Actor, writer. Warhol Superstar featured in *I, A Man* with Valerie Solanis. Former drinking buddy of Jim Morrison, who was arrested with him for violation of the Air Piracy Act during a flight to Phoenix to see the Rolling Stones. (Deceased: 1981)

Lester Bangs: Writer, musician. Former editor of *Creem* magazine. Singer: Birdland, Lester Bangs and the Delinquents. Author (posthumously) of *Psychotic Reactions and Carburetor Dung*, his collected essays, rants, and reviews. (Deceased: 1982)

Stiv Bators (a.k.a. Steve Bators): Musician. Singer: the Dead Boys, Rocket from the Tombs, Lords of the New Church. (Deceased: 1990)

Roberta Bayley: Photographer. First door person at CBGB's. Former photo editor of *Punk* magazine. Album covers include the first Ramones album and Richard Hell and the Voidoids' first album.

John Belushi: Comedian, actor. Original cast member of "Saturday Night Live." (Deceased: 1982)

Rodney Bingenheimer: Disc jockey, scenemaker. Mayor of the Sunset Strip. Host of the famous radio show "Rodney on the ROQ" on KROQ in Los Angeles. During the seventies owned Rodney's English Disco, the infamous glitter teenybopper nightclub.

Johnny Blitz (a.k.a. John Madansky): Musician. Drummer: the Dead Boys.

Victor Bockris: Writer and biographer. Author of *Uptight: The Velvet Underground Story* (with Gerard Malanga), *The Life and Death of Andy Warhol, Making Tracks: The Rise of Blondie* (with Chris Stein and Debbie Harry), *Keith Richards: The Biography,* and *Transformer: The Lou Reed Story.* In the early seventies, he was the copublisher (with Andrew Wylie) of Telegraph Books, a small press that published *Seventh Heaven,* Patti Smith's first book of poetry.

Angela Bowie: Muse, manager. Author of *Backstage Passes: Life on the Wild Side with David Bowie.*

David Bowie (a.k.a. David Jones): Musician, producer, actor. Albums include *Hunky Dory, Diamond Dogs,* and *Let's Dance.* Mixed the Stooges' *Raw Power* and produced Lou Reed's *Transformer.* Starred in the films *The Man Who Fell to Earth* and *The Hunger.*

Pam Brown: Writer, painter. Former feature writer for *Punk* magazine.

Bebe Buell: Model, singer, muse, manager. Lead singer: the Gargoyles. Solo recording artist. *Playboy* centerfold, 1974. Married to musician and actor Coyote Shivers. Mother of actress Liv Tyler.

Clem Burke: Musician. Drummer: Blondie.

William Burroughs: Writer, painter. Author of *Naked Lunch, Queer, Nova Express, Junky,* and numerous other novels.

David Byrne: Musician. Lead singer and guitarist: Talking Heads. Solo recording artist.

John Cale: Musician, producer. Viola, bass, and keyboard player: the Velvet Underground. Produced the Stooges' first album, *The Stooges;* Patti Smith's first album, *Horses;* and three Nico albums: *The Marble Index, Desertshore,* and *The End.*

Jan Carmichael: Painter.

Jim Carroll: Poet, musician, author. Books include *The Basketball Diaries*, *Forced Entries*, and *Living at the Movies*. Lead singer: the Jim Carroll Band.

James Chance (a.k.a. James Siegfried, James White): Musician. Singer, saxophonist: the Contortions, James White and the Blacks, and Teenage Jesus and the Jerks.

Bill Cheatham: Roadie. Replaced Dave Alexander as bass player of the Stooges for a few weeks.

Stephanie Chernikowski: Photographer. Books include *Dream Baby Dream*.

Leee Black Childers: Photographer, manager. Former vice president of MainMan, David Bowie's management company. Former manager of the Heartbreakers and Levi and the Rockats.

Cheetah Chrome (a.k.a. Gene O'Connor): Musician. Lead guitarist: the Dead Boys.

Paul Cook: Musician. Drummer: the Sex Pistols.

Alice Cooper (a.k.a. Vincent Furnier): Lead singer: Alice Cooper. Solo recording artist.

Diego Cortez: Entrepreneur, scenemaker, writer. Books include *The Private Elvis*.

Elvis Costello (a.k.a. Declan Patrick McManus): Musician, singer, songwriter. Albums include *My Aim Is True*, *Blood and Chocolate*, and *Spike*.

Jayne County (formerly Wayne County): Musician, actor. Lead singer: Queen Elizabeth, Wayne County and the BackStreet Boys, and the Electric Chairs. Advice columnist for *Rock Scene* magazine. Author of *Man Enough to Be a Woman*.

Pam Courson (a.k.a. Pam Morrison): Former girlfriend of Tom Baker. Common-law widow of Jim Morrison. (Deceased: 1974)

Peter Crowley: Former booking agent at Max's Kansas City. Former manager of Wayne County.

Jackie Curtis: Actor, drag queen, playwright, Warhol Superstar. Star of the John Vaccaro plays *Cock Strong* and *Femme Fatale*. (Deceased: 1985)

Ronnie Cutrone: Painter. Former Warhol studio assistant. Whip dancer for Andy Warhol's Exploding Plastic Inevitable.

Damita (a.k.a. Damita Jayrudi, Damita Richter): Stripper, groupie.

Candy Darling (a.k.a. Jimmy Slattery): Actor, drag queen, Warhol Superstar.

Jay Dee Daugherty: Musician. Drummer: Patti Smith Group.

Clive Davis: Entrepreneur. Former president of Columbia Records. President of Arista Records. Signed the Stooges and Patti Smith.

Michael Davis: Musician, painter. Bass player: MC5 and Destroy All Monsters.

Miles Davis: Musician. Father of "cool jazz." Fan of the Stooges. (Deceased: 1990)

Tommy Dean: Entrepreneur. Former owner of Max's Kansas City during the seventies after Mickey Ruskin moved on to other restaurants.

Tony DeFries: Entrepreneur, manager. Former president of MainMan, David Bowie's management company. Former manager of David Bowie, Mott the Hoople, and Iggy Pop.

Ari Delon: Illegitimate son of Nico and French film star Alain Delon.

Pamela Des Barres: Author of *I'm with the Band* and *Take Another Piece of My Heart*. Former member of the GTO's (Girls Together Outrageously), the Frank Zappa-sponsored groupie group.

Jimmy Destri: Musician. Keyboard player: Blondie.

Ged Dunn (a.k.a. George Edgar Dunn): Entrepreneur. Former publisher of *Punk* magazine.

Bob Dylan (a.k.a. Robert Zimmerman): Musician, singer, songwriter, poet.

Eric Emerson: Musician, scenemaker, actor. Lead singer: Eric Emerson and the Magic Tramps. (Deceased: 1975)

Brian Eno: Musician, producer. Former member of Roxy Music. Produced Television's first demo tape.

Mick Farren (a.k.a. Michael Farren): Writer, musician. Lead singer: the Deviants. Performed in the rock opera *The Last Days of Dutch Schultz* with Wayne Kramer. Books include *Armageddon Crazy*, *Elvis and the Colonel*, and *Black Leather Jacket*.

Billy Ficca: Musician. Drummer: the Neon Boys, Television.

Danny Fields: Former "company freak" at Elektra Records. Former executive at Atlantic Records. Former editor of *16* magazine. Former *SoHo Weekly News* columnist. Former manager of the Stooges. Former manager (with Steve Paul) of Jonathan Richman and the Modern Lovers. Former manager (with Linda Stein) of the Ramones and Steve Forbert. Manager of Paleface.

Tom Forcade (a.k.a. Thomas King, Gary Goodson): Radical entrepreneur, drug smuggler. Founder/publisher of *High Times* magazine. Former financial backer of *Punk* magazine. Produced *D.O.A.*, the Sex Pistols movie. Accused of being a CIA agent by Abbie Hoffman and Allen

Ginsberg and was put on trial by the Yippies, which resulted in an apology from Abbie Hoffman. (Deceased: 1979)

Jane Forth: Warhol Superstar. Widow of Eric Emerson.

Kim Fowley: Producer, songwriter. Creator and producer of the all-girl punk band the Runaways.

Cyrinda Foxe: Actress, model. Mother of Mia Tyler.

Chris Frantz: Musician. Drummer: Talking Heads, and Tom Tom Club. Married to Tina Weymouth.

Dennis Frawley: Former columnist (with Bob Rudnick) of the *East Village Other*.

Ed Friedman: Poet. Artistic director of the Poetry Project at St. Mark's Church-in-the-Bowery.

Jane Friedman: Manager. Former manager of the Patti Smith Group and John Cale.

Gyda Gash (a.k.a. Gyda Braveman): Musician. Bass player: TranSisters.

Patti Giordano: Photographer. Former roommate of Johnny Thunders. (Deceased: 1995)

John Giorno: Poet. Owner of the Bunker, William Burroughs's infamous Bowery loft. Books include *You Got to Burn to Shine*.

Bill Graham: Promoter. Former owner of the Fillmore West and Winterland in San Francisco, and the Fillmore East in Manhattan. (Deceased: 1991)

James Grauerholz: Musician, writer, producer. Manager of William Burroughs. Singer, guitarist: Tank Farm.

Albert Grossman: Entrepreneur. Former manager of Bob Dylan, the Band, and Janis Joplin. (Deceased: 1986)

Bob Gruen: Photographer, filmmaker. Directed the New York Dolls video documentary *Looking for a Kiss*. Books include *Listen to These Pictures*, *Chaos! The Sex Pistols*, and *Sometime in New York City* (with Yoko Ono).

Brion Gysin: Artist, writer. Former collaborator of William Burroughs. (Deceased: 1986)

Eric Haddix: Former Stooges road manager.

Duncan Hannah: Painter, actor, rock & roll fan. Former president of the Television Fan Club. Star of the Amos Poe films *Unmade Beds* and *The Foreigner*.

Steve Harris: Entrepreneur, theatrical producer, manager. Former vice president of Elektra Records. Former A&R director of Columbia Records. Former manager of Carly Simon.

Mary Harron: Writer, filmmaker, journalist. Former feature writer for

Punk magazine. Former television host and documentary maker for the BBC's "The Late Show." Writer and director of the independent feature film *I Shot Andy Warhol*.

Debbie Harry (a.k.a. Debbie Blondie): Musician, actress. Lead singer: Blondie. Solo recording artist. Films include *Union City* and *Videodrome*. Author of *Making Tracks: The Rise of Blondie* (with Chris Stein and Victor Bockris).

Bill Harvey: Former vice president of Elektra Records. (Deceased: 1978)

Richard Hell (a.k.a. Richard Meyers): Musician, poet, writer, actor. Bass player, singer, songwriter: the Neon Boys, Television, the Heartbreakers, and Richard Hell and the Voidoids. Films include *Smithereens* and *Desperately Seeking Susan*. Books include the novel *Go Now*.

Gail Higgins (a.k.a. Gail Higgins Smith): Manager. Former assistant to Heartbreakers manager Leee Black Childers. Former roommate of Johnny Thunders.

Abbie Hoffman: Radical, writer, fugitive. Founder of the Yippie Party (with Jerry Rubin). A member of the Chicago Seven, who were charged with conspiring to cause a riot at the 1968 Chicago Democratic National Convention. (Deceased: 1990)

John Holmstrom: Cartoonist, writer, editor, publisher. Cofounder and editor of *Punk* magazine. Founder and editor of *Stop* magazine and *Comical Funnies*. Former publisher of *Nerve* magazine. Current publisher of *High Times* magazine. Creator of the *Scholastic* magazine comic feature "Joe."

Jac Holzman: Entrepreneur. Founder and president of Elektra Records. Retired.

Tony Ingrassia: Writer, film and theater director.

David Johansen (a.k.a. Buster Poindexter, David Doll): Musician, singer, songwriter, actor. Lead singer: the New York Dolls. In the eighties changed his name to Buster Poindexter and became a cabaret star. Costarred in the films *Car 54, Where Are You?* and *Scrooged* (with Bill Murray). Married to photographer Kate Simon.

Brian Jones: Musician. Guitarist, multi-instrumentalist, and co-founder: the Rolling Stones. (Deceased: 1969)

Mick Jones: Musician. Guitar player for the Clash. Leader of Big Audio Dynamite.

Steve Jones: Musician. Guitar player for the Sex Pistols.

Peter Jordan: Roadie, musician. Bass player: the New York Dolls (temporarily replaced Arthur Kane). Retired from rock & roll after a near-fatal stabbing incurred on the Upper West Side in the late seventies.

Ivan Julian: Musician. Guitarist: Richard Hell and the Voidoids. Former roommate of Richard Hell.

Arthur Kane (a.k.a. Killer Kane): Musician. Bass player: the New York Dolls, and the Corpse Grinders.

Lenny Kaye: Musician, writer, record producer. Lead guitarist: the Patti Smith Group. Compiler of the original *Nuggets* album. Produced Suzanne Vega's hit second album. Books include *Waylon: An Autobiography* (with Waylon Jennings) and *Rock 100* (with David Dalton).

Scott Kempner (a.k.a. Top Ten): Musician. Rhythm guitarist: the Dictators. Guitarist, singer, songwriter: the Del Lords; the Little Kings (with Dion).

Eliot Kidd: Musician. Lead singer, guitarist: the Demons.

Ivan Kral: Musician. Guitarist: the Patti Smith Group; Iggy Pop. Currently a Czech rock star.

Wayne Kramer (a.k.a. Wayne Kambes): Musician. Lead guitarist: MC5, Gang War (with Johnny Thunders), and Was (Not Was). Solo recording artist.

Hilly Kristal: Nightclub owner, manager, musician. Owner of CBGB. Former manager of the Dead Boys and the Shirts.

Harvey Kurtzman: Cartoonist. Creator of *Mad* magazine, which was taken over by Bill Gaines, the publisher. Creator of the long-running *Playboy* magazine cartoon feature "Little Annie Fannie." Founder and editor of *Help* and *Trump* magazines. (Deceased: 1994)

Allen Lanier: Musician. Rhythm guitarist, keyboard player: Blue Oyster Cult. Former boyfriend of Patti Smith.

Sam Lay: Musician. Legendary blues drummer who tutored Iggy Pop on drums (pre-Stooges).

Mickey Leigh (a.k.a. Mitchell Hyman): Musician. Guitarist: Tangerine Puppets (with Johnny Ramone), Birdland (with Lester Bangs) and the Rattlers. Currently in Stop. Joey Ramone's younger brother. Former Ramones roadie.

Neon Leon (a.k.a. unknown): Musician, scenemaker. Lead singer, guitarist: the Neon Leon Band. One of the last people to see Nancy Spungen alive.

Richard Lloyd: Musician. Lead guitarist: Television. Solo recording artist. Session work includes Matthew Sweet's album *Girlfriend*.

Matt Lolya: Former Ramones roadie.

Charles Ludlam: Playwright, actor, director. Founder of the Theater of the Ridiculous theater company.

Walter Lure: Musician. Guitarist, singer: the Heartbreakers, the Demons. Currently with the Waldos.

Steve Mackay: Musician. Saxophonist: the Stooges.

Laurie Maddox: Groupie.

Jeff Magnum: Musician. Bass player: the Dead Boys.

Gerard Malanga: Poet, photographer. Former studio assistant to Andy Warhol. Former whip dancer for the Exploding Plastic Inevitable (with Ronnie Cutrone and Mary Woronov).

Handsome Dick Manitoba: (a.k.a. Richard Blum, China Cat, the Handsomest Man in Rock & Roll): Musician. Lead singer: the Dictators, Manitoba's Wild Kingdom.

Charles Manson (a.k.a. Charlie, No-Name Maddox, Jesus Christ, Satan): Former leader of the Charles Manson Family, a hippie cult that ended up murdering film director Roman Polanski's pregnant wife, Sharon Tate, as well as almost a dozen others. The Tate-LaBianca murders, as they came to be known, effectively killed off the hippie movement in the United States.

Ray Manzarek: Musician, producer. Keyboard player: the Doors. Produced L.A.'s leading punk band, X.

Robert Mapplethorpe: Photographer. Photographed covers for Patti Smith's first album, *Horses*, and her fourth album, *Dream of Life*, as well as Television's first album, *Marquee Moon*. His explicit photographs of gay sex were denounced on the floor of the United States Senate and caused conservative politicians to declare war on the National Endowment for the Arts. (Deceased: 1989)

Philippe Marcade: Musician. Lead singer: the Senders. Drummer: Gang War. Friend of Nancy Spungen.

Jim Marshall (a.k.a. The Hound): Writer, rock scholar, disc jockey. Currently hosts a popular radio show on WFMU.

Steve Mass: Entrepreneur. Former owner of the Mudd Club.

Glen Matlock: Musician. Bass player: the Sex Pistols. Author of *I Was a Teenage Sex Pistol*.

Malcolm McLaren: Impresario, clothing store owner, manager. Unofficial manager and clothier of the New York Dolls. Manager of the Sex Pistols, Bow Wow Wow, and Adam Ant. Solo recording artist.

Legs McNeil (a.k.a. Eddie McNeil, Roderick McNeil): Writer. Former resident punk at *Punk* magazine. Former senior editor at *Spin* magazine. Former editor-in-chief of *Nerve* magazine.

Jonas Mekas: Founder of the Anthology Film Archives. Former director of the Film-Makers' Cooperative.

Monte Melnick: Former Ramones road manager.

Geri Miller: Actress, groupie, Warhol Superstar. Member of the *Pork* cast.

Noel Monk: Road manager of the Sex Pistols' first U.S. tour. Author of *Twelve Days on the Road with the Sex Pistols*.

Jim Morrison: Musician. Lead singer: the Doors. (Deceased: 1971)

Patricia Morrisroe: Author of *Mapplethorpe*, a biography of Robert Mapplethorpe.

Paul Morrissey: Filmmaker. Former collaborator with Andy Warhol on numerous films; directed *Trash* and *Heat*.

Billy Murcia (a.k.a. Billy Doll): Musician. Drummer: the New York Dolls. Died of a drug overdose on the Dolls' first trip to London.

Billy Name (a.k.a. Billy Linich, Kronk): Artist, photographer. Unofficial manager of Andy Warhol's Factory who lived in the darkroom for two years and didn't come out. Author of *Stills from the Warhol Films*.

Bobby Neuwirth: Scenemaker, musician, painter. Costarred in *Don't Look Back*, D. A. Pennebaker's legendary *cinéma vérité* documentary on Bob Dylan. Recently released *Last Day on Earth*, an album of collaborations with John Cale.

Nico (a.k.a. Christa Päffgen): Model, actress (most famous for her walk-on in Fellini's *La Dolce Vita*), musician. Singer: the Velvet Underground. Solo recording artist. (Deceased: 1988)

Nitebob (a.k.a. Robert Czaykowski): Former sound man for the Stooges and the New York Dolls. Producer. Acquired the name "Nitebob" because there was a "Daybob" at the rehearsal studio.

Jerry Nolan: Musician. Drummer: the New York Dolls (replaced Billy Murcia), the Heartbreakers. (Deceased: 1992)

Andrew Loog Oldham: Entrepreneur, manager, producer. Former manager and producer of the Rolling Stones. Produced Nico's first single.

Ondine: Speed freak, actor, Warhol Superstar. (Deceased: 1989)

Terry Ork (a.k.a. Noah Ford): Entrepreneur. Former manager of Television. Former manager of the bookstore Cinemabilia. Former president of Ork Records.

Andi Ostrowe (a.k.a. Midge): Musician. Former personal assistant to Patti Smith.

Patti Palladin: Musician. Johnny Thunders's former collaborator.

Susan Pile: Former assistant to Gerard Malanga and Andy Warhol at the Factory. Ari Delon's baby-sitter. Currently vice president of worldwide publicity at MGM/UA Pictures.

Anya Phillips: Entrepreneur, dominatrix. Former manager of James Chance and the Contortions. (Deceased: 1985)

Amos Poe: Filmmaker. Director of *Blank Generation*, *Unmade Beds*, *The Foreigner*, and *Alphabet City*.

Brigid Polk (a.k.a. Brigid Berlin): Artist, Warhol Superstar. Appeared in the Warhol film *Chelsea Girls*.

Eileen Polk (a.k.a. Eileen Revenge): Photographer. Former roommate of Anya Phillips.

Iggy Pop (a.k.a. James Osterberg): Musician, actor. Lead singer: the Stooges. Solo recording artist. Author of *I Need More* (with Ann Wehrer). Films include *The Color of Money* and *The Crow II*.

Howie Pyro: Musician. Bass player: the Blessed, D Generation.

Robert Quine: Musician. Lead guitarist: Richard Hell and the Voidoids, Lou Reed (*Blue Mask, Legendary Hearts, Live in Italy*). Studio musician for Matthew Sweet, Brian Eno, Marianne Faithfull, and others. Solo recording artist.

Rachel (a.k.a. unknown): Transvestite. Former girlfriend/boyfriend of Lou Reed. (Deceased: unconfirmed)

C. J. Ramone (a.k.a. Christopher Joseph Ward): Musician. Bass player: the Ramones (replaced Dee Dee Ramone, 1989).

Connie Ramone (a.k.a. Connie Gripp): Groupie, prostitute. Claimed to be a former member of Frank Zappa's conceptual girl group, the GTO's (Girls Together Outrageously). Girlfriend of Arthur Kane and Dee Dee Ramone. (Deceased: 1990)

Dee Dee Ramone (a.k.a. Douglas Colvin, Dee Dee King): Musician. Bass player, singer, songwriter: the Ramones. Solo recording artist. Costar of the film *Rock 'n' Roll High School* (with Joey, Johnny, and Marky Ramone, P. J. Soles, Paul Bartel, and Mary Woronov).

Joey Ramone (a.k.a. Jeffrey Hyman): Musician. Lead singer, songwriter: the Ramones. Costar of *Rock 'n' Roll High School*.

Johnny Ramone (a.k.a. John Cummings): Musician. Guitarist: the Ramones. Costar of *Rock 'n' Roll High School*.

Marky Ramone (a.k.a. Marc Bell): Musician. Drummer: Dust, Wayne County and the Back Street Boys, Richard Hell and the Voidoids, the Ramones. Costar of *Rock 'n' Roll High School*.

Richie Ramone (a.k.a. Richie Beau, Richard Reinhardt): Musician. Drummer: the Velveteens, the Ramones (1983–1986).

Tommy Ramone (a.k.a. Tommy Erdelyi): Musician, producer. Drummer: the Ramones (1974–1976).

Vera Ramone (a.k.a. Vera Boldis, Vera Colvin): Ex-wife of Dee Dee Ramone.

Genya Ravan (a.k.a. Genushka [Goldie] Zelkowitz): Musician, producer. Lead singer: Goldie and the Gingerbreads (who toured with the Rolling Stones in 1965), Ten Wheel Drive. Solo recording artist. Produced the Dead Boys' first album, *Young, Loud and Snotty*.

Lou Reed: Musician. Guitarist, singer, songwriter: the Velvet Underground. Solo recording artist. Godfather of punk.

Sylvia Reed (a.k.a. Sylvia Morales): Manager, writer, entrepreneur. Ex-wife and manager of Lou Reed.

Marcia Resnick: Photographer. Ex-wife of Wayne Kramer.

Marty Rev (a.k.a. Marty Suicide): Musician. Keyboard player: Suicide. Solo recording artist.

Daniel Rey (a.k.a. Daniel Rabinowitz): Musician, producer. Lead guitarist: Shrapnel. Produced Ramones albums *Halfway to Sanity* and *Adios Amigos*.

Lisa Robinson: Writer, editor, columnist. Former editor of *Hit Parader* and *Rock Scene* magazines. Rock & roll columnist for the *New York Post*.

Richard Robinson: Producer, writer, editor, magician. Married to Lisa Robinson. Produced Lou Reed's first solo album.

Rosebud (a.k.a. Rosebud Feliu-Pettet): Scenemaker. Mother of Harley of the Cro-Mags.

Johnny Rotten (a.k.a. John Lydon): Musician. Lead singer: the Sex Pistols, Public Image Ltd. (PiL). Author of *Rotten: No Irish-No Blacks-No Dogs* (with Keith and Kent Zimmerman).

Barbara Rubin: Filmmaker, scenemaker. Former assistant to Jonas Mekas at the Film-Makers' Cooperative. Director of the underground film classic *Heaven on Earth*. Early fan of the Velvet Underground. (Deceased: 1979)

Bob Rudnick: Poet, writer, comedian. Former columnist (with Dennis Frawley) of the *East Village Other* and the *SoHo Weekly News*. (Deceased: 1995)

Todd Rundgren: Musician, producer. Produced the New York Dolls' first album and Patti Smith's *Wave*.

Mickey Ruskin: Restaurateur, nightclub owner. Former owner of the Ninth Circle (1968), Max's Kansas City (1965–1972), the Local (1974–1976), the Lower Manhattan Ocean Club (1976–1978), and Chinese Chance (a.k.a. One University Place) (1978–1982). (Deceased: 1982)

Ed Sanders: Poet, musician, writer. Singer, songwriter: the Fugs. Solo recording artist. Owner of the Peace Eye Bookstore in the sixties. Publisher of the sixties lit-zine *Fuck You: A Magazine of the Arts*. Books include *The Family*, the seminal work on the Charles Manson family.

Edie Sedgwick: Model, actress, Warhol Superstar. Appeared in the Warhol films *Vinyl*, *Screen Test*, and *Chelsea Girls*. Star of the film *Ciao! Manhattan*. Subject of the oral biography *Edie: An American Biography* (by Jean Stein and George Plimpton). (Deceased: 1971)

Steve Sesnick: Former manager of the Velvet Underground (replaced Andy Warhol in 1968).

Coral Shields (a.k.a. Coral Starr): Sister of Sable Starr.

Sam Shepard: Pulitzer Prize–winning playwright, actor. Plays include *Buried Child*, *Fool for Love* and *Cowboy Mouth* (with Patti Smith). Former boyfriend of Patti Smith, whom he left after the first performance of *Cowboy Mouth*.

Andy Shernoff: Musician, producer. Bass player, singer, songwriter: the Dictators, Manitoba's Wild Kingdom.

Jimmy Silver: Former manager of the Stooges. Health food entrepreneur.

Kate Simon: Photographer. Married to David Johansen.

Paul Simonon: Musician. Former bassist for the Clash.

John Sinclair: Impresario, poet, writer, radical, marijuana legalization advocate, disc jockey. Former manager of the MC5. Former chairman of the White Panther party.

Leni Sinclair: Photographer, archivist.

James Sliman: Former road manager of the Dead Boys. Publicist.

Fred Smith: Musician. Bass player: Television, Blondie.

Fred "Sonic" Smith: Musician. Lead guitarist, singer: the MC5, the Sonic Rendezvous Band. Married to Patti Smith. (Deceased: 1994)

Patti Smith: Poet, musician. Lead singer: the Patti Smith Group. Widow of Fred "Sonic" Smith. Books include *Seventh Heaven*, *Witt*, and *The Coral Sea*.

Todd Smith: Roadie. Brother of Patti Smith. Former roadie for the Patti Smith Group. Bottle slashing victim of Sid Vicious. (Deceased: 1994)

Richard Sohl (a.k.a. D.N.V., Death in Venice): Musician. Keyboard player: the Patti Smith Group. (Deceased: 1990)

Valerie Solanis: Writer, actress, feminist, attempted assassin. The woman who shot Andy Warhol in 1968. Appeared in the Warhol film *I, A Man* (with Tom Baker). Wrote the *SCUM Manifesto*. President of SCUM (The Society for Cutting Up Men). (Deceased: 1988)

Nancy Spungen (a.k.a. Nauseating Nancy): Stripper, groupie. Former girlfriend and manager of Sid Vicious. Believed murdered by Sid in the Chelsea Hotel. (Deceased: 1978)

Sable Starr (a.k.a. Sable Shields): Groupie.

Chris Stein: Musician, producer. Guitarist: Blondie. Produced Iggy Pop's *Zombie Birdhouse*.

Linda Stein: Manager. Former schoolteacher. Former co-manager of the Ramones (with Danny Fields). Ex-wife of Seymour Stein.

Seymour Stein: Entrepreneur. Former president of Sire Records. Vice president of Warner Bros. Records.

Michael Sticca: Roadie. Former roadie for the Dead Boys and Blondie.

Warner Stringfellow: Policeman. Former Detroit Police Department narcotics detective.

Danny Sugerman: Writer, manager. Became the Doors' manager after Jim Morrison's death. Attempted to manage Iggy Pop. Books include *No One Here Gets Out Alive* (with Jerry Hopkins) and *Wonderland Avenue*. Married to Fawn Hall.

Sylvain Sylvain (a.k.a. Sylvain Mizrahi): Musician. Rhythm guitarist: the New York Dolls. Lead singer, guitarist: the Criminals. Solo recording artist.

Marty Thau (a.k.a. Chairman Thau): Entrepreneur, producer, manager. Former vice president in charge of promotion for Buddah Records. Former manager (with Steve Leber and David Krebs) of the New York Dolls. Former manager of Suicide. President of Red Star Records.

Dennis Thompson (a.k.a. Dennis Tomich): Musician, writer. Drummer: MC5, New Order (with Ron Asheton).

Johnny Thunders (a.k.a. John Anthony Genzale): Musician. Lead guitarist, singer: the New York Dolls, the Heartbreakers, Gang War (with Wayne Kramer). Solo recording artist. (Deceased: 1991)

Tish and Snookie (a.k.a. Tish and Snooky Belamo): Sisters. Entrepreneurs. Former backup singers of the Sick Fucks and Elda and the Stilettoes (with Debbie Harry). Owners of the punk clothing store Manic Panic.

Maureen Tucker (a.k.a. Mo Tucker): Musician. Drummer: the Velvet Underground. Solo recording artist.

Steven Tyler: Musician. Lead singer: Aerosmith.

Rob Tyner (a.k.a. Rob Derminer): Musician. Lead singer: the MC5. Solo recording artist. (Deceased: 1991)

Ultra Violet (a.k.a. Isabelle Collin Dufresne): Artist, Warhol Superstar.

John Vaccaro: Theater director, playwright.

Gary Valentine: Musician. Bass player: Blondie.

Cherry Vanilla: Actress, singer. MainMan's head of radio promotion.

Alan Vega (a.k.a. Alan Suicide): Singer, artist. Lead singer: Suicide. Solo recording artist.

Arturo Vega: Artist. Owner of the loft where Joey and Dee Dee Ramone lived from 1975 to 1977. The Ramones' lighting director, graphic designer, and T-shirt manufacturer.

Tom Verlaine (a.k.a. Tom Miller): Musician. Lead guitarist, singer, songwriter: the Neon Boys, Television. Solo recording artist. Former schoolmate of Richard Hell.

Sid Vicious (a.k.a. John Simon Ritchie): Musician. Bass player: the Sex Pistols (replaced Glen Matlock, 1977). Solo recording artist. Boyfriend of Nancy Spungen, and her accused murderer. (Deceased: 1979)

Viva (a.k.a. Susan Hoffman): Actress, writer, Warhol Superstar. Appeared in Warhol films *Chelsea Girls* and *Lonesome Cowboys*. Author of *Superstar*.

Ann Waldman: Poet. Former artistic director of the Poetry Project at St. Mark's Church-in-the-Bowery.

Jack Walls: Playwright, screenwriter. Former companion of Robert Mapplethorpe. Coauthor of *Somebody's Sins*, a feature-length film about the early years of Patti Smith and Robert Mapplethorpe in New York.

Andy Warhol (a.k.a. Andrew Warhola): Artist, filmmaker, publisher of *Interview* magazine. Former manager of the Velvet Underground. (Deceased: 1987)

Vivienne Westwood: Fashion designer. Ex-wife of Malcolm McLaren.

Tina Weymouth (a.k.a. Betina Weymouth): Musician. Bass player: Talking Heads. Bass player, singer: Tom Tom Club.

James Williamson: Musician, producer. Lead guitarist: the Stooges (replaced Ron Asheton, who switched to bass, 1972–1974). Produced Iggy Pop's *New Values*.

Russell Wolensky: Musician. Lead singer: the Sick Fucks.

Holly Woodlawn (a.k.a. Harold Ajzenberg): Actor, drag queen, Warhol Superstar. Star of Warhol film *Trash*. Author of *A Low Life in High Heels: The Holly Woodlawn Story* (with Jeff Copeland).

Mary Woronov: Actress, painter, author. Former whip dancer for the Exploding Plastic Inevitable. Starred in *Rock 'n' Roll High School* (with the Ramones) and *Eating Raoul*.

Andrew Wylie (a.k.a. Bill Lee): Poet, publisher, literary agent. Former publisher of Telegraph Books (with Victor Bockris). Former contributor to *Punk* magazine. Books include *Yellow Flowers*.

Dorian Zero: Musician. (Deceased: 1994)

Jimmy Zhivago: Musician, producer. Keyboard player: Wayne Country and the Back Street Boys.

More Depraved Testimony

...

More Innocence Lost

Ask Not What Your Boy Scout Can Do for You: Ron Asheton Interview, Tape One, June 27, 1994, Ann Arbor

RON ASHETON: The first person that I ever met who bowled me over was John F. Kennedy. He was campaigning in Davenport, Iowa, and I was part of the Boy Scout Honor Guard. We were only kids and the cops were holding us back, and when Kennedy's car got up to me, the crowd surged forward—and I'm freaking. I'm wearing my Boy Scout uniform, and the Secret Service man grabs me by my shirt. He's pulling my little metal zipper and it's choking me, and the Secret Service guy goes, "Take it easy, little kid . . ."

And I stuck my hand out, and Kennedy's standing right there. My head was right by his dick, man, and I shook hands with him. Well, more like one of those finger-touching moments—he looked so fucking beautiful, man.

So I'm pushing people back because the policeman's three-wheeled motorcycle is coming, and I couldn't get back far enough, and the back wheels ran over both my feet. I didn't feel it; I was in such a daze. I forgot about getting my ride home. I walked the five miles or whatever.

The next day, I was like, "Oh, no, why are my toenails black?" I felt no pain because I was totally bedazzled.

Book of Revelations: Jim Carroll Interview, Tape One, June 16, 1995, New York City

JIM CARROLL: The biggest effect on me growing up was the Cuban Missile Crisis. That explains my total drug thing, and nihilism, and why I felt I was running out of time.

The Brother in Catholic School said, "Don't worry, if those sirens start ringing, by ten this morning we will all be down in the gymnasium and we'll have three months of concentrated wafers and water to last three months."

I thought, "Don't worry? We'll be living on fucking crackers for three months in the gymnasium. Great."

The old Ground Zero for where the Russians would drop their missiles was Forty-second Street, and then they'd draw circles around it showing which areas would be hit the hardest. They'd say, "If you're in this circle, you're going to be incinerated immediately, and if you're in this circle, you're going to die within two days of radiation sickness . . ."

I lived in Manhattan in the first fucking zone, you know, so I was going to be incinerated. It was certainly good incentive for youthful nihilism. So I thought—just like with the first blackout, years later—that the Russians were coming.

Oh, it was a total trauma, man. My brother, who was a year older than me, had a totally different make-up, because he would be teasing me before we went to sleep, saying things like, "I heard that all the Soviet ambassadors and all the Cuban ambassadors are getting planes out of town. Boy, the bombs are coming."

I said, "Why are you kidding about that?"

I was totally shitting my pants. So I said to him, "At least I don't fucking wake up crying after *Creature Features*!"

My mother would not want us to watch *Creature Features* because my fucking brother always had these fucking wimpy nightmares. I'd never have nightmares after the horror movies on Friday night. So it pissed me off that he was pulling my chain about a nuclear holocaust.

This was the *real* business, you know?

I Want to Hold Your Hand: Richard Hell Interview, Tape One, March 22, 1989, New York City

RICHARD HELL: I was always interested in girls, as far back as I can remember. The first girl whose name I can remember was in the third grade.

Mimi McCullen. I was nuts about her. Of course, in third grade, you can barely talk to girls. One night I was lying in bed thinking about her, how gorgeous and irresistible she was, and I remember thinking, I wish she was there when I got hit by a car.

Then I could say to her, "Mimi, I'm dying, would you hold my hand?" Ha ha ha.

A Shock to the System: John Giorno Interview, Tape One, June 14, 1995, The Bunker, New York City

JOHN GIORNO: Andy Warhol and I were sitting on the Tiffany couch amongst the clutter in his brownstone on Eighty-sixth Street, watching the live TV coverage from Dallas. We heard Walter Cronkite say, "President Kennedy died at 2:00 P.M. on November 22nd, 1963."

We started hugging each other, pressing our bodies together and trembling. I started crying, and Andy started crying. We wept big, fat tears. It was a symbol of the catastrophe of our own lives. We kissed and Andy sucked my tongue—it was the first time we kissed—and it had the sweet taste of kissing death. It was exhilarating, like when you get kicked in the head and see stars. I didn't particularly like Kennedy and I had never voted, but his assasssination changed all that—they shot my man.

Then Andy and I thought, "This is the best thing he's ever done— dying." The whole world had stopped, and it was all live. Jackie was at the hospital with JFK and they would say, "She still has JFK's blood and some of his body parts on her dress." An hour later, she was on the airplane going back to Washington, and that serious Walter Cronkite voice was saying, "She still has the same dress on, with the blood on it." And I was thinking, "She is so great. This is the best thing she's ever done!"

That was the symbol of the beginning of the '60s and '70s. It was so exhilarating. It was as though you had just sniffed something new—I'm talking about great clarity. Coming out of the 1950s, it was like being released from prison—you had spent your entire life in jail and you thought you would never get out—and the only way out would have been to commit suicide. Everyone I know tried to commit suicide a few times, including myself.

But the day Kennedy was shot was one of those traumatic times when you've cried and cried, and it does something to your nervous system which shocks it, and suddenly everything has this great clarity.

...

More Sex

Discretion Is the Better Part of Valor: Danny Fields Interview, Tape One, January 5, 1994, New York City

DANNY FIELDS: Edie Sedgwick was close with all those people who were close to the Kennedys. Edie had affairs with a couple of them, didn't she? I think one would come in the front door and the other brother would go out the back. So it was at the same time, but not the same minute. Everyone knew that.

I loved Bobby Kennedy. He was my political idol. Sometimes Edie would say about Bobby, "Oh, he was so cute and cuddly," but I wasn't going to ask her about him. I mean, what are you going to ask, "Does he have a big dick?"

Take a Walk on the Wild Side: Jim Carroll—Interview, Tape Two, June 16, 1995, New York City

JIM CARROLL: I knew Jackie Curtis from the old days at Max's when I was a little more wild. We always had this weird thing, especially when she was in her drag period, before she went into the James Dean thing. We had this flirtation. We went out the back door of Max's a few times, and I'd get blow jobs and shit.

Yeah, she did give some good head actually, ha ha ha. Guys always give good head, man, especially if they have no teeth, ha ha ha.

She had teeth, but it was good anyway.

The Uncensored Lenny Bruce: Rosebud Feliu-Pettet Interview, Tape One, May 17, 1995, New York City

ROSEBUD: The first time I met Lenny Bruce he called me into the bathroom. I had been warned. Somebody told me, "Oh, that's his main move. He always does that."

So he calls me into the bathroom, where he was shooting up, and he goes, "Hey, I just thought of something really great. Why don't you blow me while I'm getting off, and I can like get off and come at the same time? I bet that'd be really far out!"

I thought, "Oh, poor thing, I guess he needs this for his fantasy world." So I did start giving him a blow job, but he was directing me, you know, "Oh, a little slower . . ."

I just said, "Do it yourself," and left. He got really upset, very insulted. But it didn't really stand in the way of our friendship.

Took a Little Down About an Hour Ago: Scott Asheton Interview: Tape Three, February 15, 1995, Ann Arbor

SCOTT ASHETON: Iggy was over visiting my brother's apartment, had taken acid and quaaludes, and ordered from three different restaurants massive amounts of food, delivered. And there was a girl there hanging out that just loved Iggy—thought he was the greatest thing in the world. So he's sitting in the chair in front of the TV eating all these to-go foods on acid and quaaludes, and Iggy always had lousy manners. It was something that my mother didn't like about him. He'd come over to the house, open the refrigerator door, open a carton of milk, and start drinking out of it. He used to disgust her. If there was a cake on the counter, he'd go lift the lid off, just take his fingers and gouge out a big handful, whack!

My mom didn't like that.

Anyway, Iggy passed out eating all this food in front of the TV, and this girl realized he was passed out so she pulled his pants off, she got his shit out, and she started working on it. But he's passed out. I was there laughing and she's looking at me, you know, "Oh, man!"

No, nothing was working. Ha ha ha.

Broken Glass, Part One: Iggy Pop Interview, Tape One, June 6, 1995, New York City

IGGY POP: The stitches were happening, let me tell you. They were great big black things, and they had like bits coming out of them. For a long time after that when girls would say, "Are you so-and-so?" And I'd say, "Yeah," then they'd say, "Oh yeah? Well, let me see your scars . . ."

So I seem to have fallen into a good thing there, quite literally, you know?

Sleeping in the Barnyard: Richard Hell Interview, Tape One, March 22, 1989, New York City

RICHARD HELL: The first girl I actually had sex with was a waitress at Jerry's Drive-In. I was about fifteen, and she was like eighteen, nineteen. I told her that I was a medical student. She was living in an apartment near

Jerry's. I started visiting her. It wasn't too much fun. She was really frigid, and she really fought me. She did her duty, because I insisted. It took a few weeks to soften her up.

I think her name was Rachel. She looked and sounded like a hillbilly. She was. Brown hair. She had freckles all over her body. People always ratted their hair, teased it then.

I'd meet her after work. Eventually I got keys to her apartment, and that's what caused our break-up. One time I took another girl back there, and she came in and found us. She was really mad. She called up my mother, and my mother got really worried. She claimed she was pregnant, and she kept calling my mother's boss. She really went nuts.

Not long after that, I made a date with this girl who lived down the street. I was going to sneak out of the house with a bottle of liquor, and she was going to steal the keys to her mother's car. I didn't know how to drive yet, and her mother's car was a Volkswagen with a stick shift. I could handle an automatic, even though I didn't have a driver's license. All the cars I'd ever stolen and driven had automatic transmissions.

It was hard getting the car out of the driveway. We had to roll it down to the corner before we started the engine. We had this idea that we'd go visit friends who lived on a farm in the country. We almost got to their house. It was a little ways away. We even got to their street, but we couldn't tell which house was theirs. We had to drive up people's driveways to get a closer look—farm driveways with the houses set in the back. We drove up this one driveway. It was the wrong house, and there was no circular driveway. I had to drive backwards all the way out. We got back to the road and ended up in an eight-foot ditch. There was no way to get the car out, and it was two o'clock in the morning. We ended up sleeping in this barnyard. I said to the girl, "Look, we have to hold each other close because maintaining our body temperatures is the only way to stay warm."

A cop woke us up the next morning. Somebody had to drive out to get us. My mother came to get me. I think that was the time she got so mad at me she pulled the car over to the side of the road and started beating her head against the steering wheel. I just sat there and said to myself, "What's the correct behavior for this situation?"

I really didn't feel at all. I guess I was a sociopath.

Synchronized Swimming: Scott Asheton Interview, Tape One, February 15, 1995, Ann Arbor

SCOTT ASHETON: Sable used to dye her pubes green. She used to swim on her back and do this back arch so she'd stick it right up in the air, like a big green mop. Ha ha ha.

• •·•

MORE "53RD & 3RD"

Midnight Cowboys: Duncan Hannah Interview, Tape Four, May 3, 1994, New York City

DUNCAN HANNAH: In the fall of 1974 I moved into this railroad flat with this Chinese Columbia student named Eric Lee, who was in the Marbles. He was really pretty; he had shaved his eyebrows off and had the tightest pants and the highest shoes. So we were a couple of Dolls fans. And he was also a classical pianist. He's the guy that auditioned for Patti Smith.

I guess it was summer of '75, and we're sitting in our apartment, drinking. It was about one hundred degrees, and we were drinking cheap something . . . We used to drink this stuff called "Duncan Scotch." It was like $4.50 a quart. It was so bad. I mean, instant hangover. Forget the drunk, it was just like drinking a hangover.

So we're drunk, and Eric couldn't drink much—he'd get all flushed. I was working at Sutters, which was a French pastry shop on Tenth Street that Patti Smith and Tom Verlaine used to come to, and I'd give them free tuna platters.

But Eric didn't have a job. He couldn't find a job, so I started singing him, "53rd & 3rd," the Ramones song. He said, "What is that?"

I said, "Whatta you think?"

He said, "But, but what is it?"

I said, "That's what Dee Dee does, or did."

He said, "Whatta you do?"

I said, "Well, haven't you ever been by Fifty-third and Third?"

See the only time I'd go uptown is to see French movies at those theaters across from Bloomingdales. I'd pass Fifty-third and Third, and I'd see the hustlers standing there. And I'd see the cars slow down, and the hustlers get in, and I just thought, "Weird."

So he just said, "Whatta you, whatta you know?" And I told him everything I knew, and then he was just gone. He came home at dawn with all this money. He was so homophobic, that was the weirdest thing.

I don't know how much money he made. I don't think he knew what to charge. And just to prove that he wasn't, you know, abnormal, he stopped at a whorehouse on the way home and slept with a black girl. It was some place that actually had a red light. I don't know how he found it, but he found the red light district.

He was just laughing, and I said, "I can't believe it. What did you do?"

I guess he gave guys blow jobs in their cars.

Yeah, he kept going back. He became a male hustler. I mean, it was just funny if you knew the guy, because he was, you know, this nice Taiwanese kid, Columbia math whiz, classical pianist. So here he is, giving blow jobs to tourists on Fifty-third and Third all because of a Ramones song.

So I guess it's true. Rock & roll is a bad influence, isn't it? Later he became good friends with the Heartbreakers, which probably wasn't a real good idea either.

And now he's dead.

• • •

MORE DRUGS

I'm Waiting for My . . . Bartender: Danny Fields Interview, Tape Three, February 9, 1994, New York City

DANNY FIELDS: To me, Lou was someone who sang about heroin. Everyone did some speed, but I never saw him speeding the way I saw Rotten Rita speeding, or Ondine speeding, or the great speed people. I think Lou was more about singing about it than doing it. I'm sure he did some dope, but I don't remember him as a nodding junkie. He was always functional. He was probably into the romance of the ritual. Waiting for the man.

I never saw heroin. I never saw drugs at the Factory at all. Lou Reed was basically a drinker. People romanticize. They decide to tell you they used all the hard stuff, but so often they were just drunks.

New York Junkie Slang: Phillipe Marcade Interview, Tape One, April 22, 1995, New York City

PHILIPPE MARCADE: The first time I met Sid Vicious, something really funny happened. I was walking on Twenty-third Street. I was going to a shop where I had my vacuum cleaner fixed. So I'm walking right in front of the Chelsea, and Nancy Spungen came out and yelled, "Philippe!"

I haven't seen her since she went to England, for several months, so I say, "Hey, man, how you been?"

She says, "Sid is right behind me. You gotta meet him."

So Sid Vicious comes walking out of the Chelsea, you know, wearing a dog collar and everything. Nancy says, "Sid, this is Philippe. He's my friend that I told you about in England."

We say hi, and I'm standing there, and she says, "What're you doing?"

So I say, "Well, I'm on my way to pick up something, something really stupid, my vacuum cleaner."

Sid's eyes kind of lit up. He got near me and he goes, "What are you picking up?"

I said, "Ahh, you know, a vacuum cleaner."

His eyes got really bugged, and now he was very interested. He got right in my face and said, "Vacuum cleaner, right. What's that?"

Ha ha ha, he figured it was some junkie New York slang for dope, like *vacuum cleaner*.

So I say, "You know, a vacuum cleaner. It's this thing that you clean the rug with. You know, you plug it in and you go like EEEEEHHHHH," and suddenly it occurred to me, Oh, man, I'm explaining to Sid Vicious what a vacuum cleaner is, ha ha ha. And he's looking at me like, What the fuck is this guy talking about? Like, Oh, yeah, great, okay.

Ha ha ha, so that's when I met Sid Vicious.

• • •

MORE ROCK & ROLL

The Fat Fonzie: Handsome Dick Manitoba Interview, Tape Four, June 11, 1990, New York City

HANDSOME DICK MANITOBA: We played with the Who's Who of American rock artists. I mean, at least one gig or more, we played with Kiss, we played with Bob Seger, we played with AC/DC, we played with Cheap Trick, we played with the Dead Boys, we played with Styx, we played with Uriah Heap, Foreigner, we played with Rush. Everybody were assholes except for AC/DC.

Gene Simmons might be the single biggest asshole I have met in my fifteen years of rock & roll. We got thrown off the Kiss tour because I talked Yiddish. I talked like Jewish words to Gene Simmons, who's like a serious religious Jewish guy.

Plus I heard their rap onstage one night, and I thought it was so lame. I think Paul Stanley was going, "You want to *rock?*" So the next night I did his rap and that was our last show of the tour. They said something like I was like a fat Fonzie, ha ha ha.

It was great. It couldn't have been more of a compliment.

Sorry Mom: Peter Jordan Interview, Tape Two, September 22, 1994, New York City

PETER JORDAN: When I was first starting to play, about 1965, I was standing alone in my room with a guitar, and my little amp turned up to fucking top volume, screaming, "FUCK YOU," over and over, at the top of my lungs, just fucking wailing on the guitar.

My mother opened the door. I'm in my bedroom, in my house, and it was like, "What are you doing?"

I was like, "FUCK YOU! FUCK YOU! FUCK YOU! FUCK YOU! Oh, sorry, Mom."

She was like, "What are you doing?"

I didn't know what to say. I couldn't explain what fucking motivated me to fucking act in such an antisocial way.

Music Machine: Scott Asheton Interview, Tape Three, February 15, 1995, Ann Arbor

SCOTT ASHETON: The first time I met Johnny Rotten was in England after the Sex Pistols had broken up. This was when me and Fred Smith and Gary Rasmussen were backing up Iggy. I think it was the *Lust for Life* tour, because I refused to do "Nightclubbing"—I thought it was too drippy. And we refused to do "China Girl." I didn't like that song. Iggy wanted to do it, but we hemmed and hawed until he got the message.

We were playing at the Music Machine, and after the show Bowie and Rotten came backstage. They're all sitting around a big table, and Bowie and Iggy just kept telling Johnny flat out what he should do. You know, "You should do this, get rid of these guys, straighten up your act, go talk to this person . . ." And he's just sitting there not saying a thing. Finally Johnny just stood up and said, "Fuck you guys. You're full of shit."

He walked toward me and Fred and Gary—Fred had a fifth of Jack—and he said, "Can I get that?" Then he goes, "You're the guys I wanna talk to."

Before that, I didn't think much of the guy. After that, I go, "This guy's all right. He just told Iggy and Bowie to fuck off."

Room Service: Leee Black Childers Interview, Tape Seven, January 26, 1994, New York City

LEEE CHILDERS: Have you seen the back of the LAMF cover? With the fingerprints? Did it ever occur to you to wonder why it was a bunch of fingerprints? Well, here's why. I wasn't on the road with them, but Gail told me.

I think they were in Leeds. She was in the room with a couple of the band members, when there was a knock on the door. This guy came in with a gun.

He said, "Don't worry, don't worry, don't anybody worry. I'm with MI5. We're looking for a terrorist."

So Gail said, "Okay."

Then he said, "I'm gonna have to hold you people in this room for a while, for your own security."

Gail said, "Okay."

And the hours went by, and he sat there with this gun trained on them, saying very little. Gail was trying to make small talk, and not getting very far. Walter called up from the lobby and says, "Gail, we're starving. Come down here and sign for our breakfast."

Gail was saying things to him like, "I'm being *held up* right now. I feel like a *gun* is being *pointed* at me. I am so *held up*."

Walter said, "You're talking crazy. I'm just gonna come up there."

So up came Walter. Knock-knock-knock, then he came in the door, and the guy with the gun took Walter prisoner, too. That's what happened with every band member. It was like a Marx Brothers movie, right? Eventually they all came to Gail's room, because Gail had the only money.

So they're all sitting there at gunpoint, and to give Gail great raving credit, she never snapped. She just kept talking to him.

She said, "What on earth is going on here? Are you nuts? We're a rock & roll band, we're not terrorists. You have to stop this in the next twenty minutes because we have to get sound-checked."

He said, "You just keep quiet, ma'am."

Eventually he stood up and said, "All clear now. I'll go," and out he went. Apparently this guy was a notorious nutcase who'd been doing this for a while.

When the police came, they had to fingerprint everyone in the room so they could hunt for his fingerprints, as the extra fingerprints.

Of course, the police said there was nothing they could do, but they were very nice, because Gail said, "Oh, these would be nice souvenirs. Can I just have them?" And they said, "Sure." So she gave them to Chris Stamp, and he put them on the back cover.

• • •

More Degradation

Psycho-Nazi-Rich-Jewish-Girls: Ron Asheton Interview, Tape Five, June 27, 1994, Ann Arbor

RON ASHETON: Iggy was such a mess. He was doing this whole thing of hooking up with rich Jewish girls. He had this really rich Jewish girlfriend whose name was Alex. And Alex had a sidekick named Georgia. Iggy started bringing them over, and he'd be so fucked up that they started digging on me, because I had all the Nazi stuff. They became like psycho-Nazi-rich-Jewish-girls.

So I usurped Iggy.

That's when I got to understand Iggy a bit more—of how he was using these people, and then they'd get sick of him. So I would end up using them and their limousines. I would go to Alex's house—"The Giant House"—and I would say, "Gee, what if your father comes in?"

Alex said, "Hey, the house is so big that he has the whole other wing, and he don't care. Do you want me to buzz the maid to bring shit up?"

And I'm going, "wooooow!"

You know, this is Iggy's world. And he'd really burn these girls. If I ever said anything, Iggy would be like, "No, I don't, man."

Iggy never showed up at Alex's house while I was there. He was banned. And when you're banned by Alex, you're banned. He was problem-ed out. When Iggy stumbled down a flight of stairs in my apartment building, Alex went, "Tsk tsk. I hope he's dead."

So that was the beginning of Alex's and my relationship. She said, "I'm sick of him. He's too stoned all the time. He can't fuck. He's no fun. He can't do anything but get high."

So I obliged her.

Broken Glass, Part Two: Jan Carmichael Interview, Tape One, Date Unknown, Phone Interview

JAN CARMICHAEL: At the beginning of the tour with David Bowie and Blondie, Iggy was trying desperately not to do drugs. And so me being from the Midwest, I think Iggy saw me and thought, "Well, if I bring this innocent girl into my life, I'll have a shot at a normal life."

A magazine was interviewing him during that time, and he said, "Cincinnati's beautiful. My girlfriend's from there—my Ohio find; fresh, natural, no other deals, no big trips."

I mean that was it. I was Iggy's attempt to stay straight, but it was totally stupid. After the tour I went to Los Angeles to visit Iggy. He was renting a beach house in Malibu. It took me about a week to realize that he wasn't sleeping at all, he was just completely deranged on coke.

One night we went to dinner at some posh place in Beverly Hills with Hunt and Tony Sales. Iggy was completely and utterly psycho during dinner, and he actually kept proposing marriage to me. He was just completely out of his mind; it was obviously not to be taken seriously. He was just kind of frantic and babbling, completely nonsensical.

After dinner Iggy was driving, and he smashed into a parked car. I hit the windshield. I got a gash near my hairline, so we went to the hospital and Iggy had a plastic surgeon sew it up.

That was like the end of that whole deal. I spent a couple of days at Iggy's manager's house and then flew home. I wasn't pissed off at all. I honestly watched everything happen from the beginning to end with detachment. I mean, I was amazed that this guy was interested in me. I was amazed that I got to go along for the ride. But it also made it apparent to me that fame is not all that it's cracked up to be.

I honestly felt sorry for those guys. Fame is its own cage.

• • •

MORE GREAT MOMENTS

Peer Pressure Defined: Danny Fields Interview, Tape One, January 5, 1994, New York City

DANNY FIELDS: The first time I met Andy Warhol—on that particular day, during that particular twenty-four hours—he was extremely famous because his Campbell Soup cans had made it to the lead story of the *New York Times*. I can date the party where I met him because it was the day that the lead story in the *New York Times* was illustrated by a painting of rows of Andy Warhol's Campbell Soup cans. I don't remember what the story was—"A New Movement in Art" or "Is This the Art of Tomorrow or Today?"

When I arrived at the party, Andy was sitting on the couch with Gerard Malanga and Ivy Nicholson, who was *Vogue*'s "Girl of the Year." And Ivy Nicholson was getting drunk and started crawling across the floor to Andy on her belly. She sort of squiggled across the floor and started pawing at Andy's leg—rubbing his knee—saying, "Oh, Andy, I love you, I love you!" I don't know if she said, "Put me in a movie," or not. She probably did. She probably said, "I love you, comma, put me in a movie."

And Andy tried to kick her away with his foot—his leg was crossed—and every time she would rub his leg, he would sort of kick her off like, "Go away!" She was like an annoying pet, like a dog who was trying to hump you. So Ivy went over to the window—she let down the top sash—then she climbed up on the windowsill and she put one leg over. Then she stuck her head out. And then she put her arm over—she was going out the window.

Everyone else was just sort of watching her, but I was nervous she was going to jump. So I went over to her and I said, "Don't do that. You mustn't do that, come back inside, everything will be all right." So she came back inside, and I thought people would say, "Oh, aren't you a hero, you saved her life."

And Andy says, "Oh, why did you do that? Why didn't you let her jump?"

I thought to myself, Oh, these people are *much* cooler than me.

Sunday Morning: Duncan Hannah Interview, Tape Three, May 3, 1994, New York City

DUNCAN HANNAH: One Sunday morning—I was still at One Fifth Avenue so it had to be 1974—Danny Fields calls me up and says, "Hey, Nico's coming over today. Would you keep an eye on her? She's so exhausting. I'm just sick of her shtick. She's a dear friend, but she's too much."

I said, "Are you kidding? I'm there."

C'mon, Nico? She lived in Ibiza, she was somebody you never even hoped to see, right? She was like, gone. So I said, "Yes."

So I raced up there, and she shows up in all these Moroccan robes and stuff, and he warned me she was an opium addict. She'd been living with

Kevin Ayres on this little island and she was really out there. She was all in these bells and Patchouli oil, and she was real giggly and plump.

But she was . . . I mean, she was cool, right? She was *Nico*.

Danny said he had something to do, so it was just Nico and me. I was playing records for her, all the new bands and stuff. And she was very receptive. This was fun for her, right, because she didn't know anything. So I was like, Wow, spinning platters for Nico. So I said, "Oh, you must love Roxy Music." And she said, in a deep, slow, German-accented-Nico-voice, "I . . . don't . . . know . . . what . . . this . . . is . . ."

I said, "Oh, Roxy Music, they're . . . look, this guy in the band, Eno? He says that you are the premier rock singer, ever."

She said, "What is this boy's name?"

I said, "Brian Eno, and he just said that in the last issue of . . ."

I was always reading *Melody Maker* and *Sounds* and *NME*, and I said, "Well, Eno says that you are just the tits." And so I'm playing her, you know, "For Your Pleasure," and we're just having this great old time, and we're getting drunk. We're drinking grapefruit and vodka. And she goes in the kitchen to make us a couple new drinks and I'm thinking, God, I can't believe it, you know, sitting here, playing Roxy Music records for Nico.

Then I heard a huge crash.

So I go in the kitchen and Nico's sitting on the floor—not sitting, she's like splattered on the floor—and there's vodka all over the place and she just, I don't know, stepped on a banana peel or something, just like, BOOM!

And so I look at her and she looks at me and I'm like, very tense, right? And then, very slowly, she starts going, "Ha . . . ha . . . ha . . . ha . . ."

And so I started laughing and then we were both like laughing hysterically. It was great.

She said everything so slow. Danny did this great imitation of her. It was really funny. So it was hard not to be like in hysterics all day long, right? And then Danny made us some dinner and I said, "Hey, look, there's the band I've been telling you about, that kinda sounds like your old band. You know, they're playing tonight, and we should all go."

She said, "Ja, let's go."

So then Danny Fields, Nico and I went to see Television. On the way, I asked her about the Velvet Underground, you know, "Remember your band?"

She said, "Oh, ja . . . With Louuu . . . Suuure . . ."

But I'd ask her something and she'd say, "I can't remember." Then after a long pause, "I think I've taken too many drugs." You know, stuff like that. It was really funny.

So we got to CBGB's and there was Eno, who was doing a demo of Television. There was some plan for him to be their producer. So there's Eno and I'm thinking, Wow, well, I got to do it.

I'd met him once, so I go, "Hey, ah, ah, Brian?"

He turns around and says, "Yeah?"

I said, "I'm Duncan, yeah, we met through Lance Loud, yeah, I just wanted you to meet my friend, um, Nico."

It was like the Great Moment.

Eno was like, "Oh, my God!"

So I stuck them together. And then he took over, right? That's the last I saw of Nico. And then Eno wound up producing Nico's next record.

I was thinking, you know, you admire something from afar, all the way from Minneapolis, where I'm from, right? And then suddenly, you're like in it. I mean, I didn't do anything, but, you know, I did it. They were like fictional characters. It's like talking about the Tin Man and The Cowardly Lion, but then suddenly you're right there and you're like sticking them together.

Sweet Smell of Excess: Wayne Kramer Interview, Tape Five, July 11, 1994, Los Angeles

WAYNE KRAMER: When they got Iggy into macrobiotics he lost like forty pounds. I mean, he just shriveled up into this shadow of his former self. One day at Stooge Manor, I went upstairs to the attic to see Iggy, and I said, "What's up, man?"

He said, "Oh, this brown rice, macrobiotic thing, it's so great, my shit don't stink."

I said, "Get outta here, man."

He said, "No, I know it sounds funny, but my shit doesn't stink now."

Moe, Larry, Cheese! Moe, Larry, Cheese! Ron Asheton Interview, Tape Three, June 27, 1994, Ann Arbor

RON ASHETON: One night I was at the Whiskey-A-Go-Go, and all the GTO's were hanging all over Max Baer, who played Jethro on the television show, *The Beverly Hillbillies*.

Everyone was calling him Jethro, and he kept saying, "Don't call me Jethro! My name is Max!"

I was standing there with a drink. I said, "What are you drinking?"

I think he had a screwdriver. I had to be a little buzzed because I would never have done this to anybody, because I hate it myself, but I was poking his chest with my finger, my index finger, going, "But you know, you were the star of that show! Jethro, you were the star of that show!"

Then I just went and sat down. And somebody came up and said there was a girl in the audience that says her grandfather is one of the Three Stooges. I said, "Oh, get her up here." And it was Chris Lamont, who was Larry Fine's granddaughter. So the next day she took me to the Motion Picture Rest Home and I met Larry.

He had had a few strokes, and when I first met him, I could hardly understand a thing he said, but I wanted to keep going back, and Chris didn't want to go back as much as me, so I finally called him up and said, "Hey, Larry, can I come by?"

Larry said, "Oh, yeah."

I used to go and sit with him all afternoon, swap tales. He let me smoke cigarettes and he's going, "Oh, that smells good, man. I wish I could have a cigarette . . ."

He told me all the Stooges stories—Moe was the business guy, and Curly was the party guy—all the great Stooges stories. And I did all this fan mail—I licked and addressed the envelopes. He had a form letter. He'd sign them and I'd send them out. I paid for the postage with my own money. I helped him decorate his place, which is cinder block walls painted white. The kids would send him so much mail. I'd say, "Well, let's see what we got here, man." The kids would draw Three Stooges stuff, so we plastered his walls with all the drawings the kids sent him. It was great.

I wound up talking to him so much that his speech improved, but I didn't really even notice it because I'd been with him so much. One time I was leaving, and the doctor comes up to me and goes, "Oh, I've really got to thank you, you've so improved Larry's speech. He's so much better. I'd really like to thank you for spending time with him."

For me, it was my honor to hang out with one of my idols. I always liked Moe the best. I always fancied myself as Moe when I was a kid pretending to be Stooges, but a chance to be with Larry—it was wonderful. He only had three people that came to visit him. Ed Asner was one, Moe Howard would come a couple times a week, and myself.

But I always missed Moe. Every time I came by, Larry would go, "Ah, you missed Moe, he was just here."

"Oh, fuck."

So I never met Moe. But I'd go anytime I could get a ride out there, or bum somebody's car. I wound up taking buddies out there, and it really made Larry happy. I got a lot of snapshots of Larry poking me in the eyes—doing Stooges routines—and I'm doing Moe Howard stuff, like slapping Larry.

A Little Something to Remember Me By: Bebe Buell Interview, Tape Three, July 22, 1994, New York City

BEBE BUELL: Upon his death, Stiv wanted to be cremated and then he wanted all of his close friends to do a line of his ashes. And a few people did. Caroline Bators did and said it was really painful, so she said to me, "You don't have to snort yours," and I was like, "Thank you."

I think Stiv would understand. I didn't look at it, I just folded the paper it was in and put it in a heart-shaped box.

• • •

MORE GOOD-BYES

Death on the Installment Plan: Richard Lloyd Interview, Tape Three, June 24, 1994, New York City

RICHARD LLOYD: I mean, some people climb Mount Everest, are they less nuts? People die on Mount Everest—they get frostbite, they come out with no hands, no toes, dead, they get crushed by avalanches. Other people get shot to the moon and blown up in a space shuttle. For what? To float in weightlessness and look back on earth?

So I took things that made you do that without going anywhere. Yes, people died, but was it any more insane than the pursuits which are put on pedestals by ordinary human beings?

You can look at it as adventuring. Maybe someone is on a path where they're seeking a certain knowledge, and in order to get it they have to go the way of great danger with the possibility of grievous damage to themselves. But that's where the hidden secret is, you know? I'm not saying that people don't get lost, but if you have a compass that's hidden from view, and everyone else is going the other direction and you're going this way, who's to say that they're not a lemming and that your other way is not the way of sanity? That everyone else is falling off the cliff at the end of the world, but they don't know it. It's about a certain sense of . . . maybe the flock of birds is flying in the wrong direction.

It's a real razor's edge. You and I have emerged both terribly and virtually unscathed. That's as deep a paradox of human experience as any. It was a religious experience to have gone through that.

The Final Word: Wayne Kramer Interview, Tape Seven, July 11, 1994, Los Angeles

WAYNE KRAMER: Ben Edmunds called me the morning after Rob Tyner died and told me. This whole business of grieving—you know, these guys were my brothers and I'd lost them. So I told Ben that I couldn't go to the funeral because I'd wrenched my leg playing racketball. I hate to say that—the poor guy dies of a heart attack and I'm playing racketball—but I couldn't see myself fucking hobbling through airports. Plus, it was more than I could deal with—emotionally I couldn't deal with Fred Smith.

Fred and I had a tremendous rivalry going on. We were like brothers. When we were together on shit, we were unbeatable, but we were also at odds a lot because I was always trying to make things happen, which, in turn, would make Fred feel powerless. So to balance the situation out, Fred would become passive-aggressive, like being late, or not showing up and being difficult.

But I told Ben I'd do the benefit concert later on because Ben was telling me that Rob didn't have any insurance, he had left three kids, and of course having been in the MC5 did not leave any of us independently wealthy. So I got Dennis's number and Michael's number and Fred's number and I called them up, and said, "Look, man, I'm gonna go up there and play, man. You wanna play with me?"

Dennis was hurt that no one had even bothered to ask him if he wanted to play on the show, but he was very happy to hear from me and wanted to participate in the thing. And Michael re-upped just like that, real cool, and Fred—Fred was real obstinate about it.

When I got to Detroit, what was left of the MC5, and the band Soundgarden, was being inducted into the Michigan Rock & Roll Hall of Fame, which is this cheap hustle for this restaurant in Detroit. It was kind of embarrassing—we had to put our hands in cement.

I was kinda worried about being in the same room with Fred. I just know he's gonna be drinking, and if anyone's capable of pushing my button, Fred is. And I was at the stage of my life where I didn't want to end up in a boxing match with this motherfucker, you know? So I just stayed away from him and I didn't drink, and Fred was drinking nonstop all day. He looked real bad—I mean, his skin had kind of drooped down, it was like he had some kind of palsy. All his teeth were rotted and he looked scary, man. Me and Michael went out to dinner together and we said, "Man, did you see Fred's face? Oh, Jesus, man, what happened to the guy?"

We had a rehearsal the next day. The rehearsal was called for four o'clock, but everything ran a little bit late. Dennis had been there waiting, me and Michael got there about 4:35, and we all sat around for about two hours waiting for Fred to show up. We jammed. I mean, it was really fun. I'd been trying to explain how to play free to musicians for the last fifteen years, since the MC5 broke up—you know, go off the beat and the key—but these guys—we all learned how to do this together, so we were fucking playing, rhhhaaaa-jam-jam-jam-jam. We were having fun—this was old, old friends and we were getting into it. And finally Fred shows up, "He's here, he's here!" All the guys from the studio were saying, "He's here, he's here!"

They all scurried out and they carried in his gear for him and here comes this frail old guy. Fred sits down and these other guys are tuning his guitar for him and plugging everything in—and he sits down with two bottles of wine and commences to knock one off before we start playing. He sets a mike up and he's saying, "Wells, a-huh, I'm sorry I'm late, I, I'm, I, I feel like shit, but anyway . . ."

So we start to rehearse what we're gonna do and Fred can't play his guitar, he don't remember the parts: "Wayne, what did I play? You know what I used to play?"

I was like, "Yeah, I think you played—it went like this, it's seventh fret, doo-do-da, like that, you know?"

He said, "Oh, I don't remember anything, after the band broke up I, I don't remember anything."

This was like where we left off when the band broke up in 1972. It was now 1991, except worse. It was like a gross caricature of the dynamic that existed then. I mean that kinda shit don't change over time. I just sat there and let Fred talk and talk and talk because my rules were: A) Do not drink with the guy, because that's gonna turn into a disaster, and B) It's not my job to change him or to try to bring him up to speed or to do anything except make this show as good as I can make it.

Fred commenced to get plastered, and Dennis was so funny. He got so angry at one point, he said, "Come on, can we get on with it? I have more fun at the dentist!"

Finally we finished the rehearsal. The rehearsal was ridiculous, we might as well not have rehearsed for what good it did. So we get to the gig, and of course everyone's waiting for Fred to get there. He arrives late and then it's time for us to play. The stage is dark and the gear is ready and we're waiting; we're sitting backstage and Fred won't go on.

Fred's drinking wine out of a coffee cup and waiting. Michael goes out onstage and plugs his bass in and the kids go, "Hooray," and they see it's Michael Davis and no one else is behind him, so he comes back. Then Dennis goes out and gets his drums going. The kids all cheer, "Yeeaaahhhh," and he's all alone. I knew there was no point in going out there until Fred was ready to go. When Fred's ready to go, that's when we're gonna go. I wasn't gonna try to convince the guy that we gotta go on. What's the point? So I just sat and waited, while Dennis and Michael kept coming backstage. They were getting increasingly frustrated and angry, but it was just that Fred Smith thing, you know, that passive-aggressive thing. When people are late and they hang you up, you know, it's about power and control.

Michael and Dennis both kept coming in: "Come on! Let's play, let's play, let's play!"

But Fred wouldn't play and then at one point, they left the room and Fred looked at me and said, "Fucking amateurs," which was an old joke. So Fred finally finished his wine and we went on and played "Rambling Rose" and "Black to Comm." Then Fred said, "Well, you know, I'm gonna have some remarks for the audience."

I said, "Fine, me, too. I've got some things I wanna say."

So Fred told the audience, "If we know anything, we're only here for a minute and you've got to make your mark and Rob certainly made his mark . . ." And then he told this story about a drinking contest in Germany, and how Rob'd finally gotten pissed, and it turned into a singing drinking contest and Rob sang this beautiful version of "Georgia."

I suppose it was kinda funny if he hadn't incapacitated himself by drink at the time. Then we did "Black to Comm," and Fred read this Jack Kerouac poem in the middle of it.

Then I said to the audience, "You know, I was born and raised in Detroit. And the streets that you all drive every day to go to school and go to the store and go to work, I used to travel. And when I was a little boy I wanted to grow up and be a musician, and I looked for people in my neighborhood that wanted to be musicians, too. And there was a kid that used to deliver the papers, and that's that man back there on the drums, that's Dennis Thompson."

I said, "And there was this juvenile delinquent I met at Junior High School in Lincoln Park, and that's that man right there on the guitar, that's Fred Smith.

"And there was an art school dropout from down by Wayne State University, named Michael Davis, and that's that man right there playing the bass."

Then I said, "There was another guy that I knew in the neighborhood that was into some far out shit and knew something about everything, and I learned a lot from, and his name was Rob Tyner and we were the MC5. People say that we did a lot of great things with our band, but we also did some not so great things, and Becky Tyner's here and she can testify to that."

I said, "But in the end, the worse thing that we did, was that we lost each other. The MC5 represented a lot of things. We represented possibilities—a possibility of new music, possibility of a new lifestyle, possibility that we could change the world. But in the end, the worst thing we did is that we lost each other. So tonight I'm here to reclaim those possibilities, and to reclaim my lost brothers. So Rob, if you're out there, and I know you are, and you're listening, this one is for you . . ."

And then we did "Kick Out the Jams."

The End

William Burroughs smoking a joint, The Bunker, New York City, September 21, 1995.
© *Kate Simon, 1995.*

Source Notes

The authors wish to acknowledge the following publishers and individuals for granting permission to reproduce excerpts from their books, original interviews, and other previously published works:

Jerry Nolan interviews by Doug Simmons (which appear in this book on pp. 115, 117, 117–18, 128, 131, 131–32, 191, 194 [two instances], 214, 257, 257–58, 258, 260–61, 262, 397, 405, 406, 407) courtesy of Doug Simmons/*The Village Voice*.

Nancy Spungen interview by Jeff Goldberg (pp. 150, 260, 350) used by permission of Jeff Goldberg.

Sabel Starr interviews by Mary Harron (pp. 137, 137–38, 139, 150, 151, 153, 154, 215) used by permission of Mary Harron.

John Cale interviews by Mary Harron (pp. 4, 20, 54) used by permission of Mary Harron.

Nico interviews by Mary Harron (pp. 10, 19) used by permission of Mary Harron.

Damita interviews by Victor Bockris (pp. 284, 300, 301–02) used by permission of Victor Bockris.

Patti Smith interview by Victor Bockris (pp. 100, 107–08, 110, 114, 159, 160, 161, 162) used by permission of Victor Bockris.

John Vaccaro interview by Eugenia Bone (pp. 89, 90) used by permission of Eugenia Bone.

Excerpts from *The Velvet Underground* by Dave Thompson (Sterling Morrison: p. 3; Lou Reed: pp. 12, 17; John Cale: pp. 4, 20, 54) copyright © 1989 by Dave Thompson. Reprinted by permission of Omnibus Press.

Excerpts from *I Need More* by Iggy Pop (pp. 33, 38 [two instances], 52, 53, 54, 57–58, 74, 125, 255) copyright © 1996. Reprinted by permission of 2.13.61 Publications, Inc.

Excerpts from *Nico: The Life and Lies of an Icon* (Nico: pp. 8, 12–13, 13, 30; Ari Delon: pp. 402–03, 403; John Cale: p. 9) © 1993 by Richard Witts. Reprinted by permission of Virgin Publishing.

Excerpts from *Up-Tight: The Velvet Underground Story* by Victor Bockris and Gerard Malanga (John Cale: p. 21; Sterling Morrison: p. 23) copyright © 1983 by Victor Bockris and Gerard Malanga. Reprinted by permission of Omnibus Press.

Excerpts from *New York Post* (pp. 350, 352, 353, 357) © 1978 and 1979 by The New York Post. Reprinted by permission of The New York Post.

The authors also wish to acknowledge that excerpts from the following appear in this work: *Aspen*, vol. 1, no. 3, December 1966. (Lou Reed: p. 3).

John Wilcock with a cast of thousands, *The Autobiography & Sex Life of Andy Warhol*. Devised, created, and produced by Other Scenes, Inc. (New York: 1971) (Lou Reed: p. 22).

Lou Reed, "Fallen Knights and Fallen Ladies" from *The Penguin Book of Rock & Roll Writing*, ed. Clinton Heylin (Penguin Books, 1992). © Lou Reed. (Lou Reed: p. 24 [last two paragraphs of quote]).

Intransit: The Andy Warhol—Gerard Malanga Monster Issue. (Lou Reed: pp. 6, 14 [two instances], 24 [first two paragraphs of quote]).

Michael Wrenn, ed., with Glen Marks, *Lou Reed: Between the Lines* (London: Plexus Publishing, 1993) (Lou Reed: pp. 3–4, 7, 20, 23).

Debbie Harry, Chris Stein, and Victor Bockris, *Making Tracks: The Rise of Blondie* (New York: Dell, 1982) (Debbie Harry: p. 208).

Andy Warhol and Pat Hackett, *POPism: The Warhol '60s* (New York: Harcourt Brace Jovanovich, 1980) (Andy Warhol: pp. 16, 17).

Lester Bangs, *Psychotic Reactions and Carburetor Dung*, ed. Greil Marcus (New York: Vintage, 1988) (Lester Bangs: pp. 281, 282).

Frank Rose, *Real Men: Sex and Style in an Uncertain Age*, photographs by George Bennett (New York: Doubleday, 1980) (Linda Stein: p. 363 [third and fourth paragraphs of quote]).

Per Nilsen with Dorothy Sherman, *The Wild One: The True Story of Iggy Pop* (London: Omnibus Press, 1988) (Iggy Pop: pp. 123, 225; Leee Childers: p. 141).

Pam Brown, "An Afternoon with Iggy Pop," *Punk*, vol. 1, no. 4, July 1976 (Iggy Pop: pp. 49, 50, 57, 80 [two instances], 125, 211–12, 222–23).

Excerpt from Lenny Kaye review in *Rock Scene*. p. 146.

Legs McNeil, "Richard Hell," *Punk*, vol. 1, no. 3, April 1976 (Richard Hell: pp. 281–82).

Tom Baker, "Jim Morrison: When the Music Is Over," *High Times*, June 1981 (Tom Baker: p. 28).

FOR THE BEST IN PAPERBACKS, LOOK FOR THE

In every corner of the world, on every subject under the sun, Penguin represents quality and variety—the very best in publishing today.

For complete information about books available from Penguin—including Puffins, Penguin Classics, and Arkana—and how to order them, write to us at the appropriate address below. Please note that for copyright reasons the selection of books varies from country to country.

In the United Kingdom: Please write to *Dept. EP, Penguin Books Ltd, Bath Road, Harmondsworth, West Drayton, Middlesex UB7 0DA.*

In the United States: Please write to *Penguin Putnam Inc., P.O. Box 12289 Dept. B, Newark, New Jersey 07101-5289* or call 1-800-788-6262.

In Canada: Please write to *Penguin Books Canada Ltd, 10 Alcorn Avenue, Suite 300, Toronto, Ontario M4V 3B2.*

In Australia: Please write to *Penguin Books Australia Ltd, P.O. Box 257, Ringwood, Victoria 3134.*

In New Zealand: Please write to *Penguin Books (NZ) Ltd, Private Bag 102902, North Shore Mail Centre, Auckland 10.*

In India: Please write to *Penguin Books India Pvt Ltd, 11 Panchsheel Shopping Centre, Panchsheel Park, New Delhi 110 017.*

In the Netherlands: Please write to *Penguin Books Netherlands bv, Postbus 3507, NL-1001 AH Amsterdam.*

In Germany: Please write to *Penguin Books Deutschland GmbH, Metzlerstrasse 26, 60594 Frankfurt am Main.*

In Spain: Please write to *Penguin Books S. A., Bravo Murillo 19, 1° B, 28015 Madrid.*

In Italy: Please write to *Penguin Italia s.r.l., Via Benedetto Croce 2, 20094 Corsico, Milano.*

In France: Please write to *Penguin France, Le Carré Wilson, 62 rue Benjamin Baillaud, 31500 Toulouse.*

In Japan: Please write to *Penguin Books Japan Ltd, Kaneko Building, 2-3-25 Koraku, Bunkyo-Ku, Tokyo 112.*

In South Africa: Please write to *Penguin Books South Africa (Pty) Ltd, Private Bag X14, Parkview, 2122 Johannesburg.*